# Sentencing

Theory, Law and Practice

# Sentencing

## Theory, Law and Practice

Second edition

Nigel Walker

*and*

Nicola Padfield

*H* HAVERING COLLEGE
OF FURTHER & HIGHER EDUCATION
LEARNING RESOURCES
CENTRE

**Butterworths**
London, Dublin & Edinburgh
1996

408244
201691

344.205772
A9

| United Kingdom | Butterworths a Division of Reed Elsevier (UK) Ltd, Halsbury House, 35 Chancery Lane, LONDON WC2A 1EL and 4 Hill Street, EDINBURGH EH2 3JZ |
|---|---|
| Australia | Butterworths, SYDNEY, MELBOURNE, BRISBANE, ADELAIDE, PERTH, CANBERRA and HOBART |
| Canada | Butterworths Canada Ltd, TORONTO and VANCOUVER |
| Ireland | Butterworth (Ireland) Ltd, DUBLIN |
| Malaysia | Malayan Law Journal Sdn Bhd, KUALA LUMPUR |
| New Zealand | Butterworths of New Zealand Ltd, WELLINGTON and AUCKLAND |
| Singapore | Reed Elsevier (Singapore) Pte Ltd, SINGAPORE |
| South Africa | Butterworths Publishers (Pty) Ltd, DURBAN |
| USA | Michie, CHARLOTTESVILLE, Virginia |

All rights reserved. No part of this publication may be reproduced in any material form (including photocopying or storing it in any medium by electronic means and whether or not transiently or incidentally to some other use of this publication) without the written permission of the copyright owner except in accordance with the provisions of the Copyright, Designs and Patents Act 1988 or under the terms of a licence issued by the Copyright Licensing Agency Ltd, 90 Tottenham Court Road, London, England W1P 9HE. Applications for the copyright owner's written permission to reproduce any part of this publication should be addressed to the publisher.

Warning: The doing of an unauthorised act in relation to a copyright work may result in both a civil claim for damages and criminal prosecution.

Any Crown copyright material is reproduced with the permission of the Controller of Her Majesty's Stationery Office.

© Reed Elsevier (UK) Ltd 1996

A CIP Catalogue record for this book is available from the British Library.

First edition 1985

ISBN 0 406 06325 7

Printed by Mackays of Chatham plc, Chatham, Kent

# Preface

A great deal of water has flowed under several bridges since the first edition. The principles of sentencing have been clarified—if not to everyone's satisfaction—by the 1991 and 1994 Acts. The Court of Appeal (Criminal Division) has handed down many a guideline and practice direction. Unit fines have been introduced—and then hastily abolished. Parole and remission have been combined and overhauled. Prison sentences can no longer be partly suspended, and wholly suspended only in special circumstances. Extended sentences have been replaced by 'longer than commensurate sentences'. New regimes have been introduced in prison service establishments. More demanding forms of treatment in the community are now on offer. Juvenile courts are now youth courts.

As before, our aim has been not merely to describe respectfully the powers which the law gives to sentencers, but to discuss the theories on which they are based and—even more important—what actually happens when they are used. Theories can be found in books and *Hansard*, but it takes laborious empirical research to discover what is really done to offenders as a result of what courts decide should be done. Researchers have been less prolific than legislators during the last decade, at least so far as sentencing has been concerned. The explanation is partly that attention has been diverted in other directions, such as crime prevention, policing and victims; partly that funds have been more grudgingly granted for studies of a kind which in the past have yielded unpalatable findings. Consequently some fairly old studies are still the most apposite; but we have taken note of more recent research which seems relevant, up to 1995. For statistics, however, we have usually had to be content with publications relating to 1993.

A new aim has been to keep the size of the book within bounds, while adding to the information it contains. Several appendices have been omitted because the information in them is available elsewhere or has been summarised in the main text. Some chapters have been amalgamated, with economy. Others have been more or less rewritten. One—on discrimination and mercy—is new.

Nigel Walker                                                          Nicola Padfield
*January, 1996*

v

# Acknowledgments

In the preparation of this edition we have had generous help from the Home Office, the Department of Health, the Prison Service, the Transport Research Laboratory and the Magistrates' Association; from colleagues in the Cambridge Institute of Criminology (Betty Arnold, Tony Bottoms, Loraine Gelsthorpe, Adrian Grounds, Jean Kenworthy, Helen Krarup, Alison Liebling, Nancy Loucks, Jean Taylor, David Thomas, Donald West); and from David Garton of the Cambridge Employment Service, Philippa Helme of the House of Commons, Peter Johnson of West Yorkshire Probation Service, Jill Peay of Brunel University, Mark Richards of Cambridgeshire Probation Service, Roger Shaw of Powys Probation Service, Peter Tak of the Catholic University of Nijmegen, and Mandy Young of Comberton. Both of us owe special thanks to Michael Potter of Fitzwilliam College for patient help with our word-processing problems.

# Contents

## PART I

## General

CHAPTER 1

## Sentencing procedure and appeals   3

CHAPTER 5

**Discrimination and mercy   61**

PART III

Non-custodial measures

CHAPTER 15

Diversion and nominal measures   213

CHAPTER 16

Financial measures   230

CHAPTER 17

**Community penalties   257**

CHAPTER 18

## Philosophies and effectiveness of supervision   275

CHAPTER 19

## The control of stigma   286

PART IV

# Special categories

CHAPTER 20

## Young adult offenders   299

CHAPTER 21

**Mentally disordered offenders   312**

CHAPTER 22

## Dangerous offenders 343

CHAPTER 23

## Traffic offenders 360

CHAPTER 24

## The executive and the judiciary    378

APPENDIX A

## Examples of statutory maxima for determinate prison sentences    381

APPENDIX B

## Rehabilitation periods    385

APPENDIX C

## The Offenders Group Reconviction Scale    391

# References

Abt Associates (1980) *American Prisons and Jails* (5 vols), US Government Printing Office, Washington DC.

Advisory Council on the Penal System (Chairman of Sub-Committee: Baroness Wootton) (1970) *Non-Custodial and Semi-Custodial Penalties: Report etc*, London, HMSO.

Advisory Council on the Penal System (Chairman Sir Kenneth Younger) (1974) *Young Adult Offenders* London, HMSO.

Advisory Council on the Penal System (Chairman: Baroness Serota) (1977) *The Length of Prison Sentences: Interim Report etc*, London, HMSO.

Advisory Council on the Penal System (Chairman: Baroness Serota) (1978) *Sentences of Imprisonment: a review of maximum penalties etc*, HMSO, London.

American Bar Association (1986) Section of Criminal Justice: *Report to the House of Delgates*. Chicago, American Bar Association.

American Friends Service Committee (1971) *Struggle for Justice*. New York, Hill and Wang.

Andenaes, J (1974) *Punishment and Deterrence*. Ann Arbor, The University of Michigan Press.

Andrews, J (1979) *Hostels for Offenders*. Home Office Research Study No 52, London, HMSO.

Archbold, J F (1995 ed) *Pleading, Evidence and Practice in Criminal Cases*, London, Sweet and Maxwell.

Ashworth, A J (1992) *Sentencing and Criminal Justice*, London, Weidenfeld and Nicolson.

Ashworth, A J (1994) *The Criminal Process: an evaluative study*, Oxford, Clarendon Press.

Ashworth, A J, Genders, E, Mansfield, G, Peay, J, Player, E (1984) *Sentencing in the Crown Court: report of an exploratory study*. Oxford Centre for Criminological Research.

Babst, D V and Mannering, J W (1965) 'Probation versus imprisonment for similar types of offenders' in *Journal of Research in Crime and Delinquency* 2 (July): 60-71.

Barclay, G C, Tavares, C and Prout, A (1995) *Information on the Criminal Justice System in England and Wales,* London, Home Office.

Barry, K (1991) *Probation Hostels and their Regimes: a comparative study*, Cambridge, Institute of Criminology.

Baxter, R and Nuttall, C (1975) 'Severe Sentences: no Deterrent to Crime?' in *New Society*, vol 31, pp 11-13.

Bennett, T and Wright, R (1984) *Burglary: prevention and the offender*, London, Gower.

Bentham, J (1789) *An Introduction to the Principles of Morals and Legislation.* London, Payne.

Berg, I *et al* (1978) 'The Effect of Two Randomly Allocated Court Procedures on Truancy' in *British Journal of Criminology, 18, 3, 232ff.*

Berkowitz, L and Walker, N (1967) 'Law and Moral Judgments' in *Sociometry, 30, 4,* 410-422.

Beyleveld, D (1980) *A Bibliography on General Deterrence Research.* Westmead, Saxon House.

Blennerhassett, F (Chairman) (1976) *Report: of the Departmental Committee on Drinking and Driving*, London, HMSO.

Blumstein, A, Cohen, J, Gooding, W (1983) 'The Influence of Capacity on Prison Population: A Critical Review of Some Recent Evidence' in *Crime and Delinquency,* 29, No 1.

Bolton, N, Smith, F V, Heskin, K J, Banister, P A (1976) 'Psychological correlates of long-term imprisonment' in *British Journal of Criminology, 16, 1, 38ff.*

Bottomley, A K and Coleman, C A (1981) *Understanding Crime Rates: police and public roles in the production of official statistics.* Farnborough, Gower.

Bottoms, A E (1980) *The Suspended Sentence after Ten Years: A Review and Reassessment*, Occasional Paper No 4. University of Leeds, Centre for Social Work and Applied Social Studies.

Bottoms, A E (1990) 'The Aims of Imprisonment' in *Justice, Guilt and and Forgiveness in the Penal System* (ed D Garland) Edinburgh, Centre for Theology and Public Issues.

Bottoms, A E (1995) *Intensive Community Supervision for Young Offenders: outcomes, process and cost*, Cambridge, Institute of Criminology.

Bottoms, A E and Brownsword, R (1983) 'Dangerousness and Rights' in Hinton, J (ed) *Dangerousness: Problems of Assessment and Prediction*, Allen & Unwin, London.

Bottoms, A E and McClintock, F H (1973) *Criminals Coming of Age.* London, Heinemann.

Bottoms, A E and McWilliams, W (1979) 'A Non-Treatment Paradigm for Probation Practice' in *British Journal of Social Work, 9, 2, 159ff.*

Brown, S (1991) *Magistrates at Work: Sentencing and Social Structure,* Milton Keynes, Open University Press.

Bukstel, L H, Kilmann, P R (1980) 'Psychological effects of imprisonment on confined individuals; in *Psychological Bulletin, 88, 2, 469ff.*

Burgh, R (1987) 'Guilt, Punishment and Desert' in *Responsibility, Character and the Emotions* (ed F Schoeman) Cambridge, Cambridge University Press.

Butler, Lord (Chairman) (1975) *Report of the Committee on Mentally Abnormal Offenders* (Cmnd 6244). HMSO, London.

Canada (1976) *Our Criminal Law,* Report of Law Reform Commission, Ottawa.

Carson, W G (1970) 'White-collar crime and the enforcement of factory legislation' in *British Journal of Criminology, 10,* 4, 383.

Carson, W G (1982) *The Other Price of Britain's Oil,* London, Martin Robertson.

Cavadino, M and Dignan, J (1992) *The Penal System: an introduction,* London, Sage.

Clarke, R V G (1980) ' "Situational" crime prevention: theory and practice' in *British Journal of Criminology, 20,* 2, 136ff.

Cleckley, H (1941) *The Mask of Sanity: an attempt to reinterpret the so-called psychopathic personality,* St Louis, Mosby.

Cohen, S, and Taylor, L (1972) *Psychological Survival,* Harmondsworth, Penguin Books.

Coker, J B (1983) *Life Imprisonment : Release Procedures and Supervision on Licence.* Unpublished thesis in University of Southampton Library. (Summarised in a letter to the *British Journal of Criminology, 23,* 3, 307.)

Coker, J and Martin, J P *Licensed to Live,* Oxford, Blackwell.

Commission on Human Rights (1952) *Convention for the Protection of Human Rights and Fundamental Freedoms,* Strasbourg.

Committee for the Study of Incarceration (1976) *Doing Justice.* New York, Hill and Wang.

Cook, D (1989)*Rich Law, Poor Law,* Milton Keynes, Open University Press.

Corden, J and Nott, D (1980) 'The Power to Defer Sentence' in *British Journal of Criminology, 20,* 4, 358ff.

Council of Europe (1973) *Standard Minimum Rules for the Treatment of Prisoners.* (Adapted from the United Nations Standard Minimum Rules for the Treatment of Prisoners, (1955)) Strasbourg, Council of Europe.

Council of Europe (1976) *Work in Penal Institutions,* Strasbourg, Council of Europe.

Criminal Law Revision Committee (1980) *Fourteenth Report: Offences Against the Person* (Cmnd 7844) London, HMSO.

Croall, H (1991) 'Sentencing the Business Offender' in *Howard Journal, 30,* 4, 280ff.

Cross, Sir Rupert (1975) *The English Sentencing System,* London, Butterworths.

Darbyshire, P (1980) 'The Role of the Magistrates' Clerk in Summary Proceedings': 4 articles in *Justice of the Peace, 144,* 186ff, 201ff, 219ff, 233ff.

Davies, M (1969) *Probationers in their Social Environment.* Home Office Research Studies, No 2, London, HMSO

Davies, M (1970) *Financial Penalties and Probation.* Home Office Research Unit Report No 5, London, HMSO.

Department of Trade and Industry (1984) *A Revised Framework for Insolvency Law* (Cmnd 9175) London, HMSO.

Devlin, K M (1970) *Sentencing Offenders in Magistrates' Courts.* London, Sweet and Maxwell.

Devlin, P A, Lord (1979) *The Judge,* Oxford, University Press.

Ditchfield, J A (1976) *Police Cautioning in England and Wales,* Home Office Research Study 37, London, HMSO.

Ditchfield, J and Lock, M (1994) 'The prison disciplinary system: effects of the 1 April 1992 changes' in *Home Office Research Bulletin 36,* London, HMSO.

Ditton, J (1977) *Part-time Crime: an Ethnography of Fiddling and Pilferage.* London, Macmillan.

Dix, M C and Layzell, A D (1983) *Road Users and the Police.* London, Police Federation.

Dollard, J and Miller, N (1939) *Frustration and Aggression.* Newhaven, Yale University Press.

Donovan, T N (Chairman) (1965) *Report of the Interdepartmental Committee on the Court of Criminal Appeal* (Cmnd 2755) London, HMSO.

Dronfield, L (1980) *Outside Chance: The New Alternatives Project.* Radical Alternatives to Prison, London.

Dunlop, A (1975) *The Approved School Experience.* (Home Office Research Study 25), London, HMSO.

Durant, M et al (1972) *Crime, Criminals and the Law: a study of public attitudes and knowledge, carried out for the Home Office.* Office of Population Censuses and Surveys, London.

Dworkin, R (1977) *Taking Rights Seriously.* Duckworth, London.

Ehrlich, I (1975) 'The deterrent effect of capital punishment: a question of life or death' in *American Economic Review, 65,* 397ff.

Evans, R (1994) 'Cautions: counting the cost of retrenchment' in *Criminal Law Review,* 566ff.

Evans, R and Williams, C (1990) 'Variations in police cautioning, policy and practice in England and Wales' in *Howard Journal, 29,* 155ff.

Fairhead, S and Banks, C (1976) *The Petty Short Term Prisoner.* Chichester, Barry Rose.

Fairhead, S and Wilkinson-Grey, S (1981) *Day Centres and Probation* (Home Office Research Unit Paper 4). London, Home Office.

Farrington, D P and Dowds, E A (1984) 'Disentangling criminal behaviour and police reaction' in Farrington, D P & Gunn, J (eds) *Psychopaths, Dangerousness, and Reactions to Crime.* Chichester, Wiley.

Farrington, D P and Morris, A M (1983) 'Sex, Sentencing and Reconvictions' in *British Journal of Criminology, 23, 3,* 229ff.

Farrington, D P and Nuttall, C (1980) 'Prison size, overcrowding, prison violence and recidivism' in *Journal of Criminal Justice, 8,* 221ff.

Faulkner, D (1989) 'The future of the Probation Service: a view from the Government' in *The Criminal Justice System: a central role for the Probation Service* (eds Shaw, R and Haines, K), Cambridge, Institute of Criminology.

Feinberg, J (1970) *Doing and Deserving,* Princeton, University Press.

Findlater, D (1982) *The Ancillary Worker in the Probation Service* Norwich, University of East Anglia.

Fisher, R and Wilson, C (1982) *Authority or Freedom? Probation Hostels for Adults*, London, Gower.

Floud, J and Young, W (1981) *Dangerousness and Criminal Justice*. London, Heinemann.

Folkard, M S, Smith, D E and Smith, D D (1976) *IMPACT: Intensive Matched Probation and After-Care Treatment*, HOR Study No 36. London, HMSO.

Fyvel, T R (1961) *The Insecure Offender*, London, Chatto and Windus.

Gardiner, Rt Hon Lord (Chairman) (1972) *Living it Down: the Problem of Old Convictions*. The Report of a committee set up by Justice, the Howard League for Penal Reform and the National Association for the Care and Resettlement of Offenders. London, Stevens & Sons.

Gelsthorpe, L and Raynor, P (1995) 'Quality and effectiveness in probation officers' reports' in *British Journal of Criminology, 35*, 2, 188ff.

Gender, E and Player, E (1987) 'Women in prison; the treatment, the control and the experience' in *Gender, Crime and Justice* (eds Carlen, P and Worrall, A) Milton Keynes, Open University Press.

Gibbens, T C N, Soothill, K L and Way, C K (1981) 'Sex Offences Against Young Girls: a Long-Term Record Study' in *Psychological Medicine, 11*, 351-357.

Goffman, E (1961) *Asylums*, New York, Doubleday & Co Inc.

Gordon, R A (1977) 'A critique of the Evaluation of Patuxent Institution ' in *Bulletin of the Academy of Psychiatry and the Law, 5*, 2, 210ff.

Gowers, E (Chairman) (1954) *Report of the Royal Commission on Capital Punishment* (Cmnd 8932) London, HMSO.

Greenwood, P W (1979) *Rand Research on Criminal Careers: Progress to date*. Rand Corporation, Santa Monica, California.

Griew, E (1988) 'The future of diminished responsibility' in *Criminal Law Review, 75*ff.

Griffiths, R et al (1980) *Incidence and effects of police action on motoring offences as described by drivers*, Supplementary Report 543, Crowthorne, Transport and Road Research Laboratory.

Gross, H (1979) *A Theory of Criminal Justice*, London, Oxford University Press.

Gross, H (1992) 'Preventing Impunity' in *Jurisprudence: Cambridge Essays,* (eds H Gross and R Harrison) Oxford, Clarendon Press.

Grünhut, M (1963) *Probation and Mental Treatment*, London, Tavistock.

Hammond, W J (1960) 'A comparison between the effectiveness of short-term imprisonment and other penalties for first offenders in Scotland' in *The Report of the Scottish Advisory Council on the Treatment of Offenders: Use of Short Sentences of Imprisonment by the Courts*, Edinburgh, HMSO.

Hann, R G (1976) *Deterrence and the Death Penalty: a Critical Review of the Research of Isaac Ehrlich*. Ottawa, Research Division of the Solicitor General of Canada.

Hann, R G, Harman, W G and Pease, K (1991) 'Does parole reduce the rate of reconviction ?' in *Howard Journal, 30*,1, 66ff.

Harré, R and Secord, P (1972) *The Explanation of Social Behaviour*. Oxford, Blackwells.

Harris, R J (1977) 'The Probation Officer as Social Worker' in *British Journal of Social Work*, 7, 4, 433ff.

Harris, R (1992) *Crime, Criminal Justice and the Probation Service*, London, Routledge.

Hart, H L A (1959) 'Prolegomenon to the Principles of Punishment' (Presidential Address to Aristotelian Society: reprinted in his *Punishment and Responsibility* (1968) London, Oxford University Press).

Haxby, D (1978) *Probation: a changing service*, London, Constable.

Hebenton B and Thomas T (1993) *Criminal Records: State, Citizen and the Politics of Protection*. Aldershot, Avebury.

Hedderman, C (1993) *Panel Assessment Schemes for Mentally Disordered Offenders*, Home Office Research and Planning Unit Paper 76, London, Home Office.

Hedderman, C and Hough, M (1994) *Does the criminal justice system treat men and women differently ?* London, Home Office (Research Findings No 10).

Henham, J (1994) 'Attorney-General's references and sentencing policy' in *Criminal Law Review*, 499ff.

Henry, S (1978) *The Hidden Economy: the context and control of borderline crime*, Oxford, Martin Robertson.

H M Inspectors of Probation (1995) *Dealing with Dangerous People: the Probation Service and Public Protection*. London, Home Office.

Hill, G (1985) 'Predicting recidivism using institutional measures'. In *Prediction in Criminology* (eds Farrington, D P and Tarling, R, Albany) State University of New York Press.

Hines, J et al (1978) 'Recommendations, Social Information and Sentencing' in *Howard Journal*, 17, 2, 91ff.

Hirsch, A von (1976): see Committee for the Study of Incarceration (1976).

Hirschi, T (1980) 'Labelling Theory and Juvenile Delinquency: an Assessment of the Evidence' in Gove, W *The Labelling of Deviance* (1980 ed) Sage, London.

Hodgson, Sir Derek (Chairman) (1984) *The Profits of Crime and their Recovery: Report of a Committee*. London, Heinemann.

Hogg, R (1977) *A Study of Male Motorists' Attitude to Speed Restrictions and their Enforcement*, Supplementary Report 276, Crowthorne, Transport and Road Research Laboratory.

Hoggett, B (1990 ed) *Mental Health Law*, London, Sweet and Maxwell.

Home Affairs Select Committee (of House of Commons) (1995) *Report on the Mandatory Life Sentence for Murder*, London, House of Commons.

Home Office (annually) *Offences relating to motor vehicles* (in Statistical Bulletin series) London, HMSO.

Home Office (1982) *Report of the Working Group on Magistrates' Courts*, London, Home Office.

Home Office (1984a) *Cautioning by the Police: a Consultative Document*. Home Office, London (not on sale).

Home Office (1984b) *Intermittent Custody* (Cmnd 9281) London, HMSO.

Home Office (1990) *Partnership in Dealing with Offenders in the Community: a decision document,* London, HMSO.

Home Office (1990) *Crime, Justice and Protecting the Public,* London, HMSO.

Home Office (1991) *Custody, Care and Justice: the way ahead for the Prison Service in England and Wales.* London, HMSO.

Home Office (1991) *The National Collection of Criminal Records,* London, HMSO.

Home Office (1995) *Strengthening Punishment in the Community: a consultation document,* London, HMSO.

Honderich, T (1976 ed) *Punishment: the supposed justification.* London, Peregrine Books.

Hood, R G (1962) *Sentencing in Magistrates' Courts,* London, Stevens.

Hood, R G (1972) *Sentencing the Motoring Offender: a Study of Magistrates' Views and Practices* (Cambridge Studies in Criminology, 31), Heinemann, London.

Hood, R G (1974) *Tolerance and the Tariff: some reflections on fixing the time prisoners serve in custody.* NACRO Paper. London, NACRO.

Hood, R G and Shute, S (1994) *Parole in Transition: evaluating the impact and effects of changes in the parole system: Phase One: Establishing the base-line,* Oxford Centre for Criminological Research.

Hood, R G and Shute, S (1995) *Paroling with New Criteria: evaluating the impact and effects of changes in the parole system: Phase Two,* Oxford, Centre for Criminological Research.

Hood, R G and Sparks, R F (1970) *Key Issues in Criminology,* London, Weidenfeld and Nicolson.

Hood, R G and Taylor, I (1968) 'Second Report on the Effectiveness of Pre-sentence Investigations in Reducing Recidivism' in *British Journal of Criminology,* 8, 4, 431ff.

Hough, J M (1996) 'People talking about punishment' in *Howard Journal* (forthcoming)

Hough, J M and Mayhew, P (1983) *The British Crime Survey: 1st Report.* Home Office Research Study No 76. London, HMSO.

Hough, M and Moxon, D (1985) 'Dealing with offenders: popular opinion and the views of victims' in *Howard Journal,* 24, 3, 160ff.

Humphreys, S A and Roy, L (1995) 'Driving and psychiatric illness' in *Psyciatric Bulletin,* 19, 12, 747ff.

Hutter, B (1988) *The Reasonable Arm of the Law,* Oxford University Press.

Jacobs, F G (1975) *The European Convention on Human Rights,* Oxford, Clarendon Press.

Jardine, E and Moore, G (1983) 'Community Service Orders, Employment and the Tariff' in *Criminal Law Review,* 17ff.

Jones, S (1983) 'Deferment of Sentence: an appraisal ten years on' in *British Journal of Criminology,* 23, 4, 381ff.

Kassebaum, G, Ward, D, Wilner, D (1971) *Prison Treatment and Parole Survival,* New York, Wiley.

King, R D and Elliott, K W (1977) *Albany: birth of a prison, end of an era*, Routledge and Kegan Paul, London.

King, R D and McDermott, K (1995) *The State of our Prisons*, Oxford, Clarendon Press.

Knott, C (1995) 'The STOP Programme: reasoning and rehabilitation in a British setting' in *What Works : reducing reoffending* (ed J McGuire) Chichester, Sage.

Kraus, J (1974) 'A Comparison of Corrective Effects of Probation and Detention on Juvenile Offenders' in *British Journal of Criminology, 14*, 1, 49ff.

Kriefman, S (1975) *Driving While Disqualified*, Home Office Research Study No 27, London, HMSO.

Kvaraceus, W C (1966) *Anxious Youth,* Columbus, Ohio.

Lacey, N (1987) *State Punishment,* London, Routledge.

Lane, Lord (Chairman) (1993) *Report of the Committee on the Mandatory Life Sentence*, London, Prison Reform Trust.

Langdon, A J (Chairman) (1984) *Managing the Long-Term Prison System: The Report of the Control Review Committee*, London, HMSO.

Law Commission (1977) *Defences of General Application*, London, HMSO.

Law Commission (1994) *Binding Over,* London, HMSO.

Learmont, Sir John (1995) *Review of Prison Security in England and Wales and the Escape from Parkhurst Prison on 3rd January, 1995,* London, HMSO.

Leech, M (1995) *The Prisoner's Handbook,* Oxford University Press.

Leigh, L H (1982) *The Control of Commercial Fraud*, London, Heinemann.

Lemert, E (1969) *Human Deviance, Social Problems and Social Control.* New Jersey, Prentice-Hall.

Levenson, H (1981) *The Price of Justice: Costs and Defendants*, Cobden Trust, London.

Levi, M (1981) *The Phantom Capitalist*, London, Heinemann.

Levi, M (1993) *The Investigation, Prosecution and Trial of Serious Fraud,* Royal Commission on Criminal Justice's Research Study, London, HMSO.

Lewis, P (1980) *Psychiatric Probation Orders*, Cambridge, Institute of Criminology.

Lidstone, K, Hogg, R and Mawby, R (1980) *Prosecutions by Private Individuals and non-police Agencies*, London, HMSO.

Livingstone, S and Owen, T (1993) *Prison Law,* Oxford University Press.

Lloyd, C, Mair, G and Hough, J M (1994) *Explaining Reconviction Rates: a critical analysis,* London, Home Office (Research Findings No 12).

Longford, Earl of (1961)*The Idea of Punishment*, London, Chapman.

Loucks, N (1993) *Working Guide to the Prison Rules*, London, Prison Reform Trust.

McCabe, S and Sutcliffe, F (1978) *Defining Crime: a study of police decisions*, Oxford, Blackwells.

McDermott, K and King, R D (1988) 'Mind games', in *British Journal of Criminology, 28,* 3, 357ff.

McIvor, G (1990) 'Community service and custody in Scotland', in *Howard Journal, 29, 2,*101ff.

McIvor, G (1992) 'Intensive probation supervision: does more mean better ?' in *Probation Journal, 39,* 1, 2ff.

Mackay, R D (1995) *Mental Condition Defences in the Criminal Law,* Oxford, Clarendon Press.

McWilliams, W and Murphy (1980) 'Breach of Community Service' in Pease, K and McWilliams, W, *Community Service by Order.* Scottish Academic Press, Edinburgh.

Magistrates' Association (1982) *Suggestions for Traffic Offence Penalties,* London, Magistrates' Association.

Mair, G (1988) *Day Centres,* (Home Office Research Study 100), London, HMSO.

Mair, G, Lloyd, C, Nee, C, and Sibbit, R (1994) *Intensive Probation in England and Wales,* Home Office Research Study 133, London, HMSO.

Mair, G and Nee, C (1990) *Electronic Monitoring: the trials and their results,* Home Office Research Study 120, London, HMSO.

Malleson, K (1993) *Review of the Appeal Process,* Royal Commission on Criminal Justice Research Study 17, London, HMSO.

Mannheim, H (1939) *The Dilemma of Penal Reform,* London, Routledge and Kegan Paul.

Mannheim, H and Wilkins, L T (1955) *Prediction Methods in Relation to Borstal Training,* London, HMSO.

Markham, G R (1981) 'A Community Service for Elderly Offenders' in *Police Journal, 54,* 3, 235ff.

Mars, G (1982) *Cheats at work,* London, Allen and Unwin.

Martin, J P (1962) *Offenders as Employees,* London, Macmillan.

Martinson, R (1974) 'What Works? Questions and answers about prison reform' in *Public Interest* (Spring) 22ff.

Martinson, R (1976) *Rehabilitation, Recidivism and Research,* New Jersey, National Council on Crime and Delinquency.

Mathieson, D (1980) 'Social Inquiry Reports: the Status of the Defendant' in *Justice of the Peace, 144,* 46.

Matza, D (1964) *Delinquency and Drift,* New York, Wiley.

Mawby, R I (1979) 'Policing by the Post Office' in *British Journal of Criminology, 19,* 3, 242ff.

May, C (1992) *The National Probation Survey, 1990* (Research and Planning Unit Paper 72), London, Home Office.

May, C (1994) 'Probation and community sanctions' in *The Oxford Handbook of Criminology* (edd Maguire, M et al) Oxford University Press.

May, Sir John (Chairman) (1979) *Report of Committee of Inquiry into the United Kingdom Prison Service* (Cmnd 7673) London, HMSO.

Mayhew, P (1994) *Findings from the International Crime Survey,* London, Home Office (Research Findings No 8).

Meehl, P E (1954) *Clinical Versus Statistical Prediction*, University of Minnesota Press, Minneapolis.

Merton, R (1949) *Social Theory and Social Structure*, Glencoe, Free Press.

Mirrlees-Black, C (1993) *Disqualification fro Driving: an effective penalty ?* London, Home Office (Research and Planning Unit Paper 74).

Moberly, W (1968) *The Ethics of Punishment*, London, Faber and Faber.

Morgan R, and Jones S (1992) 'Bail or Jail ?' in *Criminal Justice under Stress* (eds Stockdale, E and Casale, S) London, Blackstone.

Morgenroth, E C (Chairman) (1971) *Struggle for Justice: a report on crime and justice in America.* (Report of American Friends Services Committee). New York, Hill & Wang.

Morison, R P (Chairman) (1962) *(First) Report of the Departmental Committee on the Probation Service* (Cmnd 1650) London, HMSO.

Morison, R P (Chairman) (1962) *Second Report of the Departmental Committee on the Probation Service* (Cmnd 1800) London, HMSO.

Morris, A, Wilkinson, C, Tisi, A, Woodrow, J and Rockley, A (1994) *Managing the Needs of Female Prisoners*: a report to the Home Office.

Mountbatten, Earl (Chairman) (1966) *Report of the Inquiry into Prison Escapes and Security* (Cmnd 3175) London, HMSO.

Moxon, D (1988) *Sentencing Practice in the Crown Court*, Home Office Research Study 103, London, HMSO.

Moxon, D, Sutton, M, and Hedderman, C (1990) *Unit fines: experiments in four courts*, Research and Planning Unit Paper 59, London, Home Office.

Moxon, D, Sutton, M and Hedderman, C (1990) *Deductions from Benefit for Fine Default*, Research and Planning Unit Paper 60, London, Home Office.

National Association for the Care and Resettlement of Offenders (1981) *Bridging the Gap: Report of a Working party on the Transition from Education in Penal Establishments to Education in the Community*, London, NACRO.

National Assosition for the Care and Resettlement of Offenders (1995) *Pre-sentence Reports: a handbook for probation officers and social workers*, London, NACRO.

National Swedish Council for Crime Prevention (1978) *A new penal system: ideas and proposals*, Report No 5 (English summary of *Nytt Straffsystem*) Stockholm.

Nelken, D (1983) *The Limits of the Legal Process: a Study of Landlords, Law and Crime*, London, Academic Press.

Nellis, M (1991) 'The electronic monitoring of offenders in England and Wales' in *British Journal of Criminology, 31*, 2, 165ff.

Nellis, M (1995) 'Probation values for the 1990s' in *Howard Journal, 34*, 19ff.

Newbury, T (1988) *The Use and Enforcement of Compensation Orders in Magistrates' Courts*, Home Office Research Study 102, London, HMSO.

Owen, T (1991) 'Prisoners' rights' in *New Law Journal, 140*, 1328.

Padfield, N (1993a) 'The right to bail: a Canadian perspective' in *Criminal Law Review*, 477.

Padfield, N (1993b) 'Parole and the life sentence prisoner' in *Howard Journal, 32,* 87.

Padfield, N (1995) *Texts and Materials on the Criminal Justice Process,* London, Butterworths.

Parker, H, Sumner, M and Jarvis, G (1985) *Unmasking the Magistrates,* Oxford University Press.

Parole Board *Annual Reports of,* London, HMSO.

Pease, K et al (1977) *Community Service Assessed in 1976,* Home Office Research Study No 39, London, HMSO.

Pease, K (1981) *Community Service Orders: a first decade of promise,* London, Howard League.

Pease, K (1994) 'Cross-national imprisonment-rates: limitations of method and possible conclusions', in *Prisons in Context* (eds King, R D, and Maguire, M) Oxford, Clarendon Press.

Peay, J (1989) *Tribunals on Trial,* Oxford, Clarendon Press.

Phillpotts, G J O and Lancucki, L B (1979) *Previous convictions, sentence and reconvictions: a statistical study of a sample of 5,000 offenders convicted in January 1971,* Home Office Research Study No 53, London, HMSO.

Priestley, P et al (1978) *Social Skills and Personal Problem-Solving: a handbook of methods,* London, Tavistock.

Priestley, P et al (1984) *Social Skills in Prison and the Community: problem-solving for offenders,* London, Routledge and Kegan Paul.

Prior, P J (Chairman) (1985) *Report of the Committee on the Prison Disciplinary System: Cmnd 9641.* London, HMSO.

Prison Department of the Home Office (annual)*Reports of,* HMSO, London.

Prison Department (Annual) *Statistics,* London, HMSO.

Prison Reform Trust (1995) *H M Prison, Doncaster: the Doncatraz File,* London, Prison Reform Trust.

Prison Ombudsman (1995) *Six Month Review,* London, Prison Ombudsman.

Prison Rules (1964) *Statutory Instrument 1964 No 388,* HMSO, London.

Quenault, S W (1967) *Driver Behaviour: safe and unsafe drivers,* RRL Report LR 70, Crowthorne, Transport and Road Research Laboratory.

Quenault, S W (1968) *Driver Behaviour: safe and unsafe drivers—II,* RRL Report LR146, Crowthorne, Transport and Road Research Laboratory.

Reed, J (Chairman) (1992) *Review of Health and Social Services for Mentally Disordered Offenders and others requiring similar Services: final summary report,* London, HMSO.

Richards, B (1978) 'The Experience of Long-Term Imprisonment' in *British Journal of Criminology, 18,* 2, 162ff.

Richards, M et al (1995) 'Foreign nationals in English prisons' in *Howard Journal, 34,* 2, 1158ff, and 34, 3, 195ff.

Richardson, G (1993) *Law, Process and Custody,* London, Weidenfeld and Nicolson.

Riley, D (1991) *Drink-Driving: the effects of enforcement,* London, Home Office (Research Study 121).

Robinson, P H (1988) 'Hybrid principles for the distribution of criminal sanctions' in *Northwestern University Law Review, 82,* 1, 19ff.

Ros, L H, Blumenthal, M (1974) 'Sanctions for the drinking driver: an experimental study' in *Journal of Legal Studies, 3,* 53ff.

Ross, H L (1982) *Deterring the Drinking Driver: Legal Policy and Social Control.* Massachusetts, Lexington Books.

Royal Commission on Criminal Procedure (1981a) *Report,* London, HMSO.

Royal Commission on Criminal Procedure (1981b) *Prosecutions by Private Individuals and Non-Police Agencies* (Research Study No 10) London, HMSO.

Royal Commission on the Penal System in England & Wales (1967) *First Memorandum submitted by the Council of the Law Society.* in *Written Evidence* etc Vol II, Part I, 54-62.

Salem, S R (1982) 'The Psychiatric Remands Process in Magistrates' Courts', unpublished Report to Home Office, copy in Cambridge Institute of Criminology Library.

Salleilles, R (1898) *The Individualisation of Punishment* (translated by R S Jastrow, 1911) London, Heinemann.

Sallon, C and Bedingfield, D (1993) 'Drugs, money and the law' in *Criminal Law Review,* 165ff.

Sanders, A (1985) 'Class bias in prosecutions' in *Howard Journal, 24,3,* 176ff.

Sanders, A and Young, R (1994) *Criminal Justice,* London, Butterworths.

Sapsford, R J (1978) 'Life sentence prisoners: psychological changes during sentence' in *British Journal of Criminology,* 18, 2, 128ff.

Schagen, I P and Heygate, S B (1983) 'Assessing the risk of re-offending' in *NASPO News* (newsletter of the National Association of Senior Probation Officers) 4, 10ff.

Schichor, D (1995) *Punishment for Profit,* London, Sage.

Schwartz, R D and Orleans, S (1967) 'On legal sanctions' in *University of Chicago Law Review,* XXXIV, 274ff.

Scott, P D (1964) 'Approved school success-rates' in *British Journal of Criminology, 4,* 6, 525ff.

Sellin, T and Wolfgang, M E (1964) *The Measurement of Delinquency,* New York, Wiley.

Shapland, J (1981) *Between conviction and sentence: the process of mitigation.* London, Routledge and Kegan Paul.

Shaw, I (1980) *Community Service Attitudes and Practice.* South Glamorgan Probation Service.

Shaw, R (1991) 'Supervising the dangerous offender' in *National Association of Senior Probation Officers' News, 10,* 4, 3ff.

Shaw, S (1982) *The People's Justice.* Prison Reform Trust, London.

Sinclair, I (1971) *Hostels for Probationers.* Home Office Research Unit Report, London, HMSO.

Smith, D, Austin, C, Ditchfield, J (1981) *Board of Visitor Adjudications*. Available from Home Office Research Unit, London.

Smith, R (1979) *Children and the Courts*, London, Sweet and Maxwell.

Softley, P (1978) *Fines in Magistrates' Courts*. Home Office Research Study No 46, London, HMSO.

Softley, P (1982) *Fine Enforcement: an evaluation of the practices of individual courts* (Home Office Research and Planning Unit Paper 12) London, HMSO.

Stace, M (1976) 'Name Suppression and the Criminal Justice Amendment Act 1975' in *British Journal of Criminology, 16*, 4, 395ff.

Stallybrass, W T (1945) 'A comparison of the general principles of criminal law in England with the "Progetto Definitivo di un Nuovo Codice Penale" of Alfredo Rocco' in *The Modern Approach to Criminal Law* (eds L Radzinowicz and J W C Turner), London, Macmillan.

Steer, D (1973) 'The elusive conviction' in *British Journal of Criminology, 13*, 4, 373ff.

Steininger, E H (1959) *Changes in the MMPI profiles of first prison offenders during their first year of imprisonment* (Doctoral dissertation in Michigan State University Library: cit Bukstel and Kilman, qv).

*Stone's Justices' Manual* (1995) , London, Butterworths.

Sutherland, E (1947) *Principles of Criminology*, Philadelphia, Lippincott.

Sykes, G M (1958) *The Society of Captives*, Princeton, University Press.

Sykes, G M and Matza, D (1957) 'Techniques of Neutralisation: a Theory of Delinquency' in *American Sociological Review, 22*, 664ff.

Tannenbaum, F (1938) *Crime and the Community* (reprinted 1951) New York, Columbia University Press.

Tarling, R (1979) *Sentencing Practice in Magistrates' Courts*, Home Office Research Study 56, London, HMSO.

Thomas, D A (1972) 'Increasing Sentences on Appeal' in *Criminal Law Review*, 288ff.

Thomas, D A (1970, 1979) *Principles of Sentencing in the Court of Appeal*, Heinemann, London.

Thomas, D A (1982) *Current Sentencing Practice*, London, Sweet and Maxwell. (2 loose-leaf volumes, regularly updated).

Thomas, D A (1983) Commentary on *Skelton* in *Criminal Law Review* at 687.

Thornton, D, Curran, D, Grayson, D and Holloway, V (1984) *Tougher Regimes in Detention Centres*, London, HMSO.

Tittle, C (1980) 'Labelling and Crime: an evaluation' in Gove, W (ed) *The Labelling of Deviance* (1980 ed) London, Sage.

Tremblay, R E (1984) 'Treatment of hard-core delinquents in a residential establishment' in *British Journal of Criminology, 24*, 4, 384ff.

Turner, A (1992) 'Sentencing in the Magistrates' Courts' in *Sentencing, Judicial Discretion and Training* (edd Munro, C and Wasik, M) London, Sweet and Maxwell.

Victim Support (1993) *Compensating the Victims of Crime: report of an independent working party*, London, Victim Support.

von Hirsch, A (1976): see Committee for the Study of Incarceration.

Walker, H and Beaumont, W (1981) *Probation Work*, Oxford, Blackwells.

Walker, M A (1978) 'Measuring the Seriousness of Crimes' in *British Journal of Criminology, 18*, 4, 348ff.

Walker, N (1969) *Sentencing in a Rational Society*, London, Allen Lane.

Walker, N (1973) *Behaviour and Misbehaviour*, Oxford, Blackwells.

Walker, N (1980) *Punishment, Danger and Stigma*, Oxford, Blackwells.

Walker, N (1981) 'The Ultimate Justification' in *Crime, Proof & Punishment: Essays in Memory of Sir Rupert Cross*, (ed C Tapper) London, Butterworths.

Walker, N (1981) 'A note on parole and sentence-lengths' in *Criminal Law Review,* 829ff.

Walker, N (1993) 'Legislating the transcendental: von Hirsch's proportionality', in *Cambridge Law Journal, 51*, 3, 530ff.

Walker, N (1995 ed) *Why Punish ?* Oxford, Oxford University Press.

Walker, N (ed) (1996) *Dangerous People*, London, Blackstone.

Walker, N and Hough, J M (1988) *Public Attitudes to Sentencing: surveys from five countries,* Aldershot, Gower.

Walker, N and Marsh, C (1984) 'Do Sentences Affect Public Disapproval' in *British Journal of Criminology, 24*, 1, 27ff.

Walker, N, and McCabe, S (1973) *Crime and Insanity in England, Vol II: New Solutions and New Problems*, Edinburgh, Edinburgh University Press.

Walker, N, Farrington, D P F, and Tucker, F (1981) 'Reconviction Rates of Adult Males after Different Sentences; in *The British Journal of Criminology, 21*, 4, 357ff.

Walmsley, R (1993) *The National Prison Survey, 1991: main findings,* London, Home Office (Research Findings).

Ward, D (1987) *The Validity of the Reconviction–Prediction Score*, London, Home Office (Research Study 94).

Wasik, M (1993) *Emmins on Sentencing* London, Blackstone.

Watts, G R and Quimby, A R (1980) *Aspects of Road Layout that Affect Drivers' Perception and Risk-Taking*, Report 920, Crowthorne, Transport and Road Research Laboratory.

West, D J (1963) *The Habitual Prisoner*, London, Macmillan.

West, D J, Farrington, D P F (1977) *The Delinquent Way of Life: Third Report of the Cambridge Study in Delinquent Development*, Cambridge Studies in Criminology, vol 35, London, Heinemann.

Widgery, Lord Justice (Chairman of sub-committee) (1966) *Reparation by the Offender, Report of the Advisory Council on the Penal System*, HMSO, London.

Wilkins, L (1964) *Social Deviance*, London, Tavistock.

Wilkins, G (1979) *Making them Pay: a study of some fine-defaulters, civil prisoners and other petty offenders received into a local prison*, London, NACRO.

Wilkinson, G (1995 ed) *Road Traffic Offences*, ed Halnan, P and Spencer, J, London, Oyez Longman.

Willett, T C (1973) *Drivers after Sentence*, London, Heinemann.

Williams, M (1970) *A Study of Some Aspects of Borstal Allocation*, Prison Department Chief Psychologist's Report 33 (unpublished).

Wolfgang, M and Ferracuti, F (1967) *The Subculture of Violence: Towards an Integrated Theory in Criminology*, London, Tavistock.

Woolf, Lord Justice (1991) *Prison Disturbances April 1990: Report of an Inquiry by the Rt Hon Lord Justice Woolf (Parts I and II) and His Honour Judge Stephen Tumim (Part II)*, Cmnd 1456. London, HMSO.

Wootton, Baroness: (1970): see *Advisory Council on the Penal System*.

World Health Organisation (1990) *International Classification of Disorders*, 10th edition, Geneva, World Health Organisation.

Wright, M (1982) *Making Good: Prisons, Punishment and Beyond*, London, Burnett Books.

Younger, Sir Kenneth (Chairman) (1974) *Young Adult Offenders: Report of (a committee of) The Advisory Council on the Treatment of Offenders*, London, HMSO.

Zellick, G (1980) 'Prison Offences' in *British Journal of Criminology, 20*, 4, 377ff.

Zellick, G (1981) 'The Prison Rules and the Courts' in *Criminal Law Review*, 602ff. (and see his 'Postscript' in (1982) *Criminal Law Review*, 575ff).

# Abbreviations

To save space and avoid tediousness, the abbreviations listed below are freely used, especially for statutes and references to decided cases. 'The Court of Appeal' (or 'CA') is used without the addition of 'Criminal Division'. 'Indictable offences' includes, quite properly, those which are 'triable either way'. 'Juveniles' means 'children or young persons' (the statutory terms for those under 14 and those aged 14, 15 or 16). 'Sentence' sometimes includes 'orders' of the kind which a criminal court can use to dispose of an offender. Numbers in brackets are references to paragraphs, so that '2.12' is a reference to paragraph 12 of chapter 2.

| | |
|---|---|
| AC | Appeal Court |
| ACO | Attendance Centre Order |
| ACPO | Assistant Chief Probation Officer |
| ACPS | Advisory Council on the Penal System |
| AEO(A) | Attachment of Earnings Order (Act) |
| AG | Attorney-General |
| All ER | All England Reports |
| CA | Court of Appeal |
| CAA | Criminal Appeal Act |
| CC | Crown Court |
| CCA | Court of Criminal Appeal |
| CCRC | Criminal Cases Review Commission |
| CICB | Criminal Injuries Compensation Board |
| CICCA | Costs in Criminal Cases Act |
| CJA | Criminal Justice Act |
| CJPOA | Criminal Justice and Public Order Act |
| CLA | Criminal Law Act |
| CLRC | Criminal Law Revision Committee |
| CP(I)A | Criminal Procedure (Insanity) Act |
| CPO | Chief Probation Officer |
| CQSW | Certificate of Qualification in Social Work |
| Cr App Rep (S) | Criminal Appeal Reports (Sentencing) |
| Crim LR | Criminal Law Review |
| CRO | Criminal Records Office |

| | |
|---|---|
| CS | Community Service |
| CSEW | Criminal Statistics, England and Wales |
| CSO | Community Service Order |
| CSP | Current Sentencing Practice |
| CYPA | Children and Young Persons Act |
| DC | Detention Centre |
| DCO | Detention Centre Order |
| DH | Department of Health |
| DHSS | Department of Health and Social Security |
| DOL | Discharge by Operation of Law |
| DPP | Director of Public Prosecutions |
| DVLA | Driver and Vehicle Licensing Authority |
| ECHR | European Commission on Human Rights |
| EDR | Estimated Date of Release |
| EEC | European Economic Community |
| ES | Extended Sentences |
| FBI | Federal Bureau of Investigation |
| FEO | Fine Enforcement Officer |
| HA | Homicide Act |
| HO | Home Office |
| IA | Immigration Act |
| ICD | International Classification of Disorders, published by World Health Organisation |
| IG | Instruction to [Prison] Governors |
| ITEW | Indictable, triable either way |
| JP | Justice of the Peace |
| KPI | Key Performance Indicator (for prisons) |
| LAA | Legal Aid Act |
| LCJ | Lord Chief Justice |
| LRC | Local Review Committee |
| M(ADP)A | Murder (Abolition of Death Penalty) Act |
| MC | Magistrates' Court |
| MCA | Magistrates' Court Act |
| MHA | Mental Health Act |
| MH(PIC)A | Mental Health (Patients in the Community) Act |
| MHRT | Mental Health Review Tribunal |
| MMPI | Minnesota Multiphasic Personality Inventory |
| MP | Member of Parliament |
| MPSO | Money Payment Supervision Order |
| NACRO | National Association for the Care and Resettlement of Offenders |
| NAPO | National Association of Probation Officers |
| NASPO | National Association of Senior Probation Officers |
| NCCL | National Council for Civil Liberties (now 'Liberty') |
| NCO | Non-Commissioned Officer |
| NHS | National Health Service |
| NHSRA | National Health Service Reorganisation Act |
| NTVLRO | National Television Licence Records Office |
| OCAU | Observation, Classification and Allocation Unit |
| PA | Prison Act |
| PCCA | Powers of Criminal Courts Act |
| PE | Physical Education |
| PED | Parole Eligibility Date |
| PMO | Prison Medical Officer |

| | |
|---|---|
| POA | Prison Officers' Association |
| PSR | Pre-Sentence Report |
| PSIR | Post-Sentence Interview Report |
| RCCJ | Royal Commission on Criminal Justice |
| RMO | Responsible Medical Officer |
| ROA | Rehabilitation of Offenders Act |
| RTA | Road Traffic Act |
| RTOA | Road Traffic Offenders Act |
| RTRA | Road Traffic Regulation Act |
| SI | Statutory Instrument |
| SL | Standard List |
| SPO | Senior Probation Officer |
| SS | Suspended Sentence |
| SSSO | Suspended Sentence Supervision Order |
| TA | Transport Act |
| TIC | Taken into consideration |
| TLR | Times Law Reports |
| UK | United Kingdom |
| USA | United States of America |
| USSR | Union of Soviet Socialist Republics |
| WLR | Weekly Law Reports |

# Table of statutes

References in this Table to *Statutes* are to Halsbury's Statutes of England (Fourth Edition) showing the volume and page at which the annotated text of the Act will be found.

# Table of cases

## Q

## R

Part I

# General

# Chapter 1

# Sentencing procedure and appeals

## Preliminaries

**1.1** A defendant cannot be sentenced or otherwise disposed of by order of a criminal court unless and until

   a.   he has been found guilty[1] or pleaded guilty; and

   b.   he or his representative has been given an opportunity to put any mitigating considerations to the court.

In practice courts usually also receive

   c.   a list of his 'antecedents' (if any): that is, of those previous convictions or findings of guilt[2] which the prosecutor considers relevant to the present sentencing decision. The defendant may also ask for certain offences to be 'taken into consideration' (TIC: see 2.10).

If the offence is indictable the court is quite likely to ask for

   d.   a pre-sentence report (PSR) by a probation officer; but it hardly ever does so in the case of traffic offences or summary offences (with the exception of soliciting and indecent exposure).

If there is reason to think that the offender is mentally disordered the court is likely to ask for

   e.   at least one 'state of mind report' by a psychiatrist, and sometimes two (see 2.33; 21.37).

The court may also hear or read

   f.   oral or written testimony from one or more 'character witnesses', almost always in favour of the defendant.

Finally, it may have received

   g.   one or more claims for compensation or restitution from or on behalf of persons who have suffered injury, loss or damage as a result of the offence (see 16.41).

---

1. Exceptions are defendants found unfit to plead, not guilty by reason of insanity, their equivalent in MCs (see 21.60), or persons bound over without being found guilty (see 15.27).
2. Youth courts do not 'convict' defendants: they 'find them guilty'; but findings of guilt can be included in antecedents reports, unless the defendant was over 21 at the time of the offence for which he is being sentenced, and the finding of guilt occurred before he reached the age of 14 (s 16 CYPA 63).

## Postponement of sentence

**1.2** Normally the offender is sentenced on the day on which he is convicted unless

a. the court defers sentence: this is dealt with in the chapter on diversionary measures (see 15.17);

b. the offender has been convicted by a magistrates' court (MC) which comes to the conclusion that the offence(s) are more serious than at first appeared: the court then commits him in custody or on bail to the Crown Court (CC) for sentence (s 38 MCA 80, as amended by CJA 91)[1]. About 3 per cent of indictable offenders are so committed. The same power to commit in custody or on bail can be used by an MC if it convicts an offender of an imprisonable offence while he is subject to a parole licence (s 40(3) CJA 91; and see 14.38), so that the CC can consider whether to revoke the licence, with the result that he will be returned to prison. The CC however is not obliged to do what the MC has in mind: it can itself inquire into the circumstances of the case and deal with the offender in any way in which it could deal with him if he had been convicted by the CC on indictment (s 42 PCCA 73). Similarly, if an MC convicts an offender aged 14 or older of an offence for which it could sentence an adult to prison, if the necessary conditions for the making of a hospital order (see 21.37) are satisfied, and if it appears to the MC that if a hospital order is made it should be accompanied by an order restricting his discharge from hospital it can commit him in custody (not on bail) to the CC which may either make a hospital order with or without a restriction order or deal with him in any other way in which the MC might have dealt with him (s 43 MHA 83);

c. he is convicted by an MC which decides to remit him to some other MC which has already convicted him of 'another such offence' (but has neither sentenced him for it nor committed him to the CC for sentence for it nor dealt with him in any other way: s 39 MCA 80). This can be done only with the consent of the other MC: the aim is to make it possible for him to be sentenced by a single court on a single occasion for all the offences of a similar kind for which he has been successfully prosecuted but not yet sentenced. There is no similar express provision covering the CC, no doubt because of the fiction that it is a single court: but in practice judges do remit convicted offenders to each other for sentence;

d. the court adjourns proceedings. In the case of MCs this is usually done under s 10(3) MCA 80, 'for the purpose of enabling inquiries to be made or of determining the most suitable method of dealing with the case': such adjournments must not be for more than 4 weeks (3 if the offender is remanded in custody), but further adjournments are permissible, subject to the same time-limits.

   The CC has a common law power to adjourn before passing sentence, or to delay the pronouncement of part of the sentence (*Annesley* (1975) 62 Cr App Rep 113). It is properly used when 'all the material necessary to complete all elements of a sentencing problem is not immediately available' (ibid), or in 'circumstances of a very special nature' (*Spittle* [1976] Crim LR 698).

e.  the court remands him for medical examination and report. MCs have an express power to do this in s 30 MCA 80; but it is limited to cases in which the court is satisfied that the accused did the act or made the omission charged but feels the need of a medical report before determining how to deal with him. It was originally intended for use *before* conviction so that magistrates could take the medical report into account when deciding whether to convict or not; and in many courts it is still used, adjournments (see (d) above) being used to obtain medical reports *after* conviction. Some courts, however, use s 30 regardless of whether they have reached the stage of convicting the offender, while others use s 10 regardless. More than 95 per cent of 'medical remands' are in fact 'psychiatric remands', for reports on the mental state of the defendant or convicted offender (Salem, 1982). Psychiatric remands by CCs are based on the common law power of adjournment described in (d) above. For courts' powers to remand to mental hospitals, see 21.15.

f.  the offender has been convicted by a MC in his absence and the court is minded to impose a custodial sentence or a disqualification: see 1.4.

1.  There is a special power of committal with a view to a sentence of detention in a young offender institution exceeding the MC's powers (s 37 MCA 80 as amended by Sch 14 CJA 82).

## Sentencing the absent

**1.3** Although there is a general assumption that the defendant should be in court when sentence is being considered and passed, and should be given an opportunity to make a submission in mitigation, neither statute nor case-law lays this down. Indeed, in the case of summary offences for which the offender could not be sentenced to more than 3 months' imprisonment there is a procedure allowing him to plead guilty by post (s 12 MCA 80); but if he makes a submission in mitigation it must be read out to the court. On the other hand, if the defendant is willing and able to be present at his trial or sentence he is regarded as having the right to do so. An exception is a mentally ill or severely impaired defendant whose condition has led the Home Secretary to authorise his transfer from custody to a mental hospital before his trial (under s 48 MHA 83): the court can deal with him by means of a hospital order (but not otherwise) in his absence if it appears 'impracticable or inappropriate' to bring him to court (s 51 MHA 83; see 21.37). In the case of the CC a restriction order may be added. Nothing in the section requires that the defendant be represented in court. If the defendant absconds during the trial he is regarded as having waived his right to be present and thus given the judge discretion to allow the trial to proceed in his absence (*Jones (No 2)* [1972] 1 WLR 887).

**1.4** What an MC must not do is sentence anyone to prison or a young offender institution or activate a suspended prison sentence unless he is either present in person or represented by counsel or (more likely) a solicitor (ss 11, 122 MCA 80). Nor may an MC impose a disqualification on him in his absence, except at the resumption of an adjourned hearing (see (d) 1.2). This does not debar the court from committing him in his absence to prison for defaulting in the payment of a fine, compensation order or other payment (see 16.31), or for failure to comply with some other requirement: but since a 'means hearing' must be held in most such cases (see 16.18) it is rare for this to happen without his personal appearance.

## Sentencing in public

**1.5** On the principle that justice should be administered in public the news media and the public are not normally excluded during the sentencing stage, although the court has—and occasionally uses—the jurisdiction to exclude them (*A-G v Leveller Magazine Ltd* [1979] AC 440). On the other hand, by no means all of the information on which sentencers base their decisions is given to the public. What the defendant or his representative puts forward by way of mitigation has normally[1] to be said aloud in open court; but not the contents of reports by psychiatrists, doctors, probation officers or social workers (the defendant or his representative must be given copies of these, and what is said aloud may refer to the contents, but efforts are made not to disclose intimate information to the public or press). Police 'antecedents' reports are also submitted in writing, and while what is said aloud may refer to previous convictions the public and press do not usually hear the whole of a recidivist's record. Claims for compensation are sometimes read aloud, sometimes not.

1. An application to clear the court for this purpose in an exceptional case should itself be explained *after* the court has been cleared (*Weafer* (1981) 3 Cr App Rep (S) 296). The Criminal Procedure and Investigations Bill 95, if enacted, will give a trial judge the power to restrict reporting of 'false or irrelevant' allegations made in a speech in mitigation.

## Plea-bargaining

**1.6** Sentences can be affected by what is known as 'plea-bargaining'. When this takes the form of an agreement between defence lawyers and the prosecution it is not regarded as objectionable. The defendant may agree to plead guilty to charges 1 and 2 if the prosecution undertakes to offer no evidence on charges 3, 4 and 5. Or he may agree to plead guilty to a less serious charge based on similar evidence: for example to causing grievous bodily harm with intent instead of attempted murder. Since English prosecutors do not propose the sentence, this cannot form part of the bargain, although it is obviously affected by the nature of the charge.

**1.7** 'Plea-bargaining' which involves sentencers, on the other hand, is strongly discouraged by the Court of Appeal (CA), whose attitude is quite different from that of appellate courts in—for example—the USA: 'The judge should ... never indicate the sentence which he is minded to impose. A statement that on a plea of guilty he would impose one sentence but that on a conviction following a plea of not guilty he would impose a severer sentence is one which should never be made ... The only exception to this rule is that it should be permissible for a judge to say, if it be the case, that whatever happens, whether the accused pleads guilty or not guilty, the sentence will or will not take a particular form, e g a probation order or a fine, or a custodial sentence. Finally, where any such discussion on sentence has taken place between judge and counsel, counsel for the defence should disclose this to the accused and inform him of what took place' (*Turner* (1970) 54 Cr App Rep 352). The point of the exception—which does not amount to bargaining—is that it allows the defendant who is hesitating between a plea of 'guilty' and one of 'not guilty' to take into account the type of sentence which the sentencer has in mind. At any discussion of this kind between the judge and the defendant's counsel, the counsel for the prosecution must be present, and so, if he wishes, may the defendant's solicitor (*Turner*, ibid). A shorthand writer or tape recorder should record exactly what is said (*Smith* [1990] 1 WLR 1311). The defendant himself, however, is never present. His counsel is allowed to refer to mitigating considerations, including matters of which the defendant himself is and should be ignorant: for example that he has not long to live (*Turner*, ibid). The Royal Commission on Criminal Justice (1993) (RCCJ) recommended the partial reversal of *Turner*. They suggested that, at the request of defence counsel on instructions from the defendant, judges should be able to indicate the highest sentence that they would impose at that point, on the basis of the facts put to them. A request for such an indication might be made at a preparatory hearing called especially for this purpose, or at the trial itself. One danger with this approach is that the judge is being asked to speak with inadequate information, particularly when a PSR has not yet been prepared. Of even greater concern, such a process may lead to a presumption of guilt. Any move from the court room to the judge's chambers smacks of secrecy and administrative convenience, and a loss of due process safeguards.

### Varying the sentence

**1.8** An MC can vary or rescind a sentence or other order (e g a compensation order) which it has imposed on a convicted offender, provided that it does so within 28 days (counting the day on which the offender was sentenced or found guilty) and provided that the court is constituted in the same manner as the court which imposed the original sentence (or, where the original court comprised three or more justices, by a court which consists of or comprises a majority of them: s 142 MCA 80). The CC has a similar power (s 47 Supreme Court Act 81) with minor differences. When altering a sentence, it can substitute one which is more severe or of a different nature (*Sodhi* (1978) 66 Cr App Rep 260). After the time-limit has expired the court cannot add or alter a sentence or order, but can correct the terms of an order which is lawful in substance though defective in form (*Saville* (1980) 2 Cr App Rep (S) 26). When an alteration is made the offender should be present, and he or his counsel should be given an opportunity to address the court.

### Giving reasons

**1.9** With some exceptions, the court is not obliged by statute to give reasons for its choice of sentence. In the majority of cases the reason for the choice would simply be that it is the normal penalty for the offence. If the choice is more severe than usual, however, the sentencer is expected to justify it. The CA has expressed dissatisfaction with a prison sentence of even moderate severity when the sentencer has given no indication of his reasons for it (for example in *Newman* (1979) 1 Cr App Rep (S) 252, or *Smith* (1987) 9 Cr App Rep (S) 475, where Mars Jones J said 'This appeal is brought by leave of the single judge, who observed that he granted leave not because he thought that three years was necessarily wrong but because he believed that a person is entitled to an explanation as to why he is being sent to prison for three years. So do we, and we are quite unable to say from the observations made by the learned judge upon what basis he passed this sentence'). It is also advisable to give reasons for exceptional leniency, in case this is misunderstood by the news media. In certain situations the giving and recording of reasons is required by statute; and these are noted in their contexts in Parts II, III and IV. This requirement is often part of a provision which prohibits a custodial sentence but allows it if the court can give special reasons for it. Failure to give a reason, however, does not seem to invalidate the sentence. As Taylor CJ said in *Baverstock* (1992) 14 Cr App Rep (S) 471, referring to s 1(4)CJA 91, 'the statutory provisions are not to be treated as a verbal tightrope for judges to walk ... sentencing judges must comply with their statutory duty, but if they err, this court will not interfere with the resultant sentence, unless it is wrong in principle or excessive'. In practice, the reasons given in court are usually perfunctory: for example, Ashworth et al (1984: see 1.27) found that 'such reasons as are given tend to consist of general references to factors taken into account rather than a detailed explanation of how the judge weighed these factors in arriving at the precise sentence'.

## Advice from justices' clerks

**1.10** Magistrates may be advised by their clerks. While the justices' clerk will be a barrister or solicitor of at least 5 years' standing (see Justices of the Peace Act 79), he or she performs an increasingly managerial role, and is assisted by a team of deputy or assistant clerks. In practice therefore the clerk in court, on whom the magistrates may rely heavily, is often not professionally qualified and may not even have a law degree. The *Practice Direction (Justices: Clerk to Court)* [1981] 1 WLR 1163 includes the statement that

'3. If it appears to him necessary to do so, or he is so requested by the justices, the justices' clerk has the responsibility to
   (a) refresh the justices' memory as to any matter of evidence, and to draw attention to any issues involved in matters before the court;
   (b) advise the justices generally on the range of penalties which the law allows them to impose and on any guidance relevant to the choice of penalty provided by the law, the decisions of the superior courts or other authorities.
If no request for advice has been made by the justices, the justices' clerk shall discharge his responsibility in court in the presence of the parties.

But it adds that

4. (a) The justices are entitled to the advice of their clerk when they retire in order that he may fulfil his responsibility outlined above ...'

Thus his advice is given in private *only* if the justices retire to consider their verdict or sentence and if they invite him to join them. In practice many clerks have admitted that they influence MC's sentences to a considerable extent (Darbyshire, 1980).

## Appeals against magistrates' sentences

**1.11** The offender has the right of appeal against any sentencing decision of an MC, with the following exceptions:
  a. an order for the payment of costs (although the prosecutor can appeal: s 5 CICCA 73);
  b. an order to destroy an animal under s 2 Protection of Animals Act 1911;
  c. a legal aid contribution order (*Hayden* [1975] 1 WLR 852).
The right must be exercised by giving notice of appeal within 21 days after the day on which the sentencing decision is announced, although extensions of time may be granted by the appellate court.

**1.12** Appeals against sentencing decisions of MCs are heard by the CC (s 108 MCA 1980), unless they are appeals by way of case stated on a point of law or jurisdiction, in which case they are heard by the High Court (s 111 MCA 80). When hearing appeals the CC consists of a judge sitting with 2, 3 or 4 justices, who can outvote him, except on a matter of law (*Orpin* [1975] QB 283). The High Court consists of 2 or more judges. Bail pending the result of an appeal may be granted either by the MC itself or by the appellate court (s 13 Courts Act 71, s 113 MCA 80; *Practice Direction: (Crown Court: Bail Pending Appeal)* [1983] 1 WLR 1292).

## Appeal by way of case stated

**1.13** 'Any person who was a party to the proceedings before a MC, or was aggrieved by the conviction, order, determination or other proceeding of the court' may question the proceeding on the ground that it was wrong in law or in excess of jurisdiction, in which event he applies to the justices to state a case for the opinion of the High Court (s 111 MCA 80). This procedure confers a limited right of appeal on both prosecution and defence. The case is heard by the Divisional Court of the QBD, which may 'reverse, affirm or amend' the magistrates' decision (s 6 Summary Jurisdiction Act 1857). Even a sentence within an MC's power can be challenged in this way on the ground that it is harsh, oppressive and far outside what is normal for the offence (*R v Crown Court at St Albans, ex p Cinnamond* [1981] QB 480), although the High Court might well decline to review the sentence if the right of appeal to the CC had not been exercised (*Shepherd* (1983) 5 Cr App Rep (S) 124). But only the person convicted can appeal to the CC against an MC's sentence or order. Thus a victim aggrieved because an MC had failed to make a (satisfactory) compensation order in his favour could proceed only by way of a claim in the civil courts.

## Judicial review

**1.14** The last decade has seen a significant increase in the number of cases of judicial review of criminal justice decisions. In judicial review proceedings, the Divisional Court of the QBD of the High Court is asked to review the legality, rationality or procedural propriety of a decision. The majority of such cases do not involve the challenge of sentencing discretion, but of discretionary powers exercised by the police, the Crown Prosecution Service, Legal Aid Board, prison authorities etc. Since the normal way to correct an inappropriate sentence is through the appeal process, the Divisional Court will only change a sentence when the normal appeal process has been exhausted. Thus, for example, in *Birchall* [1990] Crim LR 352 the Divisional Court reduced fines imposed by the MC for 10 offences of overloading a goods vehicle from £7,600 to £1,300, although the CC had dismissed the appeal. The Divisional Court held that the sentence was so far outside the normal discretionary limits that there was an error of law.

## Appeals against Crown Court sentences

**1.15** A person sentenced by the CC may appeal against the sentence to the CA provided that
    a.   the sentence is not fixed by law (but s 38 RTOA 88 gives a right of appeal against non-discretionary disqualification from driving);
    b.   the sentence was passed on indictment, or, if passed as a result of committal to the CC for sentence, or the bringing of an offence to the CC to be dealt with as subject to a conditional discharge, a probation order or a suspended sentence, it fulfils *one* of the following conditions:
        i.   it is a sentence of at least 6 months custody ; or
        ii.   it is one which the convicting court has no power to pass; or
        iii.   it is a recommendation for deportation (see 5.6); or
        iv.   it is an order activating an existing suspended sentence in whole or part (see s 10 CAA 68).
Note that non-defendants cannot appeal to the CA, even if they are victims dissatisfied with a decision about compensation: their remedy is supposed to lie in the civil courts.

**1.16** No one who has the right of appeal should be without legal advice or assistance for this purpose; and legal aid orders for trials include provision for this. Solicitors are expected to instruct counsel accordingly. Immediately after conviction or sentence counsel should either advise his client about the chances of a successful appeal or promise advice within 21 days (which means the solicitors should get the advice within 14 days). The RCCJ (1993) concluded, referring to Malleson's research (1993), that vast improvements were needed in the provision of post-conviction advice, recommending 'that both branches of the profession take all necessary steps to ensure that practitioners not only perform their duty to see the client at the end of the case, as most do, but also give preliminary advice both orally and in writing'.

**1.17**   Unlike an appeal from an MC to the CC, an appeal to the CA needs leave, for which an application must be made within 28 days from the date of the sentence. Extensions can be granted by the CA, and usually are if it sees merit in the appeal. The application is considered by a single judge in private, although if he refuses leave the applicant can insist that it be considered by the CA itself. For this purpose, the Court can consist of only 2 judges (s 9 AJA 70). Usually it consists of 3, drawn from the Lord Chief Justice, Lords Justices and other judges of the QBD. Its changing composition may occasionally explain the contrasts between some of its sentencing decisions. The RCCJ (1993) recommended that senior circuit judges should sometimes sit on the CA to add their experience of CC trials to the Court. To save time, if the appeal seems meritorious, the application will be treated by the court as an appeal, in which case the applicant will be told that his sentence has been reduced or varied (ie replaced by one of another type), but that if he is not satisfied he can pursue his appeal (although this has not much hope of securing a further alteration). Bail pending the results of the appeal can be granted by the sentencing judge, by the CA or by a judge of appeal; but bail is only granted when the sentence is extremely short and the appeal seems likely to succeed.

**1.18**   The House of Lords hears only appeals from decisions of the CA which involve a point of law of general public importance, and this is rarely true of appeals against sentence. Leave is required, either from the CA, or from the House itself.

### Attorney-General's references

**1.19**   Sections 35 and 36 CJA 88 give the Attorney-General the power to appeal against an unduly lenient sentence, and in these cases the CA may increase the sentence. However, the CA has again interpreted its role very narrowly here: as Lord Lane C.J. said in *A-G's Reference (No 4 of 1989)* (1989) 11 Cr App Rep (S) 517, at 531: 'A sentence is unduly lenient, we would hold, where it falls outside the range of sentences which the judge, applying his mind to all the relevant facts, could reasonably consider appropriate'. Little research has been done into which cases are reviewed (but see Henham, 1994). Particularly useful would be a study of whether the media exert an improper influence over which cases are referred to the CA.

### Sentencing powers of the appellate court (s 9 Courts Act 71, Criminal Appeal Act 68)

**1.20**   If the appellate court decides to interfere with the sentencing decision, it may substitute any sentence or order which was within the power of the sentencer when dealing with the case, provided that its choice is not more severe than his choice. This proviso was introduced by the CAA 68 in order to prevent the CA from deterring unmeritorious appeals[¹] by the threat of an increase in the severity of the sentence. The principle was not however applied to appeals from MCs' decisions: s 9 Courts Act 71 expressly allows the CC on appeal to award any punishment 'whether more or less severe than that awarded ...', provided that it was one which was within the MC's powers. The reason for the difference is said to be that the proceedings in the CC are a rehearing of the case: but this scarcely seems to justify so obvious a departure from the principle introduced by the 1968 Act. However that may be, few sentences altered on appeal by the CC involve increases of severity; and most of these are traffic cases in which the CC reduced or removed a disqualification from driving but increased the accompanying fine.

1.  The only deterrent now open to the CA is a direction that an appellant who has been in custody should not be allowed to count the time between trial and the hearing of the appeal as part of his sentence. In a *Practice Note* of 14 February 1980 the LCJ said 'In order to accelerate the hearing of appeals in which there is some merit, single judges will ... give special consideration to the giving of a direction for loss of time whenever an application for leave to appeal is refused ... such a direction will normally be made unless the grounds are not only settled and signed by Counsel, but also supported by the written opinion of Counsel' ((1980) 70 Cr App Rep 186). This loss of time rule was challenged before the European Court of Human Rights in *Monnell and Morris v United Kingdom* (1987) 10 EHRR 205 , where the Court held by a majority that there had been no infringement of the European Convention on Human Rights. Although the RCCJ (1993) considered the power 'to be necessary as a means of discouraging appeals that have no merit', is it an undue erosion of due process rights?

## Recording and publishing proceedings

**1.21**   It is only in the CC that what is said during trial and sentencing is recorded in short-hand or on tape; and even this is transcribed only if needed for an appeal. What is said in deciding an appeal, whether by the CC, the High Court or the CA, is recorded and transcribed, but is published only if the editor of a series selects it because of its interest. The main series today include the *Criminal Appeal Reports (Sentencing)* and the *Criminal Law Review*. Transcripts of unreported CA decisions can be studied by research workers by arrangement with the Registrar of Criminal Appeals. The *Justice of the Peace* reports sentencing decisions which are of interest to MCs. The *All England Reports* include many important cases.

## Policies of appellate courts

**1.22**   When the ground of appeal is that the sentence was excessive, the Court asks itself not what its members would have imposed had they been the sentencing judge, but whether the sentence was within the appropriate 'range' of sentences. Consequently it does not usually make minor reductions. On the other hand if it is persuaded that in the particular circumstances of the case an 'individualised' measure (see 9.4) would be appropriate it will often substitute it, even though the original sentence was within the range which it considers appropriate as a punishment or deterrent. Sometimes, however, it condemns a sentence as 'wrong in principle', meaning that it disagrees with the sentencer's reasoning; and in such cases will alter the sentence even if the practical effect is small. Or again it may reduce or vary the sentence—even if only slightly—to give weight to a mitigating factor which should have but did not influence the sentencer (see 4.20ff).

**1.23** It is scarcely possible to generalise about the policies of the CC in appeals against MC's sentences, which involve judges and justices sitting in so many different places, with so little opportunity of knowing what is being decided elsewhere in similar cases. Their sentencing decisions, unlike those of the CA, are unlikely to be reported. Sometimes they are dealing with questions to which CA decisions have provided answers; but sometimes they are simply considering whether a prison sentence of, say, six months or a fine of, say, £900 is excessive in the circumstances of the case; in which event they seldom have guidance from the CA. It would not be surprising if quite different policies in such cases were followed in different parts of the country.

## The status of Court of Appeal decisions

**1.24** Even the publication of numerous decisions by the CA leaves great scope for discretion on the part of the sentencing judge. This was emphasised by the CA in *De Havilland* ((1983) 5 Cr App Rep (S) 109) when the court commented on the increasing practice of citing its sentencing decisions:

'Apart from the statutory maxima and certain other statutory restrictions, for example those on the sentencing of young offenders, the appropriate sentence is a matter for the discretion of the sentencing judge. It follows that decisions on sentencing are not binding authorities in the sense that decisions of the Court of Appeal on points of substantive law are binding both on this Court and on lower courts. Indeed they could not be, since the circumstances of the offence and of the offender present an almost infinite variety from case to case. As in any branch of the law which depends on judicial discretion, decisions on sentencing are no more than examples of how the Court has dealt with a particular offender in relation to a particular offence. As such they may be useful as an aid to uniformity of sentence for a particular category of crime; but they are not authoritative in the strict sense. Occasionally this Court suggests guidelines for sentencers dealing with a particular category of offence or a particular type of offender. *Bibi* (1980) 71 Cr App Rep 360, and *Clarke* (1982) 75 Cr App Rep 119, are recent examples of such guidelines. But the sentencer retains his discretion within the guidelines, or even to depart from them if the particular circumstances of the case justify departure. The vast majority of decisions of this Court are concerned with the facts and circumstances of the particular case before it and are directed to the appropriate sentence in that case. Each case depends on its own facts.'

It is therefore necessary to read CA decisions with care in order to distinguish those which are intended to provide general guidelines from those which are 'no more than examples'. Moreover even general guidelines do not seem to be as binding as a third category of decisions: that is, those which deal with points of law in the interpretation of sentencing statutes. For guidelines allow departures if those are justified by the particular circumstances of the case, even if the CA may turn out to disagree.

## Appeal rates

**1.25** Less than 1 per cent of defendants who are sentenced by MCs each year appeal against their sentence. The rate is higher—7 per cent—among those sentenced by the CC. On the other hand, roughly half of appeals against MCs' sentences succeed in securing some reduction, compared with a success rate of about 1 in 4 for appeals to the CA. Thus about 0.3 per cent of all defendants sentenced by MCs and 1.4 per cent of all those sentenced by the CC have at least some part of their sentences reduced on appeal. The difference between the rates for the two kinds of court is striking, but at least two things must be borne in mind. One is that in the CC prison sentences are both more likely and longer, and fines are larger, than in MCs, so that there is more scope for reduction. The other is that there may well be substantial numbers of defendants in MCs who would have a good chance of a reduction if they appealed, but who do not appeal for a variety of reasons (they may not have legal advice; they may be afraid of an increase instead of a reduction; they may not believe that appeals ever succeed).

## The prerogative of mercy

**1.26** Another procedure for interfering with a sentence is the use of the Royal prerogative of mercy, whereby, as an act of grace, the sovereign grants a free or conditional pardon, or remits the rest of an offender's custodial sentence. A pardon is granted only when it has been established that the conviction was unjustified, although, paradoxically, it does not in any sense eliminate the conviction, since only a court can quash a conviction. A person pardoned is relieved of the penalties or punishments resulting from the conviction, and may be given compensation under s 133 CJA 88. Remission does not imply that the conviction was unjustified, and its effect is merely that the offender is not required to serve any more of his custodial sentence, or complete payment of his fine or compensation order. Although the prerogative is still called 'Royal' the sovereign merely signs the document submitted by the Home Secretary, who need not consult any other minister, and whose advice the sovereign is not supposed to reject. Unlike the CA the Home Secretary does not normally make his reasons public. The need to invoke the prerogative has been gradually reduced by statutes which allow the executive more flexibility. An example is s 36 CJA 91, which allows the Home Secretary himself, if possible after consulting the Parole Board, to release a prisoner on licence before he or she becomes eligible for parole, on compassionate grounds (usually grave illness). There were six such releases in 1995. The prerogative is still invoked, however, to release prisoners early for other reasons. Usually they have given helpful information at some risk to themselves, or have intervened to save a member of staff or a fellow prisoner from attack. In 1995 there were 11 releases of this kind, and two others because the lengths of their sentences had been miscalculated. Remission of fines usually involves minor offences dealt with in MCs in which the conviction turns out to be wrongful for technical reasons, as can happen in the case of traffic offences. Mercy in a wider sense can of course be exercised by sentencers, appellate courts and other agents of the criminal justice system; and the propriety of this is discussed in 5.21.

## Criminal Cases Review Commission

**1.27** The Criminal Appeal Act 95 introduced a new and final procedure for interfering with a sentence. Before this Act, the Home Secretary had the right to refer cases to the CA 'if he thought fit'. This power will in future be exercised by the CCRC if there is a 'real possibility' that the conviction will be overturned because there exists evidence or arguments which were 'not raised in the proceedings which led to it or on any appeal or application for leave to appeal'. There is a safety valve in s 13(2) which makes clear that these limitations shall not 'prevent the making of a reference if it appears to the [CCRC] that there are exceptional circumstances which justify making it'. Section 9(3) makes it clear that the CCRC may refer sentences as well as convictions to the CA in this way. At the time of writing the detailed rules covering the CCRC had not been drawn up; the success or otherwise of the CCRC in dealing with miscarriages of justice will inevitably depend largely on the resources allocated to it and on the independence of those appointed to it.

## Studies of Crown Court sentencing

**1.28** Sentencing in the CC is done by judges, recorders and assistant recorders, whose differing ranks and functions are described by the Lord Chancellor's Department's booklet on Judicial Appointments (1990). There have been few studies of their use of the choices open to them. Ashworth et al (1984) is merely a pilot study of a rather small number of judges, since the LCJ did not allow the main study to proceed. Even so, it emphasises that many judges regard sentencing 'as an art rather than a science', and that even the system of appeals leaves individual judges room for 'idiosyncrasies' in sentencing A few years later, Moxon (1988), who sampled judges' sentences in 18 courts, found that in 80 per cent of his 2,077 cases the type of sentence was predictable when the circumstances of the case were fed into an elaborate equation. Even when the sentence was not of the type predicted it was usually of the type which the equation had indicated as next most likely. Not that judges were consciously calculating in this mathematical way; but predictability of this degree is not art as we know it. Thomas' looseleaf and constantly updated *Current Sentencing Practice* is a thorough, invaluable, study of the CA's approaches to appeals against CC sentences. This cannot be expected to reflect the normal patterns of sentences which were not the subject of appeal, still less any variations in policy between different judges or circuits, which remains in need of specific research.

## Studies of magistrates' courts

**1.29** There have been more studies of magistrates' sentencing. Apart from a few designed to answer very specific questions, the important publications are Hood, R G (1962); Hood, R G (1972) ; Devlin, K M (1970); Tarling, R (1979); Parker, Sumner & Jarvis (1985); Brown (1991), Turner, (1992). Local sentencing traditions are maintained partly by the training process and partly by the apprenticeship model, whereby a magistrates spends several years as a 'winger' before taking the chair in court (see Parker et al). Wide regional variations in sentencing practices led the Magistrates' Association to produce guidelines for the use of magistrates. The first *Suggestions for Road Traffic Penalties* were produced in 1966, and in 1989 the Association produced a *Sentencing Guide for Criminal Offences (other than Road Traffic)*, which also contained a table of suggested compensation levels. The 3rd edition (1993) sets out in a diagramm-atic form the 'entry point' for each offence, based on a first time offender pleading not guilty, as a guide for an offence of average seriousness. Although these guidelines have no legal status, justices clerks' and local liaison judges appear to be encouraging their use. According to Turner (1992), they are followed in 75 per cent of cases.

**1.30** Another reason why different benches follow different sentencing practices may stem from the way in which magistrates are chosen. Candidates can be nominated by anyone, including local magistrates. Nominations are sifted by a local panel, and some are then forwarded to the Lord Chancellor's Department, which makes enquiries about their suitability before proceeding to appoint some of them. Efforts are made to appoint magistrates who are representative of different groups, but there are difficulties. In some ethnic minorities, for example, few of those considered suitable are willing to serve; and among the young it is those who have the time and inclination for social or charitable activities who are most likely to be willing. Since they can hold office—barring misconduct or incapacity—until the age of 70 the older age-groups are over-represented among them. They are likely to be people who feel that their duty is to their local community. Their discussions show considerable sensitivity to local attitudes, especially those expressed in local newspapers.

## Stipendiary magistrates

**1.31** What has been said so far relates to lay magistrates. In many of the busiest metropolitan courts, however, the bulk of the summary trials and sentencing is conducted by full-time stipendiary (ie salaried lawyer) magistrates, sitting alone. In 1994 there were 78 full-time stipendiaries, supported by 90 acting stipendiaries. Only barristers or solicitors of at least 7 years' standing are eligible for these appointments. The RCCJ (1993) called for a 'more systematic approach' to the role of the stipendiary, and the Lord Chancellor's Department is currently producing guidelines on the respective roles of lay and stipendiary magistrates. However, to date there has been no evaluation of the merits of employing stipendiaries rather than a bench of three lay magistrates (see Padfield, 1995).

## The judiciary

**1.32** For the reasons given in 1.27, CC practices have not been the subject of thorough statistical study. Not even a comparison of different judges' or recorders' sentences seems to have been attempted or, if attempted, published. No doubt it would show variations, even when allowance was made for relevant variables: the reputations which some judges or recorders have for severity or leniency cannot be altogether undeserved. It is unlikely that the variance would be as great as that of MCs. Their educational and vocational backgrounds—most have been barristers—are much more homogeneous, and national consistency is valued.

## Relative frequencies of sentences

**1.33** A rough impression of the relative frequencies of the commonly used types of sentence can be got from Table 1A (see page 18), which has been compiled from the supplementary volumes of CSEW. Care is needed, however, in the interpretation of sentencing tables in CSEW. They show only the heaviest sentence imposed on the offender, not all the sentences. If he receives a prison sentence for one offence and a fine for another, only the prison sentence is counted[1]. CSEW also admits that since the statistics are based on returns made by police to the Home Office the reporting of the results of prosecutions in which the police are not involved (for example prosecutions by government departments and private organisations) is known to be 'less than complete'; and the same is true of motoring offences in some police areas.

1. Thus the number of disqualifications for driving has to be looked for in the special bulletin which deals with statistics for prosecuted traffic offences. If the offender receives two equal prison sentences or fines the one for the offence carrying the highest *maximum* is counted.

**TABLE 1A: Principal¹ sentences imposed on adults in 1993 (not including 'young adults' aged 18-20, the figures for whom are shown in brackets)**

| | Magistrates courts | | The Crown Court | |
| --- | --- | --- | --- | --- |
| | Indictable offences⁴ | Summary offences⁴ | Indictable offences⁴ | Summary offences⁴ |
| | % | % | % | % |
| Discharges, absolute or conditional | 27(23) | 9(18) | 7(5) | 22(21) |
| Fines | 46 (40) | 88 (67) | 6 (4) | 21 (13) |
| Probation | 10 (12) | 1 (4) | 13 (15) | 13 (16) |
| Community sentence order | 9 (11) | 1 (4) | 17 (20) | 17 (20) |
| Attendance centre | - (2) | - (1) | - (0.2) | - (1) |
| Combination order² | 0.04 (3) | 0.1 (1) | 3 (4) | 3 (5) |
| Suspended imprisonment | 0.5 (-) | 0.05 (-) | 4 (-) | 1 (-) |
| Young offenders institution | - (7) | - (3) | - (50) | - (22) |
| Unsuspended imprisonment | 5 (-) | 0.5 (-) | 49 (-) | 18 (-) |
| Otherwise dealt with³ | 3 (2) | 1 (3) | 2 (2) | 4 (2) |
| TOTALS (=100% +/- 1%) | 156,475 (45,471) | 404,463 (32,128) | 51,170 (12,191) | 1,366 (436) |

Source: the Supplementary Volumes of the CSEW.

1  Ie the most severe penalty imposed on that occasion.
2  An order combining probation and community service.
3  Chiefly hospital orders, short terms in police cells, compensation orders and recognisances.
4  Excluding traffic offences, for which see Table 23B.

# Chapter 2

# Information about the offender

**2.1** The court always has *some* information about the offender whom it is about to sentence. Even when he pleads guilty by post—as is common in the case of driving offences—the court knows his sex, his age and his address. Since the form allows him space for a statement of any mitigating considerations he can—and often does—give information (which is, incidentally, rarely checked) about his financial means in the hope that the inevitable fine will be reduced. Certain kinds of information must not be taken into account: for example, offences of which he had not been convicted and which he has not asked the court to take into consideration (see 2.10 ff).

**2.2** Some statutes lay down the sort of information about the offender which the court must have before sentencing him. For example:
  a.  In deciding whether a custodial sentence is justified, and on the length of a prison sentence, the court must obtain and consider a pre-sentence report (PSR), prepared by a probation officer or a social worker, with a view to assisting the court in determining the most suitable method of dealing with an offender (s 3(1) CJA 91). However, s 3(2) provides that no PSR need be obtained where the offence is triable on indictment only, and the trial judge takes the view that a PSR is 'unnecessary'; This provision was extended to summary offences and those triable either way by para 40 of Sch 9 of the CJPOA 94, allowing the court to avoid obtaining a PSR whenever it is considered unnecessary.
  b.  If a court is considering most community penalties, it must obtain and consider a PSR (unless it is of the opinion that it is unnecessary) (s 7(3) CJA 91).
  c.  Before passing a custodial sentence other than one fixed by law on an offender who appears to be mentally disordered, a court should obtain a medical report (unless the court is of the opinion that such a report is unnecessary) (s 4 CJA 91).
  d.  When considering whether to remand an offender to a mental hospital, or deal with him by means of an (interim) hospital order or a guardianship order, the court must have certain medical evidence. In the case of a hospital or guardianship order (but not a remand or interim hospital

order) it must also 'have regard to all the circumstances of the case including the nature of the offence and the character and antecedents of the offender, and to the other available methods of dealing with him' (ss 35-38 MHA 83).

e.  When fixing the amount of a fine the court must 'inquire into the financial circumstances of the offender' (s 18 CJA 91). Some, but not all, courts invite offenders to complete and return a statement of their means before they come to court (see 16.9).

## Antecedents reports

**2.3**  In practice, courts are usually given a report by the police on the offender's 'antecedents' before deciding on his sentence. The exceptions are

a.  minor traffic offences to which the offender pleads guilty by post; but even in such cases the court is told of any previous disqualifications or penalty points incurred (see 23.11);

b.  other summary offences prosecuted by agencies other than the Crown Prosecution Service (see 15.9 ff);

c.  offences regarded by the police as too trivial to call for a full antecedents report (as the Metropolitan Police, for example, regard an offence of drunkenness).

**2.4**  Antecedents reports vary in form and thoroughness from one police force to another. The information which should be included in an antecedents report is set out in the *Practice Note (Crime: Antecedents)* [1993] 4 All ER 863; *Interim minimum standard for the provision of antecedent information in the Crown Court*:

(a)  age and date of birth;

(b)  education, previous employment and present employment;

(c)  date of arrest and whether held in custody or on bail;

(d)  summary of previous convictions and findings of guilt, and the date of last discharge from prison or other custodial institution. This may include any offences 'taken into consideration' on a previous occasion; but offences to be taken into consideration on the present occasion are listed separately; and

(e)  a short and concise statement of domestic and family circumstances. Occasionally the report mentions facts which aggravate the offence; but unless these can be proved they are in danger of being declared improper, and may lead to a successful appeal against sentence (as occurred in *Van Pelz* (1942) 29 Cr App Rep 10).

**2.5**  Previous convictions are usually ascertained from or confirmed by the central Criminal Records Office (CRO) maintained by the Metropolitan Police (See Home Office (1991)). They will not always include all convictions which are included in local police records, unless these seem relevant. They will include any findings of guilt in a youth court, provided that these are known to the local police or recorded in CRO; but by no means all such findings of guilt are reported to the CRO by other forces. The antecedents report should also record formal police cautions. It does not of course mention prosecutions which have not ended in a conviction, except those which end in findings of unfitness to plead or a verdict of 'not guilty by reason of insanity'. Phoenix, a new criminal records database on the police national computer came into operation in 1995. It gives the police instant access to details of people convicted of all serious crimes. Data on impending prosecutions and case disposals in respect of reportable offences committed since the system came into operation are now put directly onto the database. Transfer onto the new database of the microfiche records currently held by the National Identification Service (NIS) is scheduled for completion in 1996. Phoenix will eventually be linked directly to the courts and to the CPS. For a review of the concept of an independent criminal records authority as a means of ensuring accurate and up-to-date records and effective accountability, see Hebenton and Thomas (1993).

**2.6**   The antecedents report also includes, when this is known to the police, information about any breaches of a suspended sentence, probation order, conditional discharge or parole licence, provided that these have been the subject of court proceedings. If the offender is subject to a deferred sentence which has not yet been passed, this is mentioned. If he is on bail on other charges, this too is included. If the current charge consists of or includes the theft or taking without consent of a motor vehicle, a list of the offender's previous traffic offences is included, together with other relevant facts. If the current charge involves very serious offences the police are usually prepared, if asked by the court, to describe in more detail any offences of a similar kind of which the offender has been convicted.

**2.7**   Since information about previous convictions could prejudice magistrates while they are deciding on the guilt of the accused, it is given to them only when he is found, or pleads, guilty. It should not be given to them when they are considering whether the case should, after all, be tried at the CC (*Colchester Justices, ex p North Essex Building Co* [1977] 3 All ER 567). In jury trials, however, the judge may use it in order to be on the alert for inadvertent references by witnesses which might prejudice the jury, who of course are not shown it. The relevance of previous convictions for sentencing is discussed in 4.5.

## Publicity

**2.8**   In some courts the antecedents report, with its list of previous convictions, is simply handed to the sentencer, so that the public is not told of its contents. In others, a police officer is asked to read out the previous convictions, a practice which sometimes publicises offences which the sentencer does not regard as relevant. In order to avoid this, the judge often indicates to the officer which offences are to be read out; and that if all of the previous convictions are either so stale or so different from the current offence as to make them of little relevance, none should be read aloud. To avoid suspicions of 'secret justice', and also in case of subsequent proceedings, the judge should explain publicly that only those convictions which are being read aloud are being taken into account; and the clerk should note those which are.

## Taking offences into consideration

**2.9** Along with the antecedents report the police may submit a list of offences which the defendant wishes the court to 'take into consideration' (TIC) when sentencing him. This 'convention', as it has been called by the CA, allows the offender to safeguard himself against a later prosecution for these offences at a less convenient time; for example, when he is nearing the end of a custodial sentence. It also saves the prosecutor and the court the time and trouble involved in proving every one of the charges that would be involved. It is not the prosecutor but the defendant who asks the court to TIC the offences, and his signature must be on the list when it is presented to the sentencer, although the list itself will have been prepared by the police as a result of his admissions. As a result the sentence for the offence of which he is convicted will probably be slightly more severe than it would have been, but by no means as severe as it might have been if he had been sentenced to separate consecutive sentences for each offence; and it cannot exceed the statutory maximum for the charged offence (*Hobson* (1942) 29 Cr App Rep 30). He is not convicted of a TIC offence, and there is no legal bar to his being later prosecuted for it; but this should not happen, and if it does he should not be sentenced for it (*North* (SP L3 — 1BO1)). Compensation orders can be made for any personal injury loss or damage resulting from a TIC offence, just as if the defendant had been convicted of it (s 35 PCCA 73); and mutatis mutandis the same is true of criminal bankruptcy orders (s 39 PCCA 73).

**2.10** The sentencer can refuse, however, to TIC an offence, and should do so
  a. if the offence is not one which his court is empowered to try (*Simons* (1953) 37 Cr App Rep 120);
  b. if the offence is one for which a conviction would or could lead to an endorsement of a driving licence or a disqualification from driving, since that would allow the defendant to escape those consequences (*Simons* (1953) 37 Cr App Rep 120);
  c. if the offence is one for which the offender has already been conditionally discharged or put on probation (*Webb* [1953] 2 QB 390; *Fry* (1955) 38 Cr App Rep 157);
  d. if he is a judge of the CC who is asked to TIC an offence which would normally be dealt with by a more senior judge. Indeed, it seems doubtful whether a sentencer should agree to TIC any offence which is very much more serious than the one for which he is in a position to sentence the offender.

**2.11** Some offenders claim that they have been invited by police to include in their TIC lists offences which they did not commit; and there have certainly been cases in which it was later found that they could not have committed some of those listed. The inclusion of an offence in a TIC list allows police to treat it as 'cleared up', which may have been the explanation in some instances. In others an offender who had committed a great many minor offences may have been vague in his admissions, and later retracted them. It is the court's responsibility to make sure that the offender understands the document and admits the offences listed in it.

## Sample counts

**2.12**   The TIC procedure is used when an offender is prosecuted only on 'sample counts': that is, only for a selected few of a series of similar offences (as happens when an employee has stolen or embezzled many sums over a period). If he is to be sentenced for the whole series he must ask for the uncharged offences to be TIC (*Anderson* (1978) 67 Cr App Rep 185). The list is usually agreed between the prosecution and the defence when the decision is being made as to which should be the sample counts. What happens if after conviction the offender . goes back on the agreement, and refuses to ask for the rest to be TIC, is a question which has not yet been answered. But he would usually be ill-advised to do this, since he could then be prosecuted for the rest, for which he could incur separate and probably consecutive sentences.

## Newton hearings

**2.13**   Problems arise when a defendant pleads guilty, but disagrees with the prosecution's version of the facts. Whose version should the judge accept? The issue was raised somewhat starkly in *Newton* (1982) 77 Cr App Rep 13, where the appellant, although pleading guilty to buggery, maintained that the acts complained of were consensual (even consensual heterosexual buggery being criminal until the CJPOA 94). According to the Lord Chief Justice,

'There are three ways in which a judge .... can approach his difficult task of sentencing. It is in certain circumstances possible to obtain the answer to the problem from a jury. For example, when it is a question of whether the conviction should be under s 18 or s 20 of the OAPA 1861, the jury can determine the issue on a trial under s 18 by deciding whether or not the necessary intent has been proved by the prosecution.

The second method which could be adopted by the judge in these circumstances is himself to hear the evidence on one side and another, and come to his own conclusion, acting so to speak as his own jury on the issue which is the root of the problem.

The third possibility in these circumstances is for him to hear no evidence but to listen to the submissions of counsel and then come to a conclusion. But if he does that, then ...where there is a substantial conflict between the two sides, he must come down on the side of the defendant. In other words where there has been a substantial conflict, the version of the defendant must so far as possible be accepted.'

Since in most cases the judge will choose the third option for reasons of economy, there is a danger that the defendant may be significantly undersentenced. However, the CA has recently confirmed that even where the prosecution accepts a guilty plea on the basis of an unreal and untrue set of facts, the judge is entitled to set aside the agreement and to try the factual issues involved (*Beswick* [1996] Crim LR 62)

## Pre-sentence reports

**2.14**   In most cases appearing for sentence at the CC, and in many cases in MCs, there is also a PSR by a probation officer. The 1995 *National Standards for the Supervision of Offenders in the Community* include a *National Standard* on PSRs. This states that

> 'A PSR is a report in writing, made or submitted in accordance with this standard by a probation officer or social worker of a local authority social services department, with a view to assisting the court in determining the most suitable method of dealing with an offender which imposes a restriction on liberty commensurate with the seriousness of the offence .... The purpose of the PSR is to provide a professional assessment of the nature and the causes of a person's offending behaviour and the action which can be taken to reduce reoffending.'

Prior to 1991, reports were mandatory when the accused was facing his first term of imprisonment (s 20 PCCA 73) or if an offender under 21 was facing a custodial sentence. Section 3 CJA 91 provided that a court before deciding on a custodial sentence should obtain and consider a PSR unless, when a crime was triable on indictment only, the court 'is of the opinion that it is unnecessary to obtain a PSR'. However, there has been growing concern about the amount of time that a probation officer 'wastes' writing reports. Thus para 40 of Sch 9 of the CJPOA 94 extends the court's discretion under s 3 to dispense with a report in summary cases and cases triable either way. In the case of juvenile offenders a court may only dispense with the requirement if it has a pre-existing PSR. The original s 7(3) CJA 91 provided that a court should obtain and consider a PSR before forming an opinion as to the suitability of the offender for a community penalty. This requirement was enormously diluted by the insertion of a new s 7 (3A) by para 40 of Sch 9 CJPOA 94, which states simply that s 7(3) does not apply if, in the circumstances of the case, the court is of the opinion that it is unnecessary to obtain a report. Gelsthorpe and Raynor (1995) suggest that the changes in the CJPOA 1994 'have come about because of resistance by some members of the judiciary to a perceived erosion of discretion'. While it may make sense that probation officers should be spared the task of writing reports on those going inevitably to prison, there remains a need for some form of formal assessment by the probation service prior to the imposition of one of an increasingly complicated range of community penalties.

## 'Not guilty' pleas

**2.15**   A special difficulty arises when the defendant intends to plead 'Not guilty'. The probation officer cannot then expect him to discuss freely the circumstances or state of mind in which the offence was committed (unless he admits the act but offers a legal excuse for it). Nor is his solicitor likely to advise him to enter into a discussion of this sort. Again, the result of a 'Not guilty' plea is often an acquittal (in roughly half of all cases), so that a great many PSRs on such defendants would represent a waste of officers' time. PSRs are therefore not normally prepared before trial in these cases. *National Standards* provide simply that 'an agreement or statement of preferred practice should be developed locally and should include the ... preferred basis for the commissioning of PSRs and the operation of PSR procedures'. An additional complication is that many defendants who have indicated that their pleas will be 'Not guilty' in the event plead 'Guilty', usually on counsel's advice, when they appear for trial. Sometimes, an expedited, 'same-day', report is requested to save an unnecessary adjournment. According to the *National Standards*, the objectives should be:

> 'to avoid, as far as possible, adjournments for reports, by preparing PSRs in advance of trial whenever sufficient notice of a guilty plea is given to any charge in respect of which a PSR might have to be provided (reports should be available for the sentencing judge by 1.00 pm on the day before the sentencing date so that the judge has time to read and think about them in advance)
>
> where adjournment for a PSR is necessary, to prepare the report as expeditiously as possible, especially if the trial judge wishes the report to be available quickly or there is any other reason for urgency, consistent with the requirements of this standard
>
> where adjournment would involve a custodial remand, to offer a same-day PSR unless the court agrees that the time required to prepare a PSR should be extended, for example, where an assessment by a medical practitioner (or by a local authority for the purposes of a residential placement under community care arrangements) is needed. If the case is briefly stood down the report writer should assess the complexity of the case and report to the court explaining the position, what further enquiries or assessment may be necessary and the time needed to prepare the PSR.'

2.16  Some probation areas have developed specific sentence enquiries. These are in effect the old stand down reports with proper procedural guidelines agreed with the courts. They are used where a defendant has pleaded guilty or been found guilty on the day, and the judge or magistrate wishes to proceed with a particular form of disposal. The court duty officer can then make enquiries and report to the court within the day whether the particular form of sentence is available or whether further enquiries are needed.

**Politically-motivated offenders**

2.17  The other category for which many probation officers—following the policy of their Association—are unwilling to provide PSRs, even after conviction, is that of offenders whose offences were committed for political reasons. Examples are members of the Irish Republican Army, or people who are charged with minor offences because of damage or obstruction in the course of demonstrations. In the late 1970s NAPO's policy was opposed not only to the provision of PSRs but also to the statutory supervision of offenders whose offences were determined by 'motives of a patently political character'. More recently national and local panels have been set up by NAPO, which officers are asked to consult before refusing to provide PSRs in such cases. If the outcome is a refusal, the chief probation officer is told, so that he can search for a solution.

## Refusal by the offender

**2.18** Occasionally, however, the offender himself, whether politically motivated or not, refuses to co-operate in the preparation of a report. (This is seldom the result of legal advice, since his legal advisers usually welcome the ammunition which PSRs provide for pleas in mitigation.) On the other hand, the defence sometimes welcomes the absence of a report, and invites the court to sentence without adjourning for one. *National Standards* state that:

> 'If an offender withholds consent to the preparation of a PSR (for example by refusing to attend an interview) the report writer remains under a duty to produce the most useful report possible using the information available. However, it should be clearly explained to the court in the report that the offender was unco-operative in the preparation of the report. A report should always be prepared when it is requested by the court; and provided that all reasonable steps are taken to assist the court to overcome the offender's non-co-operation, a report prepared in these circumstances will comply with this standard.'

Not all probation services are prepared to follow this *Standard*, believing that, at least before conviction, defendants have a right to withhold consent to a report.

## Preparing PSRs

**2.19** A PSR is usually prepared by the basic grade probation officer by whom the offender would be supervised if he were put on probation. A few probation services however, have specialised 'intake units' which carry out this and other kinds of assessment. Trainees are expected to prepare several PSRs as part of their practical training; but the responsibility for a PSR lies with the individual probation officer who countersigns the report, even though he is not often in court to present it. The officer usually begins by interviewing the offender, usually in the probation offices. If he is in custody the interview will take place in a special room or the visiting room of the prison or remand centre, in the sight but not the hearing of a prison officer. At some stage, however, a visit is usually paid to the offender's home, and the officer may have a talk with his parents, spouse or partner. Strictly speaking the offender's consent to this is not necessary; but probation officers prefer offenders to recognise the need for these visits. They do not usually obtain the consent of the offender's solicitors (who are normally only too glad to get a report which will save them trouble in preparing a plea in mitigation).

## Presenting PSRs to courts

**2.20** The officers who prepared the PSR is not usually in court: if they were they would not have much time for other work. Instead probation services appoint experienced officers as probation liaison officers, whose main responsibility is to see that courts are supplied with the necessary or requested PSRs, and that copies of these reach the defence, the clerk to the court, and—if the offender gets a custodial sentence - the establishment to which he is sent. In busy courts, where several cases are being tried or sentenced in different places, probation liaison officers are usually assisted by 'probation assistants', who are neither trainees nor qualified probation officers, but who have enough experience to handle the paperwork and send for the liaison officer when he or she is needed. Even he is sometimes obliged to send for the writer of the PSR if the questions put to him by the defence or the sentencer are searching: but most courts see the need to avoid this unless the questions are crucial. The PSR itself must not normally be read aloud, but there is sometimes discussion of an item in the report, and of course the defence must be allowed to cross-examine the officer if it wishes to challenge information or opinions.

## Offenders' access to PSRs

**2.21** The *National Standard* makes clear that the offender should be given a copy of the report by the probation service or social services department, and it should be read aloud to those who cannot read, or read in translation to those whose first language is not English. The offender should be offered an explanation of possible disclosure of the report (e g to prison officials). Another copy is given to his or her legal representative and, in the case of a young offender a copy should be given to his or her parent(s) or persons with parental responsibility.

## Contents of PSRs

**2.22** The *National Standard* on PSRs states that reports should be set out under the following headings:
* Introduction
* Offence analysis
* Relevant information about the offender
* Risk to the public of reoffending
* Conclusion.

The introduction should include sources of information used by the author, including a statement of whether the author had seen the CPS documents. Most probation services are now supplied at the adjournment stage with CPS documents which allow the officer to explore with the offender the circumstances of the offence, and not just to rely on the offender's account. *National Standards* also emphasise the need to include the victim's perspective in the report, including an analysis of the impact of the offence on the victim as set out in victim statements or other papers.

## Recommendations in PSRs

**2.23** The conclusions may contain a proposal inviting the court to consider the merits of a suitable programme which could be arranged within a community sentence, if judged appropriate by the court. The NACRO (1995) guide to probation officers usefully suggests factors which may be relevant in assessing the suitability for the offender of a particular sentence, such as the need and scope for intervention, the maturity or stage of development of the offender, the need for work to confront offending behaviour, the composition of groups in any group activity to which a referral is being considered etc. Where the report writer does not consider a community penalty to be appropriate, the report should make it clear that such a programme cannot be proposed and why. The *National Standard* spells out the details which should be given in any recommendation. For example:

> 'Where the proposal envisages a probation order or supervision order including additional requirements, the requirements should be set out in the precise terms proposed. Where the proposal envisages a probation order including a requirement for treatment for a mental condition or for drug and alcohol dependency this should reflect the consultation with the relevant practitioner. The court should be given the name of the practitioner undertaking the necessary assessment, the results of the assessment, the treatment proposed including confirmation of the acceptance of the offender for treatment by a named practitioner; and what will be required of the offender under the condition of the order ...
>
> Where the proposal envisages a probation order, supervision order or combination order, the report should include an outline of the supervision plan proposed for the offender. This should contain a description of the purposes and desired outcomes of the proposed sentence; the methods envisaged and the activities likely to be undertaken; a time scale for achieving each objective in the programme; the intensity of supervision envisaged; and the likely effect on other members of the family. If an appropriate order is imposed by the court, the plan will subsequently be of use to the supervising officer in establishing a more detailed plan which will need to be developed, supplemented and regularly reviewed in line with probation, supervision and combination order standard requirements.'

**2.24** What made sentencers in the past sceptical of the value of recommendations was the belief that they were one-sided, in the sense that they were seldom in favour of custodial sentences. However, since the CJA 91 there seems to have been a sea change in PSR writing, with probation officers being more willing to accept that custody is a serious consideration for the court. Therefore although probation officers still rarely positively propose a custodial sentence, they may acknowledge the likelihood of such a sentence, and give information which, for example, assists the sentencer on the length of a custodial sentence. Sometimes the judge or magistrates will give the probation officer a preliminary indication on how the court is thinking in terms of seriousness, and such guidance will be of great help to the author of the report.

2.25 Whether the probation officer should base her recommendations solely on its likely consequences for the offender, or should have regard to the consequences for the public is a question which has been the subject of conflicting comments. On one view it is for the sentencer, not the probation officer, to take into account the consequences for the public. Another view, that the recommendation must be sufficiently realistic to take account of public safety and public reaction, is suggested by the *National Standards*. The aim of the section on risk to the public of reoffending is 'to distil ... a concise statement of the report writer's professional judgement of the risk of reoffending and the risk of harm to the public which the offender ... now poses. The risk element has two dimensions: the nature and seriousness of possible further offences, and the likelihood of their occurring'.

## The influence of PSRs

2.26 In practice PSRs usually but not always include recommendations as to the sentence or disposal of the case. Contrary to popular impressions, it is a minority of PSRs which recommend probation: probation officers are fairly selective. When probation is not recommended it is seldom ordered, although this sometimes happens, especially if the PSR is not specific. Agreement between recommendations and the court's decision is usually attributed to the influence of the recommendation, although it could also be due to the fact that the information in the PSR leads both the writer and the reader to the same conclusion, or even to a tendency on the part of the writer to recommend what he thinks the court will find acceptable. An experiment in South Yorkshire, however, by Hines et al (1978) strongly suggested that magistrates, at least in a 'sentencing exercise', were genuinely influenced in their disposals by the information in PSRs even when they did not include recommendations, but were influenced even more when they did. In his CC study, Moxon (1988) found that only one third of reports in the CC were in line with the eventual sentence.

## Do PSRs improve sentencing decisions?

2.27 Many years ago Hood and Taylor (1968) asked this very pertinent question. The Sunderland magistrates adopted a scheme in 1961 under which they received PSRs to help them in sentencing most indictable offenders, whereas previously they had sentenced most such offenders without PSRs. Hood and Taylor compared the 2-year reconviction rates of 100 males sentenced before the increased use of PSRs with the corresponding rates for 100 males sentenced in the first two years of the scheme, and another 100 sentenced in its third year. They found some improvement in the rates but seem to have regarded it as rather disappointing in magnitude. In fact all that could be expected was a small improvement. The number of offenders whose prospects of being reconvicted are really affected by the choice of sentence (and especially the limited choices open to MCs) is probably small. In some such cases the

Sunderland MC probably made the same choice with an PSR as it would have without one. In cases in which the choice made a difference, and the PSR did result in a different choice, it could hardly be expected to select the best available choice every time. Davies (1969) found that, in his sample of 507 young male probationers, those who were the subject of PSRs were as likely to be failures in their first year of supervision as those who had not been the subject of PSRs. A modest improvement in reconviction rates is the most that PSRs can be expected to achieve (see 7.37ff).

**2.28** This raises the question whether probation officers are in fact expert at predicting the likely consequences of a sentencing decision for the offender. What does seem to be true is that experienced officers who are willing to say whether this or that offender will be reconvicted or not turn out to be right a good deal more often than they would by chance. But that is not the same as saying 'He is more likely to be reconvicted if imprisoned than if fined'; and there is no hard evidence that probation officers do better than chance if they make statements of that kind. In practice they usually avoid predictions about reconvictions, preferring to make them about other consequences: for example about the effect of imprisonment on the offender's family and employability.

**2.29** That point apart, it can safely be said at the moment that PSRs have one important effect. If courts did not have them they would make much more use of custodial measures than they do; and the same is probably true of fines. If the avoidance — or even the postponement — of an offender's first custodial sentence is seen as a desirable policy, probation officers' reports contribute to it. For some probation officers, who see custodial sentences as doing more harm than good, this alone is enough to justify the very large number of hours which they have devoted to PSRs. Others, who see themselves as more impartial advisers of the court, are not satisfied by merely preventing a custodial sentence, without regard to the offender's later career.

## Post-sentence use of PSRs

**2.30** The use of the PSR does not stop at the court appearance. If the offender is sentenced to custody it follows him to the establishment to which he is allotted. The official recipients there are the governor and the prison probation officer; but the governor may give copies to the chaplain, the education organiser, the prison medical staff and those concerned with security and discipline. The court duty officer should prepare a post-sentence interview report (PSIR), which will be attached to the PSR. The PSIR will contain additional information such as the offender's intended address on release and any immediate medical or welfare problems requiring attention. When the offender becomes eligible for parole the PSR may be used to compile the parole assessment report which is sent to the Parole Board. The PSR may also influence decisions to allot the offender to an establishment of a different sort. As a result, preserving its confidentiality is difficult, and there is even a possibility that a copy which is not locked up will be seen by a prisoner who is trusted to work in administrative parts of the prison. Even if the offender is disposed of non-custodially the PSR will be filed by the probation service by which it was prepared, and used by any officer who has to supervise him, or prepare a PSR for another court appearance. (The defence solicitor may file his copy, and use it on a later occasion, although the risk that it will then be out of date is considerable.) If he is sent to a probation hostel a copy is likely to follow him. Occasionally a PSR reaches the police, either in court or through the police liaison officer who is informed of impending releases from custody (see 14.26); and PSRs are sometimes sent to the police officers who run attendance centres (see 20.15). PSRs also follow offenders who are sent to psychiatric hospitals, although we have less information about their use there. The *National Standard* states that reports should be treated as confidential documents and should not be disclosed more widely than to a custodial institution without the offender's consent.

## Lifers

**2.31** The PSIR prepared by the Probation Service on anyone sentenced to life imprisonment is sent not to the prison establishment but to the Prison Service's headquarters, where copies are distributed to the governor and probation officer at the lifer's prison, as well as to the Home Office division responsible for the release of such prisoners (see 22.16ff). These reports are therefore particularly thorough. In cases involving serious sexual and other violent offences the supervising probation service must arrange for the victim or victim's family to be contacted within two months of sentence and offered the opportunity of being kept informed of the sentence.

## Medical and psychiatric reports

**2.32** Medical reports are generally prepared on any offender charged with murder, manslaughter, a serious violent or sexual offence, or arson. Otherwise psychiatric examinations take place only in cases in which they are requested by the defence (the most frequent initiator) or suggested by a probation officer or the police. Occasionally sentencers themselves are so puzzled by the nature of the offence or the offender's behaviour in court that they initiate this step. If the court requests a medical report it pays for it, as it usually does when it is suggested by the police or the probation officer; and the defence often asks the court to do this instead of paying for it out of private means. Unless the defence has obtained a report before the court appearance the defendant has to be remanded for examination. The most reliable information about the use of psychiatric reports is provided by Salem (1982), a thorough study of some 600 cases in 14 MCs in different parts of England. It does not deal with the CC's use of such reports; but many of its findings—for example about the initiation of reports, which usually takes place in the lower courts—are relevant for the CC.

**2.33** Salem estimated that in 1980 there were some 8,000 custodial remands for psychiatric examination, plus an unknown number of remands on bail. Less than a quarter led to a psychiatric disposal: that is, to a court order involving psychiatric care or treatment (see chapter 21). This was not because the courts were too zealous in suspecting mental disorder. In Salem's sample only 7 per cent of remands resulted in a diagnosis of 'no mental disorder'. In other words, most psychiatric remands result in a diagnosis of mild mental disorder but not in a psychiatric disposal. This does not mean that they are wasted, since a positive diagnosis usually influences the court against punitive measures even if the psychiatrist cannot offer treatment.

**2.34** A court should give the psychiatrist its reasons for requesting a report. It should, for example, make it clear whether it has in mind the possibility of a hospital or guardianship order (see 21.36ff), although that would not preclude the psychiatrist from recommending instead a psychiatric probation order, or indeed some other disposal. (If he recommends a hospital order, however, he must use a prescribed form for his report). On the other hand, what the court may want to know is whether the defendant is mentally fit to be tried: whether he can understand the proceedings sufficiently to make a proper defence, and understand the substance of the evidence (Butler, 1975). Occasionally the court needs to be told (even if it has not asked) whether the defendant knew the 'nature and quality of his act' or knew that it was legally wrong, or was under a delusion which, if true, would have excused his act: in other words, whether an insanity defence is, or would be, justified. If the charge is murder the report will usually be expected to say whether the defendant's 'mental responsibility' at the time of the killing was 'substantially impaired' by 'abnormality of mind' (the defence of diminished responsibility: see s 2 HA 57 and 4.21). If the defendant is a mother who has killed her child within 12 months of its birth, the question will usually be whether 'the balance of her mind was disturbed' by reason of her not having fully recovered from the effects of giving birth to the child (the defence of infanticide: see s 1 IA 38).

**2.35** Like the probation officer, the psychiatrist is sometimes expected to prepare a report on a defendant who has not admitted his guilt, and intends to plead 'not guilty'. This is most likely when he has been committed for trial on some very serious charge. The defendant may consent to an examination and interview, yet deny that he was the person who committed the crime, or claim that his actions were defensible because of the behaviour of other parties. The psychiatrist must be clear as to whether his report (and his oral evidence) is to form part of the evidence on which the defendant's culpability will be assessed (as for example when the defence is diminished responsibility) or whether it will be used only at the sentencing stage. Even in the latter case his assessment of the offender's dangerousness must depend to a considerable extent on the opinion which he has formed about the state of mind in which the offence was committed. He must be particularly careful about references to any other offences which the offender may admit to him, if he is not sure whether the latter has been convicted of them or admitted them to the police.

**2.36** Whatever the circumstances, the report is expected to include an opinion as to

a.   whether the defendant suffers from any form of mental disorder;
b.   if so, whether he is in need of or capable of benefiting from treatment;
c.   where and by whom this treatment can be given;
d.   whether it should be in-patient treatment;
e.   the prognosis, when this is possible (HO Circular 1/1975).

**2.37**   Reports should make clear the sources of the information which they contain, especially when it is obtained from the defendant, from his relatives or (as is often the case) from an PSR. The main source of information is usually the defendant himself, together with any physical tests—such as electro-encephalograms—which seem necessary. If the offender has been remanded in custody the psychiatrist should also have the benefit of notes by hospital officers or nursing staff on his behaviour while 'inside'. If 2 or more psychiatrists have to report they usually consult each other, chiefly in order to avoid apparent contradictions as a result of different terminologies.

**2.38**   A psychiatrist's report is given to the clerk of the court, and to the defence solicitor. The liaison officer may or may not receive a copy, depending on local arrangements, even if the proposal for a psychiatric examination originated from the probation service. It must not be read aloud, although occasionally there is a discussion in court of something that is said in it. If the offender is sentenced—or remanded again—to custody it does not automatically follow him—unlike a PSR—although the prison medical officer can usually obtain a copy for his file. The file is not accessible to other custodial staff, with the possible exception of those employed in the PMO's office. The offender himself is seldom shown it by his solicitor or the examining psychiatrist.

**2.39**   A distinction, however, must be drawn between the confidentiality of a psychiatrist's report to a criminal court and the confidentiality which he—or any medical practitioner—would feel obliged to observe when writing about a patient. The defendant is not his patient, even if the report has been requested by the defence; and the distinction should be made clear to him. Some psychiatrists however make a practice of asking him whether he has disclosed anything to them which he would prefer the court not to know. If he is about to plead 'not guilty' the psychiatrist may be in the same difficulty as the writer of a PSR (see 2.16): he may feel unable to discuss the most relevant part of the defendant's behaviour with him, or the defendant himself may be unwilling to discuss it. If he does in effect admit his guilt to the psychiatrist it is for the latter to decide whether he should mention this in his report.

### Reports by prison staff

**2.40**   Prison Service establishments no longer provide courts with routine reports (as they used to do in the case of ex-borstal inmates). On the other hand, if any member of staff—such as a prison medical officer—notices anything which is obviously of importance from a sentencer's point of view, the governor should report this to the court. The CC may ask the establishment for a report, for example on the offender's behaviour while in custody; but it is unusual for a MC to do so.

## Evidence as to character

**2.41**   During a trial, but more usually at the sentencing stage, the defence may produce written or oral evidence to the effect that the offender is of good character. If this is done during the trial the aim is to persuade the court that the accused is unlikely to have been the person who committed the act, or—if that is not denied—that he did so innocently or excusably. More often the evidence is used to support a plea in mitigation, for example, where an employer is called to say that he is prepared to continue employing the defendant. Character witnesses are seldom cross-examined.

## Pleas in mitigation

**2.42**   Sentencers must always give a convicted offender the opportunity to submit a plea in mitigation, even when he pleads guilty by post (see 1.3). The offender may submit this in person, unless he is legally represented (and he may dismiss his legal representative in order to speak in person). Most pleas in mitigation are based chiefly on information in PSRs, sometimes supplemented by what the offender tells his solicitor or counsel. Shapland's (1981) study of counsel's pleas in mitigation found striking variations in the points made by 30 barristers when presented with the same fictitious case. There were marked differences both in the amount of information which each barrister elicited from the brief and from the interview with the 'client' (a part played by Dr Shapland herself), as well as in the choice of items on which the plea would be based. She recommended, inter alia, training for barristers in this part of their work. Such training as now is offered by the Council for Legal Education seems to be having little effect: McConville et al's (1994) study of solicitors' firms concluded that, in MCs, solicitors 'join hands' with prosecutors and routinise pleas and mitigation. The authors called for a 'cultural transformation in the values of criminal defence work' (p 296). It may well be, as Wasik (1994) points out, that the structure provided by the CJA 91 to the sentencing decision will be increasingly mirrored in pleas in mitigation (see chapter 4). Perhaps training too would be more effective if it could be based on empirical studies of the influence which different kinds of information have on sentencers; but so far the only such studies in England which have been published have been limited to lay magistrates and special types of offence. Hood's (1972) experiments with magistrates involved only motoring offences; Taylor's (1972) involved only sexual offences. Research in CCs has not been permitted (see 1.28).

## Reports for magistrates' courts

**2.43**   Not all that has been said so far applies to MCs. The information which they are given about traffic offenders is dealt with in chapter 23. In the case of summary non-traffic offences the nature of the information which courts are given depends chiefly on

a. whether the prosecutor is the CPS or some other agency. In CPS prosecutions it is usual to give the court an antecedents report, listing all known previous convictions other than traffic convictions; but if the offence is trivial—for example an unaggravated offence of drunkenness—some police forces do not submit an antecedents report. Other official agencies, such as local authorities, may submit only a list of previous convictions resulting from their own prosecutions, or may ask the local police to supply a list of other convictions (especially if the offence being prosecuted involves dishonesty or violence);

b. whether the offender is offered the opportunity of pleading guilty by post. If so, the letter with this offer should tell him of any previous convictions of which the sentencing court will be informed. Because pleading guilty by post is intended to save the time of all concerned, and is confined to minor offences, such letters often do not list previous convictions of which the court could have been told; and when this is so the court must not of course be told of them.

Other kinds of information about the offender, of the sort provided by comprehensive antecedents reports or PSRs, are not usually provided when he is being sentenced for a summary offence, although there are exceptions (for example when a young prostitute appears in court on her first charge of soliciting). In practice, a PSR will only be prepared after a finding of guilt and following an adjournment.

**2.44** Even when magistrates are dealing with an offence which must be tried on indictment, or is triable either way, they may or may not be provided with a PSR. They are very likely to be if

a. the offender is already known to the local probation service. That service will have been provided with a list of those due to appear before the court, and should have had time in which to prepare a PSR of sorts, based chiefly on the information already in their files;

b. the nature of the charge suggests to the local probation service that a PSR should be prepared, in which case a probation officer can propose a remand;

c. something about the case suggests to the clerk or the magistrate that a PSR is needed, in which case a remand is usual.

Shortage of time usually prevents the report from reaching the clerk of the court 24 hours in advance, as it should do in the CC. If the offender is being committed to the CC for trial or sentence it is left to the probation service to prepare a PSR for that court, and the magistrates do not see it.

# Chapter 3

# The relevance of explanations

**3.1** Reports on the offender may throw some light on the reasons for his law-breaking; and many sentencers—like members of the public—feel the need for explanations of some kinds of offence (but not of some other kinds: an important fact which is emphasised in 3.3). The need may even drive them to look for literature on the subject, in the hope of deepening their understanding of the cases which come before their courts.

If they do not find the literature completely satisfying, there are several good reasons[1]. First most explainers write in very general terms, being under the impression that they are formulating scientific laws of human nature. In order to gloss over the cases which these laws clearly do not fit they have to be expressed in very imprecise terms, or qualified by many exceptions. The result is vagueness. Secondly, most human behaviour[2] cannot be described intelligibly as if it were determined by natural laws in the same way as the movements of a machine. It is better described as following *rules*[3]. Some rules are unwritten· or even unarticulated: examples are those concerned with ways of eating, speaking, defecating, dressing, copulating, insulting, apologising. Some are codified, as in football, chess, bridge, medical practice. Some are not only codified but backed up by the official threats of the criminal justice system.

1. For a fuller discussion of explanations (and pseudo-explanations) see Walker (1973). This short chapter is confined to points of relevance for sentencing.
2. Exceptions, which can be described as law-determined, are movements such as those of an epileptic fit or a tic.
3. For a thorough exposition of this point of view see Harré and Secord (1972).

## Rule-following and states of mind

**3.2** Sometimes the straightforward explanation of a breach of the criminal law is simply that the offender was following some other sort of rule. An example is an assault of the kind which is regarded in some circles as the correct response to an insult. More often the explanation is not that the offender was following an unofficial rule but that he was acting in breach of one (or of the law itself) because the circumstances were such that

i.   he did not regard the rule as applying to the situation. For example, he may have trespassed in order to save a child from an obvious danger, or committed a minor sexual assault by touching a woman in a way to which she unexpectedly objects;

or

ii.   he was aware that he was breaching the rule, but felt justified in doing so, either because of the special circumstances—for instance, extreme provocation—or because of his strong political or religious views, terrorist violence being an example. The justification may be a delusion: for example that he is defending himself against the devil. Again, he may regard the rule as pointless or anachronistic, as some regard the law which forbids the use of cannabis. Common ways of excusing violence or theft have been described by sociologists such as Sykes and Matza (1957);

or

iii.   he was overcome by a desire or emotion—aggressive, sexual, or acquisitive—so strong that the relevant rules were forgotten or brushed aside with no thought of justification. If the desire or emotion came on him suddenly his act is usually called 'impulsive'; but it may instead be 'compulsive'—a chronic or recurrent itch to steal, expose himself, provoke someone. He may do this in situations which make detection and arrest highly probable; or he may be able to control himself for a short time until he finds a less risky opportunity. A capacity for doing the latter does not always negative 'compulsion'. On the other hand, the common assump-tion that abnormal desires—sexual, sadistic or acquisitive—are always compulsive is a mistake: many people experience but resist them;

or

iv.   the rule was one which had no moral force for him, and the reward for breaking it seemed to outweigh the (perhaps unlikely) consequences of being detected in doing so. This is the state of mind of many acquisitive offenders—burglars, thieves, embezzlers and frauds; but it is also the state of mind of many drivers of motor vehicles. Many rules about ownership or traffic have no moral force for a large number of people who are not amoral in other ways[2];

or

v.   he broke a rule for the sake of doing so, perhaps as a demonstration, perhaps because he resents being told not to do something, perhaps because he enjoys the excitement of risking arrest. He may even want to be arrested, whether to achieve martyrdom, to get a bed and a meal, or to escape from problems[3].

1.   Obviously, states of mind have to be inferred from what offenders say—usually to police, probation officers or solicitors—although sometimes their behaviour is a more reliable indicator. Some offenders are very skilled in presenting themselves favourably; others have so little verbal skill that they cannot be honest either. The court has to be content with the interpretation given to it by defence counsel or probation officers who have their own reasons for presenting it in a way which is favourable to the defendant. This is another reason why, in real life, sentencers are bound to take explanations with a little salt.
2.   There are of course rarer sorts of people who seem to be unable to share the moral feelings which most people have about some rules. They are aware that others have such feelings, but have not experienced them. The classic description of such people is Cleckley's (1941), who

called their condition 'semantic dementia'. preferring this term to the vaguer label 'psychopathic personality'; but the latter prevailed.
3. See Bennett and Wright's (1984) accounts of what their burglars said.

## Situations

**3.3** These subdivisions are very broad and can be subdivided further. They are enough however to illustrate how it is possible to distinguish the states of mind in which offences are committed without saying—and perhaps without being able to say—how they came about. Not that this is usually difficult. Often they are unsurprising responses to situations: to a provocation in a bar, to the discovery of a radio on a park bench without an owner in sight, to the sight of an empty motorway when one is driving a powerful car. In some situations it is a strict observance of the law that is surprising.

## Dispositions

**3.4** It is when we think that most people would not have broken the law—whether for moral or prudential reasons—that we feel a real need of explanation. What is then offered may invoke the notion of a disposition, or it may rely on a narrative. Examples of dispositions are a hair-triggered temper, a weakness of self-control, a love of fast cars. Some of these dispositions are attributed by psychologists to upbringing, or by sociologists to the values of the social group to which the offender belongs. Some are attributed by psychiatrists to mild or severe forms of mental disorder, or occasionally to cerebral damage. There may even be genetic explanations of some cases of weak self-control.

## Narratives

**3.5** Dispositional explanations are most plausible when it is known that the offender has repeatedly behaved in a similar way. If this does not seem to be the case, if there is no other evidence of a disposition, and if a 'situational' explanation seems inadequate, a narrative account is the third resort. A driver who ignored a red traffic light may have left home later than he planned, to keep an important appointment, or to catch a train. Coming to the light-controlled junction he may have seen that there was no chance of a collision, and no police in sight. He may have reasoned that obedience to traffic lights is required solely in order to prevent accidents, and could on this occasion be waived with safety and no real immorality. An explanation of this kind, relying partly on the immediate situation as he perceived it, partly on preceding events as experienced by him, may seem quite adequate. Sometimes, when the offence is of a more serious kind, it may be necessary to invoke a disposition as well—for example a liking for risks—in order to make the account entirely plausible: but sometimes the disposition is so prevalent that it is not worth special mention.

## The positivist fallacy

**3.6** This emphasises a subtle fallacy of positivism to which Walker (1973) drew attention. It is the assumption that explanations of rule-*breaking* ought to tell us why it was, in the circumstances, inevitable or at least highly probable. Most rule-*following* can be explained in this more or less scientific way; but in many cases of rule-breaking the best that can be offered is an answer to the question 'How *could* he have done that?', an answer which tells us how it was psychologically *possible*, not probable, far less inevitable. Only if he (or she) repeatedly breaks the rule is it sensible to ask for a probability-explanation. Otherwise we accept possibility-explanations in real life. The scientistic fallacy is to attempt probability-explanations of rule-breaking when there is no reason to suppose that the rule-breaking *was* probable.

## General theories

**3.7** All this should be enough to discredit any 'general theory' which offers to explain 'crime', or some broad category of it, in terms of a single concept. Yet there have been many attempts. 'Differential association', 'anomie', 'the amplification of deviant values', 'frustration', 'insecurity', 'subcultures', 'drift', 'labelling'—the galleries of criminology are museums for these megaliths, each decorated with its esoteric runes and critical graffiti. Obvious exceptions to each general theory are met by defining the central concept yet more widely or vaguely. The fallacy of regarding 'crime' as a homogeneous social phenomenon which could conceivably have a unified explanation should be as plain as the naivety of seeking a single explanation of 'disease' or 'poverty'. What is less obvious, but equally true, is that not even a fairly specific type of offence is in every case attributable to the same state of mind, let alone the same process of causation. Even indecent exposure, or sadistic killings, are committed in varied moods, with varied intentions, and as a result of different kinds of experience.

## Selection and magnification

**3.8** Even when it is a single offence that is being explained, the sort of explanation that is appropriate varies according to the purpose for which it is needed. Explanations are not usually expected—except sometimes in psychologists' laboratories—to detail all the sufficient conditions of human action: if they did so they would be impossibly complex. What they normally do is to select those conditions, in the situation or in the individual's past, which stand out either because they seem abnormal or because they appear to point to some way in which he or she could be influenced to behave differently. Psychologists and psychiatrists look for experiences or physical disabilities which can be counteracted. Sociologists look for economic, environmental, social or political conditions which can be improved. From the strictly scientific point of view the result is to overemphasise whatever factor is selected for attention: to apply a magnifying glass, as it were, to one part of the whole picture. Even the 'situational approach' of Clarke (1980), which rightly holds that the best way of reducing most types of crime is to reduce opportunities for them, may not attach enough importance to the differences between individuals who are not prepared to take advantage of opportunities, those who are, and those who look for or create them.

## The purposes of selective explanation

3.9   If what has to be satisfied is scientific curiosity, rather than the desire to do something effective, an exhaustive, unselective explanation may be the ideal. That is not, however, the sentencer's requirement. He wants either

i.   an explanation which will give him some indication of the probability that the offender will behave likewise again. This is especially important if the offence is of a kind against which the public demands protection (see chapter 22);

or

ii.   one which will point to something that can be done to reduce that probability. It may be social work, individual deterrence, psychiatric treatment or — in the last resort — incapacitation (see chapters 7, 21 and 22);

or

iii.   one which will help him to assess the offender's culpability. Some explanations aggravate, some mitigate and some completely excuse the offence. The courts' approach to aggravation and mitigation is the subject of the next chapter; but it is worth pointing out here that the explanations which they accept as excuses or mitigating considerations are often — perhaps usually — answers to the question 'How could he ?' rather than the question 'Why did he have to?'.

## Abolishing causes of crime

3.10   This chapter may have made it clear why so much less is written nowadays about the causes of crime. Yet sentencing policy is still subjected to the naive criticism that it does not attack those causes. The critics seem to have in mind a medical model in which disease is abolished by preventive methods. Needless to say, this seldom happens in real life, even in medicine; and it is an even more visionary hope where human rule-breaking is concerned. In any case, the sentencer has to deal with the end-products of an imperfect world. If the end-product is a persistent offender the causes of his behaviour lie far back in his past; and often the most that can be done is to discourage him, or find some *modus vivendi* which will enable society to tolerate the nuisance which he represents. Even when a psychiatrist is able to offer treatment with good prospects of success, he is not usually offering to remove the cause of the abnormal behaviour: much more often he counteracts it, for example with drugs. Sentencers cannot be expected to abolish causes, only to take them into account when they are relevant to culpability, to the probability of recidivism or to the likelihood that some agent of the criminal justice system will be able to have some influence on the behaviour in question.

Chapter 4

# Aggravation and mitigation

**4.1**   Murder apart, sentencers are allowed—but not obliged—to exercise a discretion to choose sentences which are more severe or lenient than normal; and until recently the statutes did not tell them how to use this discretion. Nowadays there are four specific factors which they are required by statute to take into account: pleas of guilty, the 'totality principle', being on bail at the time of the offence, and previous record. These will be discussed in the following paragraphs. It is true that statutory distinctions—for instance between murder and manslaughter, grievous and actual bodily harm, dangerous and careless driving— also reflect mitigating or aggravating considerations; but by and large the statutes leave it to sentencers to decide what aggravates and what mitigates; and merely require them to take into account '... all such information about the circumstances of the offence ... (including aggravating and mitigating factors) as is available' (s 3 CJA 91). Although this requirement applies only to decisions about the appropriateness and length of custodial sentences, it would be difficult to argue that the principle does not apply to fines and other non-custodial penalties. What is more important is that the requirement applies only to factors which are part of 'the circumstances of the offence'. Another section of the same Act, however (s 28), says that 'nothing in this Part of this Act shall prevent a court from mitigating an offence by taking into account any *such matters* as in the opinion of the court are relevant *in mitigation* of sentence'. Ashworth (1992) argues that this section allows factors which are not related to the seriousness of the offence to mitigate but not to aggravate. We shall see in 4.10, when we come to consider 'prevalence', how far the CA is prepared to stretch the meaning of 'the circumstances of the offence'.

## Pleading guilty

**4.2**   When the offender pleads guilty the court '*shall take into account*' the stage of the proceedings at which he or she indicated an intention of doing so, and the circumstances in which this indication was given (s 48 CJPOA 94). This does not tell sentencers what sort of allowance to make: only that they must take the plea into account. The circumstances in which it is made may suggest that it was a voluntary and praiseworthy decision (for example intended to save the victim of a sexual offence from having to testify), or one which was more or less forced by the weight of the evidence (in which case any allowance would be minimal). The stage at which the decision is taken is important because an early indication saves courts more time and trouble than a late one. It is interesting, however, that when, before the 1994 Act, judges made allowances for guilty pleas, late decisions seemed to earn larger allowances than early ones (Moxon, 1988). The explanation may be that *changes* of plea made more impression on counsel and judges. However that may be, Moxon estimated the average allowance at about 20 per cent of a custodial sentence; but as much as 50 per cent has been deducted when the offender voluntarily gave himself up to the police before being detected. As we have seen, the justification for taking this factor into account may be mere expediency—the encouragement of offenders to save the courts trouble—or moral credit, if the court believes that the offender's motive is genuine remorse or consideration for his victim; but since offenders are supposed to know that a guilty plea will earn some degree of leniency it is never easy to be sure about their motives. Allowances for guilty pleas are among the practices which have been criticised as 'oiling the conveyor belt' (Sanders and Young, 1994).

## The totality principle

**4.3**　Another principle now recognised by statute (s 28(2)(b) CJA 91) is the 'totality principle'. If an offender is receiving more than one custodial sentence, or more than one fine, 'nothing in this Part [of the CJA 91] shall prevent a court ... from applying any rule of law as to the totality of sentences'. This acknowledges the CA's occasional decisions that even when each of the penalties were by themselves correct they might add up to something excessive (eg in *Hunter* (1979) 1 Cr App Rep (S) 7, whose total of eight years for a series of indecent assaults was reduced to six). The justification for the totality principle cannot be that it oils the wheels of justice, or that it is likely to reduce the crime rate. Arguably it is a subtle retributive principle: that eight years is excessive because it is more than twice as severe as four years.

## Offending while on bail

**4.4**　If an offence is committed while an offender is on bail 'the court *shall treat* the fact as an aggravating factor' (s 29 CJA 91). Both the italicised words are worth noting: courts must, not may, treat, not merely take into account, offending on bail as an aggravation. By the 1990s magistrates and police were complaining loudly about the number of offenders whom courts felt compelled by the Bail Act 1976 to set free while awaiting trial, only to see them charged with fresh offences. This clause was probably intended to strengthen the hands of sentencers who regarded an offence committed in these circumstances as deserving of more severity than it would otherwise have been. As we shall see, 'abuse of a position of trust' has long been recognised as an aggravation, and offending on bail can be seen in that light.

## Previous record and non-response to earlier sentences

**4.5**  The ordinary sentencer regards previous convictions and failure to respond to earlier sentences as good reasons for choosing a more severe sentence. The ordinary offender—a simple retributivist—resents this: it is punishing him twice for earlier sins. The CA used to take a similarly retributive view: see *Queen* (1981) 3 Cr App Rep (S) 245; and the CJA 91 in its original version laid down that an offence was not to be regarded as more serious by reason of a previous conviction or failure to respond to previous sentences. The Government was soon persuaded, however, to amend this so as to allow—but not oblige—sentencers to regard both of these factors as aggravations (s 29 CJA 91 as amended by CJA 93). It certainly makes pragmatic sense to try a more severe sentence when a milder one has failed; but retributive purists who want severity to be proportional to culpability (see chapter 9) find it hard to see how culpability can be affected by previous offences, even if of a similar kind. One suggestion is that having a clean record should be regarded as a mitigation, and that with each successive conviction there is a 'progressive loss of this mitigation' (Ashworth, 1992). Treating a clean record, however, as a mitigation is very much the same thing as making an allowance for 'good character'; and it seems less artificial simply to argue that previous convictions show how little respect the offender has for the law, and justify sentencing him accordingly. Either way, it means that courts are sentencing a defendant for character as well as offence.

## Dangerousness

**4.6**  If an offence is sexual or violent, and the court is of the opinion that a custodial sentence longer than would be commensurate with the seriousness of the offence is needed for the protection of the public from serious harm from the offender, it may pass such a sentence, provided that it does not exceed the statutory maximum for the offence. In certain circumstances the CC may even pass a 'life' sentence as a precaution, or add a restriction order to a hospital order. Dangerousness is a very special kind of aggravation, and is dealt with in chapter 22.

## Non-statutory guidance

**4.7**  Other specific aggravations are listed in the LCJ's *Practice Note* of 1990 ([1990] 3 All ER 979) which guides MCs in deciding whether to commit an offence that is triable either way to the CC for trial. Factors mentioned in the context of several types of offence are
- the high value (ie worth £4,000 or more) of any property stolen, handled or damaged;

- the professionalism or sophistication of the method;
- organisation by a gang, or commission by a group;
- the vulnerability of the victim;
- the fact that the offence was a breach of trust or abuse of a position of authority or responsibility;
- the use of weapons;
- the seriousness of personal injury;

Other factors are mentioned in the context of particular types of offence:

- burglary of a dwelling: entry in the daytime when the occupier (or anyone else) is present; vandalism; the Practice Note reminds MCs that they must commit for trial if anyone in the dwelling was subjected to violence or the threat of it (Sch 1 MCA 80);
- burglary of non-dwellings: burglary of pharmacies or doctors' surgeries; vandalism on a substantial scale;
- dishonest handling, when the receiver has commissioned the theft;
- personal violence, when serious violence is caused to those whose work has to be done in contact with the public: for example, police, taxi-drivers, shopkeepers;
- public order offences: when organised, or racially motivated; when police, ambulance men and the like are attacked;
- violence to and neglect of children, when it is repeated (even if the harm is slight); when it is sadistic (it is interesting that this is the only context in which the Practice Note mentions sadism, although it might have been expected to do so in the context of other personal violence);
- indecent assault, when the assault is more than trivial and is repeated, or where there is substantial disparity in age between victim and defendant (presumably the LCJ was thinking of young rather than middle-aged victims);
- possession of a Class A drug, unless the amount is small and consistent with personal use; possession of a Class B drug with intent to supply, unless on a small scale and no payment; possession of a substantial quantity;
- criminal damage consisting of deliberate fireraising, or racially motivated;
- reckless driving, when contributed to by alcohol or drugs; when the speed is grossly excessive; when racing; or when associated with other offences;

The *Practice Note* makes it clear that the defendant's antecedents and personal mitigating circumstances are irrelevant when mode of trial is being decided, no doubt because they will be considered by the court if and when the sentencing stage is reached.

## Guideline cases

**4.8** So, of course, may any of the considerations in the *Practice Note*. Courts are also guided by a number of cases in which the CA has not merely upheld or varied the sentence which was the subject of an appeal, but has indicated what factors sentencers should take into account by way of aggravation or mitigation. Some of these cases are expressly called 'guide-line cases', but many are not, even when their advice is as detailed. The important cases are:

- manslaughter in cases of diminished responsibility: *Chambers* (1983) 5 Cr App Rep (S) 190;
- manslaughter in a fight: *Coleman* (1992) 13 Cr App Rep (S) 508;
- infanticide: *Sainsbury* (1989) 11 Cr App Rep (S) 533;
- causing death by dangerous driving: *Boswell* (1984) 6 Cr App Rep (S) 257: *Willetts* (1993) 14 Cr App Rep (S) 592: *Shepherd and Wernet* (1994) 15 Cr App Rep (S) 640 (A-G's References 14 and 24 of 1993);
- attempted murder: *Ellis* (1995) 16 Cr App Rep (S) 773;
- robbery (but not mugging): *Turner* (1975) 61 Cr App Rep 67; *Daly* (1981) 3 Cr App Rep (S) 340; *Gould* (1983) 5 Cr App Rep (S) 72;
- use of a real or imitation firearm in an offence: *Sheldrake* (1985) 7 Cr App Rep (S) 49;
- planting explosive devices: *Byrne* (1975) 62 Cr App Rep 159;
- riot and unlawful assembly: *Caird* (1970) 54 Cr App Rep 499; *Pilgrim* (1983) 5 Cr App Rep (S) 140;
- racially motivated violence: *Ribbans, Duggan and Ridley* (1995) 16 Cr App Rep (S) 698;
- kidnapping: *Spence and Thomas* (1983) 5 Cr App Rep (S) 413;
- illegally procuring miscarriage: *Scrimaglia* (1971) 55 Cr App Rep 280;
- burglary of a dwelling: *Mussell* (1990) 12 Cr App Rep (S) 607;
- breaches of trust: *Barrick* (1985) 7 Cr App Rep (S) 142;
- pilfering by employees: *Dhunay* (1986) 8 Cr App Rep (S) 107;
- rape: *Billam* (1986) 82 Cr App Rep 347;
- incest:, *A-G's Reference (No 1 of 1989)* 11 Cr App Rep (S) 409;
- unlawful sexual intercourse with girl under 16: *Taylor* (1977) 64 Cr App Rep 182;
- buggery of young man: *Willis* (1974) 60 Cr App Rep 146;
- gross indecency between men: *Morgan* (1978) CSP B4−92001;
- living on immoral earnings: *Farrugia* (1979) 69 Cr App Rep 108;
- concealing income from Inland Revenue: *Ford* (1981) 3 Cr App Rep (S) 15;
- social benefit frauds: *Livingstone-Stewart* (1987) 9 Cr App Rep (S) 135;
- dealing in heroin or cocaine: *Aranguren* (1994) 16 Cr App Rep (S) 211;
- importing Ecstasy: *Warren* (and *Beeley*) [1995] Crim LR 838;
- having obscene articles for publication for gain: *Holloway* (1982) 4 Cr App Rep (S) 128; and see *Littleford* (1984) 6 Cr App Rep (S) 272 for importation;

A guideline case of more general application is *Bibi* (1980) 2 Cr App Rep (S) 177, in which the CA advocated shorter sentences for 'the less serious types of factory- or shop-breaking, the minor cases of sexual indecency, the more petty frauds where small amounts of money are involved, the fringe participants in more serious crime'. The CA's reason was merely pragmatic: overcrowding in prisons; but when dealing with Bibi herself it took into account a consideration which will be discussed later.

## Other cases, other considerations

**4.9**  In guideline cases the CA usually confines itself to the harm done, the way in which it was done, and any features which seem to make it more or less culpable (such as premeditation or impulsiveness). Other cases, however, exemplify a wider range of considerations, although it is not always clear how widely the CA intends them to be applied. As it emphasised in *De Havilland* (1983) 5 Cr App Rep (S) 109, its sentencing decisions are not binding, and are no more than 'examples of how the Court has dealt with a particular offender in relation to a particular offence'. Guideline cases allow sentencers to retain discretion, and even depart from the guidelines if the circumstances of the case justify this.

## Prevalence

**4.10**  Even guideline cases are not always easy to interpret. The prevalence of an offence does not justify sentencing a particular offender with special severity in order to make an example of him or her (*Cunningham* (1993) 14 Cr App Rep (S) 444 at 448); but it is 'a legitimate factor in determining the length of the custodial sentence to be passed' (ibid). This must mean that prevalence justifies consistently long sentences for a whole class of offences. The CA's justification for this principle is the alarm which robberies or rapes (its examples) cause in a locality: 'the sentence commensurate with the seriousness of the offence may need to be higher there than elsewhere' (ibid). This can hardly mean that otherwise similar rapes or robberies are more serious in London than in Lincoln: it must mean that prevalence is an aggravating circumstance of the offence within the meaning of s 3 CJA 91. Cunningham's robbery, in plain words, was aggravated by the fact that a lot of other robbers were active in his locality. This shows how far the meaning of 'circumstances' can be stretched.

## The victim

**4.11**  If the victim is very young the sentence is likely to be more severe. (In the case of sexual offences this may even place the offence in a different category.) An elderly or handicapped victim has a similar effect. The underlying reasoning seems to be based on the notion that violence against able-bodied adults is in some way closer to 'fair play'. The justification must be different for increasing severity when the victim of violence is a police officer, which the Court of Appeal endorsed as a general principle in *McKenlay* ((1979) 1 Cr App Rep (S) 161). In this case the violence was committed by a picket during a strike, and the Court of Appeal may have been worried at the time by the problem of violent picketing, although they did not give this as a reason. There are other cases however in which severe sentences for assaults on police have been upheld, eg *Coleman* (1975) 61 Cr App Rep 206: *Bell* [1973] Crim LR 318. Since police are physically fit and trained to deal with violence the justification cannot be based on 'fair play': it must be simple deterrence.

## Abuse of position

**4.12** Offences involving the abuse of positions of trust or power tend to be severely sentenced. Corruption and embezzlement provide many examples; and abuse of an expense account is regarded as being in a similar category (*Woodley* (1979) 1 Cr App Rep (S) 141). A policeman is in a position of power when interrogating people, so that *Lewis* ([1976] Crim LR 144), who beat up a man for withholding information, was unsuccessful in his appeal against a 2-year prison sentence. Sexual offences against children by teachers or other people who have been given charge of them are also severely punished (an example is *Seaman* (1982) 4 Cr App Rep (S) 108).

## Professionalism

**4.13** The CA has upheld long prison sentences imposed because the offender was regarded as 'professional'. In *Brewster* ((1980) 2 Cr App Rep (S) 191) it referred to 'professional criminals, who have long records, great skill as criminals and who from time to time make very valuable hauls'. In that case the express justification for the sentence was the incapacitation of the offender. The underlying justification for treating professionalism as an aggravating feature seems to be that the 'professional' is likely to do more harm than his non-professional equivalent. This must certainly be so when his skill enables him to identify the most lucrative targets for his burglaries, robberies or frauds. Mere skill in executing them, which is sometimes taken as the evidence of professionalism, does not mean that the harm done is greater than usual. It may even mean that less physical injury is caused: it is often the inexperienced burglar who panics and seriously injures the householder, or who vandalises the dwelling.

## Likelihood of escaping detection

**4.14** Another aspect of 'professionalism' however is the likelihood that the offender has committed similar offences without being detected, or at least convicted. But unless he asks for them to be TIC the sentencer should not increase his sentence on that assumption (see 2.10 ff). What he can do, it seems, if the offence is of a kind which makes detection difficult, is to increase the sentence in order to deter those who might consider doing likewise: a consideration which is quite often mentioned with approval by the CA (for example in *Silverman* (1983) 5 Cr App Rep (S) 46). The offender is not being sentenced for unproven misdeeds, it seems: but the sentence is more than usually severe in order to make up for the improbability of incurring it.

## Premeditation

**4.15** A premeditated offence is usually regarded as morally worse than one committed on the spur of the moment, especially when it consists of violence to the person. The CA, however, does not seem to have provided a guideline case on the subject. *Horrocks* ((1979) 1 Cr App Rep (S) 119) seems to be a rather special case, in which a man provoked by his wife's infidelity might have been sentenced more lightly for his attack on her lover if he had not 'made the weapon ready before the interview'.

## Unnecessary violence

**4.16** Frequently mentioned is violence of a gratuitous or excessive nature: that is, 'violence over and above the violence necessarily involved in the act itself' (in *Roberts and Roberts* (1982) 4 Cr App Rep (S) 8): and see *Silver and Gosling* ((1982) 4 Cr App Rep (S) 48).

## Motives

**4.17** Motives matter: some are more disapproved than others. Greed is worse than need. Racial hatred is worse than football rivalry. Crimes committed as part of a campaign were especially condemned in *Cruikshank and O'Donnell* (1995) 16 Cr App Rep (S) 728: '... It must be clearly understood by activists for whatever cause that to seek to destabilise the community or exert pressure must be met with severe deterrent sentences'. Revenge, on the other hand, is more tolerable (Bacon, the 17th-century Lord Chancellor, called it 'a kind of wild justice' (1597)). *Tracey* (1993) 14 Cr App Rep (S) 666, who had had acid thrown at him by a gang, and threw acid back at them a week later, was dealt with leniently by the CA as a case of 'delayed provocation'.

## Short-term visitors

**4.18** Although being foreign is not an aggravating circumstance, visitors to England whose stay is meant to be short may find that they are dealt with slightly more severely. Foreign shoplifters are often not given time to pay fines, for the practical reason that the usual procedures for enforcing payment would be rendered ineffective by their departure. By contrast, if the sentencer is hesitating between a fine and a custodial sentence because of the nature of the offence he may decide against a prison sentence because of the problems which this would create for a tourist. On the other hand, the fact that *Mbelu* ((1981) 3 Cr App Rep (S) 157) was merely in transit at Gatwick between Nigeria and Los Angeles did not save him from an 18-month prison sentence for smuggling a substantial amount of cannabis, because of the seriousness with which courts view this offence. Discriminatory treatment of short-term visitors is discussed in the next chapter.

## Mitigation

**4.19** Mitigation, like aggravation, is usually though not always based on retributive reasoning; that is, on reasoning which concludes either (a) that the offender's culpability is enhanced or diminished or (b) that he will suffer more (or, rarely, less) than most offenders would from the usual penalty. Occasionally a court mitigates sentence for a third retributive reason: (c) that the offender has behaved in a meritorious way which, though strictly speaking it does not alter his culpability, should be taken into account in his favour. Yet even sentencers who try not to reason retributively may mitigate for other reasons. They may for example be persuaded that the offender's personality or circumstances are such that a mild or nominal measure will be sufficient to discourage him from repetition. The following paragraphs illustrate common—and some not so common—reasons.

## Diminished culpability

**4.20** The offender's culpability is often regarded as diminished by one of the following:

a. provocation or temptation, especially if the victim was to some extent responsible for either (an example is *Wilbourne* ((1982) 4 Cr App Rep (S) 163) whose daughter seduced him into incest). For an example of financial temptation see *Oakes* (1974) CSP C3–2CO1. In the case of homicide, the law (s 3 HA 57) recognises that provocation may reduce the crime to manslaughter if the 'provocation was enough to make a reasonable man do as he did'. This has until recently been taken to include only sudden loss of temper, but controversy surrounds the applicability of the defence, for example to women who kill their violent husbands (see for example *Humphries* [1995] 4 All ER 1008). When the offence is not murder the sentencer may take provocation into account by way of mitigation, and does not seem to be bound by the strict definition in the HA 57 (see, for example, *Haley* (1983) 5 Cr App Rep (S) 9).

b. mental disorder, even where a psychiatric disposal (see chapter 21) is not justified or practicable. The substantive law again recognises a defence of 'diminished responsibility' which reduces a charge of murder to that of manslaughter 'if he was suffering from such subnormality of mind (whether arising from a condition of arrested or retarded development of mind or any inherent causes or induced by disease or injury) as substantially impaired his mental responsibility for his act or omissions in doing or being a party to the killing' (s 2 HA 57). Griew (1988) argues that the unclear wording of the section allows it, paradoxically, to work effectively in practice. Nevertheless the section can be seen to leave the decision on culpability too much in the hands of psychiatrists[1], and a case such as *Tandy* [1989] 1 All ER 267 (where an alcoholic mother was not allowed the defence since her first drink of the day was not 'involuntary') suggests that the defence is in need of reform.

c. circumstances in which the offender was under stress, especially of a domestic kind (an example is *Law* (1975) CSP C3–2BO1);

d. the effect of alcohol (or occasionally some other drug, especially if it was medically prescribed) upon self-control: but not of course in cases in which the offender was risking a breach of the law by being under the effect of alcohol or drugs, as in the case of driving offences. The CA, however, is stricter than many sentencers, and usually rejects the influence of alcohol as a reason for reducing sentence, as in *Bradley* (1980) 2 Cr App Rep (S) 12. On the other hand, it is sometimes influenced by it, as in *Spence* (1982) 4 Cr App Rep (S) 175;

e.   ignorance of fact or law, even when a strict interpretation of the law does not allow these as defences. See for example the *Daily Telegraph* of 7 May 1978, reporting a case in which a man who had illegally tried to recruit for the Rhodesian Army received a conditional discharge because (as the police evidence confirmed) he did not know this was prohibited;

f.   the nature of the harm intended: in *Byrne* for example ((1975) 62 Cr App Rep 159) the explosives conspiracy was to cause damage, not loss of life, and the sentence was accordingly lenient. But failure to achieve the harm intended does not mitigate, officially at least. The Criminal Attempts Act 1981 (s 4) sets the same maximum penalties for attempts as for completed offences. Recklessness seems to be another matter, if traffic law is to be taken seriously. The maximum penalty for reckless driving was set higher if it caused death than if it did not; and the CA regards the gravity of the consequences as relevant to the sentence (*Steel* (1992) 14 Cr App Rep (S) 218). Yet when the driving is merely 'careless' the nature of the harm done by it—even when it is death—is 'not relevant to penalty' (*Krawec* (1984) 6 Cr App Rep (S) 367). It is not easy to reconcile these approaches.

and occasionally by

g.   the fact that the offender was brought up in another country in which his action would not have been criminal, or would have been regarded as pardonable (although the Court of Appeal did not accept the relevance of this in *Kang* (1982) 4 Cr App Rep (S) 152).

1.   As was pointed out in the Lane Committee's *Report on the Mandatory Life Sentence* (1993).

## Necessity

**4.21**   English law has been reluctant to recognise this as a substantive defence, and has preferred to leave the question of necessity to be taken into account by way of mitigation. However, recent cases have acknowledged the existence of the defence (see Lord Goff in *Re F* [1990] 2 AC 1). A related defence has also come to be recognised—duress of circumstances—though this defence merely excuses wrongful behaviour, and does not seek to justify it (see *Conway* (1988) 88 Cr App Rep 159; *Martin* (1989) 88 Cr App Rep 343). If the substantive law continues to evolve a defence of necessity, it will, of course, be less often necessary to raise the issue at the sentencing stage.

## Entrapment

**4.22**   Similarly, the courts have been reluctant to recognise a substantive defence of entrapment. The HL in *Sang* [1980] AC 402 upheld the decision that there was no such defence, and that the issue was relevant only in mitigation of sentence. However, many cases have resulted in the exclusion of evidence by the judge on the basis of its 'unfairness' under s 78 PACE 84 when it was clearly obtained by undercover policemen acting inappropriately (see *Bryce* [1992] 4 All ER 567; but see also *Williams* (1994) 98 Cr App Rep 209), It may be that here too English courts are moving towards the US position of recognising an entrapment defence.

## Duress

**4.23**  Duress, on the other hand, is not merely a mitigating factor, but a defence. 'The essence of [this] defence is that the will of the subject of the threats is no longer entirely under his own control because of the fear engendered by those threats' (*Ortiz* (1986) 83 Cr App Rep 173). Curiously, the HL has held that the defence is not applicable to the crime of murder (*Howe* [1987] AC 417); yet this is the one serious crime where the judge has no discretion at the sentencing stage. In other crimes, where a plea of duress may fail at the trial stage, it may still succeed in persuading the sentencer to be lenient. An example is *Taonis* (1974) 59 Cr App Rep 160, who smuggled cannabis into England after being tortured and threatened with the torture of his mistress. Since he had had time to tell tell this to the police before the smuggling duress was not accepted as an excuse, but the CA reduced his prison sentence from four to two years.

## Good character

**4.24**  Evidence that the offender is a person of good character can be heard even before conviction if it casts doubt on his guilt; but it can also be heard at the sentencing stage (see 2.43). As we have seen, the absence of previous convictions is commonly regarded as evidence of good character, and will lead to a lighter sentence unless the facts of the case—such as multiple charges or offences TIC (see 2.10)—show that the offence was not out of character. Even a substantial record of convictions can be offset by a subsequent period of (more or less) law-abiding conduct, as in the case of *Bennett*, a burglar who for the last 10 years had incurred only a suspended sentence (1981; CSP C2–2EO2). It was assumed that the suspension meant that the offence could not have been serious.

## Meritorious conduct

**4.25**  Sentencers are sometimes influenced by another principle which seems to be retributive in spirit: that deserts are reduced by meritorious conduct on the offender's part. This is most likely when the conduct consists of an attempt to undo, compensate for or reduce the harm done by the offence, especially if the attempt is made before detection. An offer of compensation when the offender is prosecuted is less likely to affect the type of sentence[1], since the court is likely to reason (i) that the mere possession of sufficient funds should not excuse the offender from the proper penalty, and (ii) that the offer of compensation at that late stage is more likely to be tactical than inspired by genuine remorse. Expressions of remorse in court have to be very convincing if they are to have much effect. *Norman* (1975, unreported: CA(CD): cit Thomas, 1979 p217)) who confessed to his thefts before being suspected, had his sentence reduced and suspended. Remorse which is manifested during a prison sentence is something which the parole authorities rather than the CA are supposed to take into account (*Waddingham* [1983] Crim LR 492). Remorse is more credible after impulsive violence than after a lucrative or sexual offence (it is worth noting that some violent offenders are so horrified by what they have done that they suffer from genuine amnesia, whereas sexual offenders hardly ever do so: the explanation probably lies in the pleasure of the offence). However that may be, remorse seldom persuades the CA to mitigate: *Norman* (1994) 15 Cr App Rep (S) 165 is a rare instance, a 50-year-old man whose seven-year sentence was reduced to five partly for this reason.

1. Although it will obviously affect the amount of a fine if the offender's means are limited: see chapter 16.

### Assisting law enforcement

**4.26** Another sort of conduct which may be a sign of a change of heart, but is more often an attempt to earn a reduction of sentence, is helping the police either to obtain evidence against other offenders or to lay their hands on stolen property. An interesting example was *Wright* (1974, unreported: cit. Thomas 1979 p218) who was sentenced by a recorder in ignorance of the fact that he had given the police helpful information, and had his sentence reduced accordingly by the CA. On the other hand that Court has made it plain that there is no 'tariff' of discounts in such cases: each case should be decided on its merits (*Rose and Sapiano* (1980) 2 Cr App Rep (S) 239). Nor can police promise a discount as an inducement: the most they can properly offer is to stress the helpfulness of the offender when they are asked for their evidence at the sentencing stage. Nor can there can be any discount for a prisoner who helps the police long after he has begun to serve his sentence (*X* (1994) 15 Cr App Rep (S) 750).

### Moral credit

**4.27** More remarkable are cases in which the court is influenced by meritorious conduct which has nothing to do with the offence. Men have had prison terms shortened because they have fought well in a war, given a kidney to a sister, saved a child from drowning[1] or started a youth club[2]. Such cases are interesting because they seem to result from two assumptions: (i) that offenders are being sentenced not for the offence but for their moral worth; and (ii) that moral worth can be calculated by a sort of moral book-keeping, in which spectacular actions count for more than does unobtrusive decency. This can be illustrated by the ambivalent remarks of the CA in *Reid* (1982) 4 Cr App Rep (S) 280: 'While this Court would not usually interfere with a sentence because the defendant had committed an act of bravery, we think that if the Recorder had known about this incident it may well be that he would have formed a different view of the appellant: he might have come to the conclusion that the appellant was a much better and more valuable member of society than his criminal activities had led him to suppose '.

1. *Keightley* [1972] Crim LR 262.
2. *Ducasse* (1974, unreported CA(CD): cit Thomas, 1979 p200).

## Remedying mistaken punishment

**4.28** Another sort of moral book-keeping is very occasionally observable. *Benstead* ((1979) 1 Cr App Rep (S) 32) had already served nearly two thirds of a six-month prison sentence when the CA was persuaded to substitute a one-day sentence. It acknowledged that, beyond ordering his immediate release, it could do nothing to put matters right, but directed that a note of what had happened should be placed on his record documents so that if he were later convicted of some other offence this could be taken into account. In plain words, his next sentence should be less than he deserved because his present one had been more than he deserved. This is certainly not a guideline case. More often the Court of Appeal simply substitutes a sentence of such length that the prisoner is due for release on the day of the decision: a good example of a contrived coincidence.

## Sensibility

**4.29** It is recognised that some offenders suffer more than most from the usual penalties. Bentham (1789) called this 'sensibility', the 18th century equivalent of 'sensitivity'. Fines are reduced for the poor (see chapter 16). Prison sentences are reduced — sometimes not imposed — because the offender is elderly, pregnant, about to emigrate or certain to lose his or her job if incarcerated. The prison sentence of *Bibi* (1980) 2 Cr App Rep (S) 177 was reduced because as a Muslim wife she would suffer more than most in prison. The plea that in prison the offender will have to be segregated for his own safety is sometimes accepted by the CA, sometimes not: compare *Holmes* (1979) 1 Cr App Rep (S) 233 with *Kirby* (1979) 1 Cr App Rep (S) 214 (which was decided by a different trio of judges). Illness is sometimes taken into account, but nowadays the CA is more likely to take the line that it is for the Home Office to use its powers (or the prerogative of mercy: see 1.26) to release prisoners if their life expectancy is short, as in *Stark* (1992) 13 Cr App Rep (S) 548, who suffered from AIDS.

## 'Natural punishment'

**4.30** Sentences are sometimes reduced because it seems that the offender has already suffered enough. In *Campbell* (1995) 16 Cr App Rep (S) 20 the CA said that 'he has punished himself in that since he was sentenced his father, to whom he was attached, has died', and reduced the sentence. German jurists used to call this *poena naturalis*. It is a consideration which is most likely to be taken into account when a careless or reckless driver has caused the death or serious injury of a relative (see the guidelines in *Boswell,* set out in 23.24).

## Age

**4.31**  Youth is treated as a mitigating consideration both in statute and case-law. Not only are there special presumptions about the mens rea of children: they and young adults (see chapter 20) are also protected by special statutes from the full severity of sentences for adults[1], and to this protection is added the principle that sentencers should deal less severely with the young[2]. This is particularly evident when the offender is under 21[3], but Thomas (1979.195) has noted cases in which men as old as 30 have benefitted. The underlying reasoning is hardly ever made clear, but is probably the assumption that the young 'don't know any better': that is, have not had enough experience to realise fully the consequences of their actions for themselves or others, although this has worn rather thin by the age of 30. At some point, too—about the age of 60—advanced age begins to be a ground for leniency, especially if combined with a blameless record. The justification is probably 'sensibility'—that the elderly suffer more in custody than do the young or middle-aged—since, as has been seen, mere shortening of life expectancy as a result of illness is usually regarded by the CA as a matter for executive discretion, not intervention by the court.

1.  With the notable exception of indeterminate sentencing: a child of 10 can receive what is in effect a 'life' sentence under s 53 of the Children and Young Persons Act 1933 (as amended) for homicide or some other 'grave crime', and can be detained for so long that he (or she, as in the case of Mary Bell) eventually becomes a prisoner in an adults' prison.
2.  Note, however, that if violence of a kind regarded as pathological and dangerous is manifested early this is regarded as especially alarming, and the person may be detained for a very long period. But that is decided by the executive, not by sentencers.
3.  It may be worth noting, however, that youth is not pleaded or accepted by way of mitigation when the offence is joy-riding or other illegal use of vehicles: in such cases youth is assumed to indicate incompetence or recklessness rather than relative innocence.

## Incorrigibility

**4.32**  It seems unlikely that an offender's incorrigibility could be an acceptable reason for mitigation: but in *Thomas* [1983] 3 All ER 756 the Court of Appeal reduced the period of a driving disqualification from 2 years to 1 (in spite of the statute which stipulated a minimum of 2 years), their reason being that he seemed incapable of obeying the disqualification for so long a period, which would thus increase the likelihood of his committing further offences. As is pointed out in chapter 5 however, traffic offences seem to be the subject of very special pleading, and it is unlikely that the CA would apply similar reasoning to other types of offence—or indeed to future cases of the same kind.

## Indirect effects of conviction or offence

**4.33**   Courts may take into account the consequences of the conviction for the offender. An example was *Richards* ((1980) 2 Cr App Rep (S) 119), a medical practitioner whose prison sentence was reduced because his conviction for making false financial claims would be the 'end of his whole career'. Even the consequences of the offence may be taken into account: in *Rimmer* ((1975) CSP C5–2AO2) the Court of Appeal suspended a six-month prison sentence on a man who had caused death by dangerous driving, because he had spent six months in hospital and, not having been insured, had to face a large financial claim. Even when the offence involves abuse of the offender's professional position the fact that he will lose that position sometimes weighs with the CA, although that court is not usually sympathetic to breaches of professional trust (an example is *Fell*, a mental nurse who had assaulted a refractory patient [1975] Crim LR 349). On the other hand, if the court takes a very serious view of the offence or the offender's record the fact that a prison sentence will ruin his career may not persuade it to interfere ((*Rees and Moss*) (1982) 4 Cr App Rep (S) 71).

## Staleness

**4.34**   Many other jurisdictions have statutes of limitation, forbidding the prosecution of an offence after a period which varies from, say, 5 years to 15 or more, according to the seriousness of the offence (Switzerland and Germany are examples). The usual justification offered is the difficulty which the defendant would have in producing or rebutting evidence after a substantial lapse of time. If so, it seems that the more serious the crime the less difficult that is supposed to be—or the less it matters. A more jurisprudential justification is that after a long lapse of time the offender is 'not the same person' (Stallybrass, 1945); or, less metaphorically, that if he has not repeated his offence in the interval he is entitled to a presumption that he is no longer a person of the sort that is capable of offending in that way. However that may be, English statutes have no general provisions of this kind. Non-indictable offences can be prosecuted only within six months (s 127 MCA 80), and a few indictable offences have a similar statute of limitation (for example 12 months in the case of unlawful sexual intercourse with a girl aged 13,14, or 15: s 37 SOA 56). Otherwise it is left to the prosecuting authority (see chapter 15) to decide whether to take the offender to court. MCs have been known to throw out cases in which prosecution seems to them to have been inexcusably delayed[1]. In the CC the typical case is a middle-aged man convicted at last of a sexual offence committed many years ago against a child in his household who has only recently decided to report it. The CC is reluctant to reduce the sentence to take staleness into account, but sometimes makes a small allowance for it (as in *Cuddington* (1995) 16 Cr App Rep (S) 246, whose prison sentence was reduced partly for this reason, but partly also because he had been a juvenile when he committed his sexual offences). The CA said in *Nicholson* (1992) 14 Cr App Rep (S) 311 that 'the mere passage of time cannot attract a great deal of discount in such cases'. Staleness is seldom mentioned in textbooks on sentencing, let alone discussed.

1.  In Germany it has been held that avoidable delay between detection and prosecution violates the provision of Art 6 of the European Convention on Human Rights concerning the right to a speedy trial. By a compromise, however, the defendant can still be given a sentence, though it must be lighter than normal. In England the practice of allowing offences to be 'taken into consideration' (see 2.10) was instituted to protect defendants against the practice of delaying prosecutions until a prisoner had nearly reached the end of a prison sentence.

## Individualisation[1]

**4.35** Especially interesting is what Thomas (1979) called 'individualisation': 'a sentence which would be considered inappropriate as an application of tariff principles may be considered entirely correct if seen as an individualised measure based on the court's assessment of the needs of the offender as an individual ...' Thus the choice of a hospital or probation order in a case in which a penalty would be justified is individualisation. It should be distinguished from mere leniency inspired by excuses or compassion, since it is a practical decision taken in order to meet a need of the offender, whether for psychiatric treatment, for case-work or for some other kind of treatment. The most striking examples are those in which persistent offenders, with as many as 40 previous convictions of dishonest acquisition, are unexpectedly put on probation instead of receiving a lengthy prison sentence. This is usually the result of a persuasive PSR, especially one which offers the offender a place in a supervised hostel (see chapter 17). An example is *McNamee* ((1979) 1 Cr App Rep (S) 126). Individualisation does not always result in leniency: it may instead mean detention—for example under a hospital order—for longer than a tariff sentence of imprisonment. There has not yet been a case in which the CA has pronounced on the propriety of this.

1.  A term which means different things in different theories. As originally used by German penologists in the 19th century it meant the adjustment of prison conditions in the light of the prisoner's age, health etc. In French jurisprudence (eg Salleilles, 1898) it meant the mitigation of penalties on retributive grounds such as the offender's age or motivation. When translated into English by Mannheim (1939) it seemed to denote corrective individualisation, which is close to Thomas' meaning.

## The effect on others

**4.36** A more awkward consideration of a retributive kind is the effect of a sentence on innocent dependants of the offender. Such situations, in which the court regards the offender as deserving imprisonment but is influenced by the suffering of dependants, illustrate the problems created by the retributive principle that the innocent should not be penalised (see chapter 9) . The result of a fine may in fact be that dependants are deprived of more than the offender will be. The result of a prison sentence may be hardship for the offender's children, who may even have to be taken into care by others if it is their mother who is imprisoned. In *Parkinson* (1976, CSP C4–2DO1) a mother's 9-month prison sentence was reduced for this reason, so that she was released. In *Franklyn* ((1981) 3 Cr App Rep (S) 65) a father was released for similar reasons. On the other hand the Court of Appeal has said 'as a matter of general interest' that even if the offender is 'a woman with a family, is in difficulty at home and is living on social security, that does not give her a licence in any way to commit crime' (5 days' imprisonment upheld: *Botfield* (1982) 4 Cr App Rep (S) 132); and this sounds like a guideline.

## Double jeopardy

**4.37** Although 'double jeopardy' usually means the retrial of a defendant who has been acquitted the CA often applies the term to Attorney-Generals' references (see 1.19), and when increasing the sentence almost always remembers to declare that it has allowed for the defendant's state of suspense. Anxiety in other circumstances—for example while awaiting a long-delayed trial—is sometimes pleaded by defence counsel, and may influence the CC, but we have not found a case in which it weighed with the CA.

## Forgiveness

**4.38** Victims sometimes forgive, and occasionally courts are given evidence of this. Although it says more about the offender's good luck than his culpability, the CA is sometimes impressed by it. Its reasoning in *Darvill* (1987) 9 Cr App Rep (S) 225 was complex. 'There is no doubt that forgiveness can in many cases have an effect, albeit an indirect effect ... It may reduce the possibility of reoffending, it may reduce the danger of public outrage which sometimes arises where a defendant has been released ... unexpectedly early, and it may enhance the evidence of provocation by the victim ...' In *Hutchinson* (1993)15 Cr App Rep (S) 134 the CA reasoned strangely: that the forgiveness of a raped ex-partner indicated that she had not suffered much harm, and it reduced the sentence accordingly. It would have been less artificial to argue that whatever the degree of harm the victim was in the best position to judge whether the rape had been to some extent excusable.

## Consistency

**4.39** If there is no sound reason for differentiating the penalties imposed on two or more offenders for the same offence, it is assumed that they should be the same; and if the offences are distinct but indistinguishable in any relevant respect the same principle applies. The CA, however, seems to speak with two voices when it has to wrestle with consistency. In *Reeves* [1964] Crim LR 67 it felt obliged to reduce what it considered a perfectly proper sentence because his accomplices had pleaded guilty in a MC and received what the CA regarded as excessively lenient sentences. In *Broadbridge* ((1983) 4 Cr App Rep (S) 269) however, it refused to reduce a prison sentence in spite of the fact that his accomplices' sentences had been suspended in another court. The judge's duty was to deal fitly with the offender before him.

## Subjective consistency

**4.40** Occasionally, however, the CA has been influenced by what might be called 'subjective consistency': that is, the offender's feeling that in comparison with others he was being sentenced too harshly. In *Bishop* (1973, unreported: cit Thomas, 1979 p71) the CA reasoned that if he got the appropriate penalty he might well 'feel that he has suffered an injustice when compared with the fate of his comrades in the crime'. This was certainly not a guide-line, for in *Large* ((1981) 3 Cr App Rep (S) 80) the court dismissed subjective injustice in a purple passage:

> '... those who prey on the public by attempting to steal with the aid of sawn-off shotguns cannot expect their disappointment about sentences to weigh heavily in the balance against the duty of the court to protect the public ... Let him who has been properly and severely sentenced rejoice in the good fortune of his companions ...'

Yet two years later the CA reduced the sentence of *Fawcett* (1983) 5 Cr App Rep (S) 158 to correspond with his accomplices' over-lenient sentence, in order not to outrage his sense of justice.

## General

**4.41** As we have seen, the usual reasoning which leads to mitigation or aggravation of sentence is retributive, based on factors which seem to reduce or increase the offender's culpability, or which make it likely that he or she will suffer more than most from the normal penalty. Occasionally the sentencer is thinking of the effect on the offender's future conduct, or of the deterrence of potential imitators. Sometimes the intention is simply to encourage offenders to co-operate with the workings of the criminal justice system. Merciful or discriminatory reasoning will be discussed in the next chapter.

**4.42** Long as the list of considerations is, it cannot be exhaustive. MCs and the CC may be lenient—or, more rarely, severe—for reasons which never reach the CA. Defendants never appeal against leniency, and A-Gs refer only extreme examples of it. Reasons which are clearly improper are mentioned in the next chapter. Occasionally even the CA's reasoning seems to be contradicted by what it has said in another case. Sometimes the explanation is a change of outlook as the years go by; but more often it simply reflects the differing views of different trios of judges.

**4.43** Some jurisdictions make greater efforts to achieve consistency. Their statutes prescribe a standard penalty for each type of offence, and list permissible reasons for leniency and severity, with strict limits to their effects. English sentencers, however, are as jealous as English doctors of their freedom to prescribe. Even the CA used to say that its guidelines were not binding, and that sentencers were free to depart from them if a case seemed exceptional. What a judge may not do, it seems, is express disagreement with the guidelines themselves. In *Johnson* (1994) 15 Cr App Rep (S) at 830 he said '... much as I respect their Lordships, I do not agree with their principles and I do not mind saying so and I am not going to act upon their principles.' The CA's comment was that incidents of this sort created an appearance of injustice:

> 'In such special cases the judge should indicate clearly the factor or factors which in his judgment allow departure from the tariff set by this court. What a judge must not do is to state that he is applying some personal tariff because he considers the accepted range of sentences to be too high or too low'.

Interestingly, the CA made it clear that but for the judge's remarks it would not have interfered with his 7-year sentence for what had been a violent mugging. As it was, Johnson, *tertius gaudens*, benefited by a 2-year reduction.

Chapter 5

# Discrimination and mercy

**5.1**   When mitigation or aggravation favours or disfavours a whole category of offenders for some unacceptable reason it is called 'discrimination', a term which once upon a time meant good taste, but is nowadays a dirty word. As will be seen, however, it is not always possible to be sure that discrimination is taking place.

## Gender

**5.2**   For example, it used to be assumed, without benefit of statistics, that women offenders gained from discrimination. It was then argued that this was a misleading impression, because although their offences bore the same legal labels as mens' they tended to be less harmful. The pendulum swung a little further when feminist statisticians noticed that higher percentages of women prisoners had no previous convictions, and it was inferred that many of them would have received non-custodial sentences if they had been men. By far the more likely explanation is that other things being equal, including the seriousness of the offence, a man is twice as likely to have at least one previous conviction. A careful study of the evidence by Hedderman and Hough (1994) showed that (i) a higher percentage of women than of men are cautioned instead of prosecuted (see 15.5ff) for serious offences; (ii) women are less likely to be remanded in custody; and (iii) women are more likely to receive lenient sentences, even when previous convictions are taken into account. What others have pointed out, however, is that if a woman is sent to prison the smaller number of establishments for females means that she has less chance of being allocated to one which is suited to her needs or close to her family.

## Being black

**5.3**   The over-representation of black men in prisons has given rise to the suspicion of discrimination, but seems not to be attributable to sentencers' prejudices. This is the finding of at least three independent studies. The latest, by Hood and Cordovil (1992) in the Midlands, allowed for a large number of variables, and found no general tendency for blacks to be imprisoned more often than whites (other things being equal). One court, at Dudley, appeared to discriminate, although the numbers were not large enough to exclude chance (p =.07). Interestingly, Asians seemed to be less likely than whites to be imprisoned (again *ceteris paribus* ). They also found that a much higher percentage of blacks (41 per cent) and of Asians than of whites (17 per cent) had legal advice at the police station, which may account for their pleading 'not guilty' more often (though their acquittal rates were not higher).

## Offenders from abroad

5.4    Short-term visitors from abroad tend to benefit from the fact that they are due to leave this country soon. They are more likely to be fined rather than imprisoned or made subject to some time-consuming non-custodial order. When fined, however, they are much less likely to be given time to pay. Major criminals apart, the courts' main objective is to get rid of them. This is an example of favourable discrimination prompted by expediency.

5.5    Custodial sentences on the other hand involve more than normal hardship for foreign offenders (of whom there were about 800 in English prisons in 1995)[1]. They may be accompanied by wives and children who will find it difficult to return home safely by themselves. Inside, they may suffer from language problems and a certain amount of xenophobia among both prisoners and staff. The food will be strange, to say the least, and they will not get a special diet unless they can plead religious or medical reasons. They will have few, if any, visits from relatives or friends. If they have any ties in this country these may be broken by deportation at the end of their sentence. But if they would prefer to serve their sentences in their own countries they can apply for repatriation under the Repatriation of Prisoners Act 1984, provided that their countries have signed the Convention on the Transfer of Sentenced Prisoners. Their sentences must be long enough to enable their cases to be considered by the Home Office and their own countries; and either the Home Secretary or the foreign country may refuse a transfer.[2] Prisoners cannot be transferred under the RPA 84 against their will; but they can be deported unwillingly when due for release.

1. For a fuller discussion of this problem see Richards (1995).
2. See *Hansard* (Lords) for 5 March 1984, coy 18, for what might be reasons for the Home Secretary's refusal.

## Deportation (Immigration Act 1971)

5.6    The Home Secretary has power (subject to appeal, under the IA 71) to deport a person who is not a British citizen if this seems 'conducive to the public good' and he sometimes uses it to deport people who have not been convicted of any offence. More often he is acting on a recommendation from a

MC or the CC following a conviction for an imprisonable offence1. The offender must be given at least seven days' notice of such a recommendation, and can appeal against it as if it were a sentence; but it does not bind the Home Secretary to deport, although he can deport without a recommendation, and his deportation order can also be the subject of an appeal. Those awaiting the result of deportation proceedings are usually remanded in custody. In *Nazari* (1980) 2 Cr App Rep (S) 84 the CA laid down guidelines for deportation recommend-ations. 'The more serious the crime and the longer the record the more obvious it is that there should be an order ... On the other hand a minor offence would not merit an order ... Shoplifting would not merit a recommendation... But a series of shoplifting offences on different occasions may justify a recommendation ... Even a first offence of shoplifting might merit a recommendation if the offender were a member of a gang carrying out a planned raid...' Citizens of Eire and Commonwealth countries who fulfil certain residence requirements (see s 7 IA 71) are exempt from deportation for 'the public good', and cannot be recommended for it.

1. The CC occasionally by-passes this procedure by simply binding the offender over to come up for judgement when called on, with a condition that he leave the country: an expedient approved by the CA (eg in *Williams* (1982) 4 Cr App Rep (S) 239). The offender must consent; and his departure is then supervised, usually by a probation officer.

## Diplomatic immunity (Diplomatic Privileges Act 1964)[1]

**5.7** Some foreigners have 'diplomatic immunity' from prosecution—and most kinds of civil suit. Immunity is conferred on 'diplomatic agents' by the DPA 64. A 'diplomatic agent' is the head of a permanent diplomatic mission or a member of the staff of a mission who has 'diplomatic rank'. 'Diplomatic rank' is not defined in the Act; but it is usual for missions to supply the Foreign Office with the names of those members of staff who are regarded as having that rank. The immunity includes 'immunity from the criminal jurisdiction of the receiving State'. It can be waived by the 'sending State' or by the head of mission (s 2 DPA 64), but not by the offender himself (an obiter dictum of the Court of Appeal in *Madan* [1961] 2 QB 1). The immunity extends to members of the family of a diplomatic agent who form part of his household, provided that they are not nationals of the receiving state. If the diplomatic agent is himself a national of the receiving state his immunity is only 'in respect of official acts performed in the exercise of his functions'. Similarly immunity is conferred on diplomatic agents in transit through the UK on journeys between their own countries and their missions in other countries, but only to the extent required to ensure their transit or return. Consular staff have a limited immunity under the Consular Relations Act 1968[1].

1. For the similar immunity enjoyed by heads of states, their families and private servants, see s 20, State Immunity Act 1978; and for the immunity granted for example to senior United Nations staff see the International Organisations Act 1988.

**5.8** The justification for adherence to the Vienna Convention is one of expediency. Without it, diplomatic agents abroad could be harassed by arrest, prosecution and imprisonment. The practical effect, however, is that diplomatic agents and members of their families can disregard the criminal law. The only threat which they have to fear is return in disgrace to their own country, either at the insistence of their own head of mission or as a result of a request from the Foreign Office; and both are steps which are taken only if the offender's behaviour is a serious embarrassment. Diplomatic agents and members of their families cannot be officially deported.[1] The House of Commons were told by the Foreign Office in 1984 that over the last 10 years 546 serious crimes, including rape, incest, blackmail, illegal possession of firearms, and causing death by reckless driving had been attributable to persons with diplomatic immunity.

1.  Not only diplomatic agents and members of their families but also members of the administrative, technical and service staff of a diplomatic mission are protected from deportation by s 8(3) IA 71.

## Commercial offences

**5.9**  'White-collar crime' is a popular term because of the assumption that a criminal way of carrying on a normally legitimate occupation is concentrated in the middle class; but as Mars (1982) and many others have shown, 'fiddles' are prevalent among wage-earners as well as salary-earners. 'Corporate crime' is also too narrow, because it excludes the self-employed. 'Commercial offences' cover any infringement of the criminal law, whether by a corporate body or by an individual, which involves or is facilitated by commercial activity. It thus includes frauds, corruption, evasions of taxes or excise duties, breaches of regulations for factories or food-sellers, mines or oil-rigs, illegal trading in drugs, weapons or rare animals, inaccurate or inadequate descriptions of merchandise, environmental pollution, and the manufacture of inadequately tested drugs.

**5.10**  Some of these activities have been the subject of special studies. British examples are Carson on safety in factories (1970), Carson on safety in the North Sea oil industry (1982), Ditton on 'fiddles' in the bakery industry (1977), Leigh on commercial fraud (1982), Levi on long-firm fraud (1981), Mars on fiddles in various occupations (1982), Martin on pilfering by employees (1962), Nelken on harassment by landlords (1983). What nearly all these studies emphasise is not only the prevalence of unrecognised commercial offences but the extent to which, even when they come to the notice of those responsible for enforcement of the law, they are disposed of by 'diversionary' methods. Chapter 15 describes these, and in particular the preference of the Inland Revenue for out-of-court financial settlements with tax-evaders. Martin (1962) makes it plain that even when employers are the victims of pilfering they often refrain from invoking the law for the sake of good relations with their labour force or in order to avoid losing a useful worker (but this leniency does not extend to the pilfering of cash). There are only a few sorts of commercial offender which have little chance of diversion, even with 'clean records': those involved in corruption, frauds, the illegal sale of controlled drugs, or illegal abortions.

**5.11**  Where sentencing is concerned, there is, of course, an important distinction between the sentencing of a corporate body and the sentencing of an individual, although in some cases both the responsible individual and his company are successfully prosecuted for one and the same offence. Where certain offences[1] are concerned, the company is virtually always disposed of by a fine, whereas individuals, though usually fined, not infrequently receive immediate or suspended custodial sentences. What CSEW do not show is the numbers of individuals who suffer a disqualification, even when this is the automatic or court-ordered accompaniment of conviction; and of course they could not be expected to show how many individuals are debarred from practising their occupation by subsequent decisions of professional bodies such as the General Medical Council.

1. Handling stolen goods; frauds; forgeries; firearms offences; revenue offences; trade description offences; health and safety offences; obscenity offences; some types of traffic offences; illegal Sunday trading; weights and measures offences; wireless telegraphy offences; illegal employment of children; illegal use of parks of other open spaces; gambling and lottery offences; labour law offences; offences concerned with cruelty to, or diseases of, animals; and—very infrequently— some other types of offence.

**5.12** Croall (1991) points out most of the difficulties involved in comparing sentences for offences by small businesses. Magistrates seem to deal so rarely with such cases that their sentences may be wildly inconsistent. Many seemed to Croall to be sympathetic to the situations of small businesses, and when the offence was one of 'strict liability' were ready to accept pleas in mitigation. Levi's study, though confined to 'long-firm frauds'[1] tried at the Central Criminal Court[2] in the 1960s and early 70s, makes several points of interest. First, the sentences are for the most part much less severe than a study of the Court of Appeal's decisions would lead one to expect (this is of course quite likely to be true of most CC sentences). Fully nine in ten prison sentences were shorter than the 5-year 'tariff' sentences which the CA seemed to have in mind (Thomas, 1970) for highly organised frauds. More than a third of the 'first offenders', and a substantial (but unspecified) percentage of the others, had their prison sentences suspended, and nearly a third were dealt with non-custodially (presumably by fines and disqualifications).

1. Levi does not expressly define the term, which is not a legally recognised one. It consists, roughly speaking, of obtaining goods on credit for resale without the intention of paying the creditors for them. Firms or companies may be used, or set up, for this purpose. It is usually individuals, however, who are prosecuted, since there is little point in prosecuting a firm without realisable assets.
2. Although Levi was to a limited extent able to compare them with sentences in the Manchester Crown Court over roughly the same period, finding that the latter seemed somewhat more severe, perhaps because that court tried fewer cases of a graver kind than did the Central Criminal Court.

**5.13** 'Principals' usually received more severe sentences than accomplices. Offenders who seemed to have been tempted into long-firm frauds in the course of legitimate trading ('slippery slope' frauds) were sentenced more leniently than those who set up firms with the intention of defrauding creditors. But the sums involved seem to have influenced the court: Levi's Table 10.6 shows prison terms of 8 and 9 years for frauds involving £200,000 and much shorter terms for those involving less than £10,000. A previous record of dishonest lawbreaking was of course an aggravation. Otherwise, however, the individual's personal history and present situation did not seem to have much influence on the judges. Levi's interviews with fraudsters convinced him that the sentencing policies of the courts did not deter those with experience:

> You can make a hell of a lot of money from l.fs., and the sentences are really low because it's got no violence ...
> When we were thinking of running an l.f. we reckoned that even if we got done, fuck all would happen to us. You get less for an l.f. in toiletries than you would for knocking off a bog roll from Woollies ...

If comments such as these reflect the attitude of many long-firm fraudsters, this seems to be an example of a non-impulsive type of offence whose perpetrators are influenced by the type of penalty which they expect, rather than by the probability of incurring it, which Levi estimated as high.

**5.14** Apart from the very exceptional long prison sentence, the only deliberately incapacitating measure employed against commercial offenders is disqualification, usually from being concerned in a company in any way (s 1 of the Insolvency Act 1986, although for some occupations other kinds of disqualification are possible: see 22.27 for examples). Whether disqualification for commerce has much effect is doubtful: dishonest businessmen seem able to find undisqualified people to act as their accomplices.

**5.15** Neither Levi nor Leigh have much to say about the ways in which courts arrived at the amounts of the fines which they imposed, although in the CC these may be very large indeed. In some cases the sentencer uses the fine in order to deprive the offender of his illegal profits. It is worth noting that distress warrants, usually regarded as ineffective against individual fine-defaulters, seemed to be used more often where firms are concerned, because they more often have goods which can be resold for substantial sums.

## Traffic offenders

**5.16** The sheer numbers of traffic offenders—and sentencers' awareness of their own driving offences—have created a system of disposal for them which appears lenient, but which is so complex that it requires a chapter to itself (chapter 23).

## Age

**5.17** The criminal justice system deals leniently with the old and the young. The old often do not go to prison because sentencers are persuaded that this would damage them physically or mentally. The young are protected from prosecution before the age of 10, from custodial sentences before 15, and from imprisonment before 21. These protections are justifiable as rules, even if some individuals seem lucky to benefit from them. What is difficult to justify is the rule that a sentence of youth custody, unlike a short prison sentence, cannot be suspended. This has been controversial ever since youth custody was distinguished from imprisonment. What motivated the legislators was therapeutic optimism—the belief that unlike imprisonment youth custody would not be a mere deterrent but a benefit, and that to suspend a benefit would be illogical. The result is that youth custody cannot be suspended even in circumstances in which a prison sentence would be. This example of discrimination against the young is less important now that suspension is limited to 'exceptional circumstances' (by s 5 CJA 91). Even so, a substantial number of prison sentences are still suspended: 3753 in 1993.

## Publicity

**5.18** Fame can be an unfair disadvantage. The news media have elephantine memories, and pay well for gossip about the possible release of any notorious prisoner. The Home Secretary, who still has the final say on the freeing of murderers, is a politician, and his directive to the Parole Board makes it clear how concerned he is 'with the wider policy implications, including the effect on public confidence in the life sentence system which release may have, ie how the public would be likely to respond to the lifer being released at that juncture' (Parole Board's Report for 1993). Altruistic or not, this is political reasoning of a kind which Home Secretaries of all parties have followed without openly saying so. Its effect is that some murderers who have made a name for themselves are less likely to be licensed than others, no less culpable, who have not. As we shall see in chapter 22 a few have been told never to expect release, and it would be reassuring if we could be certain that this is entirely due to their dangerousness and not to their notoriety.

## Mental disorder

**5.19** Discrimination is not always easy to distinguish from justifiable differentiation. In chapter 22 we shall see how the law allows the CC more freedom to impose indeterminate detention when the offender is diagnosed as mentally disordered or 'unstable'. Hospital orders with indefinite restrictions on discharge can be imposed for any imprisonable offence, whereas if the offender is non-disordered and the offence is not one which is eligible for 'life' his prison sentence must be a determinate one, however dangerous he may obviously be. Even when 'life' is allowed by statute the CA discourages the CC from imposing it unless the offender is at least 'unstable', and only in rare cases upholds it when he is stably dangerous and likely to remain so for an unpredictable period. (Yet when the crime is murder 'life' is mandatory, however strong the mitigation and however sane the murderer.) The debatable justifications for these distinctions will be found in 22.5.

## The importance of being guilty

**5.20** Discrimination can be the result of good intentions. We shall see in chapter 19 how the Gardiner Committee's preoccupation with the stigma of conviction inspired the elaborate provisions of the Rehabilitation of Offenders Act 1974, while neglecting the stigma suffered by many a defendant whose trial ends in an acquittal.

## Mercy

**5.21** Is mercy a sort of discrimination? It involves making exceptions, but usually in favour of individuals, not classes; and it is usually regarded as commendable when not motivated by corruption or favouritism. Yet it has had its critics. Aquinas and Anselm wondered whether God's mercy to sinners was consistent with his justice. Beccaria (1764) argued that a perfectly just penal code would have no need of mercy. A modern philosopher, Harrison (1992), goes further. The state, he argues, must be impartial and rational when penalising. Rationality means consistent rule-following, and thus outlaws the discretionary leniency in individual cases which is called mercy. But this cannot be the last word. Mercy towards individuals may be inconsistent rule-breaking; but there can be such things as merciful *rules*; an example is those for the repatriation of foreign prisoners. More precisely, the *initiation* of a rule—the setting of a precedent—can be an act of mercy even if honouring the precedent is mere rule-following. In modern times the exercise of the prerogative of mercy in individual cases (see 1.26) is regarded as creating rules which are to be followed, even if not every Home Secretary has followed them (Walker, 1994). But even rule-following can in some cases involve discretionary decisions. It is sometimes unclear whether a case is of the kind to which a certain rule applies. Many rules need to be supplemented by 'constitutive rules' which define the circumstances in which the main rule applies (for example, what is a 'professional foul' in football). Yet, as the CA have said more than once (eg in *Lindsay* (1993) 14 Cr App Rep (S) 239 at 242) there are types of case in which the circumstances 'vary so infinitely' that guidelines cannot be formulated. For example, how stale must an offence be, or how remorseful the offender, to earn leniency? There is a place for merciful discretion even in individual cases.

## General

**5.22** Discrimination may be prompted by stereotyping, expediency, or even therapeutic optimism. It is sometimes a reality, sometimes a widely believed myth. Sometimes it can be proved or disproved by statistics, more often by careful research. Sometimes the offences involved are so different that comparisons of the *ceteris paribus* type are just not possible. Should a lucrative fraud be dealt with as severely as a robbery with threats but no actual violence? As for mercy, although it has been criticised as inconsistent with justice, it is logically defensible if properly motivated, and need not be dismissed as a sort of discrimination.

# Chapter 6

# Background information

**6.1** As well as information about the offence, its circumstances and its perpetrator, sentencers sometimes feel the need of background information of various sorts:

a. about the sentences which other courts are choosing for offences of the same kind;

b. about trends in the frequencies of such offences; and in particular whether they are increasing sharply;

c. about the locations of such offences; and in particular whether they are especially frequent in the area where the offence with which they are dealing was committed;

d. about the effect which this or that sentence is likely to have on the offender's future behaviour (a subject to which chapter 7 is devoted);

e. about the effect which this or that sentence is likely to have on the behaviour of other people who take note of it (a subject to which chapter 8 is devoted);

f. about the ways in which this or that sentence is put into effect in practice (a subject to which much of Parts II, III and IV of this book are devoted);

g. about the attitude of 'the public' (whatever that means) to offences of that kind, and to the sentences which might be chosen for it.

Unfortunately, as will soon become clear, sentencers are not provided with adequate information about (a) or (b), and must be wary and sceptical about much of the information which is provided under the other heads.

## Judicial statistics

**6.2** It is far from easy for a sentencer to inform himself or herself about the sentencing policy of other courts. No published—or unpublished—documents provide information about sentencing which is of much use for this purpose. Consider the judicial tables in the *Criminal Statistics, England and Wales* (CSEW), and suppose that the sentencer wants to know the usual sentence for a young adult female convicted for the first time of burglary of a home on a single occasion. Table S 1.1 (D) in Supplementary Vol 1 will show the frequency with which women aged 18 to 20 convicted of this offence are discharged, fined, put on probation or community service or sent to a young offenders' institution, but it will not reveal what differentiated those dealt with in these lenient or severe ways: whether for example it was their previous records, or the harm they did. If the sentencer is a magistrate he or she may want to know what is the usual sentence for his bench, since benches value self-consistency more than consistency with other benches. For this Supplementary Vol 3 of CSEW can be consulted; but although a table there will show the sentence-distribution for certain age-groups, by sex, in the relevant police area, it does not distinguish different offence groups, let alone 'first offenders'[1] and recidivists.

1. The term used for offenders found guilty for the first time, ignoring the possibility that they have in fact offended before.

**6.3**   Suppose, however, that the sentencer knows that imprisonment is the usual choice for the sort of case before him, but would like some guidance as to the length of the sentence. He will certainly find tables (in Vol 1 for MCs, Vol 2 for the CC) which subdivide sentences for burglary into those of different lengths; and they distinguish aggravated from unaggravated burglaries, and dwellings from other premises: but they do not make the all-important distinction between burglars with and without 'records'.

**6.4**   In practice sentencers consult non-statistical publications: the Magistrates' Association's *Sentencing Guidelines* or, in the case of judges, Thomas' *Current Sentencing Practice*, although neither publication tells them what courts actually do. It would be by no means impossible to provide judges—or magistrates—with tables for each of the common offences, distinguishing first offenders from recidivists, single from multiple convictions[1], and offenders according to their age-group[2]. The cells of each table would show the percentage of each sub-group disposed of by means of absolute or conditional discharges, probation, community service, fines, compensation orders, immediate or fully or partially suspended prison sentences. Even if confined to common types of offence such tables would be voluminous: but the volume would be of value to sentencers. The present tables in CSEW are not.

1. The latter including cases in which similar offences were 'taken into consideration'.
2. At least into 'adults', 'young adults', 'young persons' and 'children'.

**6.5**   Such tables would not, of course, dictate the choice of sentence. Sentencers would be expected to make their choices in the light of the information about the individual offender and his offence, and perhaps even other kinds of background information. Their choices, however, would be better informed than they are at present. Until information of this sort is provided the best they can do is to ask experienced colleagues, whose advice may be idiosyncratic or out of date.

**6.6**   Tables of this kind are open to one important criticism: that if they are followed too closely they will halt any movement towards a different, and perhaps better, sentencing pattern. This is more likely if—as in some US jurisdictions—they simply show the usual sentence for each combination of variables. It is less likely if they show the complete sentence-distribution. Thus if, instead of indicating merely that custodial sentences are the most frequent choice for young adult house-burglars with at least one previous conviction[1], they showed that community service orders are used for a substantial percentage, this would lead some sentencers to consider that choice as an alternative.

1. This is imaginary: as has been pointed out, we are not told this at present.

## National trends of offences

**6.7** Another sort of information which sometimes influences sentencers is concerned with increases (seldom decreases) in the frequency with which offences of this or that type are committed. For this too they depend on the CSEW, or at least figures selectively quoted by the news media from Home Office summaries. These figures are based on what police forces record and report to the Home Office. They report only 'notifiable' offences: that is, indictable or triable-either-way offences plus a few summary offences which are regarded as important. In the case of other summary offences, including non-indictable traffic offences, they report only cases in which the offender was identified and dealt with by prosecution, caution or fixed penalty.

## 'Notifiable offences'

**6.8** Even the figures of notifiable offences, however, which are reported to the Home Office must be studied with several reservations. Some of them come to the knowledge of the police through their own observation: examples are violence or damage in the course of demonstrations. Records of these are usually very selective: police trying to control a crowd cannot be expected to record every blow struck at them or every window broken by a stone. Only serious injuries or serious damage are recorded. Again, the police may be stimulated by complaints to 'do something about' soliciting in some part of a town: the result is a number of recorded incidents, a very special selection from what is actually happening.

**6.9** Most recorded offences, however, are the result of telephone calls or visits—less often letters—from members of the public: parents of children, householders, shop-keepers, bus-drivers, attendants at petrol stations and so on. What they report is evaluated before it is recorded as an offence, and sometimes the decision is that it was 'no crime'. A frequent example is a complaint in the middle of the night about a noisy gathering. Complaints from wives about minor marital violence may also go unrecorded, unless the injury needs medical treatment or the wife is clearly willing to make a statement and stick by it in court. A damaged door or window may suggest an attempt at a burglary but is often not recorded.

## Unreported offences

**6.10** Even more important than non-recording is non-reporting. *The British Crime Survey 1992* (Mayhew et al 1993) confirmed the findings of earlier local studies that—at least in the case of the sorts of crimes about which respondents were asked—by no means all instances were reported to the police:

**TABLE 6A: Percentages of British Crime Survey offences reported to the police**

| | |
|---|---|
| Thefts of vehicles | 99% |
| Burglaries with losses | 92% |
| Bicycle thefts | 89% |
| Burglaries without losses | 53% |
| Thefts from vehicles | 53% |
| Robberies | 49% |
| Woundings | 48% |
| Attempted vehicle thefts | 41% |
| Other personal thefts | 38% |
| Thefts from the person | 36% |
| Vehicle vandalism | 31% |
| Other household thefts | 29% |
| Common assaults | 26% |
| Household vandalism | 25% |

6.11 Most of the percentages in Table 6A seem surprisingly low, until the victims' reasons for non-reporting are studied:

**TABLE 6B: Victims' reasons for non-reporting**

| | | *Personal offence* | *Household offence* |
|---|---|---|---|
| a. | offence too trivial: no loss or damage | 58% | 55% |
| b. | police could do nothing | 17% | 25% |
| c. | inappropriate for police: victim etc would deal with it | 11% | 12% |
| d. | fear or dislike of police | 1% | 1% |
| e. | inconvenient to report | 2% | 3% |
| f. | police would not be interested | 7% | 13% |
| g. | fear of reprisals | 1% | 2% |
| h. | reported to other authority | 4% | 6% |
| i. | other answers | 7% | 4% |

Reasons (a), (b) and (c) evidently explain most of the non-reporting: the others are infrequent. Indeed, the interesting question is 'Why are the reporting percentages for thefts of motor vehicles and bicycles so high?' The answer must be partly that one has a better chance of getting back one's car or bicycle if the theft is reported; but partly that insurance cannot be claimed unless this is done. Insurance, too, must be the main reason for the higher-than-average reporting percentage for burglary with loss.

6.12 The main relevance of under-reporting for sentencers is that an upward trend in the statistics for a notifiable offence may be wholly or partly the effect of an increase in the percentage which is reported. It is known, for example, that although the number of household burglaries recorded in 1980 was about a third higher than it had been in 1972, the General Household Surveys for those years showed an increase of only one tenth. It is probably relevant that in 1972 only about 20 per cent of the property reported as stolen had been insured; but in 1980 about 40 per cent had (General Household Survey figures). The greater the percentage of under-reporting the more room it leaves for illusory increases in the reported figures. Sharp increases (or decreases) from one year to the next in the statistics for common offences are always suspect, although it is never justifiable to conclude that there has been no change at all in the real incidence. The lesson for sentencers, however, is that they should be aware of the possibility of over-reacting to apparently sharp increases.

**6.13** A less general, but worrying, point which should occur to sentencers who study Tables 6A and 6B is this. If the reason why offences are not reported is usually their triviality, what should the sentencer do when faced with a conviction for an offence so trivial that he wonders why the incident was reported, or why the prosecutor considered it worth a prosecution? The answer must often be withheld from him: for example if it is that the offender has been suspected of a series of offences, but only one can be proved against him. There is usually a reason for the prosecution of a trivial offence.

## Homicide statistics

**6.14** The statistics which arouse most interest are those for intentional homicide, especially at times when the restoration of capital punishment is being debated. The CSEW's homicide figures are more accurate than the rest for two reasons:
  a. very few homicides are not reported to the police. Occasionally it is discovered that an apparent suicide, death from heart failure or voluntary disappearance was really murder: but it is fair to assume that the 680 or so intentional homicides recorded each year represent at least 95 per cent of those which actually occur;
  b. the figures for intentional homicide, unlike all others, are corrected whenever a further investigation or a trial leads to the conclusion that there was no intentional homicide. This reduces the figures by about 13 per cent.
When the *trends* are being studied, however, murder should not be distinguished from manslaughter, because the distinction between them is a very fine one, and the boundary line has shifted several times in living memory as a result of decisions in the CA or House of Lords. In any case, the numbers of both are so small that fluctuations are often due to chance, such as the killing of an usually large number of victims by a single crime of arson or a bomb. The larger the figure the smaller the chance element in its fluctuations. It would be unwise, however, to include the figures for attempted murders, since the decision whether to charge someone with this crime or with the intentional infliction of grievous bodily harm, or an attempt at that crime, is often dependent on the nature of the evidence.

**6.15**   The trend for intentional homicide is therefore reflected not too inaccurately in the figures shown in Table 4.1 of the CSEW. Since capital punishment for murder was abolished in 1965 they have risen from 7 per million of the country's inhabitants to just under 12 per million. It used to be said that 'murder is a crime apart' because its incidence does not rise like that of other crimes. It was probably misleading when it was said; and it would certainly be misleading now. Its rate has risen more slowly than that of non-fatal violence; but it has risen markedly, and the rise might well have been more marked if techniques for saving victims' lives had not developed, partly as a result of medical experience, partly as a result of quicker responses to 999 calls.

## Local trends

**6.16**   For local trends sentencers' main source of information is chief constables' reports. So far as statistics for recorded offences are concerned these are subject to the same limitations as the national tables; but the chief constable may reveal whether his force has been paying particular attention to some kind of crime — such as mugging — or has been distracted from its usual pursuits by incidents such as riots. Not much else is recorded on a night of riots.

## Local prevalence

**6.17**   Sentencers may also want to know whether their district suffers more than most, or more than its neighbours, from certain types of crime. If so, the CSEW no longer gives them much help. Its map in Figure 2.5, based on rates of notifiable offences per 100,000 inhabitants, shows sharp contrasts between black, grey and white police areas, but does not distinguish between types of offence. Nor does it reflect the fact that crime rates for a police area are largely determined by its cities. The Northumbrian moors are not as black as they are painted. Supplementary Table S.3.1, on the other hand distinguishes types of offence, but without relating the figures to the populations. In any case the recorded figures for some types of offence, as we have seen, can be suspect. A special study by Farrington and Dowd (1984) found that Nottinghamshire's apparently high rates for several kinds of notifiable crime were due to unusually conscientious recording by its police force: its real rates, judged by victim surveys, were not very different from those of neighbouring counties. The lesson is that comparisons of figures compiled by police with different 'book-keeping' methods are unreliable. Comparisons of figures for different districts of the same force are likely to be sounder; but even so there may be variations in the way in which different stations handle complaints from the public.

## Public attitudes

**6.18**   In theory sentencing decisions are influenced only by officially approved considerations, whether embodied in statute, practice direction, case law or

Whitehall circular. In real life most sentencers admit to having some regard to what they believe to be public opinion. Their beliefs are usually based not on scientifically planned surveys of opinion but on occasional protests in the news media against a sentence which has struck a reporter as exceptionally lenient or severe. A magistrates' bench is sometimes the target of criticism—usually for leniency—from a local newspaper. Now and again national papers take a judge to task, usually again for leniency. To what extent such criticisms by the news media reflect public opinion, and to what extent they shape it, is a complex question. The point is that sentencers are not systematically supplied with anything better.

**6.19** This is not for want of systematic surveys. These are usually of the 'plebiscite' type, in which interviewees are questioned about 'crime' or, somewhat more sensibly, 'violent crime', 'sexual crime' and so forth; and are invited to choose between a number of alternatives designed to ascertain their 'attitude'. The aim is usually either to measure the 'seriousness' which they attribute to crimes of different sorts, or to find out what sort of penalty or disposal they would choose for the criminal.

**6.20** Surveys concerned with 'seriousness' have had a respectable history since the pioneering example set by Sellin and Wolfgang (1964). They tend to pro-duce consistent comparisons of the seriousness which different sub-groups of the population attribute to different kinds of offence committed in different circumstances. None of the findings—at least of English surveys[1]—seem to present sentencers with a challenge to their assumptions about relative serious-ness.

1. Durant et al (1972); Sparks et al (1977); M A Walker (1978). The last was concerned mainly with methodological aspects of the subject.

**6.21** For sentencers the more relevant 'plebiscites' have been those which questioned respondents about the choice of penalty or other disposal for the offender. The best-known have been those conducted by Gallup Polls at irregular intervals during the last quarter of a century to find out what Britons think about capital punishment. Other market research organisations have been commissioned—usually by newspapers—to question the public about other sorts of penal measures. What the papers have published, however, have usually been crude and selective percentages, often based on questions whose wording has more public appeal than precise meaning. ('Can we afford to do without hanging?') Even if the questions are better drafted, such surveys usually suffer from several serious defects. One is the eliciting of 'pseudo-views', from respondents who are not really concerned about a subject, but who are manoeuvred into giving answers by interviewers who have been trained to minimise the numbers of 'don't knows'. Another is lack of 'specificity'. Questions are asked about 'crime', or some very wide category such as 'violence', and no effort is made to ascertain what sort of crime the respondents has in mind when he gives his view or pseudo-view.

## Victims' views

**6.22**  A group, however, whose responses are unlikely to include many pseudo-views is respondents who have been the victims of the crime in question. The British Crime Survey of 1982 identified substantial numbers of victims of fairly common crimes, and asked them 'In your opinion what would have been a suitable punishment for a court to impose?' and 'In your opinion what should have happened to those who did it?'[1]. The findings were interesting. Taking burglaries and vehicle thefts as examples, victims did not seem to be more punitive than non-victims (Hough and Moxon, 1985); but there were, as might be expected, marked differences between the 'punitiveness' of victims who had reported the crime and those who had not. In the case of 49 per cent of the reported burglaries the victims thought that the offenders should be imprisoned (45 per cent) or birched (4 per cent), whereas for the unreported burglaries the corresponding percentage was only 16 per cent (including 1 per cent for birching). Almost all vehicle thefts were reported, and the corresponding percentage for them was 35 per cent (including 3 per cent for birching). Other proposals varied from probation or community service to the restitution of the property or, simply, 'nothing'; but the only one proposed with frequency was a fine (for 1 in 4 reported burglaries and 1 in 3 reported vehicle thefts). Victims whose losses had been high or whose property had been damaged usually suggested more severe penalties than others. For instance, when burglars had caused any damage, or loss worth more than £250, half the victims would have liked to see them imprisoned: otherwise only a quarter. Not surprisingly, victims were more likely to be punitive if they had been very upset by the crime (Hough, 1984). Women over the age of 40 were less punitive—at least where burglaries or motor vehicle thefts were concerned—than younger women or men.

1.  The responses were combined.

## Personifying the public

**6.23**  There are faults of interpretation as well as design. One is the ascription of a view to 'the public' when it is merely the view of a majority—or even of the largest minority. When asked in the Prison Reform Trust's survey (Shaw, 1982) 'What do you personally think is the main purpose of sending people to prison?' respondents replied

| | |
|---|---|
| 'to punish the criminal' | 42% |
| 'to reform criminals so they can fit into society' | 25% |
| 'to keep criminals apart from society' | 21% |
| 'to deter would-be criminals' | 12% |
| other or 'don't know' | 5% |

This scarcely justifies the report's statement that 'the public views the main purpose of imprisonment as punishment or just deserts'. Only something close to unanimity would justify that.

## Ranking sentences
**6.24** A subtler variant of personification is the use of 'mean ranking'. Respondents are asked to rank items—such as types of sentence—in order of, say, severity. When Walker and Marsh (in an experiment described in 8.25ff) did this the result was Table 6C.

**TABLE 6C: Ranking of types of sentence**

|  | *most frequent ranking* | *mean ranking* |
|---|---|---|
| Imprisonment for 12 months | 1st (959) | 1.2 (1st) |
| Imprisonment for 6 months | 2nd (900) | 2.2 (2nd) |
| A fine of £100 | 3rd (451) | 4.0 (3rd) |
| A fine of £40 | 4th (364) | 5.3 (6th) |
| Community service | 5th (261) | 5.0 (4th) |
| Probation | 6th (309) | 5.0 (4th) |
| Suspended sentence | 7th (401) | 5.4 (7th) |

The table shows how mean rank order can be misleading. In this case it would lead to the claim that respondents ranked a £40 fine below community service and probation, whereas the other column shows that it was most frequently placed 4th. The explanation is that an affluent minority ranked it very low. Again, while there was considerable agreement that 12 months' imprisonment was 'toughest', not quite so many agreed that 6 months' imprisonment came next: for some it was the £100 fine. The most revealing column is that which shows the most frequently assigned places: the numbers decline until we come to the suspended sentence, which a substantial 401 respondents ranked 'mildest' (as indeed it is if one expects to avoid a further conviction). On the other hand, a minority gave it much higher places, next to imprisonment or a £100 fine: they may have been influenced by its symbolic or hypothetical toughness. In this sense, the suspended sentence spoke with forked tongue. Omitting it from the list would have resulted in greater agreement. In other words, if a sentencer chooses a suspended sentence with the intention of signifying the seriousness of the offence, this will be understood by some; but most others will see it the most lenient of all choices. Mean ranking can be a misleading attempt to personify 'the public'.

**6.25** The surveys so far mentioned were of the usual door-to-door kind, in which interviewers subjected representative respondents to questionnaires carefully (if sometimes naively) designed by researchers with some knowledge of the criminal justice system. Hough (1996) adopted a new technique. 'Focus groups' of representative adults in various parts of England were formed, and 'warmed up' by asking them to discuss the crimes that worried them most. They were then asked to work their way through 10 categories of crime. The main findings were that
  i.  'respondents were highly cynical about the ability and performance of sentencers, and thought that in general sentences are far too soft';

  ii. they tended to be misinformed about sentencing practice, often substantially underestimating the extent to which prison sentences are used;

  iii. the sentences they themselves advocated were often in line with sentencers' actual practice, at least as regards *type* of sentence;

  iv. but many expressed highly punitive views about serious crimes such as rape and grievous bodily harm, and advocated longer sentences than were in use for such crimes;

  v. many wanted a closer correspondence between nominal lengths of prison sentences and periods actually served;

  vi. some wanted sentences to include a reparative element, but this was often in combination with prison sentences rather than an alternative;

  vii. they lacked any clear understanding of probation and reformative sentences.

Respondents were also given some details of examples of nine of the types of crime they had discussed, the examples being based on cases actually considered by the CA. In general they found the CA's sentencing decisions 'within the bounds of acceptability', although a majority thought the CA too lenient in the cases of rape, drug supplying and street robbery. Some were angered by the offender's decision to appeal.

### Punitiveness

**6.26** These findings do not support assertions that the English public is less punitive than its sentencers. In any case, as we have seen, it is misleading to personify 'the public' in this way. Hough, Lewis and Walker's (1988) experiment, which used faked newspaper cuttings to maximise specificity, found substantial variations in punitiveness between age-groups, social classes and those whose education ended early or late. Young men were more punitive than young women, but the middle-aged of both sexes were equally punitive. What interested the researchers, however, was what their respondents thought of sentencers' typical sentences for the offences in their faked cuttings. Only about half regarded them as 'about right'. More interestingly, very few of the other half thought the sentences 'too tough': most opted for 'a little too soft' or 'much too soft'. Nor were most of these pseudo-views, for they felt that 'something should be done about it'. Tolerance of severity was commoner than tolerance of leniency. And when an international survey asked European and United States citizens for the most appropriate sentence for a recidivist burglar of 21 the percentage of English respondents who chose a prison sentence (38 per cent) was higher than in any other country surveyed except Northern Ireland (44 per cent), the United States (53 per cent) and Czechoslovakia (63 per cent) (Mayhew, 1994). Where sentencing is concerned leniency is not popular in England.

# Chapter 7

# The efficacy of correctives

**7.1** Law-breakers may desist for adventitious reasons—premature death or disablement, the influence of a law-abiding partner or religious mentor, enlistment in the armed services or the merchant navy: even, in a few cases, the financial success of their illegal enterprises. What sentencers often hope, however, is that their interventions will induce desistance before it would otherwise have occurred. One of the major problems of penology is to identify the types of intervention— if any—which seem likely to fulfil this hope.

**7.2** Efficacy must not be confused with efficiency. We know roughly how efficiently fixed penalties for traffic offences are administered—that is what percentages of them are paid (see 23.8)—but we have no idea how effective they are in deterring the offenders. Terminology can cause other sorts of imprecision. There is a tendency to ask, for example, whether prison ever reforms, using 'reform' to mean 'improving a person's character so that he is less inclined to offend'. (Sometimes the word 'rehabilitation' is used instead of 'reform', although it is better to reserve 'rehabilitation' for efforts to make it easier for offenders not to reoffend: eg by finding them jobs.) The difficulty in answering questions about reform lies in the problem of distinguishing between non-offending which can be attributed to a change of character and non-offending which is due to the desire not to repeat an unpleasant experience: ie individual deterrence. In the case of some penalties it is highly unlikely that they could reduce offending by reformation. Fines, if they do reduce offending, could hardly be doing so by any means but deterrence. In the case, however, of prison, community service and even probation it is unsafe to make assumptions about the nature of the process by which they achieve an effect, if any. We need to find a convenient term for effectiveness in reducing offending which does not beg questions: 'corrective efficacy' seems to serve. The next step is to find out whether penalties 'correct'; and only if the answer is that some do need we go on to ask what form the correction takes.

## Criteria for correction

**7.3** The next problem is the criterion of correction. Unless there is agreement about this those who believe in the efficacy of a measure—such as community service—can appeal to any sort of evidence they like, from the statements of offenders to the impressions of their supervisors. These are not worthless; but they are so liable to be influenced by optimism or scepticism that some more objective criterion must be found. The choice seems to lie between the avoidance of further offences (or offences of certain kinds) and some more general kind of improvement.

**7.4** The Morison Committee on the Probation Service faced this problem in the early 1960s. It was presented with rather discouraging statistics about the effectiveness of probation in terms of reconvictions, when compared with other sentences. Instead of dealing realistically with them, it reacted by offering a different criterion:

'... But the avoidance of offences is a poor, and even *misleading*, measure of the rehabilitation of the offender and of the degree to which he had learnt to overcome anti-social traits and attitudes, to live happily within the limitations imposed by society, and to meet, or reconcile himself to, material and environmental difficulties that accompanied and, perhaps, occasioned his delinquent behaviour. Conversely, the commission of another offence may mark no more than a temporary relapse in the rehabilitative process. Further, on a wholly material level, it is difficult to regard the offence as showing a total failure with the probationer if, in the period of supervision, he has met difficulties to which he would otherwise have given way or accepted responsibilities which he would otherwise have avoided. No penal treatment can do more than the delinquent's limitations permit and with many offenders periodic breakdowns in behaviour must be expected ...'. (1962.9: our italics)

## Social adjustment

**7.5** Reconvictions undoubtedly have unsatisfactory features, and they will be discussed in a moment. The Morison Committee, however, was intent on arguing that they were 'misleading' because there was a better criterion. Paradoxically, the Report offered a much more ambitious objective for probation officers, but seemed to imply that they would come out better on this test. What it did not discuss was how the sort of adjustment to society which it described could be measured.

**7.6** What is more, by calling the avoidance of offences a 'misleading measure' it seemed to imply, subtly, that probationers who would be classed as successes on the criterion of adjustment would appear as failures if judged by further offending, and vice versa. It may seem unfair to read so much into the word 'misleading': but some people still believe that the effectiveness of probation should not be assessed by looking at probationers' further law-breaking, and the point must be discussed.

**7.7** Obviously, it is very difficult, perhaps impossible, to find a way of measuring social adjustment in a way which makes it a relatively 'hard' criterion instead of a 'soft' one. (A soft criterion is one which depends so much on the judgment of individuals that in a substantial number of cases two independent assessors will disagree as to whether the criterion is met. A hard criterion is one which leads to few or no disagreements.) Reconviction is a fairly hard criterion. Is it possible to find a measure of social adjustment which could be called 'hard'? The Home Office team responsible for the IMPACT Project found this very difficult (see 18.21), although they used not only personality tests and probation officers' ratings of the severity of probationers' problems but also employment records. Bottoms and McClintock's study of the inmates of Dover Borstal did not include personality tests, but dealt very thoroughly with regularity of employment, conflicts with parents or wives, use of leisure, abuse of alcohol or drugs, and the presence of personality problems or mental disorder. They combined these in a 'social problem score' (and found, by the way, that the scores of some inmates were better after than before their time in borstal, while others' were worse) (1975).

## Social problem scores

**7.8** One interesting finding of the Dover study, which is the most thorough that has been published in this country, was that the social problem score of ex-inmates in their first year after release was closely related to the numbers who had been reconvicted within 18 months of release; and that the two criteria sorted the ex-borstal youths into much the same groups. Those who prefer the social problem score as a criterion of success can argue that reconvictions would wrongly have classed as failures about 1 in 5 young men who had few identifiable problems, and wrongly classed as successes a roughly equal percentage who had a lot of problems. (It is interesting to speculate whether the relationship would have been even closer if it had been possible for an omniscient researcher to record all offences committed by the ex-inmates, and not merely those which had resulted in reconvictions). This finding does not justify the view that reconvictions are a *misleading* measure of social adjustment: merely less than perfect.

**7.9** In fact a case can be made out on sounder lines for adopting criteria other than law-breaking, but only if the argument is limited to one or two kinds of special circumstances. Every criminal court encounters offenders whose offences seem to matter less than the situation which they disclose. Examples are young delinquents who are found, as a result of petty thieving, to be under serious stress because of the behaviour of their parents; or adult offenders who are found to be suffering from mental disorders, especially if these can be alleviated by treatment or good nursing. In such cases a court might well feel justified in choosing a measure which in effect 'transports' the individual, not out of the country but out of the penal system and into the care of some other system, such as the National Health Service, in the hope that it will alleviate his or her handicaps. When this is done—whether the hope is justified or not—it seems fair to argue that the criterion of success or failure should be those used by the service to which the individual is 'transported', and not his later law-breaking. In the case of the probation service, however, it cannot often be argued that the individuals entrusted to it are in this special category. Indeed it could be argued that since the probationer is still liable to be sentenced for breach of the requirements of his order he is still within the ambit of the penal system, and that his success or failure must be judged by its criteria. Both arguments seem to go too far: there are probationers whose offences are quite overshadowed by the magnitude of their social problems, and in whose cases the probation officer is entitled to claim that he is achieving some improvement even when they reoffend. But this is a claim which must not be made too often.

7.10    The case for using law-breaking, however, instead of social adjustment rests not only on
   a.    the laboriousness of ascertaining social problems; and
   b.    their comparative softness as a criterion;
but also on
   c.    the argument that it is law-breaking which sentences are intended to reduce.
This last argument can of course be challenged, and not only by the punisher who judges sentences by their retributive rightness. Arguably, even a reductive penal system should not limit its aims to the reduction of law-breaking but should use the right to intervene in people's lives in order to benefit them: what we have called 'occasionalism' in chapter 21. One can accept occasionalism or object to it, for example by equating it with paternalism; but even if accepted it is not a sound reason for rejecting law-breaking as a criterion of success. All it justifies is the use of *additional* criteria, provided that these can be measured reliably.

**What sort of law-breaking?**

7.11    A decision in favour of law-breaking as a criterion may be the end of one argument: but it is only the beginning of another. Should the success of a sentence be judged by the commission of *any* further offence, or only by the commission of another of the same kind? In practice, as we shall see, the limitations of sources of data exclude consideration of most summary offences, unless researchers have the resources and permission for the use of local police files. Most follow-ups are concerned with cohorts of men sentenced for standard list[1] offences—dishonest acquisitions, malicious damage, sexual offences, personal violence—so that reconvictions for drunken behaviour, minor motoring offences, or peccadilloes involving TV licences do not seem very relevant. Yet if one is following up a sentenced robber how relevant is a conviction for an assault committed in a quarrel over a girl?

1.   The 'standard list' (SL) includes all indictable offences, plus non-indictable offences which resemble indictable offences (eg assaults), and driving offences serious enough to be dealt with on indictment.

7.12    The obvious answer may turn out to be rather superficial. If a sentence for robbery is regarded as a way of facilitating some sort of treatment which is meant to be a specific for robbery—or, if that seems unfair, for acquisitive offences—then nobody should expect it to be a prophylactic against losing one's temper. It would be more realistic, however, to hope that what the burglar will learn is self-control, or even some consideration for others, so that he will be less likely in future to break the law in ways that have serious consequences. It might be more realistic still to hope merely that he will learn to think of the risks involved in law-breaking, and to consider less risky ways of getting what he wants. If so, it is reasonable to count not only subsequent robberies but also assaults, burglaries, car thefts and so on as indications of the failure of the sentence.

**7.13** That is why most follow-up studies—both in this country and abroad—do not limit their criteria of correctional failure to 'cognate' offences (a useful Scots term). But there are minor awkwardnesses to be considered before moving on to more technical problems. Suppose that a man's next offence is very trivial, yet technically means a conviction for a SL offence? Suppose that after being imprisoned for burglary he is convicted of sexual intercourse with a girl under 16? Is it possible to define the criterion to deal with this sort of case, without lapsing into hopeless subjectivity, and—a practical consideration—without becoming deeply involved in the details of each offence? Some research workers cope with this fairly sensibly by distinguishing reconvictions which lead to custodial sentences, those leading to non-custodial measures, and those which result in a mere discharge. There are other solutions to this problem: see Scott (1964), Pease et al (1977), Kraus (1974), Dunlop (1975).

## Technical problems

**7.14** There are also technical problems. The first is the ascertainment of subsequent convictions. Because adult and young adult offenders are mobile, follow-ups in local police or other records are not reliable. The usual source nowadays[1] for national follow-ups covering England and Wales is the Offenders' Index, a computerised data-base of criminal records involving SL offences which is maintained by the Home Office for research and statistical purposes. It is not however exhaustive, since

    i.   it does not record many kinds of summary offence (for which local police records would have to be consulted if comprehensiveness were considered all-important);

   ii.  it does not normally record cautions[1] for admitted offences (see 15.5ff);

  iii.  it does not, as a rule, include convictions in courts outside England and Wales;

  iv.  offenders who do not want to be linked to their previous convictions, for fear of a more severe sentence, are sometimes able to avoid this by giving false names, although known aliases are recorded, and most offenders are nowadays finger-printed.

---

1. The Criminal Record Office (CRO) of the Metropolitan Police (now called the National Identification Service or NIS) used to be a source for authorised researchers, but was laborious to utilise. In 1995 Phoenix, a police computer system covering the same data (and intended eventually to include cautions) went live, and should some day become an important source of information about reconvictions.

## Inaccuracies of reconviction data

**7.15** A more serious defect (at least from the point of view of research) is that most sources do not record cases in which the offender has been suspected of a later offence but not cautioned or prosecuted, or if prosecuted has been acquitted. (Nor of course could they possibly record offences of which he is not even suspected.) The detection rates for most types of acquisitive offence are low, and the acquittal rates of most offences are high. There is good evidence of the 'incompleteness' of reconvictions as a criterion. West (1963) collected a sample of 'habitual prisoners' with apparently crime-free gaps of at least four years in otherwise criminal careers. His aim was to find out why these gaps had occurred; but interviews with 59 such men in Wandsworth disclosed that in at least 24 cases the interlude had not been as virtuous as the records suggested: they had merely escaped detection through luck or skill. Conversely, as Lloyd, Mair and Hough discovered (1994) there are also 'pseudo-reconvictions'—convictions during a follow-up which are the results of offences committed before the sentence which is the subject of the follow-up. These can inflate the apparent failure rate by as much as 7 per cent. Finally, there is what can only be called 'underconvicting'. Plea-bargaining, deficiencies of evidence, and juries' doubts or sympathies can result in a defendant's being convicted of an offence less serious than the one which he or she actually committed: for example, of actual bodily harm instead of attempted murder, of indecent assault instead of attempted rape, or careless instead of dangerous driving. This is an awkward problem for researchers who want to use the seriousness of subsequent convictions as a measure of failure.

**7.16** These are among the reasons why most US researchers prefer 'rearrests' as a criterion of recidivism. Since inevitably some rearrests are mistaken this exaggerates what it tries to measure, but probably by less than 'reconvictions' underestimate it. It is noticeable in McLaren's (1992) review of correctional research that the use of rearrests seems to reveal sharper differences between control samples and treatment samples than does the use of reconvictions. It is a pity that the English system does not lend itself to such comparisons.

**7.17** It would be excusable to conclude that reconvictions fall so short of reflecting reoffending that they are useless as a measure of efficacy, except perhaps where crimes with very high detection rates are concerned. But this is probably too pessimistic. Even reconvictions for offences with low detection rates show systematic differences which are difficult to explain without the hypothesis that they reflect real differences in frequencies of reoffending:
  i.   the more previous SL convictions a person has the more likely it is that he or she will incur another. A conceivable explanation is that the offenders who are found guilty more often are simply those who are easier to detect; but it is unlikely that this explains the whole of the difference;
  ii.  young males are more likely than young females to be convicted and reconvicted, although this difference seems to taper to vanishing point by the age of 30;

iii. after the late teens SL reconviction rates, like SL offending rates, decline—though only gradually—with increasing age. Again this could in *theory* be an index of greater skill in avoiding prosecution, but it is consistent with what we know about the decline in the real frequency of offending as people age;

iv. there are differences between reconviction rates for types of offences which are *not* consistent with the hypothesis that all they reflect is different detection rates. For example, offenders convicted of burglary or criminal damage, which have low detection rates, have high reconviction rates in comparison with others.

To sum up, the most likely explanation of these systematic differences (which repeat themselves again and again in all sorts of samples) is that they reflect real differences in the frequencies of reoffending, however dimly they reflect them and whatever else they reflect. This is supported by self-reported information about law-breaking.

## Self-reported law-breaking

**7.18** It would obviously be better if reconvictions could be supplemented by information about offences which did not result in reconvictions: for example, by cautions and acquittals. Best of all would be self-reports of offences. West and Farrington (1977) have shown not only that these can be got (provided at least that subjects have become used to being interviewed); but also that they add a great deal to the accuracy with which people can be classified as offenders or non-offenders. For example, when 389 of their subjects were interviewed at the age of 18 or 19, 42 of them admitted to having burgled in the last three years, although only 26 of the 42 (62 per cent) had been convicted for doing so. The percentages for other offences against property were even lower. Yet their data also show that while reliance on findings of guilt misclassifies substantial numbers of teenaged offenders as non-offenders, it still distinguishes between those who are committing relatively few offences and those who are committing a lot. In other words, reconvictions for offences, even those with low detection rates, can be used to distinguish males who are committing rather few offences from those who are frequent law-breakers.

## Follow-up periods

**7.19** Almost all follow-ups cover limited periods: one, two, three or more years. The reason is not simply impatience on the part of research workers. It seems to be the case that if an offender is going to be reconvicted at all this is more likely to happen in the first few years than later. This is neatly illustrated by Phillpotts and Lancucki: see Figure 7A. Clearly, if a man is going to be reconvicted this is most likely to happen within three years of his sentence. Note how even by the end of the fourth quarter the reconviction rates distinguish between two groups of offenders: those on probation or under suspended

**FIGURE 7A: Males convicted of standard list offences in January 1971: cumulative proportion reconvicted by sentence and time since January 1971 conviction[1]**

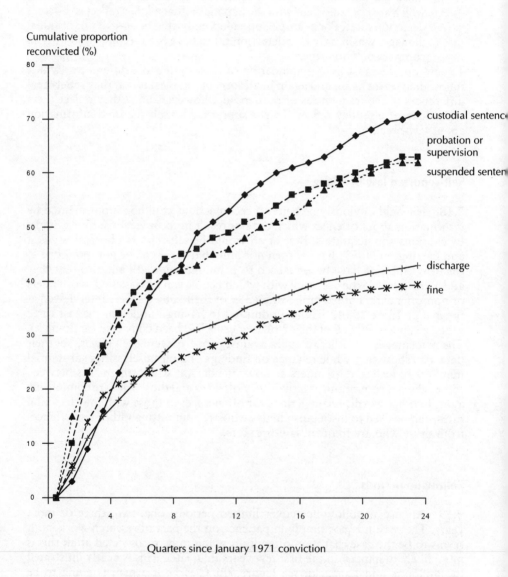

Cumulative proportion
reconvicted (%)

custodial sentence

probation or
supervision

suspended sentence

discharge

fine

Quarters since January 1971 conviction

1.   Source: Phillpots and Lancucki, 1979.

sentences and those fined or discharged. (It should not be inferred at this stage that any of these disposals is more effective than another, for reasons which will soon be discussed).

**7.20**   The graph also makes another point: that if any members of a cohort receive custodial sentences, a follow-up which covered only a year would be misleading, because most of them would have spent a substantial part of it 'inside'. It is not until the end of the third year that the curve for ex-prisoners has established its position well above the rest. By that time 84 per cent had been at liberty for two years or more: but if the cohort had included a very substantial number of long-term prisoners it would have been necessary to extend the prisoners' follow-up so as to allow them the full six years at risk of being reconvicted[1].

1.   Phillpotts' and Lancucki's Table 3.6 and Figure 3.2 show the corrections which had to be made when this was done. Even with these corrections, only a follow-up of at least three years would show the full extent of the difference between ex-prisoners' rates and the others.

**7.21**   The worst kind of follow-up is (i) very short and (ii) fails to ensure that each individual has had more or less the same time in which to incur the risk of reconviction. Again, the shorter the follow-up the more it is necessary to look not at the date of reconviction but the date of reoffending, since the periods between offending and being sentenced can vary considerably. In a short follow-up two men could reoffend and be detected and charged, yet only one of them might be recorded as reconvicted because the other had not yet made his final court appearance.

**7.22**   It is also possible to be critical of follow-ups of probationers which cover only two years (or in some cases less). During most of that time they will have been under supervision. Certainly if the question is whether probation induces long-term improvements in law-observance the follow-up ought to outlast probation. But
  i.   people also want to know about the effectiveness of probation in keeping probationers out of current trouble;
  ii.   the curve in Figure 7A does not suggest that probationers are any more inhibited during probation than men under suspended sentence. Both groups have curves which rise both steeply and smoothly. Neither curve shows any marked increase at the two-year point, the end of the operational period for the suspended sentence and of most probation orders (if they have not already been ended by reconviction!).

**7.23**   To sum up, two years seems to be the minimum acceptable period for a follow-up intended to assess corrective efficacy. If the cohort includes people sentenced to substantial periods of custody, either they must be followed up for at least two years after release or the follow-up period for the whole cohort must be at least three years. If the cohort includes probationers the presentation of the findings should distinguish reconvictions which occur during probation from those which were incurred after it. It should also be clear by this stage that to talk about the 'success rate' of any measure betrays one's ignorance. It is less misleading to refer to '*known failure rates*'. More precise would be 'the known (3)-year failure rate in terms of SL convictions'.

## Absolute and comparative efficacy

**7.24**  The problem is how to use such rates to measure efficacy. Ideally what we should want to assess is 'absolute efficacy', which can be defined as the difference between the subsequent frequency of offending by offenders to whom no measure has been applied and the frequency among offenders to whom the measure in question has been applied. It is necessary to adopt a definition on these lines because of the likelihood that there is a natural decrease in offending as offenders become older, more prudent, perhaps even more considerate of the interests of others. Thus a slight decrease in failure rates among sentenced teenagers might be attributable simply to this natural process.

**7.25**  It is obviously impossible to know whether an identified individual offender would have ceased to commit offences at some stage if he had not been detected and sentenced. At most it might be possible, by means of interviewing and reinterviewing undetected offenders at intervals, to arrive at a rough estimate of the percentage of, say, young adult males, living in areas of high (or low) unemployment and committing acquisitive offences, who within, say, five years cease to do so without official intervention in their lives. The Cambridge Family Development Study (West and Farrington, 1977) achieved a series of interviews with both detected and undetected offenders over nearly two decades; but it was not designed with such estimates in mind, so that the questions asked about undetected offences differed at different stages.

## Comparing failure rates

**7.26**  Failing such estimates, most follow-up studies have been content with trying to compare known failure rates for two or more types of measure, in the hope of finding that one rate is markedly lower than another, thus indicating which measure is preferable, at least in terms of corrective efficacy. The awkward possibility that some offenders would do as well if merely detected but not sentenced, or even if not detected at all, remains more or less unexplored.

**7.27**  Comparisons of failure rates, however, have to solve other technical problems. The chief of these is that certain characteristics of offenders which are known to be associated with higher or lower reconviction rates also make it more likely that offenders will receive one kind of sentence than another. As we have seen, being a female under the age of 30, and having few or no previous convictions, are associated with low reconviction rates; and they are also characteristics which tend to lead courts to choose non-custodial sentences. It is therefore not surprising that non-custodial sentences appear to have lower reconviction rates than imprisonment. Age, too, seems to be associated both with choice of sentence (partly because of legal restrictions on the sentencing of the young) and with different reconviction rates, although if the whole of a cohort is over 20 years of age these associations are not very strong. Someone who is unemployed at the time of conviction is both more likely to be reconvicted and also to get a sentence other than a fine (Softley, 1978), a factor which must be taken into account when the efficacy of fines is being assessed.

## Random allocation

7.28 Comparisons of the failure rates of different measures have to take account of such factors either by random allocation or by statistical techniques for comparing slightly biased samples. Because of the obvious ethical objections, experiments with random allocation are rare, and those that have been tried have usually succumbed to interference after they have begun: see for instance Ross et al (1974). An example of a fairly successful one is described by Berg et al (1978). In this the juvenile court randomly dealt with cases of truancy either by assigning the case to social workers or by requiring the family to reappear before the court for reports six months later. Although the main interest was subsequent truancy it was found that the 'adjourned' cases did better not only in terms of school attendance but also as regards other kinds of delinquency.

7.29 The ethical objections likely to be made to random choice of measure are negligible when the measures are of the mild sort involved in Berg's studies but much greater if one measure seems to be much more drastic. It is arguable that if offenders have knowingly risked or deserved imprisonment it is not unfair to substitute a lesser penalty for a random selection of them; but that does not satisfy objectors who regard this as inequitable discrimination between the lucky and the unlucky. Nor are they appeased if it is pointed out that the same offenders, if sentenced in another court, might well get a non-custodial penalty. Apparently discrimination for a useful purpose is ethically worse. However that may be, other people's objections are everyone's political facts.

7.30 It is sometimes acceptable to randomise when it is possible to arrange that a cohort of offenders who have received the same official sentence are assigned to regimes of different kinds, as was done with borstal inmates in the Pooled Allocation Experiment (as a result of which one type of borstal appeared to have a lower failure rate than others: Williams, 1970). There is an all-important difference, however, between the evaluation of sentences and the evaluation of regimes; that is, of the ways in which sentences are applied in practice. Most comparisons of regimes have been done in North America (at considerable cost) with results that have been summarised by McLaren (1992). Broadly speaking, her conclusions were that it is a waste of special resources to devote them to 'low-risk' offenders; but that the recidivism of 'high-risk' offenders can be reduced by 'interventions' which recognise their relevant needs but also take into account their abilities and ways of learning. Unlikely to be effective are regimes based on the notion that offending is a sickness (the medical model), or on 'open communication and friendship' approaches, non-directional counselling, offender-run projects, or plain deterrence. (She could have instanced the English finding that toughening the regimes of detention centres for teenagers did not reduce their reconvictions (Thornton et al. 1984).)

**7.31** Regimes, whether custodial or non-custodial, can be designed so as to observe these principles. Sentences cannot. Fines apart, whatever option a sentencer chooses will hand the offender over to practitioners—probation staff, prison staff, hospital staff—whose approaches will vary, sometimes very widely, and cannot be controlled by the sentencer. The natures of regimes are apt to change when staff are replaced or retire. Prisoners are shuttled from one establishment to another, or from one wing to another. Even psychiatrists are mobile and mortal.

**7.32** Yet there is still some point in comparing the reconviction rates of different types of sentence (if only to discredit the wilder claims of penal reformers); and this is what English research has tended to do. It has usually relied on what might be called 'unplanned randomness': the differences between the sentencing policies of different courts, which means that sometimes similar offenders receive dissimilar sentences. That means using statistical techniques to compare cohorts. The crudest is matching, and the crudest kind of matching is group-matching. We are sometimes told that those who received custodial sentences had a mean age of, say, 18.3 and a mean of 1.7 previous convictions, and that these means do not differ significantly from the means of those who were, say, fined. But means can conceal important differences. In one group most of the offenders might have ages close to the mean, while the other group consisted of two groups, one under 16, and the other over 20. One group might contain some people with no previous convictions, some with one, some with two and so on, while the other group consisted of people who had either none or more than four. Group matching of this kind is too crude for most purposes. Individual matching means pairing individuals in one group with members of the other who correspond in age, previous convictions and any other variable that seems unavoidable. (Matching men with women is always inadvisable; but it is usual to avoid samples of mixed sexes in penal studies, for reasons which should by now be obvious). The trouble with individual matching is that there are almost always some unmatchable individuals who have to be discarded. If a lot have to be discarded the result may be that one or more of the cohorts to be compared is atypical of people who receive the sentence in question.

## Base expectancies

**7.33** What most professional evaluators prefer nowadays is to calculate the 'base expectancy' of reconviction for all the offenders in a cohort who received a sentence of the same type (say imprisonment), for all those who received another type (say a fine) and so on. The calculation of base expectancies takes into account the effect of variables such as previous records and type of offence which are associated with differences in the probability of reconviction. (An example is the Offender Group Reconviction Scale offered by the Home Office to writers of PSRs: see Appendix C). Evaluators can compare the 'expected' numbers of reconvicted offenders with the actual numbers, and if these are lower by a significant margin (see 7.38ff) this is regarded as encouraging. It must be remembered, however, that this technique does not measure absolute efficacy: it only compares the efficacy of different measures. It could be a measure of absolute efficacy only if the sample on which the expected reconvictions were based were mainly composed of offenders who had not been subjected to any measure.

7.34   With these reservations, Table 7B is presented here because it shows the result of applying the 'expectation method' to the best follow-up data for English and Welsh SL offenders. The cohort was a 1 in 6 sample of SL offenders sentenced in courts throughout the country in January 1971, and followed up for the next six years. Phillpotts and Lancucki (1979) presented some of the results, but allowed Walker, Farrington and Tucker (1981) to analyse further the data for men aged 21 or older, with the results shown in Table 7B. The variable used in calculating expected numbers was type of offence (age is not strongly associated with reconviction probabilities after the teens). The important figures in the table are those which show whether the number of reconvictions for a given group (e g probationers with no previous SL convictions) was greater or less than expectation: 1.88 indicates that it was 88 per cent more (whereas for example 1.00 indicates that it was exactly the expected number, and 0.69 indicates that it was 31 per cent less).

**TABLE 7B: Actual and expected reconvictions of adult men in the Phillpotts-Lancucki sample**

| | *Number of previous standard list convictions* | | | |
|---|---|---|---|---|
| | *None* | *1* | *2, 3 or 4* | *5 or more* |
| Discharge | 0.97 | 1.15 | 1.40 | 0.98 |
| | (19% of 113) | (50% of 24) | (90% of 20) | (85% of 13) |
| Fine or compensation | 0.96 | 0.93 | 0.92 | 0.97 |
| | (19% of 578) | (41% of 181) | (61% of 221) | (84% of 77) |
| Probation | 1.88 | 0.94 | 0.85 | 1.00 |
| | (38% of 36) | (46% of 26) | (54% of 48) | (88% of 24) |
| Suspended sentence | 1.24 | 1.21 | 1.10 | 1.00 |
| | (27% of 60) | (56% of 64) | (73% of 112) | (88% of 59) |
| Immediate imprisonment* | 0.69 | 1.02 | 1.04 | 1.02 |
| | (15% of 47) | (51% of 49) | (69% of 148) | (90% of 169) |
| All disposals above | 21% of 834 | 47% of 334 | 66% of 549 | 88% of 342 |

Actual reconvictions are shown as multiples of corrected* expected reconvictions (see text). The numbers in brackets represent individuals at risk of reconviction, and the bracketed percentages are their actual reconviction rates. Community service orders were not a permissible method of disposal in 1971.

*   Reconvictions of imprisoned offenders were 'corrected' by estimating (from other data) how many additional ex-prisoners would have been reconvicted if their follow-up had covered a full 6 years from release: but most of the prisoners received sentences of a year or less.

7.35   The table confirms the strong association between number of previous convictions and the rates of reconviction. For men with no previous SL convictions the reconviction rate was only 21 per cent, whereas for men with more than four it was 88 per cent. Not surprisingly the rates were very high whether these recidivists were discharged, fined, put on probation or given suspended or immediate imprisonment: in no case did it differ from expectation by more than one or two cases. At the other extreme, there were considerable differences between reconviction rates for the different sentence-groups of men with no previous SL convictions. For probationers and those given suspended sentences they were high, and well above expectation. For fines and discharges they were only slightly below expectation; but for immediate imprisonment they were markedly below expectation. This last difference cannot be explained[1] as due to differences in the kinds of offences for which men tend to be sent to prison or fined, since offence-type was the variable used to calculate expected numbers. The low reconviction rate for immediate imprisonment will startle those who are used to being told that reconviction rates after imprisonment are high; but it must be realised that such rates usually fail to distinguish those without previous convictions from the recidivists who make up the majority of prisoners. It is worth noting too that even for recidivist prisoners the reconviction rates are not much above expectation.

1.  Nor is it very likely to be due to sampling error. The odds are 95:5 that the imprisoned 'first offenders' *subsequently* differed from the rest in some way that affected their likelihood of being reconvicted.

7.36  The figures for suspended sentences, whether used for 'first offenders' or for recidivists, are disappointing. So are those for 'first offenders' put on probation, but not those for recidivist probationers: a finding which raises the question whether probation is a wise choice for the first sentence for an adult male. All the other figures are very close to expectation: it would require only one or two reconvictions more or less to bring them into line. In short, with the exceptions mentioned, what the table emphasises is how little difference the choice of sentence made to an adult male's general probability of reconviction, when this was calculated from his type of offence and previous record. But since the base expectancies were calculated from a sample which did not include men who had not been subjected to any measure the table merely *compares* the efficacy of different measures; and does not measure absolute efficacy. For all we know, even the suspended sentence might have been better than nothing— merely not as effective as the other measures.

7.37  Since the Philpotts-Lancucki follow-up sentencers' options have changed in one or two respects. Suspended sentences are now supposed to be reserved for exceptional cases. Community service is now an option, as is probation with special activities (see chapter 17). Recently Lloyd, Mair and Hough (1994) followed up nearly 18,000 men and women aged 17 or older who in 1987 were either released from a custodial sentence or dealt with non-custodially. The follow-up covered two years. Expected numbers of reconvictions were calculated using gender, age and criminal histories. Table 7C shows how they compared with actual reconvictions.

**TABLE 7C: Expected and actual reconviction percentages in the Lloyd-Mair-Hough two-year follow-up**

|  | Actual | Expected | Numbers |
|---|---|---|---|
| Custodial sentences | 54% | 53% | 9,615 |
| Probation | 43% | 45% | 2,448 |
| Probation with special requirements | 63% | 60 % | 3,354 |
| Community service | 49% | 52% | 2,394 |

It has to be remembered that since this sample did not include offenders who had avoided being sentenced these percentages do not allow us to estimate absolute efficacy: only to compare efficacy. For all we know, all four types of sentence reduced recidivism to some extent, in which case the percentages simply show which were the most effective. Yet the differences between expected and actual percentages are disappointingly small. Sentencers (and the probation officers who advise them) when faced with a choice between these measures must wonder how often their decision makes any difference to an offender's likelihood of reoffending. The answer must be 'not very often'. On the most optimistic assumption that the whole of the differences between expected and actual reconvictions was attributable to the choice of sentence, that choice was right or wrong in only a few hundred cases out of nearly 18,000. On the more realistic assumption that the differences were only partly due to the choice of sentence (and partly to factors which could not be ascertained or quantified) the cases in which the choice mattered were even fewer than that. We shall return to this comparison in 18.20.

## Significance

**7.38** Whatever technique is used to compare the subsequent careers of offenders subjected to different measures, numerical differences will raise the question of their significance. If, after precautions have been taken to ensure that the difference between the reconviction rates of finees and ex-prisoners is not due to variables such as age and recidivism, there is still a moderate difference, can this be taken at its face-value? The problem arises from the fact that every cohort of sentenced offenders is merely a sample of all sentenced offenders. A sample, however carefully drawn, cannot be relied upon to reflect with complete accuracy the proportions of characteristics in the 'population' from which it is drawn, although by repeated sampling the accuracy of estimates can be increased. Consequently if a cohort of finees is found to have a reconviction rate of 50 per cent and a cohort of ex-prisoners a rate of 60 per cent it is *possible* that both are drawn from populations whose real reconviction rate is the same: say 55 per cent. If so, the difference would be an illusion due to sampling error. Not even statisticians can rule this out: but they can calculate, from the numbers involved and the magnitude of the difference, how probable it is that a difference of that magnitude could be the result of mere sampling error. If the probability is small — say .05 or less — it is regarded as safe to assume that *some* of the difference is *not* due to sampling error; but only some of it: a point that is usually overlooked.

**7.39** For the appropriate ways of calculating the significance of differences statistical textbooks must be consulted. Even experienced users of such tests, however, sometimes fail to distinguish

a. studies in which there are small differences between small samples. The only inference that can be drawn from them is that larger samples are needed, to see whether the smallness of the differences was due to sampling error, and whether there is in fact no difference or a larger difference between the 'populations' which are being sampled;

b. studies in which the difference between the samples is considerable, but because the samples are small the probability that it is due to sampling error is too great. Again the only useful inference is that larger samples are needed;

c. studies in which the difference between samples is small, but because of their large numbers very probably reflects a real difference between populations. As has been seen, such findings are of little direct help to practitioners who have to decide between one sentence and another, or one regime and another;

d. studies which find differences which are both significant and large.

Even research workers who are aware of these important distinctions may commit the fallacy which converts a finding of 'no significant difference' (as in studies of type (a) or (b)) into a finding of 'no difference'. Only very large samples, or a series of substantial samples yielding similar findings, could justify the assertion that two populations do not differ at all in the relevant respect. Finding of type (c) and (d) on the other hand do indicate that there is a difference between the populations being sampled; but in case (d) it is probably important while in case (c) it is probably not.

**7.40** There are other inferential banana skins. If many comparisons are being drawn between the same samples, and if the level of significance adopted is, say, .05, this means that roughly one in every 20 comparisons will spuriously satisfy the significance test by mere chance. In that situation either a more stringent level of significance must be adopted or — better — all the comparisons should be examined to see whether the apparently significant one is supported or discredited by the comparison of other variables which one would expect to vary in a consistent way.

## Non-methodological pitfalls

**7.41** Even a research project which avoids methodical weaknesses, and manages to collect the relevant information with great thoroughness, may be defeated by human factors:

i. the random allocation of individuals to the chosen measures is liable to interference when the allocators come face to face with an unusual case, for example because it seems too dangerous to assign the case to the measure dictated by lot. Again, once the offender has been allocated, his behaviour may make it necessary to withdraw him from the experiment, as happened to some subjects in the Pooled Borstal Allocation Project (see Williams, 1970).

More serious still are the following possibilities:

ii.  a measure which is intended as a test of a specific regime may be applied half-heartedly or even cynically by staff who may either have been sceptical from the outset or become discouraged by the experience of applying it. A good illustration of this is the test of group counselling described by Kassebaum et al (1971), which for this reason cannot be regarded as discrediting the regime;

iii. staff who have an interest in demonstrating the superiority of some technique may succeed in reducing its apparent failure rate, for example by under-reporting adverse information or by influencing law enforcement agencies to refrain from prosecuting. This is less likely than (i) or (ii), but is said to have occurred in at least one Californian project concerned with the success of non-custodial supervision. At least one project has been suspected of falsifying data (see Tremblay, 1984).

## Conclusions

**7.42** In a famous review of correctional research in 1974 Martinson came to the conclusion that 'nothing works'. It is true that two years later he published a partial retraction, and that reviews of more recent research—for example by McLaren (1992)—have been much more encouraging, at least when comparing regimes. Sentences, however, do not determine regimes, and this chapter must have demonstrated why it is so difficult to advise sentencers with any confidence that in this or that sort of case one of the permissible choices is more likely to 'correct' than the others. Reconviction rates vary significantly with gender, previous convictions, type of offence and—at least in youth—with age; but not much with type of sentence. There are several possible explanations, none of which exclude the others:

(i)   that reconvictions are too insensitive an index of reoffending and thus fail to reveal rather small differences between the correctional efficacy of different types of sentence;

(ii)  that in the case of most offenders whether they reoffend or not depends almost wholly on factors unaffected by the choice of sentence (such as character, associates and economic situation);

(iii) that sometimes the sentence chosen does reduce the offender's law-breaking, but that the frequency with which this happens is roughly equalled by the frequency with which the choice actually increases other offenders' tendency to offend.

Comparisons of regimes instead of sentences (perhaps using arrests or charges instead of reconvictions) might yield less neutral findings. Neither sentences nor regimes, however, are like standard doses of medication. Sentencers are not doctors, and cannot prescribe or even predict what will be done to offenders as a results of their sentences.

# Chapter 8

# General deterrence and education

**8.1** Whatever effect the sentencer expects to have on the future conduct of the offender, he must also have in mind the likely effects of the sentence upon the conduct of other people. The effects which sentencers most often hope for are deterrence and education.

## General deterrence

**8.2** Many legislators as well as sentencers believe that the penalties which courts impose discourage potential imitators. Research in the last two decades or so has shown that this sort of discouragement affects fewer people, or lasts for less time, than used to be assumed; but it has not justified the statement of some critics that 'deterrents never work', which is prompted by dislike of deterrents rather than hard evidence. The dislike is understandable. The use of a deterrent means the deliberate infliction of hardship, if not harm; and if the benefit is invisible and unquantifiable — as it must be when unidentifiable people are deterred from offending — it is not easy to weigh it against the visible penalising of an identified individual.

## A fallacy about capital punishment

**8.3** This is especially so when the penalty is drastic. When the advocates of capital punishment offered deterrence as a justification for it, one result was to associate deterrence with inhumanity in people's minds, so that it was assumed that all deterrents involve the infliction of irremediable harm (which need not be so, fines being an example). The other result was that when the opponents of capital punishment pointed to statistics which showed that the use or non-use of the death penalty was not associated with differences in homicide rates[1] a naive inference was drawn: that the death penalty does not deter anyone. The most that could be inferred was that the death penalty deterred no more potential homicides than did the substitute for the death penalty, which is very long imprisonment. Not only are most homicides committed in a state of mind in which the likely penalty is not a consideration: even when it is considered, it seems, the prospect of being incarcerated for a very long time discourages as many[2] people as the prospect of being executed. This may sound unlikely to people who feel sure that they would choose incarceration rather than execution; but there is no contradiction. It is fallacious to assume that in order to deter an equal number of people deterrents need to be *equally* feared. They need only be *sufficiently* feared. Pedestrians avoid motor cycles as well as buses.

1.  The most striking comparisons were those in the report of the Gowers Commission (1954). Ehrlich's much later (1975) analysis of homicide rates in the USA, which purported to show that each execution saved the nation about 8 homicides, has been the subject of telling criticism, particularly by Hann (1976).
2.  Probably but not necessarily the same people.

## Demonstrating ineffectiveness

**8.4**   The argument that deterrents do not deter because the death penalty does not seem to affect homicide rates is thus based on a misinterpretation of statistics. Nor have other attempts to show that deterrents never work been much more successful. This would in the nature of things be a very difficult thing to demonstrate. To deter someone from doing something is to influence him by a threat or threats so that he refrains from doing it, postpones doing it, does it somewhere else, gets someone else to do it[1], or finds some other way of achieving his desire. To demonstrate by statistics that the use of a deterrent is not having *any* of these results would obviously be very difficult.

1.  As when would-be shoplifters persuade children under the age of criminal liability to do their stealing for them.

## Demonstrating effectiveness

**8.5**   On the other hand, it is occasionally possible to point to demonstrations that some potential offenders are discouraged from some types of offence by the threat of legal consequences. Sometimes these demonstrations are accidental results of abrupt changes in the likelihood of detection. When police forces are put out of action—as they were for seven months in Nazi-occupied Denmark (see Andenaes, 1974)—there are spectacular increases in reports of robberies and thefts, but not of frauds and embezzlements; and on rare occasions on which police forces have been on strike similar increases have been reported.

**8.6**   Conversely, an abrupt increase in what seems to be the likelihood of detection has been shown to have a beneficial effect on the frequency of driving under the influence of alcohol. The introduction of breath-testing[1] in Britain in 1967 was followed by a marked drop in serious road accidents, especially on week-end evenings when most heavy drinking takes place. What was also demonstrated, however, was that the effect of a spectacular technological innovation of this sort may wear off with time. Drivers who liked to drink heavily probably came to realise that their likelihood of being detected and convicted had not increased quite as sharply as they had thought. Either drinking drivers became acceptant of a higher recognised risk, or experience reassured them that the risk was not as great as they had thought (or both processes took place).

1. For a review of the effects of 'Scandinavian-type' legislation in various jurisdictions, including the 'Cheshire blitz' in 1975, see Ross (1982).

**8.7** Yet a quarter of a century later a survey by Riley (1991) was less discouraging. It involved interviews with some 1,700 leisuretime car drivers, and compared those in police districts where breath-tests were very frequent with those in adjoining districts where tests were relatively infrequent. Drivers were not told whether they were in 'high-enforcement' or 'low-enforcement' districts, and their estimates of their chances of being stopped by police while driving 'over the limit' seemed to be much the same whichever sort of district they were in. Nevertheless the attitudes to drink-driving and the self-reported driving behaviour of drivers in high enforcement districts were markedly better than those of drivers in low-enforcement districts. Riley concluded that 'the long-term effects of high levels of police activity are achieved not by increasing drivers' estimates of detection risks but by mobilising concern about being found out by family and friends and about the impact of alcohol on safe driving'. Certainly his drivers in the high-enforcement districts had shown more concern about such aspects of drink-driving; but it is not easy to see how high enforcement could have achieved this without affecting their estimates of risk. It is possible that those estimates were in fact affected to an extent that was not measured by the interviewers' rather crude questions (see Walker, 1992); or that even the high enforcement rates had not been high enough to affect their estimates, and that the difference in attitudes was due to some subtler process of education.

**8.8** An interesting experiment in the USA compared the effect of reminding people of penalties with the effect of appealing to their civic consciences. Schwartz and Orleans (1967) arranged interviews with nearly 400 Illinois taxpayers. These were divided into four matched groups, whose interviews differed in content. The 'sanction' group were asked questions designed to remind them indirectly of the penalties which they might suffer if detected in tax evasion. The 'conscience group' were asked instead questions designed to arouse their civic sense and feelings of duty. The 'placebo group' were asked only neutral questions which avoided both these topics. The fourth group were not interviewed at all, in order to see whether even a placebo interview produced some effect. The interviews took place in the month before the taxpayers were due to submit their statements of income for 1962. Without disclosing information about individuals the Internal Revenue Service compared the returns of the four groups for 1961 and 1962. The reported gross incomes of both the 'sanction' and the 'conscience' groups had increased in 1962, whereas those of the 'placebo' and uninterviewed groups had slightly decreased. Not many taxpayers seemed to have been influenced by the interviews; but whereas a significant number of the 'conscience' group had declared more of their incomes the number of the 'sanctions' group who did so was not significant. The authors also found, by the way, that it was not only declared gross incomes which increased: so did claims for deductible expenses: a finding which is consistent with the assumption that the taxpayers had a low estimate of the likelihood of being detected.

8.9  It seems that deterrence does not occur unless potential offenders believe that the risk they run is high. It might be more precise to say 'without a sufficiently high level of subjective probability', and admit that we have no basis for knowing what is a sufficiently high level. The threshold must vary from one individual to another, and be affected by his or her experience, anxiousness, the situation, the degree of deliberation with which he or she decides to commit or refrain from the offence, and the strength of his or her desire to commit it.

## 'Undeterribility'

8.10  Low subjective risk is not the only antidote to deterrence. Others are lust, greed, anger and the desire for revenge. Some offenders suffer from compulsions, for example to expose themselves, or to steal, which they cannot always resist, even in high-risk situations. Some people, of course, are so moral that they can refrain from temptation even when it would obviously be safe to yield to it. At the other end of the scale, however, is 'undeterribility', a subject which has received too little attention from research workers, although there are abundant examples of it in custodial institutions. Some have pathologically weak self-control, which makes resistance to any sort of temptation unlikely. Addictions can be powerful enough to lead to high-risk behaviour. Mental illnesses can preoccupy or mislead sufferers to an extent that makes the consequences of their actions irrelevant. Some sane men and women have experienced fines and imprisonment so often, and have so little to lose, that the prospect of another sentence is merely dispiriting rather than alarming. Some even welcome short periods of humane incarceration. For some young offenders the risk involved is even an attraction: joy-riders are an example. Finally there are law-breakers who are confident of their ability to avoid detection, or at least conviction: a confidence which is sometimes justified.

## The nature of the penalty

8.11  Important as the subjective probability of detection is, it cannot be inferred — as it sometimes is — that the nature of the consequences of detection is unimportant. There is evidence, from comparisons[1] of felony rates in different US jurisdictions, that the rates are lower where the probable penitentiary sentences are longer. Again, Norwegians and Swedes believe that their compliance with prohibitions on drinking and driving are largely due to the fact that detection usually means a short prison sentence[2]. What is doubtful is whether legislation which merely makes tougher sentences *permissible* has much effect, at least in England, where courts have their own norms (see 23.23). Even when tougher measures are made obligatory, as has happened with disqualification from driving, courts seem very ready to be persuaded to make exceptions (see 23.12ff).

1. Reviewed by Beyleveld (1980) and more recently Lewis (1987).
2. See Andenaes (1974). Although Ross (1982) is sceptical, it is unlikely that the compliance is due to the probability of detection.

## General versus individual deterrence

**8.12** It is at this point, however, that the distinction between general and individual deterrence becomes important. General deterrence is any discouraging effect which threats have upon people who might otherwise commit offences: individual deterrence is the discouraging effect of actually experiencing what is threatened. A sentencer is often confronted with an offender who seems either undeterrible or unlikely to break the law again: yet he may feel obliged to consider the need for general deterrence. In practice this usually means that he imposes the 'tariff' penalty for fear that if he is more lenient the number of people who commit similar offences will increase. When he reasons thus he is assuming that the news of his sentence will reach a substantial number of potential but deterrible offenders. In fact, the chances that the case will be reported by the national news media are very small, unless it involves a spectacular crime or a well-known person. It has a somewhat better chance of being reported by local newspapers; yet even so it is not the sentence which makes an impression, but the nature of the offence and the identification of the offender by those who know him (Walker and Marsh, 1984).

## Publicised leniency

**8.13** The important exception is a choice of sentence which strikes the news media as extremely lenient. When a woman is put on probation for the manslaughter of a husband or lover, or when a rapist is merely fined, considerable publicity is almost inevitable. But whether cases of this kind weaken any general deterrent effect is doubtful. Public criticism of the sentence—whether ill-informed or not—may well have the effect of emphasising that the usual penalty is a substantial prison sentence.

**8.14** What the sentencer must seriously consider is whether he is sentencing an offender with criminal acquaintances who will take note of any leniency. Some offenders belong to social networks along which the news of their sentences travels with much more speed and precision than through the perusal of the *Criminal Statistics, England and Wales*. If a sentencer takes this into account he has to face a moral question. Is he discriminating unfairly if, having evidence that the offender belongs to a criminal network, he rejects mitigating considerations which he would otherwise take into account? The moral issues raised by a policy of general deterrence are discussed in 8.20ff.

## Exemplary severity

**8.15** Until recently sentencers would occasionally react to increases in the frequency of a disturbing type of offence by passing a sentence whose severity was intended to 'make an example' of the offender, and thus serve as a particularly powerful deterrent. The evidence which supports such hopes is anecdotal and weak. Often cited is the sentencing of nine young men to 4 years' imprisonment for their involvement in attacks on coloured people in the Notting Hill district of London in 1958. The sentences were exceptionally long when it is recognised that all but one of the youths were 'of good character', and not only were meant as exemplary but were claimed to have put an end to racial violence in the area, at least for some time. This interpretation is far from reliable. The original attacks seem to have been prompted by an inflammatory racialist broadsheet, and may have died down because a document of that kind goes out of circulation and has only a temporary effect. There was also increased police vigilance. The nine youths sentenced may have been the ring-leaders whose removal would thus account for the diminution of violence. Finally, racial violence in the area did not cease completely after the sentences.

**8.16** Nevertheless, the Notting Hill sentences are still cited, nearly half a century later, in support of exemplary sentencing. A sounder anecdote, combined this time with a genuine attempt at measurement, was provided in 1973, when a Birmingham youth was sentenced to 20 years' detention for a particularly brutal mugging. Because of its exceptional severity the sentence was well publicised in the local as well as the national press. Yet when the week-by-week frequencies of muggings in Birmingham, Liverpool and Manchester were studied by Baxter and Nuttall (1975) no decrease could be found in the weeks following the sentence. This does not *prove* that exemplary sentencing is ineffective. The most that can be said is that it is hard to find a properly documented instance of its effectiveness. However that may be, exemplary sentencing has now been declared improper. CJA 91 (s 2 (2) (a)) requires custodial sentences to be 'commensurate with the seriousness of the offence' : the only exceptions are certain violent or sexual offences offences (see 22.2 ). In *Cunningham* (1993) 14 Cr App Rep (S) 444 at 448 Lane LCJ made it clear that what that section does prohibit is 'adding any extra length to the sentence … simply to make a special example of the defendant'. What he did not rule out is the imposition of a sentence which is strictly commensurate and deliberately disregards any mitigating features of the case. (For *Cunningham's* other implications see 4.11.)

**The state of knowledge**

**8.17** It is not possible in a single chapter to review the enormous literature of research into the effectiveness of deterrents[1]. But some general comments can be made. Naive claims that deterrent policies are highly effective—or totally ineffective—have been replaced by the less exciting realisation that *some* people can be deterred in *some* situations from *some* types of conduct by *some* degree of likelihood that they will be penalised in *some* ways; but that we do not yet know enough to enable us to be very specific about the people, the situations, the conduct, or the likelihood or nature of the penalties. Equally important is the lack of knowledge about methods of manipulating people's impressions of the probability or severity of penal consequences. We can be fairly sure that they are not altered by annual statistics about clear-up rates or the use of fines or custodial sentences. Apparently they can be altered by publicity about technical improvements in methods of detection, such as breathalysers; but this effect seems to weaken with time. In any case, it would be useful if we could be more specific about the sort of people whose impressions both need to be and can be manipulated. They do not include people who refrain from the conduct in question for reasons other than the expected consequences of detection: for example, for moral reasons. Nor do they include the 'undeterribles'. It is a third group, which might be called the 'marginally deterrible', whose inclination for the conduct can be affected by such considerations.

1. For the most thorough review of research published up to the end of the 1970s see Beyleveld (1980), who repeatedly draws attention to defects of method or interpretation.

## The role of the news media

**8.18** What is fairly clear is that the news media's choice of what to report about clear-up rates and sentences is not designed to further a policy of general deterrence; and that it is only occasionally possible to make deliberate use of newspapers, television or radio for this purpose, usually by paying for the publicity. An example is the usual Christmastide campaign to discourage drunk driving. This fact, coupled with the vagueness of our knowledge about the operation of deterrents, should dissuade both legislators and sentencers from being very optimistic about this function of penalties.

## Moral aspects

**8.19** Practical considerations apart, deterrence is sometimes attacked on moral grounds, although these too need a critical scrutiny. The moral case would be unanswerable if it were certain, or highly likely, that what are intended as deterrents do not in fact deter. They would then be nothing but the deliberate infliction of suffering or inconvenience for an end which cannot be achieved. We have seen, however, that the present state of knowledge does not support so categorical an assertion.

**8.20** Consequently, moral objections must take a more sophisticated form[1]. It is possible to concede that deterrents are effective sometimes or quite often, but to argue that they involve sacrificing the interests of the person penalised to the interests of others[2]. It is not a complete answer to point out that the penalised offender himself sometimes benefits from being deterred. Too often the offender is undeterrible, and the only justification for the penalty is either the deterrence of others or the plea that he deserves the suffering . Those who accept desert as a justification for punishment are thus able to claim that they are not merely using the offender as a means of frightening others, but are according him the dignity of being treated as a responsible person[3]. For those however, who do not regard just deserts as a good or sufficient reason for inflicting suffering, it is harder to be sure that the penalty is anything but the use of the offender as an exhibit *in terrorem*. If the penalty is meant to have beneficial effects on character — as some people claim for community service — or if it is accompanied by treatment of a disorder (as a hospital order is), consciences may be salved. But it is difficult to claim that sentences of imprisonment confer such benefits; and fines can only be deterrents or retributive punishments.

1. It is necessary to mention, if not to take seriously, the argument that deterrents are used only to maintain the political status quo. Apart from the naive implication that the status quo is always worse than the status post, it is obviously untrue that political innovators never use deterrents. New regimes often enforce changes by penalties as harsh as their predecessors. Nor are deterrents always instruments of the faction in power: they are used by terrorists too.
2. An argument credited to Kant, although exactly what he meant, or what he objected to, is the subject of a discussion which is hardly relevant here. See, for example, Walker (1991). In any case, deterrents are not the only kind of penalties which can be criticised for doing this: precautionary detention is open to the same objection: see 22.29ff.
3. This is probably something like what Kant meant.

## Two kinds of deterrents

**8.21**  The moral objectors to deterrents should also however acknowledge the important distinction between those which do and those which do not inflict serious and lasting harm. In the former category are capital punishment and physical mutilation. In the latter are fines, which inflict temporary inconvenience, or at most deprivation, but hardly ever lasting harm. There are much stronger moral objections to the infliction of lasting harm than to the imposition of a temporary deprivation, although discussions of the morality of deterrents seldom make the distinction. This escapes notice because it is usually imprisonment which is assumed to be the deterrent, and because it is assumed that it does serious and lasting harm. In fact, as chapter 11 shows, the harm that it does is probably confined to long sentences, and even then has been exaggerated.

## Educative effects

**8.22**  Independent of beliefs about deterrent efficacy are theories about the educative function of sentences: that is, the hypothesis that a sentence of a certain kind can affect people's 'tolerance' or 'moral evaluation' of the offence for which the offender is sentenced.

**8.23**  These theories — which take different forms — must be distinguished from the claim that the mere prohibition of this or that kind of conduct, by means of the criminal law, influences moral attitudes. There is experimental evidence which strongly suggests that this is so, at least in the case of some types of conduct and some types of people[1]. For sentencers, however, who have to take the criminal law as it stands, the question is not whether moral attitudes are influenced by the fact that, say, failing to use a seat-belt is an offence: it is whether such attitudes are influenced by the sentence, or, more precisely, what people believe the usual sentence to be. A subsidiary, but important, question is whether attitudes are altered by publicised sentences which are markedly more lenient or severe than the norm.

1. Berkowitz and Walker (1967) found that this seemed to be so for public drunkenness, lending a car to someone without making sure that he has a licence, borrowing money without saying that it is for betting, failing to stop a suicide attempt, at least if the subject is 'traditional, conventional, and socially responsible'. Walker and Marsh (1984) found that subjects said that their disapproval of not wearing a seat-belt would increase when this became an offence. It is not easy to test such effects in the case of more serious types of conduct because most subjects express such strong condemnation of them under most experimental conditions.

## The Sargeant effect

**8.24** The belief that the penalty performs a symbolic (or 'expressive') function of this kind has been popular for nearly two centuries, not only among English lawyers but also among sociologists of a Durkheimian outlook[1]. More recently it has been seriously discussed by philosophers of punishment[2]. For English sentencers, however, the version which is most important must be that of the CA in *Sargeant* ((1974) 60 Cr App Rep 74):

> '... There is however another aspect of retribution[3] ... it is that society, through the courts, must show its abhorrence of particular types of crime ... The courts do not have to reflect public opinion. On the other hand the courts must not disregard it. Perhaps the main duty of the court is to lead public opinion.'

The clear implication is that sentences should—at least when likely to be publicised—be of such a kind as to 'lead' public opinion; that is, presumably, to increase public disapproval of the offence in question.

1. For a short history of the idea see Walker (1981).
2. For example, Moberly (1968), Feinberg (1970) and Gross (1979).
3. It is not really an aspect of retribution because it does not imply that the sentence ought actually to be carried out.

**8.25** Walker and Marsh (1984) experimented in an effort to detect the 'Sargeant effect' on adults' disapproval of five kinds of offence[1]. To maximise realism respondents were shown faked newspaper cuttings (see Figure 8A) which described the incidents. Some sub-samples were told that the offender had been given a prison sentence of six months; some that he had been put on probation; some that 'people like yourself' disapproved strongly of the offence; some that they disapproved a little; some that the judge took a serious view of the offence; some that he did not. They were then asked to show, on a 7-point scale, how much they themselves disapproved. The results did not provide any support for the belief that the disapproval levels of substantial numbers of adults were raised or lowered by information about the sentence, or about the judges' views. Respondents' disapproval levels were overwhelmingly determined by their own assessment of what they read.

1. The offences had to be of moderate or minor seriousness because pilot experiments in which more serious offences—such as a violent mugging—were described showed that respondents' levels of disapproval were so high that no such effect could be detected by the experimental method used.

**FIGURE 8A: The 'Newspaper Cuttings'**

## Ex-Boxer breaks Challenger's Jaw

A broken jaw was the result of a challenge to a fight outside a North town public house. But the man who challenged Robert Brown (30) did not know that he had been a welterweight boxer.

Brown pleaded guilty to causing actual bodily harm outside the Rose and Crown. He told the court he thought the other man knew he was a boxer.

## Computer Fraud Exposed

A bank employee who cheated thousands of customers by using his computer skills was brought to book in court yesterday. Sidney Smith (30) pleaded guilty to stealing more than £7,000 by instructing the computer to deduct any odd pence from cheques paid into customers' accounts and pay them into his own account. On his behalf counsel pointed out that his system ensured that no single person suffered serious loss.

## The Case of the Hungry Husband

Gossiping with her neighbours all day ended in violence for a Scottish house wife in Westville when her husband came home to find the house dirty and no meal ready for him.

'She had all day to get me a meal ready and clean the place up a bit' said Bertram Wilson (24), who pleaded guilty to assaulting his wife. 'It wasn't the first time, and I just lashed out'. Mrs Wilson sustained a cut lip, requiring a stitch.

## TELEPHONE VANDAL CAUGHT

A man who smashed up telephone kiosks when he could not get his calls through was identified by a traffic warden who was waiting to make her own call from a box. Pleading guilty to criminal damage, Robert Jenkins (20) said he lost his temper when his girlfriend's office refused to put him through to her.

## The Booby-Trapped Greenhouse

ARTHUR Jackson suffered so many thefts of plants and tools from his greenhouse that he bobby-trapped it, injuring a teenage thief.

Pleading guilty too causing actual bodily harm, Jackson (31) said that after putting up with repeated thefts from his greenhouse over a period of years he fixed up a piece of timber so that it would fall on anyone who opened the door without inserting a peg. Two nights later he heard a crash and found a boy lying in the greenhouse with a cut in his head that required three stitches. the boy admitted several thefts from the greenhouse.

**8.26** It is arguable that one should not expect the Sargeant effect to manifest itself as a result of a single newspaper report; and that the experiment does not refute the belief that a series of reports of similar cases in which offenders were severely or leniently sentenced would have this effect. Perhaps so: but the news media are not so repetitive in their choice of stories for publication. Nor is it usually the nature of the sentence which makes news: more often it is the unusual circumstances of the offence or the identity of a well-known defendant. Consequently the news media do not report a series of similar sentences for similar offences. If the Sargeant effect is a genuine possibility it is a possibility that is most unlikely to be realised.

**8.27** What Moberly (1968) believed was that sentences can have an educative effect on the sentencer and the person sentenced, reinforcing the former's disapproval and impressing society's disapproval on the latter. Allison Morris et al (1980) believed that it has this effect on juvenile offenders. These beliefs are not open to doubts as to whether the message reaches the addressee: and it is certainly possible that some offenders are influenced in this way. There is no empirical evidence on the point; but it seems likely that a necessary condition of being so influenced would be acceptance of the justice of the sentence. Even an offender who does accept it as just when it is passed is likely to become less acceptant in the course of his time in prison, or even in the course of paying off a substantial fine by instalments. As for the possibility that sentencers reinforce their own or each others' disapproval, not everyone would regard this as desirable.

### Possibilities of 'backlash'

**8.28** The other possibility is the opposite of a Sargeant effect: that is, that a sentence which seems too severe or too lenient will affect people's opinions of sentencers in an adverse way. Since exceptional sentences are sometimes the reason why the news media choose to publicise a case—as when a judge merely fined a man £2,000 for raping a hitch-hiker—this is to that extent more likely to happen than the Sargeant effect. It was very marked in the Walker-Hough experiment, especially when respondents regarded the sentence as too lenient.

**8.29** Again, the message conveyed by a sentence may mean different things to different people. The suspended sentence is an example. As was seen in 6.24, some of the Walker-Marsh respondents regarded it as one of the 'tougher' sorts of sentence, possibly appreciating that it is used to signify judicial disapproval of the offence, possibly aware that it would result in actual imprisonment if the offender were reconvicted. On the other hand the place most frequently assigned to it was the lowest of all. For a very substantial percentage of the public it signifies leniency, whatever the sentencer means to convey.

### 'Anti-impunity'

**8.30** The Sargeant effect, however, is not the only possible educative function. Gross (1979) offered what he called an 'anti-impunity' version of deterrence as a justification for penalising offenders; and although he has since offered a somewhat different view of the function of sentences (1992) his original view is still very plausible:

'According to this theory, punishment for violating the rules of conduct laid down by the law is necessary if the law is to remain a sufficiently strong influence to keep the community on the whole law-abiding ... Without punishment ... the law becomes merely a guide and an exhortation to right conduct ... Only saints and martyrs could be constantly law-abiding in a community that had no system of criminal liability ... The threats of the criminal law are necessary, then, only as part of a system of liability ensuring that those who commit crimes do not get away with them. The threats are not laid down to deter those tempted to break the rules but rather to maintain the rules as a set of standards that compel allegiance in spite of violations ...'

Although the claim would be hard to test, it seems very likely that penalties do perform this function: that is, that they maintain allegiance for the rules of the criminal law by demonstrating that they are not infringed with impunity. This is a comforting thought for sentencers who are disillusioned about the efficacy of deterrence. It implies that the important audience so far as sentencing is concerned consists not so much of the likely offenders as of the people whose marginal deterribility or moral restraint, as the case may be, needs reinforcement now and again.

**8.31** It seems unnecessary, however, to claim that 'the threats are not laid down to deter', when the history of penal legislation clearly says otherwise. It is enough to argue that the anti-impunity effect is a *function* of penalties: that is, an effect which they have whether or not it is or was intended. What Gross also believed, however, was that it is this function which is the only sound justification for penalising offenders. One important consequence of such symbolic[1] theories should be emphasised here. This is that the justifying function of penalties would be achieved by merely pronouncing sentence and leading the intended audience to believe that it was carried out. If so, the infliction of harm which is involved in a prison sentence or a fine would not be justified, except to the extent that it is needed to maintain the belief that sentences are in fact carried out. That would justify the actual carrying out of sentences in only a minority of cases, chiefly those which received—or could be given—publicity. We must therefore distinguish between symbolic theories which consist merely of a claim that sentences convey important messages to the public, and those which also claim that this is the only, or the main, moral justification for attaching penalties to law breaking. It is possible to believe in the anti-impunity effect (though hardly in the Sargeant effect) while holding other views about what justifies sentencing, as we shall see in the next chapter.

1. A symbolic theory is one which regards the message conveyed by the sentence, rather than its actual consequences for the offender, as constituting the justification for the sentence. For a discussion of such theories see the next chapter.

# Chapter 9

# Sentencers' aims

**9.1**  A sentencer may have studied the reports about the offender, be aware of all the available background information which seems relevant, be conversant with the findings of research into the corrective, deterrent or educative effectiveness of different sentences, and yet be uncertain about a crucial aspect of his problem: the aim which should govern his choice. This is understandable, because most sentencing decisions are determined by what the sentencer believes to be expected of him by his colleagues, whether these are magistrates or judges, and whether he calls their expectations 'the tariff', 'sentencing policy' or whatever.

**9.2**  Nor is he given much official guidance which tells him what his aim should be. Statutes are usually silent about the objectives of the measures which they permit, with a few rather vague exceptions. An absolute or conditional discharge is to be used when it seems 'inexpedient to inflict punishment': but expediency is undefined. Longer than normal sentences of imprisonment may be used to protect the public from violent or sexual offenders. Restricted hospital orders may be used when it is 'necessary to protect the public from serious harm' by a mentally disordered offender. By contrast, no statute explains the aim of an ordinary prison sentence, community service order or fine.

**9.3**  The silence of the statutes is deliberate. Legislators who want Parliament's assent to a new type of sentence are well advised not to specify its objective, but instead to leave members free to interpret it according to their individual philosophies. Nothing divides a committee like a discussion of the aims of punishment, as the ill-fated Royal Commission[1] discovered in the 1960s. A new measure owes its acceptance to the variety of aims which can be read into it. In the case of community service, for example, these were reparation, retribution, individual deterrence, correction through work and the experience of service to others, each of which appealed to different groups of proposers, legislators, sentencers and probation officers.

1. The Royal Commission on the Penal System, set up in 1964. Two years later it asked to be dissolved without producing a report.

**9.4**  Even professional sentencers—whether judges, recorders or stipendiary magistrates—seldom discuss, either officially or unofficially, the rationale of what they are doing. This does not mean that they regard sentencing as a task for an automaton. On the contrary they sometimes call it an 'art', meaning by that a skill which cannot be taught but has to be acquired by experience. Even the most tariff-minded sentencer decides on occasion that the case calls for a measure which takes account of the offender's peculiar needs or defects. When Thomas' important book, *Principles of Sentencing* (1970), called this the 'primary decision' to 'individualise' the sentence, judges were quick to acknowledge that this was indeed an important part of their rationale. But it was an academic lawyer who put it into words.

**9.5**  Even when they individualise, however, sentencers do not usually reflect or argue about their aims or the situations in which those aims are relevant. That the offender deserves punishment, or should be 'treated', or incapacitated from doing further harm, or used as an example to deter others, is usually taken for granted, or agreed in a silent consensus. This is as true of Continental as of English courts. The difference is that whereas most French, German, Dutch or Scandinavian judges have undergone a training in which the fundamental principles of sentencing have been a subject of study, their English counterparts have not. Even those who, in their early days, took academic courses in law have not always included jurisprudence among their subjects; and even if they did by no means all jurisprudence courses pay attention to theories of punishment. This omission is sometimes defended by arguing that English sentencing is pragmatic[1]: a skill which is learned by following one's more experienced colleagues, using one's own common sense and paying attention to the Court of Appeal. The CA itself occasionally lays down principles of a limited sort (usually applying them to this or that category of case), and has not attempted to outline a coherent philosophy of sentencing. If it could be asked to do so it would probably reply that this would result in too rigid an approach, which would fail to keep in pace with developments in the system and in public opinion: an argument which has some force, even if it is responsible for the serious problems which are faced at the end of this chapter.

1.  See for example Lord Devlin's *The Judge* (1979).

**9.6**  Consequently the sentencing philosophy of English courts is best described as 'eclectic'. It selects its justifications as the situation seems to dictate. The full implications of this can be appreciated only with some knowledge of the alternatives from which the selection is made. What can be said at this stage, however, is that there are two kinds of eclectic: the reflective and the emotional. Reflective eclecticism is defensible. The emotional kind is not: it alternates between retributive and reductive justifications for sentences according to the feelings which each case arouses. If the offender seems very culpable the sentencer chooses what seems to be deserved. If not, he or she chooses what seems most likely to reduce the likelihood of recidivism. As we shall see later in this chapter, however, a reasoned eclecticism is possible.

## A general justifying aim?

**9.7** It is necessary to begin with the nature of the justification for having a system of official and compulsory penalties: what Hart (1959) called 'the general justifying aim'. Why is a general justification needed? Because the infliction of something to which a person objects is regarded, at least in societies which value individuals' freedom, as morally wrong unless it can be morally defended. In some people's eyes penalising offenders can be justified by arguing that they deserve a penalty for the very reason that they have offended: this is the retributive view[1]. For others the justification is that the penalty will reduce the future incidence of such offences, whether by preventing or correcting the offender or by discouraging or educating other potential offenders: this is the reductive[2] justification. Both have important ramifications.

1.  Nowadays often called 'the philosophy of just deserts', a phrase popularised in the USA.
2.  'Reductive' is more precise than 'utilitarian' or 'instrumental'. Not all utilitarians hold that 'the greatest good of the greatest number' is achieved by reducing crime; and an instrumentalist does not necessarily hope for a *reduction* of crime: he might want to encourage or provoke it for political reasons. For a modern, if somewhat utopian, application of utilitarianism to criminal justice see Lacey (1987).

## The retributive justification

**9.8** The retributive principle can be applied in several different ways. In its positive form it asserts that we should reward people for some sorts of behaviour: for example, for self-sacrifice in the interest of others. This is not usually considered to be within the scope of the sentencing system, although occasionally—as we saw in chapter 4—sentencers are lenient with offenders who have shown bravery or altruism. More relevant for sentencers are three other retributive principles. The first is that an offender deserves punishment for his offence. Some sentencers would add 'unless the penalty would make him more likely to repeat it, or do serious harm to others—for example his family': but that is a compromise with reductivism which is possible only if retribution is regarded as a mere *right*: for traditional retributivists it is a *duty*.

## Negative retribution

**9.9** On the other hand, there are other retributive principles which even reductivists usually accept. One is that penalties (some would add 'or compulsory measures of other kinds, such as commitments to hospital') should not be applied to anyone who is not guilty of an offence. This is sometimes called 'retribution in distribution' or 'negative retribution'. It is not an automatic corollary either of reductivism or of retributivism. A retributivist who asserts that all offences should be punished may also believe that some things that are not offences—such as wicked thoughts—should be punished. A fanatical reductivist might believe that some people who are merely potential offenders would be 'all the better for a hanging'; or that whenever a serious crime is known to have been committed someone, even if innocent, should be penalised in order to convince potential offenders that they could not commit such a crime with impunity. Nevertheless, so prevalent is the retributive outlook that very few retributivists or reductivists would want to breach the negative principle. More will be said about it later.

**9.10**  The third retributive principle is that the severity of a penalty should not exceed a limit related to the offence[1], even if that would help to reduce crime. The rapist should not go to prison for more than X years, however probable it seems that he will rape again when he is released. It is this principle which troubles people when special sentences for dangerous offenders are in question: see 22.29ff. It is important to realise that for the traditional retributivist this principle is usually redundant: for his view is not that it is *permissible* to penalise the offender up to the limit, but that it is a *duty* to so do (unless of course there are mitigating moral considerations which make the offender less culpable and thus reduce the limit). It is the reductivist who has to consider whether to accept this principle or not. What most reductivists do is to accept it with exceptions, the most common exception being the offender who has done great harm and is regarded as likely to repeat it.

1.  More precisely, either to its seriousness or to the offender's culpability: both views are held.

**9.11**  The retributivist who believes in a duty to punish offenders has to solve one or two problems. One is the severity of the penalty. What should determine this? In primitive systems, where reparation is in people's minds, it is the seriousness of the harm which has actually been done. If a spear misses, no matter: if it kills, there is a death to be paid for. To the more sophisticated retributivist what matters is the harm which the offender intended to do. If he intended none, he is either completely excused or blamed for mere negligence or recklessness. If he intended it, he is equally guilty, hit or miss: but if he was provoked, or was defending himself against an attack, or was unhinged, his guilt is lessened. Yet once this step has been taken, it opens the door to all the difficulties of estimating the extent to which he is to blame.

## Commensurability

**9.12**  However that may be, the statute now expressly requires that a custodial sentence be 'commensurate with the seriousness of the offence' (s 2 CJA 91); and similarly—but using a different word—the amount of a fine must 'reflect the seriousness of the offence' (s 18 CJA 91). (There is no such statutory requirement for other sentences, such as community service, perhaps because they are regarded as non-retributive). It does not follow, of course, that there is a precise tariff or 'price list' for each type of offence. Not only does the 'seriousness' of rapes, robberies and so forth vary, but as was seen in chapter 4 sentences are adjusted to take into account factors which increase or decrease the offender's culpability or which would mean that he or she would suffer more than most from the usual penalty (what Bentham called 'sensibility', and we might call 'sensitivity'). So for most offences the statutes merely set maxima. Within these maxima the Court of Appeal's guidelines for the CC specify ranges (eg 3-5 years' custody), and even these are not binding in special cases. The Magistrates' Association's *Sentencing Guidelines* merely suggest 'entry points' (eg 'custody', 'fine', 'community penalty'), leaving benches to decide in particular cases whether they are appropriate and if so what the quantum should be.

## Proportionality

**9.13**  Problems are created, however, by 'proportionalists' who want statutes to be more specific about the nature and severity of penalties. For Hegel—and more recently Cross (1975)—proportionality meant no more than that greatly culpable offenders should be punished more severely than the less culpable. Modern proportionalists want more: a public price list. In their favour it might be said that this would sharpen any deterrent effect, since the public is vague about penalties. It might also teach people to be more censorious of some offences, although—as we saw in 8.22ff—such evidence as there is does not encourage this hope.

**9.14**  But price lists raise awkward questions. They envisage a 'typical' or 'standard' murder, rape, robbery and so forth; or, more realistically, subdivisions such as 'domestic murders', 'date-rapes', 'armed robberies'. It may be clear which is more serious than another: but not by how much the penalties should differ. Again, some murders, such as mercy-killings, seem less serious than some rapes (one reason why the fixed penalty for murder is objectionable). The CA's 'ranges' therefore overlap. Genuinely retributive price lists, designed to administer exactly 'just deserts', would require very substantial discounts and surcharges to take account of different degrees of culpability. If these discounts and surcharges were declared in the shop-window shoppers would not be impressed by criminal justice, and might even be encouraged to commit some kinds of offence. Proportionalists who want price-lists must make up their minds whether their aim is 'just deserts' or the education of the public. For a fuller discussion see Walker (1993).

## Explaining desert

**9.15**  Retributivists have to face another difficult question. Why *must* offending be penalised? The 'reducer' has little difficulty in answering this: the hope of reducing the frequency of future offences has so obvious a point that it can be questioned only by arguing that in fact penalties never or seldom fulfil this hope. The 'punisher' however, is in a more awkward position, for he is expected to explain what is meant by 'deserving' a penalty irrespective of its future utility. He must explain, that is, why the infliction of hardship or inconvenience on an offender is the morally right response to his offence even when it can lead to no benefit. This seems to be difficult for punishers. It is not too difficult to explain why so many people *feel* that a penalty is an appropriate response. This is the way they were brought up, and this is one of the assumptions of their culture. That, however, is an answer to another sort of question, a question for social psychologists. What punishers must also provide is a *justifying* explanation, which would help people from a non-retributive culture to see why there is something right about the transaction known as punishing, irrespective of any of its benefits.

**9.16** Most attempts to do this are suspect because they could be true only in a metaphorical sense. For example
i. 'the penalty "annuls" the offence: i e achieves a state of affairs in which it is as if the offence had not been committed.' Note that it is necessary to say 'as if'. It is sometimes literally possible to undo the harm done by an offence, and sometimes possible to approximate this by making the offender pay compensation: but that is reparation, not retribution, and it cannot usually undo all the harm. One cannot be unmurdered or unraped.
or
ii. by undergoing the penalty the offender 'pays a debt' to society. For a modern version see Burgh (1987). In fact there is no literal debt to pay: only a fiction that society is owed compensation for the breach of its rules or its peace.
It is arguable that these metaphorical justifications are not merely metaphors; and that what they describe is what retributive punishment symbolises for those members of society who know of and are distressed by the offence. As we shall see, however, this inadvertently transforms a retributive justification into an expressive one.

**9.17** The punisher, however, is not obliged to resort to metaphors. For example, he can claim that
iii. offenders must be penalised because they have gained an unfair advantage over their law-abiding fellow citizens, and fairness requires that they be disadvantaged (see, for example, Honderich, 1969). This is much less metaphorical than (i) or (ii); but it raises an awkward question. Suppose that someone commits or attempts an offence from which, as it turns out, he derives no advantage. Does he deserve a penalty? Apparently not, if this explanation is to be taken at its face value. Yet this seems to conflict with the punisher's feeling that a person's deserts depend on what he intended rather than what he achieved.
iv. supernatural displeasure will be averted by penalising the guilty. This belief is attributed to Kant by Cottingham (1979) on the strength of a passage in which Kant talks of '*blutschuld*' (blood-guilt). Whether Kant meant this or not, it is an incomplete explanation because it does not tell us why a supernatural being's displeasure at the commission of an offence would be averted by penalising the offender. If this cannot be explained in human language, the implication is that the supernatural being's reasoning is not understandable, and that instead of a metaphor we must accept inscrutability. In fact Kant's explanation was not superstitious but metaphysical:

v.  human beings are rational and autonomous (in his noumenal world anyway). They must be treated as ends in themselves, not means to ends. Penalties which deter or eliminate treat them as means. Treating them as ends means punishing them as they deserve.

**9.18**  There have been attempts at non-metaphorical, non-metaphysical and non-superstitious explanations. For example

vi.  offenders must be penalised if they commit offences for which the rules to which they are subject prescribe penalties. The justification is in the rule which says that doing this or that must be penalised. This view has the advantage of also providing a psychological explanation for the feeling which some people have that penalising offenders is right. Man is a rule-making, rule-following animal; and if a code of rules both prohibits some kind of action and prescribes a penalty for it, then not to penalise it seems to add to the infringement. This holds whether the code in question consists of the criminal law, or merely of the rules of some organisation, such as a profession. For a fuller discussion of this explanation see Walker (1991).

**9.19**  Two points about it, however, are important. One is that by no means all penalties are *prescribed* by codes. In many cases they are simply *permitted*, so that the responsible authority has discretion as to the need for and the severity of the penalty. In the English penal code it is only the life sentence and a few kinds of disqualification which are mandatory, and those only in certain circumstances: otherwise penalties are discretionary. If the authority entrusted with the function of penalising imposes a penalty when it is not obliged to do so, it is questionable whether its justification for doing so can be retributive. If a sentencer felt obliged to penalise in order to comply with some rule which is not embodied in the law—an agreed tariff, for example, or a private code of his own—he might be said to be acting retributively: but only if he feels that it obliges him to punish. Otherwise his justification must be of one of the non-retributive kinds: for example, the need to incapacitate, correct or deter.

**9.20**  The other point is that it does not matter *why* the rules prescribe a penalty. The reason may be so old as to be unascertainable; or it may be a recent demand for a deterrent. What makes the act of penalising retributive is the fact that it is done because the rule—or the tariff—requires it to be done. This means that even if the reason for including a prescribed penalty in a code of rules was non-retributive, a sentencer is acting retributively when imposing the penalty if he does so in order to obey the rule.

**9.21**  This explanation of desert is not, and is not meant to be, inspiring. It does not have the rhetorical appeal of a debt to society, or the annulment of wrong-doing. According to it the essence of retribution is nothing more than obedience to a rule requiring punishment: a very formal explanation, whose only attractions are its non-reliance on metaphor and its consistency with what we know about the strength of people's need for rules and rule-following. Believers in just deserts may find it disappointing because it lacks the dignity of some more metaphorical explanations. But it may well be that there is no more—and no less—to the retributive justification than this.

**9.22** Can the same be said about negative retribution, the principle that innocent people should not be punished? Is it as hard to justify as the duty to punish the guilty? Probably not. Even a reductive penaliser, who believes not in a duty to punish but in penalties for the sake of future benefits, can argue that a state of affairs in which innocent people could suddenly find themselves being subjected to penalties would be intolerable. It might well increase the efficacy of general deterrents if someone were penalised every time a robbery is committed; but it would create a large group of people with a grievance because they had been sentenced for robberies which they had not committed. What is more, it would soon become known that the 100 per cent clear-up rate for robbery was spurious, so that the policy would lose its point, and result only in grievances.

**9.23** It thus seems that a sound utilitarian case can be made out in favour of the negative principle. A utilitarian case, however, allows exceptions to be made whenever these are likely to conduce to 'the greatest good of the greatest number'. The most important example is a compulsory measure taken to prevent a person from doing serious harm at a stage before he has actually done any. Most jurisdictions have statutes which allow this in the case of mentally disordered persons whose words or actions suggest that they will harm other people or themselves. If the negative principle is based on utilitarian considerations there is nothing wrong with such precautions (so long as the subject of them is adequately safeguarded against malicious or excessive detention). It is those for whom the principle rests on a moral foundation who can, and do, object to precautionary detention, however scrupulously managed. The moral foundation, however, is less easy to outline than the utilitarian. It is discussed in 22.29ff.

### Vicarious punishment

**9.24** The most awkward feature of the negative principle of retribution, however, is the relevance of the effects of a sentence on innocent people. There may be good reason—retributive or non-retributive—for sentencing the offender to prison for a substantial time; but this may mean hardship, material or emotional, for his or her family. (Occasionally it means that he or she cannot be ordered to compensate the victim: but more of this in 9.36ff). Some sentencers protect themselves from this disturbing consideration by assuming that they are meant to consider only the offence and the offender. Yet the same assumption would rule out prison sentences whose length is justified only by the intention of protecting hypothetical future victims.

### Privatising punishment

**9.25** Finally, the moral objections to privatising prisons (see 13.5) seem to come from retributivists. Non-retributivists are understandably concerned about private prisons' security, humanity and efficiency; but these can be the subject of inspections and other precautions. In England criminal courts have for many years been committing a few mentally disordered offenders to private hospitals without raising moral hackles; but that was for *treatment*. There seems to be something about retribution which makes privatisation objectionable. For Schichor (1995) it is making a profit out of incarceration that is 'morally questionable'. Oddly, he does not find accepting a salaried post in a state prison morally questionable, but does not say why. Possibly he would not object to contracts with non-profit-making agencies, such as NACRO. The American Bar Association, however would object: 'incarceration is an inherent function of the government, which should not abdicate this responsibility' (1986). 'Abdication' is obviously a rhetorical exaggeration: it is delegation that is the issue. What is being delegated is not the decision that a person should be punished in a specified way—that remains the function of unprivatised courts — but the carrying out of that decision. All sentencing delegates this. Does it matter whether the task is delegated to government employees or to a contractor's staff ? Only if there is something mysteriously improper about a contractual relationship.

## The reductive justification

**9.26** The problems which the reductive sentencer has to face are different. His general justifying aim is not to inflict deserved punishment for a past act but to do something that will reduce the future frequency of such acts. Like the retributive sentencer he is subject to limitations. As a sentencer he can deal only with the offender. He cannot reform society, abolish unemployment or remove temptations. He can deal only with an offender who has been found guilty, only for the offence of which he has been found guilty (or had TIC), and only by means of a sentence whose severity does not exceed limits which are imposed on him by the retributive tradition.

**9.27** Within these boundaries the 'reducer' has some freedom of choice in pursuit of his general reductive aim. He may intend—although 'hope' would be more realistic—that his sentence will do one or more of the following things:
   a.   deter the offender himself, by means of the experience of a penalty, from committing similar offences, or—if the sentencer is very optimistic— from infringing any other part of the criminal law as well: this is usually called 'individual deterrence';
   b.   influence the offender's desires or attitudes in such a way that—deterrence apart—he will be less inclined to commit similar offences ; or again, if the sentencer is very optimistic, more inclined to obey the criminal law in general;
The difficulties of assessing the likelihood that a sentence will have either of these effects have been discussed in chapter 7.
   c.   deter other people who might be tempted to do what the offender did, by instilling the fear of incurring a similar sentence ('general deterrence');
   d.   increase other people's moral disapproval of the offence, or respect for the prohibitions of the criminal law, by means of the message conveyed by the severity of the sentence ('denunciation');

The likelihood that either of these aims will be achieved by a sentence have been discussed in chapter 8.

    e.   make it more difficult for the offender to commit a similar offence, either by physical restraint such as incarceration or by prohibitions such as disqualification from driving a motor vehicle ('incapacitation').

The limitations which are placed on such measures, either by notions of retributive justice or by practical difficulties, are discussed in chapter 22.

**9.28**   The reducer thus has an even less simple task than the retributive punisher. The English sentencing system offers him the same wide choice of measures, but subjects him to the retributivist's limits as well as to a shortage of resources. Partly because of this, partly because offenders are not the most co-operative or responsive of citizens, none of the choices open to him promises spectacular results. All of this makes it easy to discredit reductive sentencing, provided that one is prepared to overlook a small but important gap in the logic. It has never been shown that 'nothing works'. Even Martinson, whose semi-popular article of 1974 was responsible for this slogan, later disavowed it (1976). Since the critics cannot honestly claim that nothing *ever* works, the most they can urge is that there is an alternative aim which is demonstrably easier to achieve. That is what the advocates of 'just deserts' have tried to do, but without solving their own problems.

### Sentencing as an expressive ritual

**9.29**   One possibility has been hinted at: the denunciatory justification. The realisation that penalties signify disapproval in a particularly dramatic way is at least as old as the 18th century[1]. Usually the lawyers or sociologists who have seen value in the symbolic function of sentences have thought of it as a means of inculcating or reinforcing desirable moral attitudes to the offence in question. Unfortunately, the evidence cited in chapter 8 does not suggest that the reporting of sentences by the news media has much impact or ever could have, when the volume and nature of competing news is taken into account. In any case, the achievement of this aim by means of sentences is merely one of the possible hopes of the reductive sentencer, not an independent justification.

1.   For a short historical account see Walker, 1981.

**9.30**   But there are less instrumental varieties of expressive theory. What they have in common is that they justify official punishment as the expression of moral condemnation, a message intended for the wrongdoer. They tend to side-step the question 'Whose moral condemnation ?', or to answer vaguely 'society's'. A less vague answer would be 'legislators'; but legislation usually leaves scope for sentencers' discretion. Judges sometimes claim—with the CA's approval—to be reflecting the views of 'right-thinking members of the public' (see for instance *Cox* [1993] 1 WLR 188); but they are relying on the views of acquaintances or the news media rather than opinion polls.

**9.31**   More interesting is the question 'Why need moral condemnation be expressed in the form of sentences? Why should sentences not have purely reductive aims ?' Von Hirsch sees the force of this, but being a 'just-deserter' he wants severity to be proportional to the degree of condemnation. Gross is not a proportionalist, but says 'because we cannot tolerate letting people get away with their crimes' (1992). The most uncompromising answer is Nozick's (1981). Even when punishing the offender has no beneficial effect on him or anyone else it is justified because it 'connects' him to correct moral values. Such answers raise other questions in their turn. What if the wrongdoer already feels guilty and repentant? Or is unlikely to understand what is being signified by a fine or community service? Should punishments take a talionic form, and resemble the harm done, in order to make sure that the doer understands? Perhaps that was the point of 'an eye for an eye and a tooth for a tooth '?

**9.32** What could conceivably be offered as an independent justification, to compete with just deserts or the struggle against law-breaking, is what might be called the 'ritual' version of the denunciatory approach. In this version a sentence can be a dramatic condemnation of an offence without the claim that it will have any effect upon public attitudes or that it inflicts just punishment. Its point is merely the satisfaction which people get from a sufficiently dramatic ceremony. A funeral or a memorial service meets a need to signify regret and respect for the deceased. The sentencing of an offender can be regarded as symbolising disapprobation. Like a funeral, it may be an ill-attended ceremony or a popular one: but either way it is, according to this view, essentially a ceremony.

**9.33** It is not easy to find unambiguous statements of this theory, let alone any real discussion of it[1]. One reason may be that it seems to come very close to saying that sentencers must try to satisfy their public. Certainly the theory has unusual implications. One of these is that if and when a sentence is intended as a ritual condemnation it must be of a nature and severity which will be interpreted in this way by those who pay attention to the trial. This in turn means that it must not conflict with their notions of what the sentence should be: and these notions are usually based on retribution. What seems too lenient or too severe will discredit the ceremony. This being so, the believer in the ritual version, though he need not himself believe in just deserts, must advocate a sentence which will appeal to those who do. He is like a theologian who tells priests to do whatever will send their congregations home happy.

1. A close reading of the Law Society's First Memorandum to the Royal Commission on the Penal System (1967), or of the Canadian Law Reform Commission's Report *Our Criminal Law* (1976), suggests this interpretation, since both distinguish the symbolic function from the retributive approach, and at the same time make no claim for a beneficial effect on future crime (the Canadian Commission expressly say in this context that they are not concerned with 'organising the future').

**9.34** Another implication is that the sentence need not always be carried out: just often enough to maintain the belief that it will. This is not as heretical as it may sound. Fines are not always enforced, though for less theoretical reasons. A 10-year prison sentence does not usually mean as many years in custody. Prison sentences are little more than symbolic when they are suspended. Some countries retain the death sentence as a formality which is never allowed to become a reality. It is this point which may make it possible to distinguish between ritual condemnation and mere subservience to popular demand. The ritualist is able to maintain that while he can justify the pronouncing of a life sentence he is not required to justify literal incarceration until death. He can argue with a great deal of evidence that the public's memory is short, and that the drama of the ritual will not be impaired by statistics showing the actual lengths of life sentences. In short, he can defend a considerable discrepancy between the formality and the reality. It is this which also distinguishes him from the retributive punisher, who cannot be satisfied unless the punishment is actually inflicted.

9.35 Taken together, however, these two features of ritual denunciation make it a very cynical theory. The ritual denouncer must at the same time distance himself from the retributive punisher, and yet admit that if the audience were not retributively minded he could not give them the satisfaction which is the aim of his ritual. In effect he must concede that his theory can be true only if most people do not realise its true nature. This is not quite a reductio ad absurdum; but if that is what the theory entails it is unlikely to appeal to many sentencers.

## Reparation[1]

9.36 The part played by reparation in sentencing is another complication, which is emphasised by modern proposals to make it an important objective of law enforcement. This point of view lays stress on the fact that primitive societies were content[2] with reparation and that non-reparative sentences were often introduced by conquerors or feudal superiors in their own interests. The revival of reparation is advocated as a means of avoiding unnecessary prosecutions, and of reconciling victims to offenders. The historical argument is worth little in societies which are so different from those of pre-Norman England or nomadic tribes. The practical arguments are worth more, especially when they favour the diversion of trivial cases (see chapter 15). What must be doubted is the possibility of a wholesale substitution of reparation for the aims of retribution or reduction. A more sensible question is whether reparation should be the *sole* objective of a sentencer in any sort of case.

1. 'Reparation' is here used to include any sort of order which is directed towards remedying or reducing the harm done by the offence, whether by returning stolen goods, repairing damaged property, or compensating the victim financially.
2. Officially content, anyway. It is hard to believe that victims or their dependents were entirely consoled, and that private revenge was not common.

9.37 In a society which was both idealistic and affluent the state would compensate victims as fully as they deserved for the harm done by the offender. If ordering him to contribute to the compensation, or do what he could to undo the harm, seemed likely to correct him, this could be done by the sentencer. Present English practice is only one step in this direction. Victims of personal violence are compensated (to a limited extent) by the Criminal Injuries

Compensation Board. Otherwise, the sentencer is supposed to consider the victim's case for compensation, and, if the case is clear, order the offender to pay. Sometimes this may be a valuable corrective for the offender; sometimes it creates or increases his grievance against the victim or the system. Often he is unable to pay the full compensation due; and even more often he is able to pay it only in small instalments: in either case the victim is receiving less than he or she deserves. Quite apart from these and other practical difficulties, reparation as a primary aim is very difficult to reconcile with what most people would regard as even-handed justice. Imagine two muggers whose offences would normally earn them prison sentences. Mugger A could compensate his victim if left at liberty to earn; but mugger B could not. Should one go to prison and the other not? Or should neither go because one of them can compensate?

9.38 If the sentencer discriminates between those who can make reparation and those who cannot his policy will be regarded as inequitable. He could make it equitable only by a policy of eschewing or suspending a prison sentence in all cases in which reparation might conceivably have been due, whether or not the offender was in a position to make it in the actual circumstances: a policy which would make prison sentences very rare indeed. Even a reductive sentencer who does not feel a need to punish in a retributive sense, and rejects equity as unimportant, would have to worry about the effect of discriminating in favour of muggers who are in a position to pay compensation. Potential muggers with good jobs would be encouraged. It is only when the tariff penalty is a fine that no problem of this sort arises. The usual fine can be reduced—even to nil—by the amount of compensation which the offender can reasonably be ordered to pay (which is now approved practice: see 16.41ff).

## Consistency

9.39 The assumption that sentencing policy should be consistent has already been mentioned (in chapter 4). But the consistency principle needs examination. In a crude form it says that if two offences are indistinguishably similar the penalties for them should be the same. In a less crude form it says that they should be the same unless there is a respectable reason for differentiating them: for example, the different effects which a penalty would have on the two offenders. More important, however, is the assumption which underlies the principle: that consistency means 'justice'. Those who assume this usually have in mind 'just deserts'. In more precise terms their belief is that by sentencing consistently they are increasing the likelihood that their choice of penalty will be retributively commensurate. Yet the principle can have the opposite result. In *Reeves'* case (see 4.40) it meant that although his original sentence was regarded as commensurate by the Court of Appeal it had to be reduced in order to achieve consistency with the inadequate sentences imposed on his accomplices. This illustrates the point that consistency increases the likelihood of retributive justice only if the court is able to take as its 'bench-mark' a sentence which it 'knows' to be retributively correct. Yet if it has this knowledge, it will be guided to the correct sentence without needing to use the consistency principle; and if it does not have this knowledge consistency will not help it. What consistency can do is persuade the public, or more precisely those who look critically at sentencing policy, that sentencers' choices are not capricious or discriminatory. Even so, it can have undesirable effects. A sentencer who thinks that an unusual choice may have a desirable effect in an individual case (for example, the choice of probation for a multiple recidivist who has experienced only a number of prison sentences) is likely to be attacked for inconsistency. The even greater prejudice against 'random allocation' experiments is also rooted in respect for consistency.

## Compromises

9.40 Compromises between retributivism and reductivism are possible, especially if retributivists are prepared to regard retribution as a mere right rather than a duty. Indeed if it is only a right this implies that non-retributive considerations must decide whether the right should be exercised. Reductivists, on the other hand, are forced to accept some sort of compromise if they want to be taken seriously by the retributively minded man in-the-street. There are several kinds of possible compromise. Two are hybrids:

a.　that the justifying aim of a sentence should be reductive — for example, reform, deterrence or public protection — but that it should not be more severe than desert allows (eg Longford, 1961). This would tie the hands of courts when dealing with very dangerous offenders (see chapter 22);

b.　conversely, that the justifying aim should be desert, unless that dictates a penalty so severe as to lead to 'an intolerable increase in the crime rate' (Robinson, 1988). But retributivists would regard this as morally cynical.

The other sort of compromise is some variety of eclecticism. The sentencer is to be allowed to decide in individual cases what his justifying aim is to be. This is, in fact, what many sentencers do. The objection is that their decisions are too often based on emotional reactions to the circumstances of the case — the details of the crime, the offender's personality, or public feeling. Eclecticism, however, need not necessarily be emotional: it could be rational. It could, for example, dictate

c.　that some types of offence should be dealt with retributively, others only with the aim of reducing their frequency. The latter might consist of offences which are merely regulatory, or involve nothing more than negligence or omission. Sentencers sometimes seem to have such a distinction in mind.

A more sophisticated eclectic might propose

d.　that the sentencer must consider how likely it is that each of the possible aims could be achieved, and to what extent, and should rule out any that seem unlikely to be achieved. If this leaves him with more than one to choose from, he should choose the one which seems to have the greatest chance of being realised. (Something like this was proposed by the Supreme Court of Victoria, although not fully worked out: see Walker, 1991.)

9.41 The White Paper which heralded the CJA 91 was retributive, but with concessions to utility:

'The first objective for all sentences is denunciation of and retribution for the crime. Depending on the offence and the offender, the sentence may also aim to achieve public protection, reparation and reform of the offender, preferably in the community. This approach points to sentencing policies which are more firmly based on the seriousness of the offence, and just desserts [sic] for the offender' (Home Office, 1990)

This reads like a rather rhetorical version of compromise (b), with tricky grace-notes such as the linking of denunciation with retribution.

**9.42** To sum up: unless a sentencer is of the academic type which in every case has a single aim in view—just punishment, the reduction of crime or ritual satisfaction—he must be an eclectic. An eclectic selects his aim in the light of the circumstances of each case in which he has to sentence. His selection may be governed either by his emotional reaction to his information, or—preferably—by rules or principles which make his selection rational. One sensible rule—as the Supreme Court of Victoria pointed out—is that aims which have some chance of being achieved should be preferred to aims which do not.

Part II

# Imprisonment

# Chapter 10

# Using imprisonment

**10.1** The literature on incarceration is so enormous that it overshadows all other penalties in the minds of the public and Parliament, just as capital punishment did in the 1950s. Only 17 per cent of offenders sentenced for indictable offences (and only 6.7 per cent of those sentenced in MCs) received an immediate custodial sentence in 1994. The average sentence length for male offenders sentenced to immediate custody at all courts rose from 14.9 months in 1989 to 15.4 months in 1993, and then dropped to 14.8 in 1994. For adult males sentenced in the CC, the average sentence length was 21.6 months in 1994, compared with 20.5 months in 1989 (Barclay et al, 1995). The average time actually served is obviously considerably shorter: for adult male prisoners in 1993 the average was 8.5 months, and for adult women, 6.6 months. Yet because imprisonment is the most severe type of sentence that is open to the criminal courts[1] it understandably receives more attention from legislators, penologists and the news media than the penalty which is imposed far more frequently—the fine.

1. A recommendation for deportation (see 5.6) has more serious consequences than a typical prison sentence, but most offenders are not eligible for this.

## The nine purposes

**10.2** Imprisonment is used for nine purposes:
  a. to hold people until they can be tried, sentenced or taken to the place to which they have been sentenced, or until they can be extradited or deported. This is a task which it performs with a low escape rate, but with the infliction of inconvenience and, in some cases, hardship on people some of whom some are eventually acquitted and others who do not, in the end, receive custodial sentences: a problem which is discussed in 10.7;
  b. to coerce people into compliance with the orders of a court. The most common example is its use for non-payment of fines; and in a substantial number of cases the sight of the warrant of imprisonment, or the experience of entering prison, does result in payment. Less common, but

by no means unheard of, are committals to prison for disobeying other court orders, such as an injunction not to go near an estranged wife;

c.   as a sentence, to protect members of the public from offenders by 'taking them out of circulation'. Since escape rates are low, this purpose is achieved for the duration at least of the detention; but since this is usually rather short it often means only a postponement of the next offence. (The ethical and other problems raised by long-term detention of dangerous offenders are reviewed in chapter 22.);

d.   as a sentence, to hold a person long enough to make possible a pro-longed course of treatment. This purpose, though popular in periods of therapeutic optimism, is now questioned, chiefly because of disappointing outcomes, but also because of the lack of resources: it is discussed in chapter 11;

e.   as a sentence, to act as an individual deterrent: that is, in the hope that the memory of the experience will discourage the ex-prisoner from risking another sentence. That this hope is sometimes realised is undeniable: the question is whether it is realised in enough cases to make it a worthwhile objective (see chapter 7);

f.   as a sentence, to act as a general deterrent: that is, to discourage others who might break the law in similar ways. General deterrence has been discussed in chapter 8;

g.   as a sentence, to symbolise degrees of disapproval of the offence. Expressive theories are discussed in chapters 8 and 9;

h.   as a sentence, to inflict retributive punishment. There is no doubt that it inflicts severe inconvenience, even hardship, on most prisoners (the exceptions being those whose way of life is so precarious or desperate that imprisonment is a form of shelter). The retributive justification for penalties is discussed in chapter 9;

i.   in exceptional cases, to protect a very unpopular offender against retaliation by victims or sympathisers of victims. Not all such prisoners, however, are safe inside: some types of offence are likely to lead to attacks by fellow prisoners (see 11.20).

## Imprisonment without sentence

**10.3**   The modern presumption in England is that until an accused person has been convicted and given a custodial sentence he should be at liberty unless there are good reasons for keeping him in custody. If he is merely summoned to appear in court on a criminal charge he is automatically free until he does, and liable to arrest and custody only if he fails to do so. If he is arrested with a magistrate's warrant which is not endorsed ('backed') for bail, he must be kept in custody until he is brought before the magistrates, at which point the grant or refusal of bail becomes and remains a matter for the MC or, at a later stage, the CC. If on the other hand it is endorsed for bail, he must be released after being brought to a police station. If he is arrested without a warrant, the grant or refusal of bail until his court appearance is a matter within the discretion of the police, subject to their statutory duty to release him if they become aware that there have ceased to be grounds for further detention (s 34 Police and Criminal Evidence Act (PACE) 84).

## Police bail

**10.4** Even so, the discretion of the police is limited. Section 38 of PACE 84 specifies the conditions when the police may keep someone in detention once he has been charged. Otherwise he must be released either on bail or without bail. If his real name and address cannot be ascertained, if he is unlikely to appear in court to answer the charge, if he is likely to interfere with witnesses or further police investigations, he may be kept in detention. Section 28 CJPOA 94 added another circumstance in which the police can detain someone: where the custody officer at the police station has reasonable grounds for believing that the detention of a person charged with an imprisonable offence is necessary to prevent him from committing a further offence. Section 27 CJPOA 94 inserts a new s 3A in the Bail Act 76 to give the police the power to attach conditions to bail once a person has been charged where they consider this to be necessary to prevent a person from absconding, committing an offence, interfering with witnesses or otherwise obstructing the course of justice. The police however still do not have the power to require a person to reside at a bail hostel (see 17.38).

## Court bail (Bail Act 1976)

**10.5** As soon as the accused is brought before a MC the grant or refusal of bail becomes a matter for the court, and custody becomes the responsibility of the prison service. The court's discretion is limited by the Bail Act 76, and in particular by s 4, which lays down that, with exceptions, bail must be granted to the accused when
   a. he appears before a criminal court 'in the course of or in connection with' proceedings for the offence; or
   b. he applies for bail in connection with the proceedings; or
   c. he is being dealt with for breach of a probation or community service order; or
   d. his case is adjourned for inquiries or a report to assist the court in dealing with him for the offence.

## Exceptions to right to bail

**10.6** Most of the exceptions are detailed in Sch 1 of the Bail Act:
   i. when the court is satisfied that there are sufficient grounds for believing that if bailed he would
      a. fail to surrender to custody; or
      b. commit an offence while on bail ;
      c. interfere with witnesses or otherwise obstruct the course of justice.

ii. where the court is satisfied that he should be kept in custody for his own protection, or, if he is a juvenile, for his own welfare;
iii. when he is already in custody in pursuance of a sentence;
iv. when the court is satisfied that there has not been time to obtain enough information to enable it to decide about bail;
v. if, having already been granted bail in or in connection with proceedings for the offence, he has been arrested for failure to surrender to bail;
vi. when his case is adjourned for inquiries or a report and it appears to the court that these could not be completed without keeping him in custody;

but there are also two exceptions in s 4:

vii. proceedings on or after conviction;
viii. proceedings against a fugitive offender.

Two further restrictions were added by the CJPOA 94:

ix. no bail is to be granted to those charged with or convicted of homicide or rape with a previous conviction for such an offence (s 25).
x. the court 'need not' grant bail to people convicted or accused of committing an offence while on bail (s 26).

When deciding whether the case falls within one of the scheduled exceptions the court must have regard to such of the following considerations as are relevant:

a. the nature and seriousness of the offence or default, and the probable method of dealing with it;
b. the defendant's record in fulfilling obligations under previous grants of bail;
c. the strength of the evidence against him (except in cases of adjournments for inquiries or reports).

**10.7** The reason for these elaborate restrictions on the court's discretion to withhold bail is the degree of injustice involved in restricting the liberty of a person who has either not yet been found guilty, or not yet been sentenced to custody. In many countries (e g Canada; see Padfield (1993)) the primary ground for refusing bail is the risk that the suspect will not appear at his trial. In England, the restrictions on bail are alternatives: the statute gives no one ground for refusing bail priority over another. The injustice of witholding bail is perhaps less serious if it is known that the defendant intends to plead guilty; but even in such cases the eventual sentence may not be a custodial one. The injustice is most disturbing when he or she is eventually acquitted. Only 41 per cent of men and 26 per cent of women remand prisoners ultimately receive a custodial sentence (Prison Statistics 1992; for a fuller discussion, see Morgan and Jones (1992)). In recent years, the daily average prison population of unconvicted and unsentenced prisoners has been rising steadily, constituting about 25 per cent of the total prison population (Barclay et al, 1995). The onus is therefore on the court not merely to make it clear to the defendant that he can ask for bail, but also to have a clear reason for refusing it. The usual procedure is to ask him if he wishes to apply for it, and if he does, to ask the police whether they have objections, which must be supported by reasons.

**10.8** If bail is granted, the court can attach requirements (to be met before or after release) in order to ensure that the defendant surrenders to custody, or does not commit an offence while on bail, or does not interfere with witnesses or obstruct the course of justice, or makes himself available for presentence inquiries or reports. In most cities there are bail hostels where he can be required to stay (see 17.39), so that staff can try, without more forcible detention, to ensure that he appears in court when needed.

The court may also insist that a 'surety' be found (that is, someone who will forfeit a stipulated sum of money if the defendant fails to appear), or the defendant himself may be asked for 'security' (that is, a forfeitable sum of money), but only if he seems unlikely to remain in Great Britain until the appointed time for his court appearance. The security may be given by him or on his behalf by some other person. Routine in many other jurisdictions (such as Canada), sureties are not usually required in England.

**10.9** If the court refuses bail it must state its reasons and also—if the defendant is not legally represented—tell him that he may apply for bail to the High Court or the CC (s 5 Bail Act 76 as amended; s 81 Supreme Court Act 81 as amended). Such applications are dealt with speedily. If he is granted bail, the Bail (Amendment) Act 93 gave the prosecution the right of appeal for the first time where someone charged with a serious offence (here one which carries a maximum sentence of imprisonment for five years or more) is granted bail. As soon as the court receives oral notice of the decision to appeal, the person is remanded in custody until after the appeal decision.

## Remand in custody

**10.10** Remands in custody place the accused in the charge of the Prison Service (or in contracted-out establishments), to which he must be handed over by the police. This does not mean that the police have no access to him thereafter: they can visit him in order to ask him further questions, but the Prison Service is responsible for his safekeeping and he can refuse to be interviewed. If he is a man aged 21 or older he will be kept in the remand cells of a local prison: if he is 18–20 he will probably be moved from there to one of the remand centres intended for young adults. A woman or girl will usually go to Holloway (if charged in south-east England) or to one of the remand centres such as Risley, Low Newton or Pucklechurch if charged elsewhere. Increasingly however unconvicted and convicted prisoners are not kept separately in prisons, in order to maximise the use of different facilities by different groups of prisoners. Prison Rule 3(2) provides simply that unconvicted prisoners 'shall be kept out of contact with convicted prisoners as far as the governor considers this can reasonably be done, unless and to the extent that they have consented to share residential accommodation or participate in any activity with convicted prisoners ....'. Places for remand prisoners are increasingly being contracted out to private companies. Britain's first privatised prison (see 12.5) was the remand prison at the Wolds in Lincolnshire, and despite strong criticism the Government is committed to continuing this policy. Because of the shortage of remand spaces, some remand prisoners are held in police cells, where facilities are inevitably particularly poor.

**10.11**   The average time spent by men in custody before trial is about 6 weeks, and the average time in custody between conviction and sentence is only a day or two less (for women both averages are a few days less). They are only averages, however; and some prisoners spend many months awaiting trial at the CC, especially if the case is a complex one. Under s 22 of the POA 85, and the regulations passed under them (the Prosecution of Offences (Custody Time Limits) Regulations 1987-91), there are now time limits regulating how long a defendant may be kept in custody pending the start of summary trial, between first appearance at court and committal for trial, and between committal for trial and the start of trial. Application can be made for extension of these limits, and a right of appeal exists in respect of a MC's decision to extend or to refuse to extend the time limit. Judicial review of such decisions is equally possible (see for example *Hollstein* [1995] 3 All ER 503, where the QBD quashed a decision of a trial judge, where no trial date had been fixed, to arraign a defendant in order to evade the time limit). A defendant, however, who is acquitted has no consolation for the time spent in custody: unlike most other countries in Western Europe, Britain does not pay compensation in such cases: only for custodial *sentences* which turn out to have been based on unjustified convictions.

**10.12**   On the grounds that unsentenced prisoners, and especially the unconvicted, should not be subject to any more deprivations than are unavoidably associated with custody, they are usually allowed to wear their own clothes, have food and drink sent in from outside at their own or their friends' expense (within limits), engage in unlimited correspondence, choose whether to do prison work or not, and receive as many visitors as they please (although the Home Secretary can impose limits and conditions, for example by banning visits from criminal friends). In some ways, however, life on remand is even more unpleasant than a sentence. Where remand prisoners are segregated from the main body of prisoners, this often means greater monotony and fewer activities for the remand prisoners. Unless the defendant is working—and sometimes there is no work for remand prisoners—he spends most of the day in or just outside his cell. Unless he is in some special category he will be sharing a cell with at least one other remanded prisoner. He has no chance of a transfer to the less crowded and slightly more tolerable conditions of a training prison. Life in remand centres for young adults is often worse: there has been much concern at the high level of suicides at Risley, and the HMCIP Report (1993) on Feltham was highly critical, highlighting, for example, the lack of training and medical facilities, and the high level of bullying.

## The coercive use of imprisonment

**10.13**   Imprisonment for fine default is not technically a sentence but a threat used to enforce a sentence: the same is true of imprisonment for failure to obey other financial orders of courts, such as compensation orders or orders for maintenance of a wife or family, or for disobeying courts in other ways ('contempt of court'). The power to imprison in such cases is expressed in a warrant, and the person concerned is often told that the warrant has been signed but is being held in suspense to give him one more chance to comply. If he is in fact taken to prison this is not irrevocable: he or someone else can buy his freedom by paying what is due, or in the case of a fine that fraction of it which corresponds to the time he has still to serve; and if he is imprisoned for disobedience of other kinds he can usually secure his freedom by apologising to the court or undertaking to obey its order. While inside, however, he is treated very much as if he were a sentenced prisoner, with none of the privileges of an untried prisoner. The important part which imprisonment plays in fine enforcement is discussed in 16.19ff.

### Imprisonment as a sentence: statutory limits

**10.14** The use of imprisonment as a sentence is controlled partly by statute and partly by case-law. The CJA 91 provides the main statutory framework, but other statutory limitations still apply:

a.  many summary offences are not 'imprisonable': the statute creating or defining them provides no penalty more severe than a fine. Even so, non-payment of the fine can result in imprisonment. Table 10A lists indictable offences which are non-imprisonable together with some examples of the commoner non-imprisonable summary offences.

b.  MCs must not impose sentences of less than 5 days (s 132 MCA 80) or more than 6 months[1](for a single offence: if they impose consecutive sentences these must not in aggregate exceed 6 months, or 12 months if two or more of the offences are triable either summarily or on indictment: ss 31, 133 MCA 80). The 5-day minimum is intended to protect the prison service from an input of prisoners for whom discharge procedures would have to begin almost as soon as reception procedures had been completed. For very short periods MCs can order offenders to be detained within the precincts of the courthouse or any police station: but this must not result in detention after 8pm, or in depriving the offender of a 'reasonable opportunity of returning to his abode' on the same day (s 135 MCA 80: s 136 confers a similar power of slightly longer detention in the case of fine-defaulters, described in 16.24).

c.  imprisonment as a determinate sentence cannot be imposed on a person under 21, although he can be sentenced to the equivalent of life imprisonment if he fulfils certain conditions. Custodial sentences for young adults are one of the subjects of chapter 20.

d.  a sentence of imprisonment cannot be passed on a person for the first time unless he has been represented by counsel or a solicitor after he has been found guilty and before being sentenced (s 21 PCCA 73, with exceptions for persons who could have been legally represented had they wished). Even the offender who has previously been given a suspended prison sentence enjoys this protection, unless the sentence has been activated (see 10.28ff). As Lord Bridge said in *McC (a minor)* [1985] AC 528, 'No one should be liable to a first sentence of imprisonment ... unless he has had the opportunity of having his case in mitigation presented to the court in the best possible light. For an inarticulate defendant, such presentation may be crucial to his liberty'. Nor can the court disregard this protection because it intends to suspend the sentence (s 21(3)). On the other hand the protection does not apply to imprisonment for contempt of court (*Du Pont* (1983) 148 JP 248), or for fine default.

e. the maximum terms for imprisonable offences are usually specified in the statutes which create or define them. For some the statute allows 'life' sentences and where this is so the CC can, in theory at least, impose instead a fixed term of any length, subject only to case-law. In the case of an offence for which a statute does not specify either 'life' or a determinate maximum, the maximum is 2 years (s 18 PCCA 73). A list of statutory maximum sentences of 2 years or more will be found in Appendix A.

g. Section 48 CJPOA 94 gives statutory recognition to the discount usually given for guilty pleas (see 4.2).

1. 'Month' means a calendar month (s 24 Prison Act 52), so that the prisoner should be released not later than the first moment of the corresponding day of the appropriate month (*Migotti* (1879) 4 CPD 233). If in a short month there is no exactly corresponding day, the last day of the month is substituted. It would be less cumbersome to enact that sentences can be pronounced only in weeks or years.

**TABLE 10A: Examples of non-imprisonable offences**

Contraventions of certain provisions in the Companies Act 85: ss 99-104; s 233(5)

Dog, keeping without licence: s 12 Dog Licences Act 59

Drunkenness in a public place: s 12 Licensing Act 1872 as amended

Intoxicating liquor, selling to persons under age: s 169 Licensing Act 64

Loitering or soliciting for prostitution: s 1 Street Offences Act 59 as amended

Railway bye-laws, offences against

Unauthorised sale of tickets for designated football matches: s 166 CJPOA 94

Touting for hire car services: s 167 CJPOA 94

Sunday trading, offences connected with: s 59 Shops Act 50

Television set, using without licence: s 14 Wireless Telegraphy Act 49

Traffic offences scheduled in the Road Traffic Offenders Act 88, Sch 2:

      Breath test, failing to provide specimen for

      Careless driving or cycling

      Cycling while unfit through drink or drugs

      Driving without a required driver's licence

      Failing to stop after an accident

      Leaving vehicle in a dangerous position

      Motor-cycle, riding without protective headgear

      Racing motor vehicles on a highway

      Selling unroadworthy vehicle

      Speed-limit, infringing

      Test Certificate, using vehicle without

## The CJA 1991

**10.15** Section 1 provides that a prison sentence cannot be imposed on a person unless the court is of the opinion either:

'(a) that the offence, or the combination of the offence and one or more offences associated with it, was so serious that only such a sentence can be justified for the offence; or
(b) where the offence is a violent or sexual offence, that only such a sentence would be adequate to protect the public from serious harm from him' (s 1(2) CJA 91).

Once a court has decided that a custodial sentence is justified, it must follow the CJA 91 provisions on the length of sentences:

'(2) The custodial sentence shall be—
(a) for such term (not exceeding the permitted maximum) as in the opinion of the court is commensurate with the seriousness of the offence, or the combination of the offence and one or more offences associated with it; or
(b) where the offence is a violent or sexual offence, for such longer term (not exceeding the maximum) as in the opinion of the court is necessary to protect the public from serious harm from the offender.'

For the requirements concerning PSRs see 2.2. Within this statutory framework, however, other controls operate. Chief among these are decisions of the CA (see 1.22 ff), although informal exchanges of views between judges, and the more formal seminars organised by the Judicial Studies Board, are also influential.

## Case-law

**10.16** Decisions of the CA in recent years have resulted in greater consistency as well as a more sparing use of the longest sentences allowed by the statutory maxima. Even within the framework provided by the CJA 91, the CA has had a vital task in interpreting key concepts. Thus after the CJA came into force in October 1992, the CA gave reserved judgements in the first six cases under the Act before the end of November to give essential clarification to the somewhat 'loosely-worded' Act.

## 'Seriousness'

**10.17** The main ground for imposing imprisonment is found in s 1(2)(a): where the offence (or it and others associated with it) is so serious that only such a sentence is justified. There was no attempt in the Act to define seriousness, but the CA in both *Baverstock* [1993] 1 WLR 202 and *Cox* [1993] 1 WLR 188 applied Lawton LJ's definition in *Bradbourn* (1985) 7 Cr App Rep (S) 180, formulated in relation to s 1(4) of the CJA 82: 'The kind of offence which when committed by a young person would make all right thinking members of the public, knowing all the facts, feel that justice had not been done by the passing of any sentence other than a custodial one'. It is clear, however, that even if an offence is sufficiently serious to justify custody, the court can still take account of mitigating factors and impose a non-custodial penalty (s 28(1) CJA 91, and 4.20ff).

## 'Protection of the public'

**10.18** An alternative ground justifying the imposition of a custodial sentence is provided by s 1(2)(b): where the offence is a sexual or violent one, a custodial sentence may be imposed to protect the public from serious harm. This 'dangerousness' ground is discussed further in 22.3.

## Fixing the length of the sentence

**10.19** Under s 2, the sentence length must be commensurate with the seriousness of the offence. What does this mean in practice? Lord Taylor CJ explained in *Cunningham* [1993] 1 WLR 183, another of the first set of cases decided under the Act, that the phrase means 'commensurate with the seriousness of the punishment and deterrence which the seriousness of the offence requires' This, he had explained (in a press conference on 30 September 1992), was because 'the purposes of a custodial sentence must primarily be to punish and to deter'. The Government's White Paper, *Crime, Justice and Protecting the Public*, which preceded the Act, argued that sentencing arrangements should not be based on assumptions about deterrence. For further discussion on the aims of sentencing, see chapter 9. In any case, s 1(4) imposes a statutory duty on the judge to explain to the offender in open court and in ordinary language why it is passing a custodial sentence on him, and which ground applies.

## 'Tariffs'

**10.20** The role of the CA in issuing guideline cases is most striking when the maxima are high: the courts have evolved a 'tariff' in which the range of sentence-lengths regarded as normally permissible for each offence ends well below the statutory maximum. The 'tariff' will not be found in any official publication, although Thomas' *Current Sentencing Practice* can be regarded as semi-official. At the risk of oversimplifying, Table 10B provides some examples taken from Thomas.

**Table 10B: Normal 'tariff' sentences for serious offences**

| Offence | | Statutory maximum | Normal range |
|---------|---|-------------------|--------------|
| Voluntary manslaughter | | Life | |
| | with diminished responsibility | | 3-life |
| | under provocation | | 3-7 years |
| | in pursuance of suicide pact | | 2 years |

| Offence | | Statutory maximum | Normal range |
|---|---|---|---|
| Involuntary manslaughter | | Life | |
| | in fights | | 1-8 years |
| | in robberies | | 3-10 years |
| Procuring miscarriage | | Life | |
| | professional abortionists | | up to 8 years |
| | semi-professionals | | 2-3 years |
| | 'one-timers' | | up to 12 months |
| Infanticide | | Life | Probation |
| Aiding suicide | | 14 years | (up to ?) 3 years |
| Threats to kill | | 10 years | 1-5 years |
| Causing death by dangerous driving | | 10 years | 1-3 years |
| Attempted murder | | Life | 5-8 years |
| Wounding with intent to do grievous bodily harm | | Life | 3-8 years |
| Grievous bodily harm | | 5 years | up to 3 years |
| Assault occasioning actual bodily harm | | 5 years | community penalty–3 years |
| Common assault | | 12 months | up to 12 months |
| Assaults on police | | 6 months | up to 6 months |
| Rape | | Life | |
| | by a group or with other | | 8-life |
| | otherwise | | 3-5 years |
| Incest | | Life or 7 years | |
| | girl over 16 | | 0–3 years |
| | girl 13–16 | | 3–5 years |
| | girl under 13 | | 6–10 years |
| Indecent assault on female | | 2 years (5 if under 13) | up to 18 months |
| Buggery | | Life (lower maxima if of male over 16 etc) | 3-5 years |
| Indecent assault on male | | 10 years | up to 7 years |
| Robbery | | Life | |
| | 'mugging' in street | | 2-5 years |
| | of householder in burglary | | 3-10 years |
| | in shops, garages etc | | 3-7 years |
| | of banks etc with organisation | | 15-18 years |

| Offence | | Statutory maximum | Normal range |
|---|---|---|---|
| Obtaining by deception | | 10, 7 or 5 (see Theft Acts) | 1-7 years |
| Burglary | | 14 years (life if with weapons) | |
| | by professionals | | up to 12 years |
| | otherwise | | 1-2 years |
| Handling stolen goods | | 14 years | up to 5 years |
| Blackmail | | 14 years | 3-12 years |
| Perjury | | 7 years | 6 months - 2 years |
| Cannabis offences | | | |
| | possession | 5 years | fine |
| | importing | 14 years | 2-4 years |
| Heroin offences | | | |
| | possession | 7 years | 6–12 mths |
| | importing | life | 6-10 years |

These are examples only, and are subject to two important reservations. Being based on the results of appeals against sentence the ranges can reflect only the views of the CA on cases which are brought before it. It is likely that the practice of lower courts is more lenient than these ranges suggest, because most of their sentences are not the subject of appeals. Secondly, the table does not mean that imprisonment is regarded as always the right sentence: circumstances may justify non-custodial or psychiatric disposals. For example, in the two years 1993-4 even adult men were sometimes disposed of non-custodially for

| | |
|---|---|
| Attempted murder | 2% |
| Manslaughter with diminished responsibility | 15% |
| Causing death by dangerous driving | 30% |
| Rape or attempted rape | 2% |
| Aggravated burglary of a dwelling | 14% |
| Robbery | 8% |
| Arson | 34% |
| Incest | 22% |

The CA also makes many distinctions between sub-types of offence which are not reflected in the list. Nevertheless, it shows the extent to which the statutory maxima for most offences of the kind which attract public concern have in practice been superseded by limits adopted by the judiciary. This is not appreciated by members of Parliament who demand increases in maximum prison terms under the impression that these would result in markedly stiffer sentences. Only statutory minima would have an effect of that sort; and while this expedient is used by many jurisdictions in the USA, it has not yet found favour in England.

## Executive influence

**10.21** Home Office policies do not result in directives to judges or magistrates: that would be regarded as improper interference by the executive. The detailed circulars which inform courts of new legislation or regulations are confined to statements of the law with the minimum of interpretation. Judicial training offered by the Judicial Studies Board is judge-led, but supported by staff of the Lord Chancellor's Department. Home Secretaries, however, have occasionally made efforts to persuade sentencers, sometimes to make less use of imprisonment and to shorten sentences, or, as has been seen more recently, to impose longer or even life sentences more frequently. The extent to which judges might have been affected by 'political speeches', rather than statutory changes, is unstudied.

**10.22** Committees concerned with imprisonment, such as the Parliamentary All-Party Penal Affairs Group (1980), have also urged the use of fewer and shorter sentences. The ACPS Report (1978) proposed that for nearly every offence there should be a new maximum based on the level below which 90 per cent of CC sentences had fallen in recent years. The proposal was not adopted by the Government, whose chief concern at that time had been to find expedients to reduce the prison population, a problem which the proposal was not intended to solve (it would have meant shorter sentences for only about 10 per cent of those received into prison under sentence). More recently, the Lane Committee (1991) has urged the abolition of mandatory life sentences, but this too has fallen on deaf ears (see 22.66).

## Consecutive and concurrent sentences

**10.23** Courts tend to be sparing in the use of consecutive sentences. When passing a prison sentence on an offender who is already serving one, or has been sentenced to one by the same or another court, a sentencer may direct that it is to be concurrent or consecutive. If he makes no direction, the sentence is deemed to begin on the day when it is passed. If consecutive, it and the other sentence are added together and treated as one in the calculation of earliest release dates. The CA has held that
   a.   terms imposed for offences which arose out of the same incident should not be consecutive (*Jones* (1980) 2 Cr App Rep (S) 152);
   b.   nor should they be consecutive if passed for similar offences all committed within a few days, against the same victim (*Paddon* (1971) CSP A.5–2BO2).
On the other hand, the CA has approved consecutive sentences in several kinds of case in which the offence could be regarded as arising out of the same incident:
   i.   when a burglar assaulted a householder who interrupted his burglary (*Bunch* (1971) CSP A5-2C01);
   ii.  when violence was used against a police officer who tried to arrest an offender (*Kastercum* (1972) 56 Cr App Rep 298; *Austin* (1980) 2 Cr App Rep (S) 203);

iii. when the offender who committed a robbery or other crime of violence carried a firearm to facilitate the crime (*Faulkner* (1972) 56 Cr App Rep 594; *French* (1982) 4 Cr App Rep (S) 57);

iv. when the offender was convicted of indecent assault and perverting the course of justice (for writing to the victim while remanded in custody pending trial to dissuade him from giving evidence) (*A-G's Reference (No 1 of 1990)* (1990) 12 Cr App Rep (S) 245).

**10.24**   Even when sentences are properly made consecutive, what Thomas calls 'the totality principle' dictates that normally the aggregate of consecutive sentences should not exceed the upper limit of the normal range of sentences for the category of offences in which the most serious of the offences falls. If consecutive sentences of the appropriate length would exceed that, it is better to resort to concurrency than to shortening them. Again, when a sentencer is dealing with an offender who is already subject to a prison sentence passed by another sentencer, he should take that into account and apply the totality principle (*Millen* (1980) 2 Cr App Rep (S) 357). As we saw in 4.3 the totality principle is recognised by s 28(2)(b) CJA 91.

**10.25**   A prison sentence which is made consecutive to a life sentence is not valid. In *Foy* (1962) 46 Cr App Rep 290 the Court of Criminal Appeal (as it then was) reasoned that since a life sentence remains in force until the offender's death (even if he is released on licence before that) a sentence which is consecutive to it cannot begin to operate until his death. Nor should a life sentence be made consecutive to a determinate sentence, not because it would then be invalid, but simply because it would make no practical difference whether it was concurrent or consecutive (*Jones* (1961) 46 Cr App Rep 129). Even when determinate sentences are made concurrent with life sentences they should not be so long as to prevent the release of the lifer on licence when this is thought right (*Skelding* (1973) 58 Cr App Rep 313).

## The relevance of parole and early release

**10.26**   Until 1991, courts did not officially take notice of parole or early release rules in fixing the appropriate sentence length. Yet when new rules were introduced the Lord Chief Justice recognised that judges would have to recognise this in order to avoid a sense of grievance between prisoners sentenced before and after 1 October 1992. In a *Practice Statement (Crime: Sentencing)* [1992] 1 WLR 948 Lord Taylor said, inter alia:

'It has been an axiomatic principle of sentencing policy until now that the court should decide the appropriate sentence in each case without reference to questions of remission or parole. I have consulted the Lords Justices presiding in the Court of Appeal (Criminal Division) and we have decided that a new approach is essential. Accordingly, from 1 October 1992, it will be necessary, when passing a custodial sentence in the Crown Court, to have regard to the actual period likely to be served and, as far as practicable, to the risk of offenders serving longer under the new system than would have been normal under the old. Existing guideline judgements should be applied with these considerations in mind.'

The offenders who were most affected by the changes in the rules relating to release were those sentenced to 12 months to 4 years, since they would previously have been eligible for parole once they had served one third of their sentence. They now have to serve one half of the term. The effect of the *Practice Statement* is discussed in 14.17.

## Counting time inside

**10.27** The length of any custodial sentence is treated as reduced by any period during which the offender was in custody solely because of a court order connected with the proceedings relating to the sentence (s 67 CJA 67, as amended by CJA 91, Sch 11 para 2). In practice this usually means time on remand in custody. The effect is that at the time of the sentence the offender who has been waiting in custody for his trial or sentence is treated, as soon as sentenced, as having already served part of his sentence. He may even be due for immediate release. The section, however, does not apply to time spent in custody before a suspended prison sentence, a probation order or conditional discharge, even if the offender's later conduct leads to imprisonment for the offence, and so the sentencer should take account of the period spend in custody when fixing the length of the sentence.

## Suspended sentences

**10.28** If a court passes a sentence of not more than 2 years' imprisonment for an offence it may suspend it: that is, it may order that it is not to take effect unless during a specified period ('the operational period') the offender commits another imprisonable offence in Great Britain and a court 'activates' the suspended sentence (SS) (that is, orders that it take effect). The court must explain this to the offender in ordinary language. The operational period must be not less than 1 nor more than 2 years, but is sometimes extended as an alternative to 'activation': see 10.31.

**10.29** A SS is treated as a sentence of imprisonment for the purposes of all enactments (and instruments made under enactments) except those providing for disqualification for office, loss of office or forfeiture of pensions (s 22(6) PCCA 73). But the statutes dealing with the sentencing of offenders to prison for the first time (eg s 21 PCCA 73) also provide that a previous SS which has not taken effect is to be disregarded.

**10.30** Suspended sentences were introduced in 1967. Significant changes were made in the CJA 72, largely because experience showed that SSs were sometimes being used not as substitutes for immediate prison sentences but instead of a non-custodial sentence that would have been chosen if there had been no such alternative. The 1972 Act therefore made it clear that a SS could not be chosen unless the case appeared to the court to be one in which a prison sentence would have been the appropriate choice even if there had been no power to suspend. The sentence has become increasingly unpopular and the reforms in the CJA 91 made clear that a SS must only be imposed in 'exceptional circumstances' (s 5). The CA (in *Okinikan*[1993] 1 WLR 173; *Sanderson* (1992) 14 Cr App Rep (S) 361; *Lowery* [1993] Crim LR 225) has made clear that most usual mitigating factors will not constitute 'exceptional circumstances'. The percentage use of SSs shown in Table 1A may well decline yet further.

10.31   If the offender is again convicted of an imprisonable offence committed during the operational period, a court must consider his case, and decide whether
   a.   to order that the SS shall take effect with the original term unaltered;
   b.   to order that it take effect with the substitution of a lesser term;
   c.   to substitute for the original operational period a new one, of not more than 2 years, to run from the date of the variation;
   d.   to make no order with respect to the SS (in which case it remains in suspended force).
The court is obliged to choose (a) unless it is of opinion that it would be unjust to do so in view of all the circumstances, including the facts of the later offence. If it is of this opinion it must state its reasons (s 23 PCCA 73).

## Non-activation

10.32   A court may 'properly consider (activation) as unjust' when the later offence is comparatively trivial and is in a different category from the original one (*Moylan* (1969) 53 Cr App Rep 590). If it is in the same category, activation is not unjust. On the other hand, the fact that the later offence is of a different sort is not of itself a justification for non-activation (*Clitheroe* (1987) 9 Cr App Rep (S) 159).

## Activation with reduction

10.33   The CA has substituted a shorter term for the original suspended term in a case in which the operational period had almost expired (*Carr* (1979) 1 Cr App Rep (S) 53). Alternatively, if the activating offence merits a prison sentence, the two sentences can be made concurrent in such a case. The CA has also reduced the activated sentence because of the triviality of the *later* offence (eg in *Joshua* (1980) 2 Cr App Rep (S) 287), although the logic of this is not easy to follow. Whether the court activates the SS with its original or a reduced term, this should normally be consecutive to any prison sentence for the later offence (*Ithell* (1969) 53 Cr App Rep 210). The statute (s 23 PCCA 73) allows the court to order that it take effect immediately or consecutively; but the former is regarded as appropriate only in special circumstances (*May* (1979) 1 Cr App

Rep (S) 124). An example of special circumstances was *Carr* ((1979) 1 Cr App Rep (S) 53), whose operational period had nearly expired when he committed the activating offence. The length of any prison sentence for the later offence should be determined without regard to the fact that the offender was under a SS, and before even considering whether the SS is to be activated (*Ithell* (1969) 53 Cr App Rep 210).

## Rationale of the suspended sentence

**10.34** The theoretical reason given by English proponents of this Continental sentence was that it constitutes a more specific threat of a penalty than does probation or a conditional discharge, and would thus deter more effectively. It also appealed to 'denouncers' (see chapters 8 and 9) who thought that in some cases it was sufficient for the sentence to sound severe enough to declare society's disapproval of the offence, without actually being suffered by the offender. The practical reason why it was eventually adopted by the Government of 1967 was the expectation that it would relieve pressure on the prison population. In fact reconviction rates after SSs turned out to be higher than after any other measure, and the impact on the prison population was less than had been hoped (see Bottoms (1980)). From the point of view, however, of those who want to minimise the total number of offenders who experience a prison sentence (for example because of the harm which it is believed to do: see chapter 11), SSs are by no means a failure. Even when SSs were frequent, only about 28 per cent of those who received them became eligible for activation; and since the non-activation rate was about 25 per cent only about 1 in 5 SSs were eventually activated. It is true that in those cases the effect of activation—which usually results in two consecutive sentences—was a longer period of imprisonment than would have been served for the second offence; but for every activation there were about four SSs which were never activated. Not all of their recipients avoid the experience of a prison sentence; but the Philpotts-Lancucki follow-up (see 7.34 ff) found that 38 per cent of recipients of SSs were not reconvicted of imprisonable offences during a 6-year period; and the probability of such a conviction after six years is known to be low. On the other hand, it was pointed out in the early days of the SS that it was sometimes being used for offenders who would have been dealt with non-custodially if the SS had not been available, so that if activated it resulted in imprisonment for some offenders who would not have gone to prison. This is more likely to have happened before the CJA 72 expressly restricted SSs to cases in which prison sentences seemed appropriate; and in any case a person reconvicted of a non-trivial imprisonable offence is quite likely to be imprisoned for it whether or not he is subject to an SS. There can be no doubt that the availability of the SS prevents some offenders from ever experiencing a prison sentence. It is of course open to question whether this is an important objective; and the reconviction rates after SSs were discouraging. But to treat the SS as a failed experiment is to over-simplify. Since the CJA 91 provides that SSs are to be imposed only in 'exceptional circumstances', there is a real danger that offenders will be sent to prison who previously might never have been.

## Incompatible measures

**10.35**  By statute a court which passes a SS must not combine it with a probation order for another offence although it may combine it with a SS supervision order (see 17.30ff) if the sentence exceeds 6 months. A community service order, too, should not be imposed on the same occasion as a SS (*Starie* (1979) 69 Cr App Rep 239). It is also wrong to impose an immediate prison sentence on the same occasion as a SS (*Sapiano* (1968) 52 Cr App Rep 674); nor should a SS be imposed on an offender who is already serving an immediate term of imprisonment.

## Partial suspension

**10.36**  For 10 years, between 1982 (although introduced in the CLA 77, it was not brought into force until 1982) and 1992 it was possible for a court to impose a partially suspended sentence. If a court passed a sentence of not less than 3 months' nor more than 2 years' imprisonment on a person aged 21 or older, and if the case was one in which complete suspension appeared to the court inappropriate, it could order that after he had served part of it the remainder was to be held in suspense. The suspended part had to be not less than a quarter of the whole sentence, and the part to be served in prison had to be not be less than 28 days, although this could be reduced by time spent in custody on remand.

**10.37**  The sentence was clearly intended for serious first offenders or first-time prisoners who were bound to have to serve some time in prison, but who might have been effectively deterred by serving only a small part of even the minimum sentence appropriate to the offence, or perhaps for prisoners whose last term of imprisonment had been a considerable time previously (see *Clarke* ((1982) 4 Cr App Rep (S) 197). It was never designed, as it has been used in some countries, to enforce compensation to the victim. For example, in some African jurisdictions today part of a sentence will be suspended on condition that the offender pays a sum of money to his victim. The partially suspended sentence appears to have been abolished in this country partly because it was never popular with sentencers and partly because of the complications which partial suspension introduced into the calculation of release dates. There was no attempt to evaluate whether the sentence resulted in lower reconviction rates.

## Intermittent custodial sentences

**10.38**  A mode of incarceration which has not so far been adopted in Britain is 'intermittent custody', whether as a specific sentence or as an executive policy for carrying out sentences. It has been discussed from time to time (for instance by ACPS 1970), but rejected because of the administrative and other problems which it would raise. In 1984 as a result of renewed proposals by the Magistrates' Association and the All-Party Parliamentary Penal Affairs Group the Home Office published a consultative document, *Intermittent Custody*. This distinguished three possibilities:

a.  'daily release', to enable selected short-term prisoners who are employed when they begin their sentences to go out to work, returning to prison each evening. This would work only if it took the form of an extension of the executive's powers of temporary release. The consultative document expressed a preference for the other possibilities;

b.  'day imprisonment', involving compulsory attendance at a centre for a specified number of hours each day (perhaps excluding Sundays), in order to engage in crafts, education or work of benefit to the community:

c.  'week-end or partial imprisonment', involving continuous custody from Friday evening to Sunday evening, or on days during the week. The consultative document expressed a preference for this form. It might provide the offender with constructive or rehabilitative activities, or be 'deliberately sparse'; but its main point would be that it would 'primarily frustrate his wish to do something else'.

However, it would be necessary to look for readily available buildings, rather than use existing prisons; and it seemed doubtful whether the provision of facilities throughout the entire country would ever be warranted. Courts would have to work out what number of hours or days of day release or weekend imprisonment should be regarded as the equivalents of short continuous sentences: a not altogether easy problem.

**10.39**  The most common criticism of these ideas has been that courts would be more likely to substitute intermittent custody for non-custodial measures than for continuous sentences of imprisonment, which is regarded as an undesirable consequence. It would certainly increase the cost of sentences; but what it would do to their effectiveness cannot be assumed.

## Executing the sentence

**10.40**  An unsuspended sentence is put into effect immediately: the offender is removed from court to a local prison, or to a remand centre for transfer to a prison. If he was not already the responsibility of the Prison Service he becomes it as soon as sentenced. Even if he immediately appeals against sentence this does not usually lead to bail or a postponement of incarceration. It is worth contrasting the English system in this respect with the Netherlands, where a prison sentence leads to immediate incarceration only if the offender is already in custody, whether because he has been refused bail or because he is already serving another sentence. Otherwise, he awaits the 'call-up' to prison; and nearly 2 in 3 sentenced prisoners are dealt with in this way. The waiting time depends on vacancies in the appropriate prison: for the majority it is 3 to 4 months. When called up an offender can ask for a postponement, and if his reasons are good will get it. He can also apply for 'mercy', which at least postpones his imprisonment until the application has been considered, and could, if successful, mean the conversion of the sentence to suspended imprisonment: if he has waited a long time for his call-up this is quite likely to be the outcome. Called-up offenders go to less strict prisons than other prisoners, unless they fail to obey the call-up. About 1 in 7 do not arrive at the prison on the due date, and have to be arrested. (The number arrested has been increasing in recent years.) ACPS in its 1974 Report proposed that an English court which is imposing a custodial sentence on a young adult should in exceptional circumstances be able to postpone the commencement of the sentence, on application either by the defence or by the prison authorities (1974); but this modest proposal was not accepted. Postponement would sometimes solve the problem faced by the sentencer who wants to order compensation by an offender who could pay it out of earnings (and not otherwise), but whom he feels obliged to sentence to imprisonment.

# Chapter 11

# Imprisonment's wanted and unwanted effects

**11.1** Legislators and sentencers intend imprisonment to punish, deter and incapacitate. The Prison Service has traditionally put an optimistic gloss on those aims[1]. Encouraging and assisting inmates to lead 'a good and useful life' was the purpose declared in the Prison Rules, and survived many years of ridicule. The Prisons Board's 1984 statement of its tasks was less ambitious but more detailed and down-to-earth:

'... to use with maximum efficiency the resources of staff, money, building and plant made available to it by Parliament in order to fulfil in accordance with the relevant provisions of the law the following functions:
   (i)   to keep in custody untried or unsentenced prisoners, and to present them to court for trial or sentence;
   (ii)  to keep in custody, with such degree of security as is appropriate, having regard to the nature of the individual prisoner and his offence, sentenced prisoners for the duration of their sentence or for such shorter time as the Secretary of State may determine in cases where he has discretion;
   (iii) to provide for prisoners as full a life as is consistent with the facts of custody, in particular making available the physical necessities of life; care for physical and mental health; advice and help with personal problems; work, education, training, physical exercise and recreation; and opportunity to practise their religion; and
   (iv)  to enable prisoners to retain links with the community and where possible assist them to prepare for their return to it.' (Home Office Circular 55/1984.)

The mission statement of 1988 was simpler and more traditional:

'Her Majesty's Prison Service serves the public by keeping in custody those committed by the courts. Our duty is to look after them with humanity and to help them lead law-abiding and useful lives in custody and after release'.

The 1984 statement was franker and more realistic about the limitations imposed by Parliament, by resources and by 'the facts of custody'.

1.   For an excellent discussion of these and other formulations see Bottoms (1990).

### Individual deterrence

**11.2**   The usual hope, however, of legislators and sentencers is that the experience of imprisonment will be so unpleasant that it will discourage the ex-prisoner from risking another term: in other words, that it will be an effective individual deterrent. Prima facie this seems quite likely. For most offenders their first prison sentence is humiliating, alarming, frustrating, depressing and boring; and while they may learn how to cope with it psychologically they nevertheless fear a repetition of it. It is only some despairing 'undeterribles' for whom it has no terrors (see 8.10). Yet as the Philpotts-Lancucki follow-up demonstrated (see Table 7B), when adult male offenders have reached the stage of their second and third convictions imprisonment does not, as a general rule, have any more effect than milder measures on their likelihood of reconviction. The most that can be said is that suspending the sentence seems even less effective. It is only those imprisoned on their first conviction who seem to have been in some way encouraged to avoid another conviction, at least for the next six years; and this is unlikely to be due to anything more positive than individual deterrence. This does not justify the inference sometimes drawn: that a man who has already experienced one prison term should not receive another if he is reconvicted. Obviously any assurance of exemption would undermine the deterrent effect. What it does suggest is that a man who has experienced two or more prison sentences and yet is reconvicted is unlikely to be affected by a third. If there is any hope of improving his future conduct it must lie in doing something different to him. Occasionally a court which is faced with a man who has experienced several prison sentences resorts to probation. Otherwise, sentencers feel obliged to impose yet another prison term, sometimes in order to maintain the credibility of prison as a general deterrent, sometimes to protect others, but usually because they regard it as deserved.

**11.3**   Sentencers often make the second sentence longer than the first, and the third longer than the second, in the hope that greater length will succeed in deterring: a hope which has a little support from research. Ward (1987), who was studying the accuracy of a prediction score for parole purposes, noticed that, even when the relevant variables such as age, type of offence and previous sentences were allowed for, and even when the subjects were men who had not been paroled, reconviction rates were lower the longer the time served. In the case of paroled men the effect was similar but less marked.

### The pains of imprisonment

**11.4**   What is it about custodial sentences that deters? Broadly speaking, 'the pains of imprisonment', a useful phrase popularised by Sykes (1958)[1]. These range from the obvious to the incidental:

a. deprivation of freedom. Although it is the intention of the sentence that the offender should be confined within an institution, he also suffers restrictions on his movement within the institution. In a local prison or remand centre—and in some training prisons too—he spends much of his time in a cell. Even when allowed out of his cell, he must be either in the wing to which he belongs or in a workshop or classroom. His visits to the open air are restricted to set times or the minutes necessary to go from one building to another. These restrictions are not the intention of the sentence but are considered necessary to control large numbers of inmates and prevent escapes. Much greater freedom is allowed in open prisons; but only a minority of prisoners are entrusted to them;

b. his food and drink are limited to what is provided, with the exception of the small gifts which visitors are allowed to bring and the purchases he can afford in the prison shop. No alcohol is allowed. If he needs special food for medical or religious reasons efforts will be made to provide it; but there will be delays, oversights and complaints about the cooking;

c. his purchasing power is severely limited. Within the prison he can spend only the pittance which he earns, plus a limited amount from his private cash. He will be allowed to buy approved items such as a radio or a favourite newspaper from outside (or his family or friends can provide them). The prison shop stocks cigarettes, sweets, toiletries—more or less what one would find in a village post-office;

d. his contact with family and friends outside is very limited. More will be said about this in 11.39;

e. he is forced to associate with other prisoners, whose tastes and values may be very different from his. Some of them will be men used to violence, so that he is likely to be in greater personal danger than he would be in freedom. If he has incurred dislike—for example because of the nature of his offence, or because he is an informer—he may be persecuted as well as assaulted (see 11.20ff). If he is not very intelligent he will be exploited by cleverer prisoners. He may be 'taxed'; that is, subjected to extortion by the powerful. He may become the target of homosexual advances, although he will hardly ever be forced to submit to them: homosexual rape is rarer than it is said to be in US jails or penitentiaries. The regime does not cater for friendships, and every transfer from one prison to another means new relationships. Even if he is at home in the society of prison his choice of associates is limited;

f. he loses the power of choice in everyday matters. He must get up, wash, eat, work, exercise, read and so on at prescribed times. Even a man whose outside life is organised into routine finds the routine of prison even more inhibiting. It is even said that the lack of choice in trivial as well as important matters is psychologically damaging: that the ex-prisoner finds it hard to made necessary choices again when he is free (but see 11.26ff);

g. he also loses privacy. At the outset of his sentence he will almost certainly be made to share a cell with a stranger whose character and habits are not what he would choose. If the whole of his sentence is spent in a local prison he is unlikely to be given a cell to himself. In training and dispersal prisons, on the other hand, he will be unlucky not to. In open prisons he is likely to sleep in a dormitory like a hospital ward. Only prisoners who are segregated for their own protection or for disciplinary reasons enjoy real privacy, and even their cells have peepholes.

The modern English prison system does not try to intensify any of the pains of imprisonment, unlike military 'glasshouses'. Its slogan for the last half century has been 'Men are sent to prison *as* punishment, not *for* punishment'. If a slogan could have a footnote it might be 'except when they are unpopular with those inside'. The system cannot abolish the pains, but it can, and does, try to palliate them. It is sometimes criticised for trying too hard.

1. His list of pains was shorter: deprivation of goods and services; of heterosexual relationships; of autonomy; of security. The pains are less severe in a few respects for unsentenced inmates; but this chapter is concerned with the effects of sentences.

## Escaping and absconding

**11.5**  It even tries to alleviate the deprivation of liberty—its essential aim—by means of open prisons, unescorted work outside, 'community visits' (e g to shopping centres) and home leave. Some prisoners —about 2,000 a year—take advantage and 'abscond'; but most of them soon give themselves up (often at their homes) or are recaptured, without doing real harm. More important are 'escapes' from escorts or secure establishments, which are dealt with in 14.38ff.

## Incentives and earned privileges

**11.6**  Depriving offenders of liberty, however, is only one of the service's aims. It tries to make custody 'positive'. Its latest initiative in this direction was the introduction of a system of incentives and earned privileges in 1995. Like the old borstal system this consists essentially of grading inmates according to their behaviour and willingness to co-operate (Instruction to Governors 74/1995). The basic grade is allowed a few of the 'key privileges', such as association with others: but even these can be suspended for disciplinary reasons. The standard grade is allowed more; and the 'enhanced' grade considerably more. Since conditions vary widely between establishments governors have a great deal of discretion to decide what privileges it is practicable to grant to each grade (for example the relaxation of visiting arrangements or leave for a 'community visit' accompanied by a relative, friend or social worker). Obviously there is more scope for privileges in open or training prisons than in local or remand prisons; but all establishments must adopt the IEP policy. Research workers (Liebling et al) have already begun to study its effects.

## Sentence planning

**11.7**  Prisoners serving 4 years or more are the subjects of 'sentence planning', an important element of which is employment or vocational training.The justifications for making prisoners work, however, have become less optimistic with time and experience:

a.  it prevents 'idleness, mother and root of all vices' (a Tudor statute);
b.  it can be used to intensify the pains of imprisonment by making it 'hard, dull and useless'. This is an obsolete Victorian objective: but some prison jobs are dirty and unexciting, and a prisoner who makes himself unpopular may find himself in one of them;
c.  it helps to meet the cost of a prisoner's keep. Prisoners who cook, clean or repair save the service the cost of outside labour, and prison industry in 1992-3 contributed a little over £5m to the running-costs of the service;
d.  it fills the prisoner's day: an argument in the 1959 White Paper *Penal Practice in a Changing Society* which echoes Tudor thinking. The 1991 *National Prison Survey* (the 'NPS', by Walmsley et al, 1992) found that even in local prisons 64 per cent of sentenced prisoners worked, for an average 36 hours a week, and the percentage in training prisons was higher;
e.  it prepares prisoners for a law-abiding life after release. More than 200 vocational training courses are provided in various training prisons, and an increasing number lead to National Vocational Qualifications. The hope is that these will offer 'better employment prospects and reduce the likelihood of reoffending' (Prison Service's *Annual Report*, 1991-2). No doubt this hope is sometimes realised; but that is less likely in times of high unemployment. The NPS found that only a minority of prisoners —21 per cent—thought that their work would help them get a job outside. The others were probably the more realistic.

Unsentenced prisoners cannot be required to work without contravening Art 4 of the European Convention of Human Rights, but sentenced prisoners can, and are quite often disciplined for refusal. Long-term prisoners, however, are usually allowed to have depressed or unco-operative moods, and are dealt with leniently when they take days off.

## Work for the community

11.8  Activities that benefit others are also encouraged, especially in YOIs. Community service of various kinds was a feature of most borstal regimes in the 1950s, long before the Wootton Report recommended it as a non-custodial sentence. Many of the 'meals on wheels' for the elderly and handicapped are cooked in prison kitchens, and in some areas are delivered by volunteers. Some establishments allow selected prisoners 'temporary release' for the day to join local volunteers who provide services in hospitals, day centres and the Cheshire Homes. There are summer camps at which young adult prisoners help other volunteers to build adventure playgrounds, maintain a holiday centre for the handicapped, or perform other tasks of obvious value. Individual prisoners produce braille texts or tapes for the blind, or make equipment for local nursery schools. Apart from the benefit to the recipients, activities of these kinds are seen as introducing prisoners to what Bentham called 'the pleasures of benevolence', and also as bringing them into friendly association with the sort of volunteer who may encourage a change of attitude to life. Inevitably it is the hand-picked inmate who has the best chance of being involved in this kind of activity. Inevitably, too, the chance is occasionally abused. Only the most cynical of critics, however, would question the value of it.

## Education

**11.9** Sentence planning may also include education. The May Report (1979) recommended 'rigorous education of all kinds' for prisoners, and disciplinary punishment for idleness in class as well as at work. The Prison Rules are more realistic, and simply provide that every prisoner able to profit from the educational facilities at a prison shall be *encouraged* to do so. Until 1993 education was provided by local education authorities, who recruited part-time teachers for the purpose. Now colleges of further education tender competitively for this service. The Prison Service's Annual Report for 1993-4 claimed that standards had already improved. But such arrangements cost money, and some governors have made them a target for economies.

**11.10** About 1 in 8 inmates have real difficulties with reading, writing and arithmetic. Two in 5 left school at the minimum age (or indeed before that), and most were unenthusiastic pupils. Classes in literacy and other basic skills are provided, but are not compulsory. Basis English classes are provided in most prisons, and are the ones most often attended.There are also courses for the GCSE and A Levels, and some 300 prisoners a year are taking Open University courses. The percentage of prisoners in the NPS who thought that their classes would be useful to them after release (68 per cent) was much higher than the percentage who were optimistic about the usefulness of their work. Education in prisons, however, is very dependent on the co-operation of uniformed staff. Industrial action by officers has at times meant the suspension of most, if not all, classes. Some officers regard classes as ways of avoiding work, and criticise the service for providing prisoners with better educational opportunities than are open to children or adults outside. Other difficulties are shortages of books and teaching materials in general, and the recruitment of suitable teachers. Encouraging and holding the interest of classes presents special difficulties when most of the members of the class are people who saw little point in ordinary school classes. Even keen learners are discouraged by transfers from one establishment to another, which usually means, among other things, the loss of hard-won books and a change of teacher.

**11.11** Another discouraging aspect is the fact that very few prisoners who participate in classes continue with education after release. This was the subject of a realistic report by a NACRO Working Party (1981). It recognised that for most inmates education is little more than a way of helping time to pass. With the possible exception of those who need remedial education, it is those who have already achieved some success in education who see most benefit in continuing it. The help which they needed did not seem to be of a kind which prison teachers were usually able to give (but that was before colleges of further education took over the responsibility). NACRO itself provided an Education Advisory Service, but lack of funds brought it to an end.

## Libraries

**11.12** Every prison and YOI must have a library from which inmates can borrow books. These libraries are branches of the local authority library service.. The contents are chiefly recreational—i e novels and magazines—but include some technical publications. Prisoners can put in requests for specific books, although like other users of local authority libraries they may be disappointed. The libraries are manned by inmates, under an officer's supervision. The number of books which a prisoner can have on loan at any one time is restricted; and in a local prison a man who reads fast will probably find that his ration is exhausted before his turn for borrowing comes round again. Training prisons' libraries tend to be better stocked and managed than those in the locals; but some library services economise by sending damaged or worn-out books to prison libraries. By contrast, some library services take a great deal of trouble over prison libraries, providing popular paperbacks, books for ethnic minorities, and technical advice.

## Offending behaviour

**11.13** Not long ago an Erewhonian[1] ethos treated a prisoner's crime as semi-confidential, to be discussed with him only by professional staff, as if it were an embarrassing disease. This was understandable when it was of a kind which might provoke attacks from fellow inmates; but the convention went further, and there was a tendency to regard his punishment as entitling him not to be confronted with the harm he had done. Even in the heyday of group counselling prisoners tended to discuss their attitudes to staff and each other rather than their misdeeds. Nowadays several prisons offer courses of psychological treatment to sexual offenders which focus on their behaviour and its effects on victims, although the courses are not usually offered to those serving short sentences. The credit for experimenting with discussions which confront offenders of other kinds with the consequences of their behaviour probably belongs to the probation service, although prison psychologists played an important part in introducing this approach to YOIs and prisons. By 1992 there were 14 establishments with programmes for sexual offenders; prison psychologists had produced a manual on 'anger-management' courses, and training for staff had begun at 10 prisons or YOIs. The 'Corporate Plan for 1993-6' promised extensions of these programmes to include social[2] and cognitive skills, on lines found moderately successful in a probation setting (Knott, 1995), all of them designed to reduce offending behaviour, and especially violence.

1. In Samuel Butler's satire *Erewhon* (1872) crimes were treated as embarrassing illnesses, and vice versa.
2. Social skills courses for prisoners are not a new idea. Priestley et al produced a training manual on the subject in 1978. Their follow-up (1984) did not suggest that the courses improved ex-prisoners' behaviour so far as the law was concerned.

## Recreation

**11.14**  Most prisoners have a sparetime activity in which they invest a lot of interest and even much of their money. This is most evident in YOIs and prisons where medium or long sentences are served: the locals are too overcrowded, and their staffs too hard-pressed, to allow for much 'individualisation' of recreation. In the training prisons the variety of activities is greater. There are gymnasia, space for handicrafts, and playing fields. The educational and library staff help prisoners to get technical books and books which are not in the local libraries through a special loan system. Evening classes for hobbies, crafts and tuition in foreign languages are well attended. Limitations of course are imposed by space and security. Prisoners are allowed training in weight-lifting but not karate. Weapon-training for cadet forces in borstals was abandoned when Baroness Wootton objected, sensibly, to offenders being taught the use of firearms. There are also clandestine recreations. Gambling is popular—but forbidden, because it leads to debts and violent methods of collection. Trafficking in tobacco is also discouraged for the same reason, but is about as endemic. Since alcohol and other drugs are banned, manufacturing the former and smuggling in the latter can be both exciting and profitable. Some prisoners are involved in feuds with others, some enjoy contriving embarrassment—or worse— for their custodians.

## Coping

**11.15**  All these activities help time to pass. Inmates of any custodial institution must find ways of coping with their situations if they are not to become casualties of one sort or another (see 11.24ff) At least six ways of coping have been described (e g by Mott, 1985):
  i. 'uncertain negative retreat': difficulties in dealing with both staff and other inmates;
  ii. 'secondary comfort indulgence': simply enjoying the comforts of the prison;
  iii. 'jailing': considerable involvement in the inmate social system, with access to, and marketing of, contraband items;
  iv. 'gleaning': frequent contacts with specialist treatment staff, attending many educational courses in the hope of attaining useful qualifications;
  v. 'opportunism': exploiting both the inmate social system and the specialist staff and educational resources;
  vi. 'doing your bird': never attracting attention from staff or other prisoners, but respected by both groups, while enjoying the comforts of the regime.
Obviously some of these strategies seem 'healthier' than others: more desirable from the point of view of both prisoner and staff. Not all prisoners, however, are capable of making a rational choice of strategy, and attempts to help them choose may misfire.

## Welfare

**11.16** Many prisoners bring personal problems with them. Some of these have been created by sudden removal from freedom: a child or relative in need of care, for example, or a car left on the street. Others are of longer standing: unpaid rents, domestic discord, failing businesses. Prisons used to have 'welfare officers', but their places have been taken by probation officers seconded (not always enthusiastically) from the local probation service. They are able to advise about problems, rather like the Citizens' Advice Bureaux, and can sometimes do something about them through local contacts with the social services or other agencies. Prison officers have fought to be involved in welfare, and the result is a compromise called 'shared working', with certain tasks falling to uniformed staff. A uniformed officer is often in a position to notice and report illiteracy, low intelligence, drug abuse, bullying, or the prisoner's reaction to distressing news. Prison probation officers take part in sentence planning and what is called 'throughcare' (ie preparations for release); but now that governors are compelled to budget carefully some have decided to economise in the services of prison probation officers.

## Religious influence

**11.17** Side by side with the Victorian belief in work went faith in the remedial powers of religious exhortation. The convicts in the penitentiaries were the targets of sermons, prayers and tracts, and the subjects of many tales of conversion and redemption. Nowadays such experiences are rarer. Religious conformity is less common than in previous generations, and nowhere less common than in gaol. Prisoners are no longer compelled to attend services or even meet chaplains, although every establishment has them. Chaplains themselves are more realistic about the sincerity of religious belief and its effectiveness in keeping prisoners on the straight and narrow path. At one time, chaplains were the unofficial welfare officers of the prisons; and if prisons dispense with probation officers they may find themselves again in this position.

## Health

**11.18** The physical health of the sentenced male population of prisons and YOIs was the subject of a sample survey in 1993 (Bridgwood and Malbon, 1994), which allowed some comparisons with the English male population. The sentenced population included a disproportionate percentage who had been day-patients or in-patients of the NHS when admitted. Four times as many described themselves as heavy drinkers. Eighty-three percent of the YOI sample (and 64 per cent of the whole sample) had been using drugs illegally. Prisoners were twice as likely as non-prisoners to be smokers; and some prisons try to discourage them. Whatever else English prisons do they at least make it harder to obtain alcohol and prohibited drugs. In 1995 random-urine testing was experimentally initiated in eight prisons in an effort to make them drug-free; but, as King and McDermott observe (1995) drug-*treatment* programmes are still 'very much in their infancy'. Prison diets were overhauled in the 1980s, and most prisoners eat less fatty and fried foods than they did outside (but alas less fruit and vegetables). Only a third of the 1993 sample were overweight, compared with half of English men outside. Yet providing prisoners—and especially young men—with enough interesting exercise is not easy, especially in remand and local prisons (training prisons have gymnasia). Keeping clean no longer seems to be a problem: 66 per cent of prisoners in the NPS had unlimited access to baths or showers, and only 2 per cent claimed to have had no such facilities for a week. Every establishment has either a full-time physician or regular visits from a local general practitioner; and prisoners who ask to see one usually do so on the same day if their request is made early in the day (14 per cent of the 1993 sample said that there had been at least one occasion in the previous fortnight when they had been unable to see a doctor; but the interviewers did not ask why.)

## Health risks

**11.19** The majority of prisoners are therefore in slightly better health than before admission. Some on the other hand are exposed to specific risks. Tuberculosis has become commoner in prisons, and can be transmitted in shared cells and crowded dormitories. Hepatitis B and C and HIV can be contracted from unprotected anal sex or needles shared for drug-injecting or tattooing. Drug abusers may lose their addiction as a result of deprivation when they enter prison, but if they do not are at greater risk of becoming self-injectors than they would be outside. Immunisation against hepatitis B is offered to every member of staff and every inmate, but it may take as much as 12 months to acquire complete immunity. (Immunisation cannot be provided against hepatitis C or HIV.) Condoms can be obtained on prescription. The bleach tablets issued to inmates for hygienic purposes can be used to sterilise needles.

## Violence

**11.20** There is also the risk of assault by other inmates (and in some situations by prison officers). Homosexual rape, which is said to be frequent in American custodial institutions, is rare in English ones. It is ordinary violence which both male and female prisoners have to fear, and especially if they belong to one of four groups:
  a.  those believed to have sexually molested or ill-treated children;
  b.  those believed to be 'grasses' (i e informers);
  c.  those involved in gang feuds;
  d.  those who do not pay debts incurred in gambling or trafficking in tobacco or drugs within the prison.
The NPS found 9 per cent of prisoners who said that they had been assaulted in the last 6 months, and twice as many who admitted not feeling safe from being

injured or bullied. Bullying is most frequent in YOIs. In prisons a common motive for violence is the enforcement of debts owed for drugs or other goods.

**11.21**   Case-law says that the prison authorities have 'a common law duty ... to take reasonable care for the safety of prisoners' (*Ellis v Home Office* [1953] 2 QB 135 CA: and see 13.22). It is true that as *Ellis* and other cases have demonstrated it is not easy for plaintiffs to convince courts that this reasonable care has not been taken, but several plaintiffs have succeeded in doing so: see for example *D'Arcy v Prison Comrs* [1956] Crim LR 56 (plaintiff knifed in Parkhurst), and *H v Home Office,* in (1992) Independent, 6 May (a case in which negligent disclosure of the nature of H's offences led to his being assaulted by other prisoners). When a prisoner who is known to be a likely target for attack is received (from outside, on transfer or after a period of segregation) staff are alerted to the need to keep an eye on him, and he is supervised at work and in other places where he associates with other prisoners. Special care is taken when allocating him to shared cells, dormitories or working parties. Some prisoners have to be segregated in special wings under Rule 43, or transferred to one of the special units for vulnerable prisoners: see 12.29ff. The latter is not segregation under Rule 43, and allows the prisoner to live in association with others for the greater part of the day. In spite of these efforts violence is an everyday occurrence, and even the Prison Service's Key Performance Indicators (KPIs) concede that there is an irreducible minimum.

## Mental health

**11.22**   It is widely believed that imprisonment impairs mental health. To what extent is this true of the English system? It is necessary to distinguish two suppositions. One is that imprisonment causes some mental disorders; the other is that it leads to what is loosely called 'institutionalisation'. The notion that it *causes* mental disorder in mentally healthy prisoners rests on no sound evidence. Certainly there are many impaired, psychopathic, hypomanic, schizophrenic, over-anxious prisoners. Equally certainly impairment, mania, psychopathy, schizophrenia are not caused by events such as ordinary imprisonment, although they may first be noticed as a result of observation in prison. Most prisoners suffering from such disorders turn out to have histories of special care or treatment before their first imprisonment. One of the chronic problems of the prison health care service has been finding hospitals willing to accept the transfer of mentally disordered prisoners (see 21.52).

**11.23**   What is true is that many prisoners become very depressed on first admission, especially during the process of trial and sentence. It has to be realised, however, that some of these prisoners were of a depressive temperament in their ordinary lives: this is especially likely to be true of the heavy drinkers, whose depression can no longer be kept at bay when they are deprived of alcohol. In some other cases the depression is an understandable reaction to the prospect of conviction, stigma, loss of job, rejection by one's family and deprivation of liberty: in other words it is a natural response to the situation rather than a product of the regime. Nevertheless it may need treatment, if suicidal behaviour is to be prevented.

## Suicide

**11.24**   The male suicide rate, often attributed to mental illness, is four times as high in prison service establishments as in the general population, and the disparity is only slightly less when allowance is made for socio-economic differences. As Liebling (1995) has pointed out, however, 'Arguably the prison population is carefully selected to be at risk of suicide'. The great majority of inmates who attempt or commit suicide are not mentally disordered but 'vulnerable', coming from broken families, often in local authority care for reasons other than delinquency, truants because of bullying at school. They have difficulty in coping with life outside, and inside are overwhelmed by isolation, hostility and helplessness. Conscientious efforts are made to identify the suicide-prone as soon as they are admitted, and to keep them under close observation. Only a hunger-striker of sound mind has (so far) established his right to 'determine his future' (*Robb* [1995] 1 All ER 677). Preventive measures— apart from close observation—include special training for staff, cell-sharing, counselling, anti-bullying measures and, in extreme cases, hospitalisation. In some prisons suitable inmates are trained, Samaritan-wise, to be 'listeners', in the hope that suicidally-minded fellow inmates will confide in them.

## Institutionalisation

**11.25**   Yet if the English prison regime cannot be accused of causing mental disorder, the possibility that it leads to what is called 'institutionalisation' or 'prisonisation' must be taken seriously. This condition was first 'diagnosed' in long-term mental hospital patients; and it was only later that the possibility of a similar effect in other types of institution was mooted. It is attributed to *long continuous* periods of detention, coupled with monotony, lack of autonomy and loss of contact with the world outside. In England the average time actually served by a male prisoner is about 7 months. Only about 8 per cent are received under sentences of 4 years or more, and some (not all) of them will actually spend more than 4 years inside. Many others, however, spend considerable fractions of their adult lives inside, with only short intervals of liberty. It is the psychological fate of these minorities which is the subject of concern.

**11.26**   There is evidence and pseudo-evidence. The best-known example of pseudo-evidence is Cohen and Taylor's *Psychological Survival* (1972). This was based on their discussions with long-term prisoners in the high-security wing of Durham from 1968 to 1971, while they were supposed to be providing the prisoners with classes in sociology, but in fact holding 'unprogrammed discussions' and moving into the role of research workers. What they describe in their book is not so much the deterioration which the prisoners were suffering as the prisoners' fears of deterioration, some at least of which must have been stimulated or reinforced by the discussions and by the books with which Cohen and Taylor supplied them. *Psychological Survival* is a fascinating and insightful description of what went on in the minds of McVicar and his fellow inmates, and also of the real frustrations which they had to endure; but it is not evidence for actual deterioration. McVicar himself dismissed with contempt the suggestion that he deteriorated.

**11.27** Unfortunately few investigators have tried to measure institutionalisation in non-subjective ways, and most of those who have were more interested in special conditions than in ordinary prison life: for example in the effects of solitary confinement, or death-cell experiences. A thorough review by Bukstel and Kilmann (1980) of studies published in English found that most had serious methodological shortcomings. If these studies are disregarded, we are left with a few which bear on the following aspects of psychological deterioration.

## Intellectual performance

**11.28** Bolton et al (1976) tested and after about 20 months retested 154 long-term male prisoners, and, for comparison, 30 adult male non-prisoners. Using well-developed types of test, they found no evidence of intellectual deterioration. Indeed verbal ability seemed to have improved (perhaps because prisoners spend so much time talking). It is worth noting that many of their subjects were in the same prison as that described by Cohen and Taylor, and that the two investigations were more or less contemporary. Cohen and Taylor devoted a whole appendix of *Psychological Survival* to criticisms of this research, which, though not then complete, seemed likely to contradict some of their impressions.

## Other aspects of personality

**11.29** Using the MMPI, Steininger (1959)[1] studied the adjustment of 'first offenders' to prison life, finding that they experienced a strong 'distress syndrome' which lasted several months (i e they were unhappy). They were at first anxious to create a good impression and therefore behaved fairly well. Later their behaviour deteriorated and their distress abated, but worsened towards the end of the year of study. Jacobs (1975)[1] found that during their first year inmates became less anxious and concerned about others' evaluation of them, more manipulative, and more paranoid. As they neared release their anxiety increased again. As regards hostility towards others and oneself, the findings of various investigators conflict with each other, perhaps because different personality types were not adequately distinguished.

1. As summarised by Bukstel and Kilmann: their theses remain unpublished.

## 'Problems'

**11.30** In an English prison for lifers and long-sentence men, Richards (1978) developed a list of 20 problems which seemed to sample the areas of psychological stress experienced during longer periods of incarceration. His subjects were 11 men who were in their first 18 months of sentence (the Early Group) matched for age, types of offence and type of sentence with 11 who had served at least eight years (the Late Group) . The two groups, however, did not seem to differ in their ratings of the relative frequency and intensity of the 20 problems: The five most severe problems were:

- missing somebody;
- feeling that your life is being wasted;
- feeling sexually frustrated;
- missing little 'luxuries';
- missing social life.

Interestingly, although these problems are essentially deprivations of the perquisites of freedom, it was the men who had served at least 8 years who were more preoccupied with them: a finding which contradicts the usual picture of 'prisonisation'. Even more interesting were the five problems which they rated as *least* severe:

- losing your self-confidence;
- feeling angry with the world;
- being afraid of dying before you get out[1];
- being afraid of going mad;
- feeling suicidal.

1. Since their average age was about 30, and they were all in reasonable health, it is not surprising that they ranked this low.

**11.31** This, and the prisoners' emphasis on their capacity for self-reliance, does not support the gloomier descriptions of the state of mind of long-term inmates. Richards concedes that the prison in which this study was done had the reputation of an 'easy nick'. It is possible that the findings in a 'tough nick' would have been more discouraging; and as we shall see lifers in particular do have to fear certain things. What the study does suggest is that in one of the better English prisons long-sentence men are less likely to become psychological casualties than Goffman or Cohen and Taylor believe. It is often forgotten that the personal experience on which Goffman based *Asylums* (1961) was acquired in old-fashioned mental hospitals, although he draws on the *literature* of prisons, concentration camps, boarding schools, borstals, nunneries, barracks, in order to support a number of generalisations about 'total institutions'. The reader is led to believe, by implication rather than direct statement, that there is no difference between the degradation of a concentration camp and the somewhat spartan life in Orwell's Eton.

### Lifers

**11.32** On the other hand, it is possible that a life sentence, with its uncertainty about eventual release, has more undesirable effects than a long determinate one. Most of Richards' subjects knew that they would be released or paroled on or before a definite date. Sapsford (1978) took as his subjects 60 mandatory lifers in a different prison, with conditions of maximum security. Twenty-six had just begun their sentences; 24 had served about 6 years and had not yet been considered for licensing; 10 were men who had spent longer than the average lifer inside (i e more than about 9 years) and must thus have realised that they might be in for many years yet. His samples were what are known as 'cross-sections', and did not involve following up the same men, which would obviously have been sounder, but would have taken a very long time. He did, however, manage to match some of the third-stage men with others in the earlier groups at least so far as age at conviction, victim-type and psychiatric reports were concerned, and he made allowances for the age factor. He did not find the decline in interest in the outside world which some people predict as a result of time served, but did find that

a.  wives and girlfriends had ceased to be in contact by visits or letters by about year 7. In contrast, parents, brothers and sisters kept up regular visits, even to the long-term group;

b.  the long-term group tended to talk about the past rather than the future;

c.  the longer the man had been inside the less interested he was in social activities and 'outgoing behaviour';

d.  the longer a man had been inside the more dependent he was on routine and the less he took decisions for himself.

**11.33**  As Sapsford himself pointed out, studies of prisoners do not tell us whether changes such as (b), (c) or (d) persist after release, or whether the ex-prisoner recovers, in which case these side-effects would be a matter of less concern. There is no doubt that long-term prisoners experience a difficult period of adjustment when they come out: but that does not mean that they remain institutionalised. Coker (1983), a Deputy Chief Probation Officer who studied the supervision and resettlement of 239 ex-lifers released in the years 1960-1964 or in 1970-74, did not find much evidence of lasting institutionalisation. Their time inside had varied from 2½ to 24 years, but averaged a little over 9 years. When sentenced they had for the most part been young (18-25 years of age), from the lowest socio-economic groups, and poorly educated: a group, in other words, not well equipped to resist institutionalisation. Two in every 3 had been convicted of indictable offences before their life sentences, and 1 in 4 had already experienced custodial sentences. Yet they

'… showed no evidence of deterioration as a result of their long years in prison, in so far as this can be measured. In general, after a short period of resettlement, sometimes accompanied by restlessness, they obtained and kept work and accommodation—satisfactory by their own standards as well as those of the Probation Service and the Home Office—and many married or remarried and made new homes. In some cases men improved upon their previous levels of employment. Additionally, these lifers revealed, generally, a fierce desire for independence and a capacity to manage their own lives competently, though some valued an opportunity to discuss matters with the probation officer on a *personal basis* of mutual respect and liking.'

## Schools for crime?

**11.34**  A naive but all too common criticism of prisons and YOIs is that the reconviction rates of their ex-inmates are high. They are high largely because, as we saw in chapter 7 (e g in Tables 7B and 7C), most of the offenders who receive custodial sentences have enough previous convictions to make them likely to reoffend. But that is not the last word on the subject. There is evidence that the more often a man has served a custodial sentence the more likely he is to be reconvicted even *when his previous convictions have been allowed for* (Ward, 1987*)*. The effect is slight until he has served more than five sentences, but then becomes more marked. A sentence in a YOI is especially likely to increase the probability of an early reconviction (Lloyd et al, 1994). The traditional explanation—Sidney Smith's, for example—is that prisons are schools for crime: that prisoners acquire from each other ideas, techniques and personal contacts which lead them into subsequent offences. This belief was one of the reasons why 'stars' (first offenders or prisoners serving their first custodial sentence) used to be segregated. The belief is supported by some prisoners' autobiographies. The consolation is that the ideas, techniques and contacts which offenders acquire inside come from unsuccessful offenders, are already well known to police, and are likely to lead to petty, incompetent thefts, burglaries and robberies, with a higher than average risk of reconviction.

11.35 A more interesting question, but much more difficult to answer, is whether an offender whose orientation is on the whole law-abiding when he enters prison is likely to be less so when he leaves. It would be relevant to know whether bad drivers with otherwise clean records are more likely to be subsequently convicted of dishonest offences if imprisoned for their driving than if dealt with non-custodially: but we know of no such comparison. What we do know is that men with otherwise clean records who have served long sentences for homicide are one of the groups least likely to be subsequently convicted of SL offences of any kind. Long association with persistent offenders does not seem to affect the careers of many of these men. The so-called 'subculture of prison' is to a considerable extent imported from the subculture of petty crime outside. Whether a prisoner is assimilated to it depends on his own subcultural background and personality. It also depends on the extent to which the regime allows the prisoners to be dominated by powerful prisoners, and on the frequency of contacts which prisoners are able to maintain with outsiders of their own choice. The shortness of most English sentences means that it is a minority of prisoners who, *if they were law-abiding when they entered*, are at risk of being turned into 'enemies of society'.

## Overcrowding

11.36 Another factor which seems to have an adverse effect on reconviction rates is overcrowding. Studying the records of prisoners released in 1965 after serving medium or long sentences in 19 English closed prisons, Farrington and Nuttall (1980) found that those who had spent most of their sentences in overcrowded prisons had reconviction rates which were higher than expectation. It is not clear why this should be so. Research in North American prisons (notably by Paulus et al, 1984) found overcrowding to be associated with higher death rates from violence, suicide and natural causes, higher signs of stress among inmates, and more frequent disciplinary proceedings. Obviously it increases the 'pains of imprisonment'; but if that were all it should enhance the effect of individual deterrence, not weaken it. It may be that in some way it intensifies some men's disposition to break the law; or it may even be that it interferes with some beneficial activities or processes in prison which reduce that disposition. The former seems rather more likely.

## Grievances

**11.37** Imprisonment not only exposes prisoners to the influence of other prisoners but also places them to some extent at the mercy of staff. The rules and standing orders which restrict or prohibit activities that would be unhindered outside can be applied generously, or with bureaucratic strictness. They may even be used to harass someone who has incurred dislike. It is very difficult for officers to steer a middle course between laxity and excessive strictness, although many have or acquire the knack. What has a most undesirable effect on prisoners' attitudes is rule enforcement which they see as unnecessary or vindictive. Deliberate provocation of an inmate, or use of unnecessary force by an officer are disciplinary offences. How often they occur is hard to say: it is only exceptionally that they receive publicity, an example being the aftermath of the Hull riots. Without denying the importance of major incidents, it can safely be said that it is the minor, unreported ones which have most effect on prisoners' attitudes, and which sustain the antagonism of the prisoners' subculture towards 'screws'. (A similar antagonism can easily be found in other authoritarian settings, such as the army, where the NCOs who have to order men about are if anything more unpopular than the authorities who make the rules.) Occasionally an individual prisoner, whether through mishandling or because of his own aggressive personality, becomes more or less unmanageable; and it is these cases which give rise to proper concern. Procedures for complaining about grievances are dealt with in 13.6ff: but even a remedied grievance is a remembered one. What we do not yet know is whether antagonism to staff—either in its extreme or in its milder endemic form—spills over into the prisoner's life outside, and colours his attitude to other representatives of law enforcement.

## Relations with families

**11.38** Some families are better off without the offender, financially, physically or psychologically. But most wives, husbands and children suffer from the separation (and the stigma, which particularly affects children's lives at school). Incarceration may break up a marriage or a stable partnership, although this is more likely to happen during a long sentence (see 11.32) or the $n$th short sentence. The NPS found that while 50 per cent of male prisoners said they had been married or cohabiting before their sentence only 35 per cent claimed to have a partner at the time of the survey. There is some hard evidence that prisoners who have partners to welcome them on release are somewhat less likely to be reconvicted. In any case, the service tries to alleviate separation in several ways (and local organisations, including probation services, form groups of prisoners wives to help them with practical and psychological problems). Most prisoners can buy and use phone cards (unless they abuse them by making threatening or obscene calls). There are no restrictions on outgoing letters (with similar exceptions); and it is only in dispersal prisons that incoming mail is censored (elsewhere it is merely opened to look for illicit enclosures). Efforts are made to allocate inmates to establishments not too remote for visits by relatives, although this is often ruled out by security or other considerations. In any case most prisons for long-termers are well away from railway or bus stations. Families may, however, qualify for assisted travel for visits. Visiting conditions vary from 'closed'—with a screen between visitor and prisoner—to relaxed, for example outdoors within sight but not hearing of staff. An important anxiety of prisoners is about their partners' fidelity. In some European systems conjugal visits or frequent home leaves help to reassure them. In England the former have never been countenanced. Home leaves do not begin until fairly late in the sentence[1], and since 1994 have been granted only to strictly defined categories of prisoner. Community visits (see 11.6) last for only a few hours.

1. Compassionate leave is another matter, and may be granted at any stage of the sentence, sometimes with an escort, sometimes without. For compassionate release see 1.26.

## Women in prison

**11.39**  Although the service's declared aims do not differentiate between the sexes, the system makes one or two concessions. Women prisoners must be protected from sexual abuse by being segregated from male prisoners (but a limited number of the staffs of women's prisons are men and vice versa). But whereas young adult males are segregated from their elders this policy was abandoned for women in the 1970s at the instance of their prison governors, who argued that mixing the age-groups would benefit both young and old. In some prisons, however, intimidation of older women by young gangs is now a problem. Women prisoners were allowed to wear their own clothes long before this became a privilege in a few men's prisons. On the other hand women prisoners are to some extent disadvantaged. Because their numbers are so much smaller it is uneconomical to provide them with the same variety of establishments. Special needs are less likely to be catered for, and women with families are less likely to be located conveniently for visits by them. They are even more likely than men to be anxious about the children, partners or dependent relatives whom they have left behind them, often without time to make arrangements for their care (Morris et al, 1994).

Women are believed to suffer more than men from the pains of incarceration. More of them seem to have vulnerable or otherwise abnormal personalities, and drug abuse is common. Discipline seems to present special problems: formal charges are more frequent in women's prisons (see Table 13B) and the staff are accused of petty enforcement of minor rules, although the explanation may be that this is the easiest way of avoiding accusations of favouritism.

## 'Human warehouses'

**11.40**  Prisons have been called 'human warehouses', which merely store people. Like so much that is said of prisons it is only in extreme situations that this approximates to reality—in solitary confinement or in remand prisons which are so overcrowded that all activities stagnate. Even there, inmates are conscious, and have dealings with their custodians and each other. In prisons where medium and long sentences are spent, and in locals when overcrowding is not at its worst, prisoners are not merely fed, clothed and allowed to sleep: attempts are made to fill their waking day. It is these attempts with which most of this chapter has been concerned. But when they are not working, learning, gambling, scheming or sleeping, inmates are thinking, and talking about their thoughts: reminiscing, gossiping, fantasising, boasting, complaining, and playing 'mind games'[1] with their custodians. Prisons are not warehouses, because prisoners are not things.

1.  McDermott and King's phrase (1988).

**11.41**  One of the unfortunate results of ambitious and costly efforts to use imprisonment to achieve positive improvement in prisoners' characters has been the way in which these distracted attention from unwanted effects. The decline in therapeutic optimism has resulted in more attention to the unintended harm which incarceration is believed to inflict. Another lesson to be learned, however, from that same decline of therapeutic optimism is that beliefs about effects of any kind, good or bad, need critical examination. An example is the assumption that bad effects must be permanent. Yet the writers who assume this are also capable of pointing out that beneficial effects must be transitory because the social environment into which inmates are discharged is a more immediate and powerful influence than the carceral experience. Finally, as this chapter has demonstrated, it is possible to exaggerate both beneficial effects and unwanted side-effects.

# Chapter 12

# Administration, location, allocation

## Ministers and senior civil servants

**12.1** All powers and jurisdiction in relation to prisoners and prisoners in England and Wales are exercisable by the Home Secretary and whichever of his junior ministers has this special assignment (s 1 Prison Act 1952). (Scotland and Northern Ireland have independent prison services.) The responsibility for administering the prison system on a day-to-day basis lies with the Prison Service, which has been subject to enormous restructuring in the past few years. The senior permanent official of the Service is designated Director-General. While previously heads of the Prison Department had been career administrators with experience of other departments, Derek Lewis, the Director-General dismissed in 1995, had no civil service background.

## Agency status

**12.2** Since 1993 the Prison Service has operated as an executive agency of the Home Office. It is run by a Chief Executive (who has retained the old title of Director-General). This change resulted partly from the criticisms of the leadership of the Prison Service found in the Woolf Report (1990) and partly from the recommendations of Sir Raymond Lygo's Review of the Management of the Prison Service, commissioned by the Home Secretary in 1991. Beneath the Director-General is a 10-member Prisons Board, chaired by the Director-General, and made up of
  (i) 4 part-time, non-executive members, who are 'outsiders' appointed by the Home Secretary; and
  (ii) the heads of the six directorates: of services; of healthcare; of personnel; of finance; of custody; and of programmes.
This Board 'has no executive authority apart from that possessed by each of its individual members in their own right': its function is to discuss and formulate policy, but subject to the authority of the Home Secretary.

## Contracted-out prisons

**12.3** More controversial than agency status has been the introduction of 'private prisons' (see 9.25). The original s 84(1) CJA 91 confined the power to contract out the running of prisons to remand prisons established after the commencement date of the section. However, s 84(2) enabled the Home Secretary by statutory instrument to apply the provisions of s 84(1) to any prison, and statutory instruments in 1992 enabled the Home Secretary to contract out any type of prison. Section 96 CJPOA 94 substituted a new s 84 into the 1991 Act allowing the Home Secretary to contract out (or sub-contract) any prison or part of a prison.

**12.4** Section 85 created three new officers to manage a contracted-out prison:
  (i) a director who will be a 'prison custody officer appointed by the contractor and specially approved ... by the Secretary of State'. The director has the same functions as a governor, though without the disciplinary functions;
  (ii) a controller, a crown secretary appointed by the Home Secretary. A new Rule 98A of the Prison Rules gives the powers under Rules 43 and 45-50 to the controller not to the director;
  (iii) prison custody officers, who do not have all the powers of prison officers.

**12.5** The first privatised prison was the Wolds, a remand prison which opened in 1992, followed the next year by two new local prisons, Blakenhurst and Doncaster. The main justification for the process has been the saving of money involved and the improved conditions within these new prisons. 'Contracting out' has now been extended to existing prisons (eg Strangeways, now renamed HMP Manchester). Contracts concluded between the Home Secretary and contractors have not been published, but tender documents make clear that regime standards are intended to be better than those provided in state prisons, not least because a private contractor may be sued for breach of contract, whereas there are still no enforceable minimum standards in state prisons.

## Prisoner Officers' Association

**12.6** Another of the reasons behind the contracting out of prisons was the increasing influence of the Prison Officers' Association, a trade union affiliated to the Trades Union Congress, with a membership of about 22,000 uniformed officers. It had increasingly concerned itself in the 1980s not only with the pay and conditions of service of uniformed officers but also with the way in which prisoners are treated. Since staff in contracted-out prisons are not members of the POA, the Association's power and influence has been greatly curbed. Governors, deputy and assistant governors, and professional staff such as psychologists and medical officers are members not of the POA, but of other civil service associations, such as the Society of Civil and Public Servants and the Institute of Professional Civil Servants. Governors, through the Prison Governors' Association, hold their own annual or other conferences, and have from time to time put forward strong views on official policy or proposals.

## Inspectorate

**12.7**  Independent of the Prison Service is the Inspectorate of Prisons, with a Chief Inspector whose reports, annual or special, are submitted direct to the permanent head of the HO and through him to the Home Secretary. His inspections are concerned particularly with the conditions in establishments, the treatment of prisoners and the facilities available to them, but the Home Secretary may direct his attention to other matters. He only has power to recommend. He does not deal with complaints from individual prisoners, although similar complaints from a number of sources might alert him to a problem; nor does he enter into correspondence with MPs, organisations or the public. His reports are made available to MPs by being placed in the libraries of both Houses of Parliament, and are on sale to the public and to prisoners.

## Boards of visitors

**12.8**  Independent both of the Inspectorate and of the Prison Service is the board of visitors which the Home Secretary must appoint for each establishment. At least two members of each board must be justices of the peace; and usually more are. Any member of the board has the right to enter the establishment at any time and have free access to every part of it and to every prisoner (s 6 PA 52, as amended). The duties of boards are prescribed by the Prison Rules 1964 (as amended), and the important ones are:

   a.  satisfying themselves as to the state of the establishment's premises, its administration and the treatment of its prisoners; rendering annual reports on these subjects to the Home Secretary;

   b.  inquiring into and reporting on any matter at the Home Secretary's request;

   c.  directing the governor's attention to any matter which calls for it;

   d.  reporting to the Home Secretary any matter which they consider it expedient to report; informing him immediately of any abuse which comes to their knowledge;

   e.  in any case of urgent necessity, suspending any officer until the Home Secretary's decision is known;

   f.  hearing any complaint or request which a prisoner wishes to make (to the board or to any member);

   g.  inspecting the prisoners' food at frequent intervals;

   h.  inquiring into any report made to them that a prisoner's health, mental or physical, is likely to be injuriously affected by any conditions of his imprisonment;

   i.  arranging a rota for visits to the establishment by at least one board member between board meetings;

**12.9**  Each board of visitors is thus a sort of lay inspectorate, but with responsibilities for dealing with individual prisoners' treatment and complaints which the Inspectorate proper does not have. Until 1992 boards were required to discharge quasi-judicial duties in dealing with the more serious disciplinary charges. As a result they were seen by many prisoners—however unfairly—as part of the prison administration rather than as the impartial providers of safeguards against maltreatment which is meant to be their main function. Disciplinary charges are now heard by either the governor or the criminal courts (see 13.6ff). The latest (1995) Home Office proposals recommend that boards of visitors should be renamed advisory councils, and that a common constitution should be adopted by all boards. The role of the Prison Ombudsman, created in 1994, is discussed at 13.21.

## Regions

**12.10**  The Prison Service was reorganised in 1990 into 15 Regions, each headed by an Area Manager, who is normally a promoted prison governor. They will have entered the service either as prison officers, as professional staff or as assistant governors (who must nowadays serve for a period as uniformed officers in addition to their formal training). Their role is to secure the application of national policy within establishments and to secure the proper functioning of those establishments.

## Staff

**12.11**  The staff of prison establishments, which numbered some 38,800 in 1995 (compared with 24,000 in 1981, and 28,200 in 1987) consist of

*The governor grades* (about 500)
   Governors (of Grade I, II, III or IV, depending on the size of the prison, remand centre, youth custody centre or detention centre)
   Assistant governors (the grade of entry to the governor grades, open to selected prison officers as well as to direct entrants with suitable qualifications)

*Uniformed officers* (about 24,000)
   Chief officers (Grades I and II, including specialists in catering, hospital services, physical education and works)
   Principal officers
   Senior officers               } including specialists of the 6 kinds
   Prison officers (the entry grade) } shown below;
   Catering officers
   Dog handlers
   Hospital officers
   Physical education officers

Officer instructors
Works officers
Matrons
Prison auxiliary officers (men)
Temporary prison officers (women)
Night patrols

*Administrative and professional staff* (about 4,000)
Administrative officers
Chaplains
Civilian instructional officers
Clerical officers
Education officers (seconded from local education departments)
Farm managers
Industrial managers
Medical officers
Nursing officers
Prison probation officers (seconded from probation departments)
Psychologists and their assistants
Teachers
Typists

*Industrial civil servants* (about 2,300)
Agricultural craftsmen
Drivers
Farm foremen
Industrial craftsmen (works department)
Plant attendants
Storemen

## Location of prisons

12.12   The most economical prison system would be one which housed all its prisoners in a single building or collection of buildings, served by one kitchen, one laundry, one hospital, one library, and administered from a headquarters on the spot. At one time in some states of the USA a single very large penitentiary was the only place for sentenced male felons[1]. None of the English establishments, however, were designed to hold more than about 1,000 prisoners, and most of them are much smaller. The reason is partly the way in which the system developed out of the locally-administered gaols, partly unwillingness to spend large sums of money on huge new edifices for the undeserving. Even a relatively independent Prison Service has to get its funds from a tight-fisted and sceptical Treasury. In any case, prison administrators in this century have tended to assume that very large units have disadvantages, although it is not easy to find a thorough discussion of this subject. Recently commissioned prisons are designed for 649 prisoners (Blakenhurst) and 779 prisoners (Doncaster). The Learmont review into prison service security (1995) recommended two new 'superjails', one high security prison for about 200 high-risk prisoners, and a 'control prison' for a similar number of disruptive prisoners. Even here, the proposals are for relatively small prisons.

1.  But short sentences—of less than a year—were served in local gaols. When England built its first penitentiaries it made a similar distinction: they were for convicts in penal servitude, and imprisonment (usually of less than 3 years) was served in gaols.

**12.13**   Local prisons are almost all in the central parts of cities, having been located close to the courts which they were to serve. Even the first penitentiaries were not far from the centre of London, at Millbank and Pentonville. Dartmoor, on the other hand, was originally built for prisoners in the Napoleonic wars, and about as far from urban civilisation as it is possible to be in this small country. Later establishments were also adaptations of military buildings or unwanted country mansions, examples being the young offender institution in the old fortifications at Dover, and Askham Grange, the long-term open prison for women. Custom-built training prisons have also been located in rural surroundings, not so much from choice as because urban sites are costly and subject to planning objections. The result is that most training prisons are difficult for visitors to reach by public transport. Although the Woolf Report (1991) suggested a move towards 'community prisons', which would be genuinely local in the sense of serving the local community, the most recent contracts to build new prisons have also been given for sites in rural areas.

### Allocation to prisons

**12.14**   Given a system with about 150 geographically separated establishments, the principles on which people in custody should be allocated to them present an interesting problem. Some of the principles are based on legal status, some on theories about the undesirability of associating certain categories, some on logistics. The Rules are firm on certain points, flexible on others:

> '3(1)   Prisoners shall be classified, in accordance with any directions of the Secretary of State, having regard to their age, temperament and record and with a view to maintaining good order and facilitating training and, in the case of convicted prisoners, of furthering the purpose of their training and treatment as provided by Rule 1 of these Rules.
>
> (2)   Unconvicted prisoners shall be kept out of contact with convicted prisoners as far as this can reasonably be done.
>
> (3)   Nothing in this Rule shall require a prisoner to be deprived unduly of the society of other persons.'

### Legal status

**12.15**   The rule that the convicted and the unconvicted are to be kept as separate 'as can reasonably be done' is based on the assumption that until they are sentenced, prisoners should not suffer any more of the 'pains of imprisonment' than are unavoidable (see 11.4). The extent to which they are kept physically separate varies: sometimes they are merely housed on one 'landing', sometimes not separated at all (see 10.10). Unconvicted prisoners are allowed to wear their own clothes (unless these are verminous, filthy or otherwise unsuitable). They may send and receive unlimited numbers of uncensored letters, and have food and drink, within limits, supplied from outside at the expense of themselves or their friends. They may receive more frequent visitors than sentenced prisoners, although for the sake of security these visits may take place under 'closed' conditions, that is with a screen between prisoners and visitors. They are not compelled to work, but can if they wish and if there is work available. Deportees, prisoners committed for contempt of court and non-payers of maintenance are in the same position. Those remanded in custody for medical reports must be kept in prison hospitals. Young adults remanded in custody must be sent to remand centres, not local prisons.

**12.16** In 1993 the non-criminal population more than doubled from 270 to 630: the increase was due to an increase of 300 in the number of prisoners held under the Immigration Act 1971. 75 per cent of male non-criminal prisoners in mid-1993 were held under the IA 71 (whereas this figure was only 28 per cent in 1983). The IA 71 accounted for 37 per cent of male receptions of non-criminal prisoners, 30 per cent were received for non-payment of community charge or rates, and 15 per cent were in contempt of court. Those awaiting trial or sentence accounted for 24 per cent of prisoners (23 per cent of male and 25 per cent of female prisoners). These percentages emphasise the importance, for the prison system as well as for defendants, of efforts to reduce the average time between arrest and sentence, especially for Crown Court cases. Thus the Prosecution of Offences Act 1985 imposes time-limits regulating how long a defendant may be kept in custody pretrial (see Prosecution of Offences (Custody Time Limits) Regulations 1987-1991; and 10.11).

**Gender**

**12.17** Rule 9 lays down that women prisoners are to be kept 'entirely separate' from male prisoners: this principle has been honoured since the 18th century in order to prevent the abuse of women by men. The relatively small number of women prisoners—roughly 1 for every 28 men—means that it would be uneconomic to provide as many different kinds of establishment for them. Only about a dozen out of about 150 prisons, remand centres and youth custody centres are female establishments; and each is designed for smaller numbers than its male counterpart, it being thought even more desirable to keep women prisoners in small groups. However, the increasing number of women prisoners (1,383, excluding fine defaulters, in February 1995) has resulted in more pressures on the women's prisons, though predictions for growth in the prison population to 2001 suggest no further growth in the female population. For the additional 'pains of imprisonment' for women, see 11.39.

## Age

**12.18**   Children under the age of 17 who are refused bail are normally remanded to local authorities' secure accommodation (see 20.8). Other juveniles and young adults go to remand centres before sentence. Those who are sentenced to young offenders' institutions should go direct to their destination, but may in practice have to wait in remand centres or local prisons for a vacancy. The sentencing system for young offenders, and the establishments where they spend their custodial sentences, are described in chapter 20, where the justifications for segregation are also discussed.

## Geography

**12.19**   The local prison to which the prisoner goes is usually the one that serves the court in which he is due to appear or by which he has just been sentenced. A sentenced prisoner is transferred from court to the nearest local prison where he is considered for allocation to a suitable prison. Each region's prisons include units for nearly all sorts of prisoner, so that it is only prisoners of certain kinds who have to be allocated outside their home region: deportees, some psychiatric cases, some prisoners who need high security or segregation, and some women prisoners. The majority of prisoners are thus located so that their families can visit them and return home within the same day, although this is sometimes difficult or impossible by public transport.

## Length of sentence

**12.20**   Thus until one is sentenced to custody one's destination within the system is determined by sex, age and geography. It is after sentence that other factors come into operation. The most important of these are length of sentence and security category. Apart from men serving very short sentences and fine defaulters, both of which categories are likely to spend the whole of their time in a local prison, sentenced prisoners are processed by an Observation, Classification and Allocation Unit (an OCAU) in their local prison, unless their sentence is longer than 4 years, in which case they are dealt with by one of the Long-Term Allocation Centres (LTACs). Lifer allocations are dealt with centrally.

**12.21**   Processing by an OCAU does not necessarily mean transfer to another prison. If a man's sentence is under 18 months in length he may very well stay in the local; but at least the OCAU will have helped to decide whether he is fitted for some special kind of work, and what his educational needs are. (The prisoner's welfare needs are assessed independently by the prison probation officers).

## Security categories

**12.22**   An important consideration when a prisoner is being allocated is his security category. As a result of the Mountbatten Report (1966) prisoners are categorised soon after reception as belonging to one of 4 categories. The procedure followed is contained in Circular Instruction 7/1988. This states that only factors relating to the likelihood of a prisoner escaping should affect categorisation. According to the Prison Ombudsman (1995), many categorisation decisions which have been referred to him have been based wrongly, not on issues relating to security but on issues relating to control.

**12.23** Category A (numbering about 750 in 1995): those whose escape would be highly dangerous to the public or the police or the security of the state. Thirteen of these are considered 'exceptional escape risks', and 163 are considered 'high risk'. They are kept in special cells from the first remand in custody, and are transferred as soon as they are sentenced to one of the high security establishments called 'dispersal prisons': Frankland (Durham), Full Sutton (York), Gartree (Leicester), Long Lartin (Worcester), Wakefield and Whitemoor (Cambridge), Belmarsh (London). There is no equivalent women's prison, though Durham has a high security wing for women.

Life in a dispersal prison is both tense and restrictive. The prisoner's only relief from the company of gangsters, terrorists, spies and sadists is withdrawal to the privacy of his cell. Applications for visitors are scrutinised to make sure that they are not accomplices or people who might help him to escape. Letters and parcels are examined with particular care. As a result escapes are rare. Efforts are made to ameliorate dispersal regimes. Prisoners are allowed to brighten their cells with their own pictures, pin-ups, a carpet, bedspread and curtains, as well as a wide range of permitted personal possessions. Day rooms and recreation rooms are made as pleasant and interesting as possible. Work and education are 'individualised'. Hobbies are encouraged. Prisoners are allowed more than usual freedom to choose between spending their time in their cells or in day rooms.

**12.24** Nevertheless, the 'pains of imprisonment' are intensified for Category A prisoners, especially since most of them are serving long sentences. The procedure for placing them in this category therefore has to combine speed with care. In practice, if the police consider that an arrested person should be handled with special security precautions they tell the local prison before he is committed to it by the court; and special precautions are taken as soon as he arrives. The OCAU then confirms or downgrades his category, subject to the approval of headquarters, where the prison to which he is to be sent is decided. There are annual reviews of classifications, and since *Duggan* [1994] 3 All ER 277 prisoners have been entitled to reasons for their classification.

**12.25** Category B (numbering about 4,000 in 1995): those for whom the very highest conditions of security are not necessary but for whom escape must be made very difficult. The vast majority of those held in dispersal prisons are in Category 'B'; but there are a number who are held in non-dispersal Category 'B' training prisons where movement within the perimeter is generally less restrictive. Since the dispersal prisons have a capacity of 2,694 and only 500 prisoners are Category A, it follows that many Category B prisoners are held in conditions which are unnecessarily secure.

**12.26** Category C (numbering about 12,000 in 1995): those who cannot be trusted in open conditions but who do not have the ability or resources to make a determined escape attempt. The majority of prisoners, and prisons, are in this category. Escapes over the last four years have averaged about 60 a year, most of them short-lived. The typical escaper or absconder (see 11.5) acts on impulse, often because news of some family crisis makes the desire to go home irresistible; and he or she is usually retaken without a struggle by police who pick the prisoner up at home. Life 'on the run' is not by any means impossible in Britain, especially for the young who can locate friends in large cities; but it is full of difficulties and anxieties, and means frequent moves and petty thefts or burglaries. Quite a few Category C escapers who are not retaken at home eventually give themselves up, or are caught committing trivial offences.

**12.27** Category D (numbering about 4,100 in 1995): those who can reasonably be trusted to serve their sentence in open conditions. In 1994 there were 12 open training prisons, three of them for women, and four open young offender institutions, two of them for women. They have no perimeter defences: only a fence to indicate the limits of authorised movement. Prisoners' letters are not normally censored, and many other restrictions are relaxed. Most of the prisoners share dormitories and can relatively easily break out at any time. About 400 escape or abscond each year but, like Category C escapers, they are soon retaken without doing any but trivial harm. Unfortunately the number of prisoners who can be trusted in open conditions has decreased, and vacancies are hard to fill.

## Sophistication

**12.28** Another aim used to be to keep those who were serving their first prison sentence—known as 'stars'—away from those with more experience: it was assumed that the former would be 'contaminated' by the latter. This may have been so when stars were quite likely to be people with no previous convictions; but nowadays most offenders are not imprisoned for their first conviction. The availability of open prisons for the relatively harmless offender, and other special types of prison, means that there is now little point in separating stars; and though the term is still used here and there it is no longer an official label. Classification by 'temperament and record', however, may still determine whether a prisoner is sent to an establishment for 'hard men' or to some 'easier nick'.

## Segregation

**12.29** Some prisoners are segregated in special units, either for their own protection or in order to prevent trouble-making (the latter will be discussed in the context of discipline). The need to protect some prisoners against others is a problem which the English system takes more seriously than do, for example, many US penitentiaries. Rule 43(1) provides that

> 'Where it appears desirable, for the maintenance of good order or discipline or in his own interests, that a prisoner should not associate with other prisoners, either generally or for particular purposes, the governor may arrange for the prisoner's removal from association accordingly.'

Although this allows the governor discretion, and does not enable a prisoner to request segregation as a right, his request is unlikely to be refused. A decision to segregate has to be confirmed within three days, and the confirmation renewed monthly, by a member of the board of visitors or the Home Secretary. The medical officer can insist, on medical grounds, that a prisoner be desegregated. The Woolf Report (1991) accepted the need for segregation, but recommended that the board of visitors was not the appropriate authorising body, preferring the area manager. However the 1991 White Paper confirmed the role of the board of visitors, but accepted that 'the prisoner should wherever possible be given the reason for these decisions in writing'.

12.30   Segregation under Rule 43 is usually managed by putting prisoners in a segregation unit, or in cells on a special landing or part of a landing. If a prisoner, however, seems to be facing a continuing risk of serious assault which is unlikely to diminish in the course of time, so that a lengthy period of segregation would be needed, every effort is made to transfer him to one of the special units (eg at Gloucester, Maidstone or Wakefield). Their regimes are designed to maximise opportunities for regular association: emphasis is placed on work, education, recreation, including outdoor exercise.

### Treatment and training

12.31   During the last two decades the Prison Service's publications have grown less optimistic about treatment and training. However, some allocations are still based on the need for treatment: an obvious example is the selection of mild or moderate psychiatric cases for treatment at Grendon Underwood. On the whole however, disappointment with the results of special treatment and training regimes, coupled with difficulties imposed by under-staffing and overcrowding, has meant that this criterion is a less important allocation criterion.

### The prisoner's viewpoint

12.32   From the ordinary prisoner's point of view the most important questions are 'In which security category shall I be placed?' and 'Shall I remain in a local?'. When it is the quality of life that is in question the difference between prisons of categories B and C is not marked: some B prisons are more pleasant than some

C establishments because of the nature of their buildings, regimes or locations. It is the dispersal and open prisons which differ markedly from the rest. Most prisoners, however, are unlikely to find themselves in either. For them the important question is whether they will remain in a local prison or be sent to a training establishment. Life in a local—especially in a large local—is prison life at its most sordid. Every local has to cope with the problem of almost daily movement in and out, either to and from courts or to other prisons. Staff are preoccupied with processing and controlling the transients, and keeping the rest fed, clothed and exercised. The workshops are less interesting than those of training prisons, and recreation is hampered by sheer numbers.

## Overcrowding

**12.33** Overcrowding has also interfered with the allocation system in recent years. Although this has intensified the 'pains of imprisonment' (see 11.4 and 11.36) for a generation of prisoners, it has not been an unmixed evil. It has forced Home Secretaries, the CA, and administrators to exhort sentencers to be more selective in their use of prison sentences, and to shorten those sentences which they feel obliged to impose. It prompted legislative innovations such as parole, the suspended sentence and the partially suspended sentence. It even persuaded the Treasury to provide the funds for the building of new prisons. Whether all these innovations have been improvements is debatable, and is debated in other chapters. There are also penologists who argue that societies should not react to prison overcrowding by increasing prison capacity, because it will encourage sentencers to increase the percentage of offenders whom they imprison. In technical language, the size of the prison population is said to be 'capacity led'. This was apparently confirmed in a study by Abt Associates (1980), Vol II, 53 ff, purporting to show that an increase in the penitentiary capacity of the USA tended to be followed, two years later, by a corresponding increase in numbers of prisoners. It is risky, however, to accept this as a social law, and especially to apply it to another society. In any case Blumstein et al (1983) showed that the data did not really support Abt Associates' generalisation, partly because of errors in computation and partly because of faults of method. But the generalisation was eagerly accepted, especially by reformers who assumed that the incarceration rate should always be lower than it is. In fact, comparisons with other countries in Western Europe show that England's prison population per 100,000 recorded crimes (about 800 in 1993) was among the lowest ratios (Barclay et al, 1995). This seems more realistic than the usual comparison of prison populations per 100,000 inhabitants. For a discussion of other criteria see Pease (1994).

**12.34** Meanwhile, in England and Wales, most of the overcrowding has been deliberately confined to the locals, because this seemed preferable to disrupting the training prisons. As a result many men have had to live in twos or threes in cells meant for one, and at peak periods rooms meant for education or other activities in locals have been used for dormitories. There is not enough work for prisoners, and not enough room for other activities. Sanitation is overloaded, and so are medical and welfare staff. Yet there have always been prisoners who prefer life in a local to even an open prison. The sociable petty thief or burglar who values his family will see less of them if he is transferred to a training prison. In the local, too, he will meet more of his friends, whether they are serving short sentences or on their way to serve long ones. He knows the establishment, its officers and its possibilities. If they run a racket the prisoners are easier and safer victims than the tough, experienced long-sentence prisoners. The frequent comings and goings of colleagues and their visitors make smuggling that much easier. Life in a training prison may be less squalid, but it can also be more demanding. For an up-to-date description of all prisons, see Leech's *Prisoners Handbook 1995*.

Chapter 13

# Rules, grievances and rights

## The Prison Act and the Prison Rules

**13.1** For the provision and management of prisons and other establishments of the Prison Service, the principal statute remains the Prison Act 1952 (as amended). The PA 52 allows the Home Secretary to make rules for the regulation and management of these establishments. The Prison Rules, and their counterparts for other establishments, thus take the form of statutory instruments, although their precise status remains unclear (see 13.23). Before any new rule or amendment comes into force it must be laid before Parliament, which cannot amend it, but by rejecting it can force the Home Secretary to amend it. The main instrument at present in force is the Prison Rules 1964 (SI 1964/388), but there have been many subsequent piecemeal amendments of the Rules. The Act and the Rules are supplemented by standing orders, which consist of detailed instructions for the guidance of prison staff. They have little or no legal force except through the doctrine of legitimate expectations (see 13.24). Numerous circular instructions ('instructions to governors') are also issued to prison governors, to amend standing orders and to provide further details.

**13.2** The Rules seem to be of six kinds[1]:
   a. those expressing *general policy*. For example, 'The purpose of the training and treatment of convicted prisoners shall be to encourage and assist them to lead a good and useful life' (Rule 1); and Rule 2 is of a similar kind;
   b. those conferring a *discretionary power* on administrators or staff. For example Rule 6 allows sentenced prisoners to be temporarily released 'for any period or periods and subject to any conditions'. In practice it enables governors to let prisoners go home for a day or two to attend death-beds or other family crises (but see 14.22). Without the Rule this would contravene the law: but it does not *oblige* any governor to grant temporary release. Whenever a Rule contains such phrases as 'so far as is reasonably practicable' this makes it to a considerable extent discretionary;

c. those intended to safeguard the health and welfare of prisoners: for example Rule 24, which insists that each prisoner must have a separate bed and bedding 'adequate for warmth and health';

d. those defining the administrative structure, and the functions and duties of important members of staff. Rules 94-96, for instance, deal with the functions and duties of the board of visitors (see 12.6). Rule 77(2) obliges officers to inform the governor promptly of any abuses or improprieties which come to their knowledge. There is, however, a separate code of rules dealing with the discipline of officers: it is not a statutory instrument, not on sale, but not confidential;

e. Rules providing prisoners with specific protection against abuses[2]. The obvious example is Rule 9(1): 'women prisoners shall be kept entirely separate from male prisoners'. Less obvious is the protection provided by Rules 47 and 50, which define types of conduct that are offences against discipline, and list the kinds of punishment that can be given. The clear implication of these Rules is that no other types of conduct can be punished, and that no other kinds of punishment can be imposed. Thus, provided that he does not 'offend against good order and discipline' (Rule 47(21)), a prisoner can express any views he holds, whether of a political or moral nature, without being officially punished. Again, corporal and dietary punishments are no longer permitted, and officers detected using violence against a prisoner when this is not needed to control him are subject to disciplinary action. More will be said about discipline later;

f. those prohibiting certain conduct, usually because it is considered detrimental to security or good order. Prohibitions of such conduct by prisoners are listed in Rule 47; but other Rules say what officers and outsiders must not do: for example, bring in 'prohibited articles' (Rule 85). What are and are not prohibited are explained in standing orders.

1. This analysis follows Zellick's (1980), but with differences.
2. For the protection afforded to prisoners against psychosurgery and surgical hormone implants without their consent see ss 56(2) and 145 MHA 83, and 21.56.

## Discipline

**13.3** Of most interest to prisoners—and to other critics of prisons—are Rules 47-56, which deal with offences against discipline. Like members of the armed services, both officers and prisoners are subject to a code of conduct which imposes obligations and prohibitions beyond those of the law to which ordinary citizens are subject. This is considered necessary to enable the service concerned to function as it is meant to: in the case of the Prison Service, to prevent escapes from custody and harm to prisoners and staff. It is sometimes argued that the Prison Service at least should be able to function merely by applying the prohibitions and penalties of the criminal law; but this is more than slightly idealistic. Most prisoners are people who have amply demonstrated their disrespect of the law and its penalties. In any case the process of bringing a prisoner to trial for an offence committed in prison would in many cases not be complete before he or she was due for release. The evidence would often seem rather unsatisfactory to criminal lawyers. Prisoners are not co-operative witnesses, partly through distrust of agencies of the law, partly through fear of unofficial retaliation by fellow prisoners or staff. Courts are unfamiliar with the world of prison. Prison justice is rough and ready, as will be seen; the problem is to find practicable ways of improving it. The Prison Service issued a *Prison Discipline Manual* in 1995 which should provide a useful tool to help prisoners to understand procedures.

**13.4** Rule 47 states that a prisoner is guilty of an offence against discipline if he:

(1) commits any assault;
(2) detains any person against his will;
(3) denies access to any part of the prison to any officer;
(4) fights with any person;
(5) intentionally endangers the health or personal safety of others or, by his conduct, is reckless whether such health or personal safety is endangered;
(6) intentionally obstructs an officer in the execution of his duty;
(7) escapes or absconds from prison or from legal custody;
(8) fails to comply with any condition upon which he is so released;
(8A) administers a controlled drug to himself or fails to prevent the administration of a controlled drug to him by another person;
(9) has in his possession—
  (a) any unauthorised article, or
  (b) a greater quantity of any article than he is authorised to have;
(10) sells or delivers to any person any unauthorised article;
(11) sells or, without permission, delivers to any person any article which he is allowed to have only for his own use;
(12) takes improperly any article belonging to another person or to a prison;
(13) intentionally or recklessly sets fire to any part of a prison or any other property, whether or not his own;
(14) destroys or damages any part of a prison or any other property, other than his own;
(15) absents himself from any place where he is required to be or is present at any place where he is not authorised to be;
(16) is disrespectful to any officer or any person visiting a prison;
(17) uses threatening,, abusive or insulting words or behaviour;
(18) intentionally fails to work properly or, being required to work, refuses to do so;
(19) disobeys any lawful order;
(20) disobeys or fails to comply with any rule or regulation applying to him;
(21) in any way offends against good order and discipline;
(22) (a) attempts to commit;
  (b) incites another prisoner to commit, or
  (c) assists another prisoner to commit or to attempt to commit
  any of the foregoing offences.

The Prison Act 1952 (s 5(2) as amended) requires the Home Secretary to include in his annual reports 'a statement of the punishments inflicted in each prison and of the offences for which they were inflicted'. These statements are now to be found in the annual *Prison Statistics*, although, as the Table for 1993 (Table 13A) shows, several distinct kinds of offence are lumped together. For a detailed analysis of the offences, see Loucks (1993); Livingstone and Owen (1993); Richardson (1993).

**13.5** The offence which has been the target of most criticism is that contained in Rule 47(21). It is so widely drafted as to be a 'catch-all' offence. The Prior Committee (1985), noting that in 1984 29 per cent of the total of proved offences were charged under this provision, recommended that the maximum punishment should be only seven days' loss of remission (ie additional days, in today's language). This recommendation has not been adopted. It should also be noted that the offences do not include any provisions as to general defences or the mental element required.

**TABLE 13A: Numbers of offences against prison discipline in establishments per 100 population**

| Types of  establishment | All offences | Violence | Escapes or absconds | Disobedience or disrespect | Wilful damage | Unauthorised transactions | Other |
|---|---|---|---|---|---|---|---|
| All establishments | 224 | 26 | 3 | 104 | 12 | 39 | 39 |
| Male prisons and remand centres | 199 | 20 | 3 | 93 | 10 | 37 | 36 |
| Male young offender institutions | 402 | 72 | 7 | 187 | 29 | 63 | 45 |
| All female establishments | 345 | 42 | 11 | 145 | 15 | 37 | 96 |

Source: *Statistics of offences against prison discipline and punishments England and Wales 1994.*

## Adjudication

**13.6** A wider target for criticism over the years than the definition of the offences themselves has been the system by which disciplinary charges are adjudicated. When an officer decides that a prisoner should be charged he does not tell him so in person: the prisoner is given a 'notice of report', usually by another officer. At this stage he can be, and usually is, locked up apart from other prisoners: a procedure which makes it difficult for him to contact potential witnesses, thus handicapping a genuine defence. Not less than two hours later, but not later than the following day (with certain exceptions) he must appear before the governor (or acting governor, but not a deputy), who usually disposes of the case, there and then, unless the charge is sufficiently serious that the governor decides to call in the police so that the case is taken to the ordinary criminal courts. Until 1992, boards of visitors had had a disciplinary function, but this was removed on the recommendation of the Woolf Report (1991).

**13.7** The prisoner does not necessarily get legal advice or representation (see 13.11). At the hearing, he is asked whether he received the notice of report, whether he understands the charge and the procedure, and whether he admits the offence or denies it. If the latter, the officer concerned gives his account of the incident (reading from his report if he wishes), and the prisoner is allowed to cross-examine him, if necessary with the governor's help in formulating questions. Then the prisoner is invited to make his statement (which he can also read) and to call any witnesses to support it. Neither side, however, can compel prisoners to testify, presumably because this could place some witnesses in danger from fellow prisoners.

**13.8**   The governor decides whether to believe the officer or the prisoner; and if he believes the former makes an 'award' of one of the penalties prescribed in Rule 50. Maximum levels of all disciplinary punishments were increased by 50 per cent in April 1995 (except for cellular confinement which had already been increased in 1994): see IG 37/1995. Penalties are:

   a.   caution;
   b.   forfeiture for a period not exceeding 42 days of any of the privileges under Rule 4 (21 days for young offenders);
   c.   exclusion from associated work for a period not exceeding 21 days (the same for young offenders);
   d.   stoppage of earnings for a period not exceeding 84 days of an amount not exceeding 42 days' earnings; (for young offenders, a period of 42 days of an amount not exceeding 21 days' earnings);
   e.   cellular confinement for a period not exceeding 14 days (7 days for young offenders);
   f.   an award of additional days not exceeding 42 days (the same for young offenders);
   g.   forfeiture for any period, in the case of a prisoner otherwise entitled thereto, of the right under Rule 41(1) to have the articles there mentioned (eg books, newspapers, writing materials etc);
   h.   forfeiture for any period, in the case of a prisoner otherwise entitled thereto who is guilty of escaping or attempting to escape, of the right to wear clothing of his own under Rule 20(1).

In addition

   i.   women prisoners (adult and young) may be given extra work for a period not exceeding 21 days;
   j.   young offenders may be removed from their wing or unit for a period not exceeding 21 days.

**13.9**   The governor can suspend an award by directing that it is not to take effect unless during a specified period of not more than the next six months the prisoner commits another offence against discipline and a governor directs that the award take effect in whole or part (Rule 55). In 1994 around 15 per cent of awards were suspended. Only about 1 in 10 suspended awards are 'activated' in this way, which suggests that suspension is a useful expedient. Even a prisoner on remand or awaiting sentence can be awarded provisional additional days, to take effect if he eventually receives a sentence of imprisonment, which is reduced by a period that includes the time when he committed the offence against discipline (see 10.23). The only appeal against the governor's verdict or award is by way of a petition to the Home Secretary.

**13.10**   The relative frequency of offences punished has been increasing over the last decade for most types of establishments, and notably in establishments for women and girls, where, as Table 13A shows, it is especially high. This may reflect a more disciplinarian approach in women's prisons (see Genders and Player, 1987). Ditchfield and Lock (1994) studied the level and pattern of offences and punishments during the first year after the changes were introduced in 1992 (see 13.6). They concluded that the changes had not significantly affected prison disciplinary behaviour. The most common punishment, because it is regarded as the most effective deterrent, is additional days, as Table 13B shows:

**TABLE 13B: Types of punishments awarded in English prisons**

|  | Cellular confinement | Removal from activities | Forfeiture of privileges | Stoppage or reduction of earnings | Caution | Removal from wing or living unit | Extra work | Exclusion from associated work | Additional days |
|---|---|---|---|---|---|---|---|---|---|
| *Men* | | | | | | | | | |
| Remand centres | 65 | * | 231 | 176 | 16 | * | * | 19 | 185 |
| Local prisons | 31 | * | 87 | 77 | 14 | * | * | 9 | 106 |
| Open prisons | - | * | 11 | 45 | 16 | * | * | - | 79 |
| Closed training prisons | 21 | * | 44 | 81 | 14 | * | * | 11 | 109 |
| Young offender institutions | 26 | 8 | 160 | 203 | 16 | 30 | 25 | * | 311 |
| *Women* | | | | | | | | | |
| Local prisons | 45 | * | 177 | 130 | 36 | * | * | 21 | 115 |
| Open prisons | 6 | * | 8 | 28 | 20 | * | * | - | 166 |
| Closed training prisons | 28 | * | 44 | 143 | 67 | * | * | 15 | 104 |
| Young offender institutions | 72 | - | 94 | 334 | 144 | - | 38 | * | 360 |

Source: *Statistics of offences against prison discipline and punishments England and Wales 1994*, Table 6.

**13.11**   Criticisms of adjudications have concentrated chiefly on

a.   the prisoner's lack of legal advice or representation. In 1983 the Divisional Court decided that boards of visitors had discretion to grant legal representation at adjudications (*Tarrant* [1984] 1 All ER 799); and the decision of the European Court of Human Rights in *Campbell and Fell* (1984) 7 EHRR 165 led to an instruction to boards that they *had to* grant such representation if it was requested by a person charged with an 'especially grave' offence. The present *Prison Discipline Manual* instructs the adjudicator to ask the prisoner whether he or she wishes to have additional assistance. In deciding whether to grant representation, the adjudicator is advised to take into account:
   (i)   the seriousness of the charge and of the potential penalty;
   (ii)  whether any points of law are likely to arise;
   (iii) the capacity of a particular prisoner to present his or her own case;
   (iv)  procedural difficulties;
   (v)   the need for reasonable speed;
   (vi)  the need for fairness.

There remains concern that prisoners are inadequately advised of their right to be assisted by a lay adviser ('McKenzie's friend'[1]) even if legal representation is refused. The Prison Ombudsman in his first report (1995) highlighted the high proportion of well-grounded complaints about adjudications which appeared to show that some adjudicators are failing to follow the appropriate procedures.

b.  the limited scope for appeals. The prisoner has no hope of getting a finding of guilt reversed by a court unless he can convince the court that the governor had breached the rules of natural justice: for example by refusing to allow him to bring relevant evidence, as happened in *St Germain (No 2)* [1979] 3 All ER 545. However, this case concerned proceedings before a board of visitors. It is unlikely that courts would interfere on the same grounds — or indeed any grounds — with a governor's adjudication: see the same case. The prisoner can petition the Home Secretary, but it is very rarely that this persuades him to interfere.

1.  Ie a friend or adviser who sits beside the prisoner at the hearing, taking notes and giving advice, but not addressing the court on his behalf, so called after *McKenzie v McKenzie* [1970] 3 All ER 1034.

**13.12**   The underlying point of these criticisms is the fear that innocent prisoners are being penalised on the evidence of officers who are either over-strict or malicious. On the other hand, good governors let it be known that they prefer to see prisoners 'managed' rather than 'disciplined'. This is not to deny that it is possible for an officer to succeed with a malicious charge. This raises another question, however: whether his chances of doing so would be much reduced by any conceivable improvements in adjudicatory procedures. It may be more realistic to pay attention to officers' approaches to the problems of controlling prisoners.

### Criminal cases

**13.13**   Both the Prior Report (1985) and the Woolf Report (1991) recommended that boards of visitors should not have a disciplinary function. While the Prior Report recommended that boards of visitors' disciplinary functions should be taken over by a new independent statutory body called the Prison Disciplinary Tribunal, the Woolf proposals, which were adopted by the Prison (Amendment) Rules 1992, recommended simply that suspected criminal offences should be referred to the police. Thus the current position is that while the governor may deal with minor offences against prison discipline, all other cases must be referred to the police. Standing orders state that the governor should open the disciplinary hearing and satisfy him or herself that there is a case to answer before adjourning pending the police and CPS inquiry.

### Segregation

**13.14**   What has been the subject of the sharpest criticisms is the use of the power in Rule 43 to segregate prisoners not only for their own protection but also 'for the maintenance of good order or discipline'. Segregation on these grounds takes a much less tolerable form. For example, the cells are featureless, prisoners are allowed none of their usual possessions[1], can communicate with nobody but the officer on duty, the governor, the chaplain and the medical officer during their short daily visits. The use of Rule 43 in this way—without the preferment of a specific charge—is a step which governors should not take without discussions which involve both staff and the prisoner. The safeguard for the prisoner is that segregation cannot last for more than 24 hours without confirmation by a member of the board of visitors or the Home Secretary[2] (a confirmation which must be reviewed at least once a month); and that the prisoner can petition the Home Secretary and, if that is unsuccessful, complain to a member of Parliament or to the Prison Ombudsman (see 13.21). Since the decision in *Hague* (see 13.15) it has been clear that prisoners may apply for judicial review of the decision to segregate them. The argument for this power is that there are a few prisoners who are adept at subverting the peace of prisons by persuading others to misbehave, but are careful not to lay themselves open to specific charges.

1. They are, however, allowed books and magazines from the library, and purchases from the canteen, unlike those undergoing a disciplinary punishment of segregation.
2. Who are given the governor's report of his internal investigation.

**13.15** The use of Rule 43 in this way would have incurred less censure if the 'pains of imprisonment' had not at one time been deliberately intensified in the special segregation units. An alternative to segregation which used to be used in dispersal prisons for high security categories was transfer for 28 days to another prison (the CI 10/1974, known as the 'ghosting' procedure). This procedure was substantially amended after the CA's judgement in *Hague* [1992] 1 AC 58. Hague applied for judicial review and claimed damages for false imprisonment and breaches of statutory duty, having been transferred to Wormwood Scrubs under the 'ghosting procedure', where he was then held for 28 days in segregation. After the CA held this to be unlawful, a different circular instruction (CI 37/1990) improved procedural safeguards for prisoners. The Home Office abandoned its cross-appeal to the HL, but maintained its argument that Hague was not entitled to damages for his admittedly unlawful segregation. The HL agreed, refusing damages and rejecting a claim for breach of statutory duty.

## Prisoners' complaints

**13.16** A new prisoners' requests and complaints procedure was introduced in 1990, details of which can be found in the *Prisoner's Information Pack*, issued jointly by the Prison Service and the Prison Reform Trust, which should be issued to all prisoners. It contains general information for prisoners, explaining among other things their right to request interviews with the governor, the chaplain, the medical officer, a 'visiting officer of the Secretary of State'—ie the area manager on one of his official visits, the member of the board of visitors who must tour the establishment at some time during the week or week-end, or the full board at its monthly meetings. If prisoners request an interview through their personal officer or the principal officer of their wing—and it is not easy for them to do so otherwise—they will be asked what they want to complain about. They will usually disclose this, unless of course the subject is likely to antagonise the officer; but they are not required to tell an officer. Internal prison complaints procedures start at the prison: only if a prisoner is unhappy with the decision taken in the prison is he likely to complain to the area manager.

## Petitions

**13.17** A prisoner can also, or instead, write a petition to the Home Secretary, to the Queen or to Parliament. Although there is no specific reference to this in the Prison Act or the Prison Rules, the *Prisoners' Information Pack* states that petitions to the Queen or to Parliament have to be done in a particular way, and that prison staff should have a copy of the instructions. The book warns that this procedure will take longer than if the prisoner raised his or her complaint with prison staff first. The governor will be told of the petition; but nobody in the establishment can properly prevent it from being submitted to the Home Office. There it will be handled by a branch which exists mainly for this purpose, and which will first get the comments of the governor, the medical officer or other senior members of staff most concerned. These may enable the branch to deal with the petition; or it may have to make more enquiries. Eventually the prisoner will receive a reply, usually from a civil servant.

## Members of Parliament

**13.18** A prisoner is allowed to write to a member of Parliament of his choice about his treatment in prison. An MP's usual action on receiving a prisoner's complaint is to send it to a Home Office minister whose private secretary will send it to the Prison Service, where a reply will be prepared by the relevant area manager. This time, however, the reply must be seen by the Home Office minister to whom the MP wrote, so that this procedure ensures a close scrutiny of the Service's response to the complaint. If the MP accepts the reply he writes to the prisoner, either paraphrasing or copying it. If he does not accept it he may try to raise the matter in Parliament, the usual method being a request for an adjournment debate: but the opportunities for this are limited. If he thinks that the Prison Service may have been guilty of maladministration he can write to the Parliamentary Commissioner for Administration.

## The Parliamentary Commissioner for Administration

**13.19** This functionary is commonly known as the 'Ombudsman' because of the origins of the office in Scandinavia. His duty, under the Parliamentary Commissioner Act 1967, is to investigate complaints of 'injustice in consequence of maladministration'. 'Maladministration' is not defined, and at first was interpreted as confining him to procedural mistakes; but under pressure from a Select Committee of the Commons is now taken to include bad decisions and bad rules, as well as administrative aspects of delegated legislation (which includes the Prison Rules). He can receive the complaints only from a member of the House of Commons and his report must be made to that member, although it will later be published, together with others, as a House of Commons paper. He (or one of his officers) can investigate a complaint in any way he thinks fit. He cannot be denied information—for example by pleading public interest immunity—but he can be forbidden, under the Official Secrets Acts, to make it public. His powers are limited to investigating maladministration by the government departments specified in the Act, which include the Home Office but not the Parole Board (although he can and does investigate the Home Office's share in parole decisions: a most artificial boundary line) or local probation services (the latter being within the jurisdiction of the corresponding local authority ombudsman).

**13.20** The investigating officer is given access to any papers which he wants to see, and to any prisoner whom he wants to question; and while he sees prisoners within sight of an officer the latter should be out of hearing, unless the MP is present. The eventual report simply states what the Commissioner found to be the facts, together with his criticism or vindication of the staff concerned. It is for the Prison Service to decide what action to take; but a government department which ignored an adverse report would have to be defended by its minister in the House of Commons. In practice the Ombudsman's reports have occasionally criticised the handling of individual cases by governors[1] or administrators, or the conditions which led to certain decisions, but have not said that any of the Rules should be altered.

1. Even while conceding that the decision did not amount to 'maladministration': see e g Case 249/77.

## Prison Ombudsman

**13.21** The Parliamentary Commissioner for Administration has long been criticised for being ineffective in his influence on prison administration (see Walker (1969); Widdicombe Committee, appointed by Justice (1977); Woolf Report (1991)). The Government accepted the recommendation of Woolf that there should be an independent complaints adjudicator, but unlike Woolf, preferred the title Prison Ombudsman. The first, Sir Peter Woodhead, was appointed in October 1994. No enabling legislation has been passed, so he has no specific powers, for example to award compensation. He cannot consider complaints made by prisoners' friends or families. The Parliamentary Commissioner for Administration continues to have jurisdiction. Only time will tell whether the Prison Ombudsman proves to be more effective in dealing with brutal or oppressive treatment: as the Prison Ombudsman's first Six Month Review (1995) points out, 'some initial problems in defining the interface with the Prison Service still need to be overcome'.

## Courts in England and Wales

**13.22** Prisoners have the same status in civil courts as any other adult citizens, and can institute legal proceedings, for instance for divorce, or for compensation for wrongs. They are allowed access to lawyers of their own choice for this purpose: the only limitation is that if the suit they want to bring concerns what has been done to them in prison they must first use the normal procedure for making a complaint, so as to give the staff an opportunity to meet the complaint. Prisoners have successfully sued the prison authorities in negligence: examples include *Ferguson v Home Office* (1977) Times, 8 October, where a prisoner was awarded £15,500 for injuries caused by a circular saw which he had used with inadequate training; *H v Home Office* (1992) Times, 6 May, where a prisoner was awarded £50 for the negligence of the prison authorities in revealing to other prisoners the fact that he had convictions for sexual offences, which resulted in his being assaulted in his cell.

**13.23** Occasionally a prisoner bases a suit on the claim that what has been done — or not done — by the Prison Service in his case was a breach of the Prison Rules. In such cases the view of the courts is still that the Rules 'are regulatory directions only. Even if they are not observed they do not give rise to a cause of action' (per Lord Denning in *Becker v Home Office* [1972] 2 All ER 676 at 682). In *Hague* (see 13.14 above), Lord Jauncey expressly accepted this. However, Lord Bridge suggested that the rule-making powers conferred by s 47 of the PA 1952 were broad enough to cover the enactment of rules providing for breach of statutory duty. Therefore, as Owen (1991) pointed out, Lord Bridge left open the possibility of an amendment of the current rules in the future to give prisoners the right to sue for breach of statutory duty without the need for fresh primary legislation.

## Judicial review

**13.24** Since the late 1970s there has been a huge growth in the number of judicial reviews of decisions affecting prisoners (see 1.14). Despite clear statements from the courts to the effect that 'where any person or body exercises a power conferred by statute which affects the rights or legal expectations of citizens and is of a kind which the law requires to be exercised in accordance with the rules of natural justice, the court has the power to review the exercise of that power' (per Lord Bridge in *Leech* [1988] AC 533), it was not until the *Hague* case that the Home Office finally withdrew its argument (after the CA's decision) that the court lacked jurisdiction to review decisions taken under the Prison Rules. Lord Bridge stated in the HL that 'the availability of judicial review as a means of questioning the legality of action purportedly taken in pursuance of the Prison Rules is a beneficial and necessary jurisdiction which cannot properly be circumscribed by considerations of policy or expediency in relation to prison administration'. The fact that the Home Office amended the 'ghost train' procedure after the CA's decision demonstrates this 'beneficial and necessary' role of judicial review.

## The European Convention on Human Rights

**13.25** If, but only if, an individual prisoner (or any other individual) has exhausted all the 'domestic' procedures open to him for seeking a remedy, he may apply to the European Commission on Human Rights (ECHR) at Strasbourg on the grounds that he has suffered or is suffering from a violation of one of the rights guaranteed by the Convention. Britain is a signatory to that Convention, although unlike states which formally incorporated it into their own law she has simply undertaken that her law will not be inconsistent with it. The practical effect of the difference is thus that in the sort of case over which a British court has jurisdiction the complainant has to go through an extra stage before he can put his complaint to the ECHR.

**13.26** Standing orders provide that a prisoner's application to the ECHR cannot be stopped by anyone in the Prison Service, nor censored, although it can be *read* by a prison official. Prisoners are not to be charged with disciplinary offences by reason of anything they say in their application. Applicants may petition the ECHR direct, or through an approved lawyer empowered by them to do so. The admissibility of the application is reported on by a rapporteur, but is sometimes the subject of an oral hearing; and the government concerned can insist on such a hearing. The ECHR meets in camera. If an application is accepted as admissible it enquires into the facts and then places itself at the disposal of the parties with a view to a settlement. If no settlement results it reports on the facts, with its opinion as to whether there has been a breach of the Convention. The final decision on the question is reached either by the Committee of Ministers or by the European Court of Human Rights (and only a small minority of cases reach this stage). In that Court it is the Commission, not the applicant, and the government concerned, who present their cases. The Court delivers its findings orally, but later publishes them.

**13.27** This procedure takes time, and does not often result in a remedy for the applicant himself, although sometimes the intervention of the ECHR leads to a settlement in which he is compensated by his government. A more important result is the occasional alteration of law, procedure or administrative policy in obedience to a decision of the Court. Thus *Golder v United Kingdom* (1975) 1 EHRR 524 led to an amendment of the Prison Rules so as to allow a sentenced prisoner access to a lawyer for the purpose of civil proceedings; *X v United Kingdom* (1981) 4 EHRR 188 led to the provision in the Mental Health Act 1983 which gave Mental Health Review Tribunals the power to direct (instead of merely advising) the release from hospital of offenders committed under a restriction order (see 22.8ff); and *Thynne, Wilson and Gunnell v United Kingdom* (1990) 13 EHRR 666 led to the transformation of parole procedures applicable to those sentenced to discretionary life sentences (see 22.16).

**13.28** On the other hand, it seems from other cases that the ECHR is unlikely to intervene in the following matters: compulsory labour for sentenced prisoners (which is expressly allowed by the *Convention*), disciplinary segregation, the allocation of prisoners to one establishment instead of another, the separation of convicted from untried prisoners, pardon, or the preference of a sentenced prisoner for the services of a doctor of his own choice.

## Prisoners' rights in theory

**13.29** The ECHR and the Court of Human Rights deal only in rights which are embodied in the *Convention*. Are there rights which are not explicit in Rules, statute or common law or the Convention; and if so does imprisonment lead to infringements of them? Answers to these questions involve jurisprudence, and vary according to jurists' conceptions of the nature of rights. In Anglo-American jurisprudence a right is a rule which either (a) allows people in general, or certain categories of people (for example the parties to a contract) to behave in certain ways *if they so choose*, or (b) forbids others, again in general or in certain categories, to behave towards them in certain ways, *unless they choose to consent*. The element of choice distinguishes rights from duties. A right to free speech is a rule that those who choose may speak their minds; but is not a duty to do so. A right to property is a prohibition on the taking or damaging of it without the owner's consent; but it is not a duty to be possessive, nor a ban on giving it away.

**13.30** What is not settled by agreed definition is whether rights are 'man-made' or 'natural' rules. On the former view, they are simply rules which enlightened people have created by means of statutes or conventions, contracts or promises. Those who believe in 'natural rights', however, believe that while the codes or contracts are man-made, and some of the rights in them are creations of the codes or contracts, at least some reflect moral rules; so that it makes sense to say 'People have a right to (this or that) and the code (or contract) should embody this right'.

**13.31** Some people —almost always those who believe that rights are natural— also believe in 'inalienable' rights. In its strongest form this means rights which cannot be surrendered even when the beneficiary chooses to do so. Some people for example believe that the right to life cannot be voluntarily renounced, even by a person who has good reason to want to die[1]. This is not necessarily inconsistent with the definition of rights as involving choice; it may merely claim that there are rights which should never be renounced in a general way, only in individual cases. More common is the belief that rights can be suspended, but only with the consent of the beneficiaries. Again, many people would argue that certain people—especially those who infringe the rights of others—forfeit those rights which they have infringed, whether they consent to forfeit them or not (as outlaws were held to have forfeited their right to life because of their slayings). Thirdly, practical considerations make it necessary to concede that rights—or at least some rights—have to be 'curtailed', that is made subject to restrictions or even exceptions, in order to infringe the rights of others as little as possible. Otherwise a right to free speech could in practice allow A to shout down B. The notions of forfeiture or curtailment of rights figure in discussions of what is done to offenders, and especially prisoners (see for example 22.29 ff).

1. A difficult question for them is therefore whether anyone should knowingly sacrifice his or her life in a good cause, or to save another life.

## Rights in English law

**13.32**    Until the second half of this century English lawyers tended to assume that the only places in which to look for rights were the Bill of Rights, statutes, subordinate legislation such as the Prison Rules, the promulgated rules of associations (such as the professions), contracts and, of course, the common law, a favourite place for armchair discoveries. Philosophers such as Locke might assert the existence of rights which could not be found in these sources; but unless such rights were recognised by law—as some of Locke's were in the US Constitution—they had no legal force. The situation is less simple now that we have the European Convention of Human Rights and its Court of Human Rights, which have obliged this country to alter some of its statutes or subordinate legislation in order to comply with the Convention or with decisions of the Court. The European Convention thus has a status and force which the United Nations' Declaration of Human Rights does not.

**13.33**    English criminal law provides certain rights for defendants, both as regards the conduct of their trial (for example the right to be presumed innocent unless proved guilty beyond reasonable doubt) and as regards disposal (for example the right to be allowed time to pay a fine). Most of these rights are subject to express exceptions; for example, time to pay a fine need not be given in certain circumstances (see 16.15).

## Prisoners' rights in practice

**13.34**    It is the rights of prisoners, however, which have been the subject of most discussion, both in the USA and here, because it is in prisons that people are most drastically prevented from doing what they feel free to do outside. The common law rule, as stated by the Queen's Bench in *Tarrant* ([1984] 1 All ER 799), is that 'a prisoner retain(s) all civil rights not taken away from him expressly or by necessary implication'. By 'expressly' the court must have meant 'by statute or statutory instrument'. Examples are the right to vote in Parliamentary elections, which is withdrawn during a custodial sentence (s 4 Representation of the People Act 1969) and the right to use one's property, which is restricted by Rules 41 and 42 of the Prison Rules 1964, among others.

**13.35**    The rights which are withdrawn 'by necessary implication' are less easily identified or defined. In the first place it is far from clear which of the freedoms a prisoner enjoyed outside were his or hers by right and to what extent he or she loses them inside. Prisoners can no longer choose whether to work or not, or the kind of work they prefer: they cannot choose their doctor, or medicate themselves at will: they cannot exercise whenever and however they want to; they cannot choose their cell-mates or other associates; they have to eat what they are given or go hungry; and so on. On the other hand, the extent to which these liberties were theirs by right is debatable. Freedom of work is very dependent on the economic climate of the day. Freedom to choose one's doctor and one's medicine is by no means absolute: a doctor can refuse to treat an unpleasant patient, and a pharmacy may refuse him the drug he wants. As for choice of associates, most people enjoy this only in the privacy of their homes: elsewhere—at work, in public transport, in public houses—they have to tolerate people whom they do not fancy. In respects like these the difference between prison and the outside world is one of degree.

**13.36**  In any case those who run prisons would point out that if society wants to hold people in this way it cannot be done without restrictions which interfere in a myriad ways with the freedoms they enjoy outside. Some of these restrictions are made necessary by such objectives as security, or prisoners' health; others by the unpleasant ways in which some prisoners behave to others or to the staff. Undoubtedly there are prisoners who would, even without such restrictions, serve their sentences peaceably, healthily and without absconding; but because by no means all prisoners are like that they have to endure the restrictions (unless their sentences are long enough for transfer to open prisons). In this direction the argument is about practicalities. What restrictions are essential, given the declared objectives and the type of prisoner for which this or that establishment caters? What restrictions are simply traditional, like the now abolished 'rule of silence', which was maintained long after staff had ceased to believe in its positive value? Which are based on moral prejudices, like the ban on conjugal visiting?

**13.37**  On the other hand there is a point of view which holds that sentenced prisoners are people who have shown by their actions that they have little regard for the 'rights'—or, less controversially, the well-being—of other people, and have therefore forfeited the 'right' to the freedoms enjoyed by outsiders. In this form the assertion is too vague and sweeping. A man who has been provoked into a single violent assault is not necessarily a man who has little regard for the well-being of others: and a thief may well be someone who abhors violence. Should they forfeit different freedoms? And if the argument is based on the notion of forfeiture should not the statute make clear exactly what is forfeited by what sorts of offences, so that the forfeiture would be an expressly declared part of the penalty?

**13.38**  There is thus a choice between a doctrinaire approach to 'prisoners' rights' and the approach founded on 'humane pragmatism', which merely tries to avoid the imposition of hardships and restrictions which are not inseparable from the deprivation of liberty. The weakness of humane pragmatism is that habit or punitiveness may preserve rules or standing orders which once seemed necessary but are no longer. Yet it is more likely to accept change than a penal code which prescribes the forfeiture of freedoms.

## Rule drafting

**13.39** What is extremely doubtful is whether the language of rights is the most effective one to use when rules are being drafted for the conduct of establishments. If the intention is to ensure that each prisoner receives certain things or services, then simply to declare that they are rights does not make it clear who is at fault if he or she does not receive them. Although the Prison Rules do not use the word 'right' some of them are phrased in a 'right-like' way: for example 'A prisoner ... shall be given exercise in the open air for not less than one hour in all, each day, if weather permits' (Rule 27). This does not lay an obligation on any designated member of the staff to ensure that every prisoner gets his or her open-air exercise. Contrast this rule with Rule 21(5): 'The medical officer shall regularly inspect the food both before and after it is cooked, and shall report any deficiency or defect to the governor'. This makes it clear whose obligation it is to ensure that food is fit for consumption, instead of merely declaring that prisoners have a right to fit food. If a similar obligation were laid on a specified member of staff to ensure that every prisoner got his outdoor exercise, it would be overlooked less often. The language of duties may be more effective in a rule-run organisation than the relatively vague language of rights.

## European Prison Rules

**13.40** In 1973 the Council of Europe adopted Standard Minimum Rules for the Treatment of Prisoners (based on a 1955 UN Resolution). The European Prison Rules superseded these in 1987. The European Prison Rules are not binding, but intended as guidelines for national administrations. In their pre-amble to the Rules (Recommendation (87)(3)), the Committee of Ministers 'recommends that governments of Member States be guided in their internal legislation and practice by the principles set out in the text of the European Prison Rules ... with a view to their progressive implementation...'. It is worth noting that the Prison Rules in England and Wales still fall short of many of these (often vague) standards (see Loucks, 1993).

## The movement towards enforceable standards

**13.41** Calls for enforceable standards have increased ever since the May Committee (1979). Paras 1.186-1.187 of the Woolf Report (1991) stated:

'In order to achieve justice within prisons there must be required standards of conditions and regimes within prisons. After proper consultation, the Home Secretary should establish a series of national Accredited Standards applicable to all prisons. It would then be the responsibility of every prison establishment to reach at least that standard. Area managers ...would be responsible for ensuring that, over a period of time, each prison in their area fulfil all the national Accredited Standards. The area manager would certify when a prison had reached a required standard. When it had fulfilled all the standards, it would be granted Accreditation Status by the Home Secretary, on the recommendation of HM Chief Inspector of Prisons. For the time being, the national standards would have to be aspirational. Once they are achieved, that would be the time to consider whether it was necessary to make them legally enforceable. We would, however, expect that at that stage they would be incorporated in the Prison Rules and so would be legally enforceable by judicial review.'

The move towards privatisation is leading to enforceable standards, imposing as it does contractual obligations on the service providers. However, there remain many calls for the overhaul of the 40-year-old Prison Act 1952. Thus Richardson (1993), in condemning the poverty of legislative involvement in drawing up policies for prisoners, says: 'If Parliament is to delegate large areas of policy formulation to other agencies, that delegation should be express; it should provide the clearest guidance possible as to the principles which should govern the emergent policy, and it should specify the processes to be followed by the agency in reaching its formulation. With regard to prison policy, virtually no attempt is made to meet these conditions.'

Chapter 14

# Getting out

**14.1**   Most of this chapter is about the release of prisoners who are serving sentences: fine-defaulters and other categories will be dealt with briefly in passing. The use of the royal prerogative of mercy to release prisoners has already been mentioned in chapter 1.

### Early release

**14.2**   The CJA 91 abolished the old system whereby prisoners had been allowed remission of part of their sentence. Remission had developed out of the regal power of pardon, which was originally exercised in order to set free transported convicts after years of labour. The new system means that prisoners serving sentences of under four years are released (or deported in the case of deportees) automatically halfway through their sentences provided that they do not have extra days added for misbehaviour (see 13.10). Those serving four years or more become eligible for parole at the halfway point of their sentence, and must be released after serving two-thirds of the sentence. 2,000 offenders were granted parole in 1994 (43 per cent of those considered), and at the end of 1994, approximately the same number were under parole supervision in the community (Barclay et al, 1995). The release procedure for life sentence prisoners is discussed in chapter 22.

### Fine defaulters

**14.3**   Offenders imprisoned in default of payment of fines, compensation or maintenance are eligible for early release. They may also, however, secure their release if any or all of the sum due is paid before they become eligible for early release, in which case they are released after serving a fraction proportionate to the unpaid fraction of the sum due. Early release is allowed only on the period for which no payment in part has been made. It is not uncommon for a fine-defaulter's partner to appear at the prison, with the sum due, the day after his or her reception, so that he or she is released at once; and fine-defaulters are allowed to telephone their families for this purpose. Wilkins (1979) found that roughly 1 in every 5 of the fine defaulters released from Winson Green Prison in Birmingham in 1977 had spent less than 3 days there, presumably because all or part of their fines had been paid. Thus even the small percentage of fines which is officially recorded as resulting in imprisonment (see 16.33 ff) gives a slightly exaggerated impression. Payment of a fine-defaulter's fine can be made by anyone, and there have been cases in which people who have been fined for some act of protest, have deliberately incurred imprisonment for non-payment, and been unwillingly released because their fines had been paid anonymously.

### Parole pre-1992

**14.4**    Parole was introduced by the CJA 67, which gave the Home Secretary power—not a duty—to release a prisoner from a determinate sentence after he or she had served a third of it or 12 months, whichever was the longer. The Home Secretary could exercise this power only in cases in which it was recommended by the Parole Board or in certain types of case by a local review committee of the prisoner's establishment; but such a recommendation did not oblige him to follow it, and occasionally he did not. The prisoner himself could decline consideration for parole, in which case he was not released until his due date. If paroled he was on licence until the date on which he would have been released on remission, but with exceptions. The parole licence meant that he was released under supervision by a probation officer and would be liable to recall to prison to serve the remainder of the sentence if he broke the conditions of his licence.

### Local review committees

**14.5**    Until recently, there was a local review committee (LRC) for every prison in which there were prisoners who were eligible for release on licence. It included:
   a.   the prison governor (although he was allowed to be, and often was, represented at meetings by a deputy governor). It could not include any other 'officer of a prison';
   b.   a probation officer who was not a prison probation officer (a probation officer who works in a prison might be thought subject to the influence of prison staff);
   c.   a member of the prison's board of visitors;
   d.   two persons who were neither (b) nor (c).
The LRC discussed all cases in which the prisoner's parole eligibility date (PED; at one third of the sentence) was imminent and their recommendations went to the Parole Unit of the HO. In *Payne v Lord Harris* [1981] 1 WLR 754, the CA held that neither the LRC nor the Parole Board had to give reasons for their decisions. Since release is now automatic for those sentenced to less than 4 years' imprisonment, the need for LRCs diminished from 1992. Once the transitional arrangements for the new scheme are completed, LRCs will become obsolete, their role being taken over exclusively by the Parole Board.

## The Carlisle Report

**14.6**   Various changes in the details of the parole system over the years led to the realisation that substantial differences in sentence lengths often in reality disappeared when prisoners were released on the same date. Thus when the minimum qualifying period for parole was reduced to six months by s 33 CJA 82, a prisoner serving nine months would be released after six months, but so would a person serving 18 months if he or she were granted parole. This widening gap between the sentence which was announced in court and the term actually served by the offender led the Government to set up a review of the operation of the parole system as it applied to fixed-term prisoners, chaired by Lord Carlisle.

The main recommendations of the Carlisle Report (1988) were:

i.    the abolition of discretionary early release for those sentenced to less than 4 years' imprisonment;

ii.   the end of the Home Secretary's responsibility for releasing determinate sentence prisoners;

iii.  the abolition of LRCs;

iv.   statutory criteria for release;

v.    a more open parole procedure: eg disclosure of material relied on by the Parole Board.

The White Paper *Crime, Justice and Protecting the Public* (1990) accepted the main recommendations of the Carlisle Report and the changes were introduced in the CJA 91. However, some key proposals such as statutory criteria for release and the end of the Home Secretary's involvement were not accepted. It is worth noting that the Carlisle Committee was not asked to examine parole for life sentence prisoners.

## Automatic unconditional release

**14.7**   All those sentenced to less than 12 months must be released unconditionally after serving half of their sentence (s 33 (1)(a) CJA 91). Their release may be delayed if they have been found guilty of a disciplinary offence under the Prison Rules and have been given additional days in prison as a punishment (s 42, and see 13.8). They may be returned to prison if they commit any offence punishable with imprisonment before the date on which they would (but for their release) have served their sentence in full (s 40).

## Automatic conditional release

**14.8**   Prisoners sentenced to 12 months or more but less than 4 years are released on licence. As with all other prisoners, their release may be delayed if they have been awarded additional days in prison as a punishment. The licence remains in force (unless revoked or suspended) until the date on which he or she would (but for his or her release) have served three-quarters of his sentence. Short-term prisoners who fail to comply with the conditions of their licence are guilty of an offence (s 38) and may be punished with a fine. They may also be recalled to prison for as long as six months (s 38(2)) but must in any event be released unconditionally after they have served three-quarters of the sentence originally imposed (s 33(3)) unless the offence is a sexual one and s 44 applies, in which case they may be recalled for the whole of the remainder of the sentence (see 22.4). A short-term prisoner may be released on licence on compassionate grounds at any time and the Parole Board need not be consulted by the Secretary of State (s 36(1) and (2)).

## Discretionary conditional release

**14.9** A long-term prisoner (one sentenced to 4 years or more) must be released on licence after he or she has served two-thirds of his or her sentence (s 33(2)), and may be released after serving one-half of the sentence if the Parole Board recommends it. The Home Secretary may release the prisoner if the Parole Board so recommends but he is not obliged to do so (see 14.16). Section 50 CJA 91 gives the Home Secretary the power to transfer the final decision to the Board in certain classes of case. He has used this power to make an order transferring this function in cases of prisoners serving 4 years but less than 7 years. The practical effect is that a recommendation from the Parole Board to release a prisoner serving between 4 and 7 years is binding upon the Home Secretary, but a recommendation to release a prisoner serving 7 years or more remains subject to his discretion.

## Criteria for discretionary conditional release

**14.10** The criteria which the Parole Board should bear in mind when considering whether to recommend release for prisoners were revised by the Home Secretary's directions in 1992. The basic underlying principle is that 'the decision whether or not to recommend parole should focus primarily on the risk to the public of a further offence being committed at a time when the offender would otherwise be in prison. This should be balanced against the benefit, both to the public and the offender, of early release back into the community under a degree of supervision which might help rehabilitation and so lessen the risk of reoffending in the future'. The directions continue:

'Before recommending parole, the Parole Board should be satisfied that:
   a.   the longer period of supervision that parole would provide is likely to reduce the risk of further imprisonable offences being committed. In assessing the risk to the community a small risk of violent offending is to be treated as more serious than a larger risk of non-violent offending;
   b.   the offender has shown by his attitude and behaviour in custody that he is willing to address his offending and has made positive efforts and progress in doing so;
   c.   the resettlement plan will help secure the offender's rehabilitation.'

Hood and Shute (1995) point out that the replacement of the former criteria for refusal by criteria for release 'has inevitably shifted the focus of decision-making from considerations which could be either positive or negative to a presumption that parole will not be granted unless all three criteria are met'.

**14.11** Under the title 'Training Guidance', the Parole Board is instructed to take into account the following factors when making a recommendation about parole. (The weight and relevance attached to each factor differs and may vary according to the circumstances).

   a. the offender's background, including any previous convictions and their pattern, and responses to any previous periods of supervision;
   b. the nature and circumstances of the original offence;
   c. where available, the sentencing judge's comments and probation and medical reports prepared for the court;
   d. any risk to the victim or possibility of retaliation by the victim, victim's family or local community;
   e. any risk to other persons, including persons outside the jurisdiction;
   f. any available statistical indicators as to the likelihood of reoffending;
   g. attitude and behaviour in custody including offences against prison discipline;
   h. attitude to other inmates and positive contributions made to prison life.
   i. remorse, insight into offending behaviour, attitude to the victim and steps taken, with available resources, to achieve any treatment or training objectives set out in a sentence plan;
   j. realism of the release plan and resettlement prospects, including home circumstances and the likelihood of co-operation with supervision, relationship with the home probation officer, attitude of the victim and local community, extent to which the release plan continues rehabilitative work started in the prison and the extent to which it lessens or removes the occurrence of circumstances which led to the original offence;
   k. any medical or psychiatric considerations;
   l. any other information, including representations by or on behalf of the offender, which may have a bearing on risk assessment.

## The Parole Board

**14.12** The Parole Board contains about 86 members, most of them serving for three years, although this period is occasionally extended. Members are appointed by the Home Secretary, and are paid for sessions which they attend, although some full-time members were appointed for the first time in 1993. The volume of 'home-work' is heavy, and invitations to serve on the Board part-time are not infrequently declined. The Chairman, too, is appointed by the Home Secretary, and receives a part-time salary. By statute (Sch III CJA 67) the Board must include

   a. a person who holds or has held judicial office (not necessarily in the UK);
   b. a registered medical practitioner who is also a psychiatrist;
   c. a person with knowledge and experience of the supervision or after-care

of discharged prisoners (usually a serving or former probation officer);

d.   a person 'appearing to the Secretary of State to have made a study of the causes of delinquency or the treatment of offenders' (a 1967 attempt to define a criminologist);

e.   independents.

Members cannot at the same time be members of Parliament: an attempt to keep the Board free of the political influence to which some parole boards in the USA have been susceptible. Several of the Board's chairmen, however, have been members of the House of Lords. The Secretary of the Board is a civil servant, who is seconded from the Home Office, as are the other staff of the Board.

**14.13**   Any three or more members may deal with a case (though the rules are different for discretionary lifer panels: see 22.16). The Carlisle Committee warned that reducing panel size would impair the inter-disciplinary nature of panels, and this appears to have happened (see Hood and Shute, 1995). The prisoner has no right to an oral hearing; but the Parole Board has a discretion to arrange for one of its members to interview the prisoner before it reaches its decision. What is said is confidential, although the news media seem able on occasion to get wind of discussions of notorious cases. The research currently being carried out by Hood and Shute is the first major study of the way in which the Board arrives at decisions since the reforms of 1991.

**14.14**   The decision of the Board must be given in writing, with reasons. The prisoner may make a written application to call witnesses and must be given reasons in writing if this request is turned down. The CA in *Wilson* [1991] 2 All ER 576 confirmed that the applicant is entitled to be informed of all reports that will be placed before the Board, though rule 5(2) allows the Board to withhold information from the prisoner that 'would adversely affect the health or welfare of the prisoner or others'. As Hood and Shute (1994) point out, both prisoners and staff have high expectations of the new system and it is important to evaluate whether this increased openness will lead to greater satisfaction with the process.

**14.15**   If the prisoner's application is unsuccessful, he may also be told that his case will be reviewed again, either within 14 months (as it must if he is still in prison custody) or earlier. Standing orders allow extensions in exceptional circumstances such as unlawful absences from prison, stays in hospital or new criminal proceedings.

## The role of the Home Secretary

**14.16**   Recommendations for parole go to the Home Office's Parole Unit, which has to accept an unfavourable recommendation but can advise the minister not to accept a favourable one if the sentence was for 7 years or more. All favourable recommendations are considered in the light of the Home Secretary's 'wider responsibilities', and in practice he appears to be rejecting only a small number of cases (16 of the 1,603 recommended in 1994), He has also made it clear that some mandatory life sentence prisoners will never be considered for parole (see 22.18).

The Home Secretary also has significant powers in relation to the revocation of licences. Under s 39(2) he may revoke any licence where 'it appears to him that it is expedient in the public interest to recall that person before such a recommendation [by the Parole Board] is practicable'. Although the CJA 91 had given the Home Secretary the power to transfer to the Parole Board exclusive power to recall prisoners, this power was repealed by s 150 of the CJPOA 94. There is now only one recall system, operated by the Home Secretary. Thus, the Government has made clear that the Home Secretary will continue to play a significant role in the release of prisoners. Whether a politician should play such a key role remains a much-debated question (see Home Affairs Select Committee, 1995).

### Practice statement on early release

**14.17**    Pre-1992 many fixed term prisoners were eligible to be considered for release at the one-third point in their sentence. From 1992, no-one was eligible for release until they had served one half of their sentence. There was therefore concern that many prisoners (particularly those sentenced to between 12 months and 4 years) would now serve in practice significantly longer in prison than those sentenced to similar terms under the old system. When the CJA 1991 came into force, Lord Taylor issued a *Practice Statement (Crime: Sentencing)* [1992] 1 WLR 948 which stated, inter alia:

'It has been an axiomatic principle of sentencing policy until now that the court should decide the appropriate sentence in each case without reference to questions of remission or parole. I have consulted the Lords Justices presiding in the Court of Appeal (Criminal Division) and we have decided that a new approach is essential. Accordingly, from 1 October 1992, it will be necessary, when passing a custodial sentence in the Crown Court, to have regard to the actual period likely to be served and, as far as practicable, to the risk of offenders serving longer under the new system than would have been normal under the old. Existing guideline judgements should be applied with these considerations in mind.'

This was discussed in *Cunningham* [1993] 1 WLR 183. Lord Taylor CJ stressed that the *Practice Statement* did not require 'an arithmetically precise calculation to be made'. Although in *Cunningham*, a case of armed robbery in a small shop, the CA reduced the sentence from 4 to 3 years, the guidance seems unlikely to encourage shorter sentences: 'where the length of a custodial sentence is challenged, this court is unlikely to be moved by nice arithmetical comparison between periods under the old and the new regimes'. Hood and Shute (1995) calculate that sentences would have to be cut by an average of 21 per cent if prisoners were not to serve longer than they would under the pre-1991 system.

## Sex offenders

**14.18** The CJA 91 treats sex offenders whom the original sentencer identifies as a 's 44 sex offender' differently from other offenders. They are then required to remain under supervision following their release until the end of their sentence, and not just until the three-quarter point. The sentencer should only order that s 44 applies having regard to the need to protect the public from serious harm and the desirability of preventing the commission of further offences and of securing the prisoner's rehabilitation. Thus it is not meant to be punitive, though it can be punitive in its effect: a sex offender who is recalled to prison for breach of his licence may be liable to remain there until the end of his sentence.

## Life sentence prisoners

**14.19** The Carlisle Report looked simply at fixed-term prisoners. But a ruling of the European Court of Human Rights forced the Government to introduce a very different system for discretionary life sentence offenders. In *Thynne, Wilson and Gunnell v United Kingdom* (1991) 13 EHRR 666, the ECHR ruled that once the 'tariff' period set by reference to the offence has expired, any subsequent detention on grounds of public protection should be capable of being challenged through proceedings in a court or tribunal which is independent of the executive. The three applicants were all sentenced to discretionary life sentences, and the Court held that neither proceedings before the Parole Board nor judicial review satisfied the requirement of Art 5(4) that:

> 'Everyone who is deprived of his liberty by arrest or detention shall be entitled to take proceedings by which the lawfulness of his detention shall be decided speedily by a court and his release ordered if the detention is not lawful.'

The CJA 91 therefore introduced a more open procedure governing the release of discretionary life sentence prisoners. The trial judge is encouraged by s 34 to state in open court the 'tariff' period, and a *Practice Direction (Imposition of Discretionary Life Sentence)* [1993] 1 WLR 223 made clear that judges should indeed do this in every case. The Government has maintained its position that mandatory lifers remain subject to the principle that release is dependent on the Home Secretary's exercise of discretion. What happens in practice is described in 22.16-19.

## Justifying parole

**14.20** As a matter of historical fact, one of the aims with which parole was introduced for determinate sentences in the 1960s was the reduction of the prison population. Various justifications for it were put forward, however, most of them more high-minded. 'We doubt the value of keeping men in prison after they have learned their lesson: at this point the cost ... is no longer justified'

(Longford Study Group, 1964). Nowadays there is less confidence about the possibility of knowing when a prisoner has learned his lesson. Again, 'Every additional year of prison progressively unfits [prisoners who are not dangerous, unstable or immature ... They] are more likely to be made into decent citizens if before completing the whole of the sentence they are released under licence with a liability to recall ...' (HO White Paper of 1965). This avoids the assumption that 'ripeness' can be diagnosed, but rests on assumptions about 'prisonisation' which are not very precise (see 11.25ff). Years later, the Parole Board itself said (in its Report for 1977) that 'imprisonment can become expensive and wasteful of human resources. There should be some system whereby a prisoner can have his case reviewed to see whether his continued detention ... is necessary, or whether an alternative non-custodial form of treatment may be safely substituted ...'. This is a plain economic argument. The Board also reasons that if release is inevitable by a fixed date it is better that the early stage of liberty should be under licence. The last of these arguments is supported by empirical evidence. The best analysis of the English data is by Hann et al (1991), who found that paroled offenders were reconvicted less often than the non-paroled, and came to the conclusion that this could not be wholly explained as the effect of selecting better risks for parole. The evidence did not make it possible to tell the extent to which the better behaviour of parolees was attributable to supervision and the extent to which it was due to the threat of recall to prison. But one way or the other, being on licence improves behaviour.

**14.21** That is not an argument, however, for a system of discretionary selection for early release. Parole used to be criticised by desert-minded penologists as resentencing (eg by Hood (1974)), and defended by utilitarian penologists (eg Walker (1974) who thought that resentencing was no bad thing if done by qualified people in the light of the prisoner's progress). However that may be, the Carlisle reforms rendered this controversy slightly passé. Instead of resentencing all prisoners who were serving more than minimal terms, the role of the PB is now confined to deciding which long-term prisoners can be set free before their due dates without undue risk to others. Assessing its performance of this task will not be easy. It will eventually be possible to count the numbers of parolees whose behaviour is alarming enough to lead to recall, and the numbers who are convicted of serious offences against the person during the time when they could have been kept in prison. What will not be countable will be the number of prisoners whose parole was refused or delayed but who would not have committed any such crimes if released. This problem besets estimates of 'dangerousness' and is discussed in 22.29 ff.

## Home leave and temporary release

**14.22** Some prisoners are temporarily released on 'temporary licence', under Rule 6 of the Prison Rules. The Home Office's current policy is contained in Instruction to Governors 36/1995. This introduced a new system of tighter controls over temporary release. The instruction states that

'The system of release on temporary licence is designed to ensure that suitable prisoners are released only for precisely defined and specific activities, which cannot be provided in Prison Service Establishments. Governors have an overriding duty when considering any release to ensure that both public safety and public confidence in the system are maintained.'

Release on specific compassionate grounds is known as compassionate leave; release for education, training or work experience, or for a limited variety of official purposes, is known as facility licence; release towards the end of a sentence to assist prisoners in reintegrating into the community is known as resettlement licence. Until 1992, the security classification of the prison where the prisoner was detained determined his or her eligibility for home leave, but now it is the prisoner's own classification. Category A prisoners are ineligible for any form of release on temporary licence, and category B are not eligible to apply for facility licence. Morris et al (1995) in their report 'Managing the Needs of Female Prisoners' point out that home leave often comes too late: relationships may have already deteriorated or changed irrevocably. The Parole Board expressed dismay about the curtailment of these 'opportunities to demonstrate reliability on licence' (Parole Board, 1994).

**14.23**   When temporary release is granted the prisoner is given a return rail warrant or bus fare, and if necessary a small sum for meals en route. Prisoners who want to marry are usually allowed to attend the church or registry office under escort, and are then brought back to prison on the same day. In this respect the English system is much less generous than, for example, the Swedish or Hungarian systems, in which prisoners, except for those who are in the highest security category, are eligible for regular home leave.

## Preparing for release

**14.24**   As the *National Standard on Supervision before and after release from Custody* makes clear, prison governors and probation officers have now to work closely together on joint arrangements to develop plans for the offender. 'Sentence planning forms the basis for effective throughcare' (para 9). Before release a supervision plan is drawn up, as a continuation of the sentence plan (for which, see 11.7). According to the *Standard*:

'The plan should
- identify the offender's motivation, pattern of offending, relevant problems—needs, the risk of reoffending or serious harm to the public and the requirements of the licence
- identify work to be done to make offenders aware of the impact of the crimes that they have committed on their victims, themselves and the community
- **describe the purpose and the desired outcomes** of the supervision for the offender
- set out an **individual programme** which addresses the **objectives** for

supervision and the individual circumstances of the case, sets individual objectives for the offender and identifies the methods to be tried
- set out the **nature and frequency** of contact during the licence (in accordance with the standard)
- identify a time scale for achieving each objective in the programme.'

Most training prisons hold classes at which prisoners can discuss practical and other post-release problems with staff or visiting specialists; and even some local prisons manage to do so. If a prisoner has no home to go to the supervising probation officer may manage to find him a place in a hostel (see 17.38 ff), or as a lodger with someone who is prepared to accept an ex-prisoner. If he wants advice on job-finding he can ask to see a specialist officer from the local job centre.

**14.25** For some prisoners there is the possibility of a place in the prerelease employment scheme for the last 6 months of their time inside. Under this scheme prisoners live either in a special part of a prison or in a hostel outside, and go to work for an outside employer, with a strict obligation to return by a specified time. They are paid ordinary wages, but must hand over part of these to the prison staff for their keep and for their family's maintenance if necessary. Selection for this scheme depends mainly on behaviour during sentence. Places are fewer than they used to be, partly because good risks may be paroled earlier in their sentences, partly because the use of parts of prisons in this way has been limited by overcrowding and security problems. Many more prisoners apply for the scheme than can be accepted. Holloway has a scheme whereby prisoners may attend external colleges on a 'day-temporary' release basis, yet Morris et al (1995) found that few women were able to obtain temporary release for such a purpose.

## Release

**14.26** Most prisoners are discharged from local prisons, although those released after remands in custody are freed at the court[1]. Those who have spent the last part of their sentences in training or special prisons are released from them, unless they have been transferred to a prerelease hostel or to a prison near their homes, for example to enable them to meet potential employers.

1. Their belongings always accompany them to court so as to save trouble in case they do not return to the prison, however unlikely this is. If released they are not entitled to discharge grants, fares or subsistence payments, although they may receive cash from charitable funds held by the magistrates, or from the Probation Service.

**14.27** On the day before his (or her) release the prisoner sees a member of the Governor Grade, who tells him what he will be given by way of money and travel warrants. He goes to the hospital wing for a medical examination, hands back books to the Library or Education Officer, and asks the latter for a 'gate pass' to authorise him to take away any article that he has made in prison, which may also be examined by the security officer in case he is smuggling anything out. Any original writings have to be seen by the library staff before removal.

**14.28** On the day of discharge he is taken at about 7.30am to 'reception', where he changes his prison clothes for his own. If his own are unfit to wear they are replaced; and men who have served a sentence of more than 4 years receive a complete set of new clothing and even a razor and toothbrush. He gets back his 'property', including any money which he had on arrival, minus any part of it which he has been allowed to spend during his sentence. He signs a receipt for these, an acknowledgment that he is debarred from possessing a firearm under s 21 of the Firearms Act 1968, and a statement that he has no complaints (for example about the return of his property and cash). If he is being released on licence he is given the licence and required to sign a statement that he understands it. If it seems likely that the press will be waiting for him outside the gate he is told that he can delay his departure until later in the day. Otherwise he walks out about 8am. The police are told in advance about all releases.

**14.29** At the prison gate he is handed his bus fare or a rail warrant to get him to the address to which he is going, and a small sum in cash for meals en route. If he has been a civil prisoner or fine-defaulter, or has served a sentence involving less than 15 days inside[1], he must go to the Department of Social Security (DSS) Benefits Agency for further help with money. But with certain exceptions, he is eligible for a discharge grant[2]. The grant may be supplemented by a subsistence allowance if the DSS Benefits Agency is not open on the day following his release.

1. Time spent inside on remand, which usually counts towards his sentence, does not count for this purpose.
2. Standard discharge grants from 1 August 1995 were £46.75 (for prisoners aged 25 and over) and £37.00 (for those aged 18-24): see IG 71/1995.

## Social security benefits[1]

**14.30** While imprisoned as a sentenced prisoner or as a fine-defaulter a person does not receive social security benefits such as a state pension, unemployment or incapacity benefit. Remanded prisoners lose benefits only if the criminal proceedings end in the imposition of a penalty. Wives or other dependants may of course be entitled to benefits. Ex-prisoners are as eligible as any other person for any social security benefits which their payment of contributions or their circumstances justify. They will of course have ceased to pay National Insurance contributions while inside; and in the case of a person who has served a substantial sentence it will be some months before he becomes reentitled to unemployment or incapacity benefit, even if he gets a paid job at once. Most ex-prisoners have to rely on income support until they find paid work; and their first step in obtaining this is to visit their local office of the Benefits Agency of the DSS, which will record their particulars as a preliminary to arranging for the first payment. If they have not already registered at the local job centre they will have to do so before payments are authorised.

**14.31** On his first visit to the Benefits Agency, however, he (or she) may be in immediate need of money if he has received no discharge grant. Ex-prisoners may for instance have found lodgings but be unable to pay the first week's rent in advance. If so, they must take a note from the landlord to the Benefits Agency who may send them (or the hostel warden or landlord) a giro cheque from the Social Fund. The Benefits Agency is entitled to question claimants about their means, and if they have come from prison they will be asked for the document given to them at the gate, which shows how much money they had in their property and how much was given to them by way of discharge grant or subsistence allowance.

1. The details of these rules may change in October 1996 if the Government's proposed job seekers' allowance is introduced.

## Jobs

**14.32** If he pays a post-release visit to a job centre, an ex-prisoner is seen by a specialist officer, who will ask him about his qualifications and history of employment. He may try to conceal the fact that he has come from prison, for example by pretending to have worked abroad; but this seldom succeeds, and most ex-prisoners recognise this. The specialist officer knows which kinds of employer are or are not prepared to consider applicants with criminal records, and so can advise the ex-prisoner whether it would be a waste of time to apply for this vacancy or that. It is for the employer, not the job centre, to decide whether to reject an applicant because of his record, or for any reason: what the job centre will not do is assist the applicant to conceal his record. The fact that it is easier for offenders who have not just emerged from custody to conceal their records is not the job centre's business. The specialist officer may advise the applicant that his best chance of a job is as a labourer with a building or civil engineering firm, which is unlikely to ask searching questions if he seems likely to be a good worker. Otherwise he may advise him to seek help from the local probation department, which knows employers who are sympathetic to offenders. (The problems raised by stigma and the fear of it are discussed in 19.18 ff.) He may refuse an offered job, especially if he finds that the pay is less than the standard supplementary benefit. But any benefit claimant under 45 who remains unemployed for 6 months will be summoned to an interview by the Benefits Agency to find out whether he is genuinely available and willing to work. As a result his benefit may or may not be discontinued. If he gets a job and needs special clothing or tools not provided by his employer the Benefits Agency will help him to buy these: ex-prisoners' needs in this respect are readily acknowledged.

**14.33** Faced with difficulties in finding a job, the ex-prisoner may embark on a 'self-employed' occupation, legitimate or illegitimate. Window cleaning and gardening are common choices. This choice will not allow him to qualify eventually for unemployment or sickness benefit, or for a contributory pension. Without these, he must rely on supplementary benefits—or on a restricted non-contributory invalidity pension—to help him when he has no income. At times of high unemployment, however, or when offered jobs at rates below those of supplementary benefit, self-employment has attractions, not the least of which is that it is easily concealed when making claims for supplementary benefit. In general, fraudulent claims for social service benefits by ex-prisoners are not uncommon. DSS staff are on the alert for these, but at the same time exercise considerable discretion in prosecuting for minor dishonesties.

## The first few weeks

**14.34**    The first few weeks of freedom are said to be the most stressful for ex-prisoners. If they return to family life both they and their families must readjust to each other. They must either find work or reconcile themselves to living on benefits. Wives may find that they benefit less from benefits when their husbands are free and spending. Men who were optimistic about job-finding while in prison are faced with the realities of high unemployment. The leisure of freedom may prove to be only a degree less boring than the leisure of incarceration.

**14.35**    The first few weeks of freedom are also believed to be the period in which ex-prisoners are most likely to commit thefts or acquisitive offences, because of the economic or other difficulties in which they find themselves. This is not supported by any sound statistical evidence; indeed such evidence as there is casts doubt on the belief. Hill followed up a sample[1] of male prisoners from south-east England, most of whom were reconvicted after release, and in many cases received non-custodial sentences. She was able to trace not only those reconvictions, but also those which followed the next custodial or non-custodial sentence. She distinguished early reconvictions (i e those incurred within one month of a non-custodial sentence or one month of release from prison) and found that they were no more frequent after custodial sentences: the same was true of reconvictions within three months[2]. The onus of proof thus seems to lie on those who believe that ex-prisoners reoffend sooner than finees or probationers. This may be so; but at present the belief seems to be based simply on the stronger impression which ex-prisoners' reconvictions make.

About a quarter of Morris et al's (1995) women prisoners had reoffended within six months of release. Unsurprisingly, the women who reoffended were more likely than those who appeared not to have reoffended to report unsatisfactory accomodation, financial diifculties and drug and alcohol problems.

1.   She used Fairhead and Banks' (1976) sample of the prison population of south-east England, as part of a doctoral research project at the Cambridge Institute of Criminology.
2.   She allowed for the differing numbers of previous convictions in the sample. What she could not completely rule out was the possibility that after a custodial sentence an offender is more likely to be committed to a higher court for trial, thus delaying the date of reconviction (only information about the dates of offences would rule this out). But her analysis of her data made it unlikely that any bias of this sort was substantial.

## Enforcement of licence

**14.36**    A supervision plan (see 14.25) will be agreed with the offender on release. This will include the conditions of the licence, including any special conditions.

Standard conditions are that

'While under supervision you must:
i.   keep in touch with your supervising officer in accordance with any reasonable instructions that you may from time to time be given;
ii.  if required, receive visits from your supervising officer at your home at reasonable hours and for reasonable periods;
iii. live where reasonably approved by your supervising officer and notify him or her in advance of any proposed change of address;
iv.  undertake only such employment as your supervising officer reasonably approves and notify him or her in advance of any proposed change in employment or occupation;
v.   not travel outside the UK without obtaining the prior permission of your supervising officer;
vi.  be of good behaviour and not take any action which would jeopardise the objectives of your supervision, namely to protect the public, prevent you from reoffending and secure your rehabilitation.'

The aims of enforcement are not simply to secure compliance with the requirements of the licence, but also to recognise where that cannot be secured and to take appropriate action (*National Standard*, para 46). Probation officers are encouraged to give formal warnings to offenders who fail to comply with the terms, and at most two warnings within a 12-month period may be given before breach proceedings are instituted.

## Breach action and recall to prison

**14.37**   For those sentenced to over 4 years, breach proceedings are normally initiated by the Parole Board. In 1993, 773 parolees on determinate sentences, and 12 lifers had their licence revoked. Only half are revoked because they commit other offences: many parolees simply failed to keep in touch (Parole Board Annual Report, 1994). A court when sentencing an offender for a subsequent offence may also revoke a parole licence. According to Barclay et al (1995), 300 parolees were recalled to prison in 1994 for breaching their licence conditions, equivalent to 10.7 per cent of the average number on parole in 1994.

## Escapes

**14.38**   One way of leaving is by escaping. Between 1 and 2 per cent of the prison population absents itself unlawfully each year. Most of the escapes—about 3 in 4—are 'abscondings': that is, take place while the prisoner is not under lock and key or under the eye of an officer. Usually this happens at an open prison, where there are virtually no physical restraints, or when a trusted prisoner is allowed to work outside. Escapes in the strict sense are rarer, because of the security precautions in closed prisons, although when they happen they receive a great deal of publicity. A common opportunity for escape is a visit to a court, because prisoners are then in civilian clothing and not handcuffed: juries must not be prejudiced by guessing that the man in the dock or the witness box has come from prison. Strangely it seems that key performance indicators for prisons today recognise an allowable quota of escapes: for HMP Doncaster, a privately-managed prison opened in 1994, the first two KPIs were:

1. Escapes from prison—no more than 2 by the end of the first year of operation: thereafter no more than 1 in each year of operation.
2. Escapes from escort—no more than 8 in each of the first three years and no more than six in the fourth year of operation (see Prison Reform Trust, 1995).

Escapes by forging keys or breaking through bars are uncommon, but catch the public imagination (as did the high profile escape by helicopter from Gartree in 1989). The escape of two category A prisoners from Brixton Prison in the summer of 1991 shifted political priorities from the 'justice' issues highlighted in the Woolf Report (published in April 1991) towards the security concerns which were the priorities of the Government's White Paper, *Custody, Care and Justice*, published in the autumn of 1991. The escape of six prisoners from Whitemoor in September 1994 led to an enquiry by Sir John Woodcock, and a further review of prison security was carried out by General Sir John Learmont following the escapes from Parkhurst in January 1995. Whether or not the proposed high security prison recommended by Learmont materialises will doubtless depend on funding priorities within the Home Office.

**14.39** Most escapees and absconders are quickly recaptured—usually within a day or two—because they head for their homes. Most escapes are impulsive[1], the result of anxieties about bad news or lack of news from families, or occasionally fear of attacks by fellow prisoners. Only a few escapees harm people during their escapes, although they may pilfer clothes, food and money, or break into houses for shelter. The penalty for escaping or absconding is usually added days, unless the prisoner is prosecuted and sentenced by a court. (They may also of course be prosecuted for an offence committed during their escape or absence). Absconders from open prisons are usually transferred to closed establishments.

1. A curious phenomenon is escapes or attempted escapes by prisoners who are close to their dates of release, sometimes because they want to prolong their detention.

Part III

# Non-custodial measures

# Chapter 15

# Diversion and nominal measures

**15.1** The chapters in this part are concerned with measures which do not entail custody, although it must be appreciated that some of the offenders to whom they are applied have been in police custody or on remand in prisons before it is decided to dispose of them non-custodially. Separate chapters are devoted to supervisory and financial measures; but first it is necessary to review ways of disposing of the offender which either avoid prosecution altogether — 'diversion' — or involve prosecution but not the imposition of any penalty, activity or restraint — sometimes called 'nominal disposals'.

## Non-prosecution

**15.2** The simplest form of diversion is a decision not to prosecute: every potential prosecutor takes such decisions now and then, with or without additional steps such as official or unofficial warnings to the suspect. At an early stage a police officer may decide not to proceed against a suspect. Once someone has been charged, it is the Crown Prosecution Service (CPS) who have the sole power to decide whether the prosecution should proceed (Prosecution of Offences Act 1985; *R v Chief Constable of Kent, ex p L; R v DPP, ex p B* [1993] 1 All ER 756 (see 15.35)). Prosecutions for offences such as bribery and corruption of officials, and the use or possession of explosives, may require the Attorney-General's consent and others — for example for incest — need the consent of the Director of Public Prosecutions (DPP). Some crimes, such as treason and murder, are always prosecuted by the DPP, who heads the CPS.

**15.3** A discussion of diversion should start with the Code for Crown Prosecutors, which was designed to encourage greater consistency in prosecution policy throughout the criminal justice system. The Code makes it clear that there are two stages in the decision to prosecute:
   a. The evidential test: Crown prosecutors must be satisfied that there is enough evidence to provide a 'realistic prospect of conviction' against each defendant on each charge. It is an objective test: whether a jury or

bench of magistrates, properly directed in accordance with the law, would be more likely than not to convict. If the case does not pass the evidential test, it must not go ahead no matter how important or serious it may be.
b.   The public interest test: The Code lists:

'*Some common public interest factors in favour of prosecution*

6.4. The more serious the offence, the more likely it is that a prosecution will be needed in the public interest. A prosecution is likely to be needed if:
- (a)   a conviction is likely to result in a significant sentence;
- (b)   a weapon was used or violence was threatened during the commission of the offence;
- (c)   the offence was committed against a person serving the public (for example, a police or prison officer or a nurse);
- (d)   the defendant was in a position of authority or trust;
- (e)   the evidence shows that the defendant was a ringleader or an organiser of the offence;
- (f)   there is evidence that the offence was premeditated;
- (g)   there is evidence that the offence was carried out by a group;
- (h)   the victim of the offence was vulnerable, has been put in considerable fear, or suffered personal attack, damage or disturbance;
- (i)   the offence was motivated by any form of discrimination against the victim's ethnic or national origin, sex, religious beliefs, political views or sexual preference;
- (j)   there is a marked difference between the actual or mental ages of the defendant and the victim, or if there is any element of corruption;
- (k)   the defendant's previous convictions or cautions are relevant to the present offence;
- (l)   the defendant is alleged to have committed the offence while under an order of the court;
- (m)   there are grounds for believing that the offence is likely to be continued or repeated, for example, by a history of recurring conduct; or
- (n)   the offence although not serious in itself, is widespread in the area where it was committed.

*Some common public interest factors against prosecution*

6.5 A prosecution is less likely to be needed if:
- (a)   the court is likely to impose a very small or nominal penalty;
- (b)   the offence was committed as a result of a genuine mistake or misunderstanding (these factors must be balanced against the seriousness of the offence);
- (c)   the loss or harm can be described as minor and was the result of a single incident particularly if it was caused by a misjudgement;
- (d)   there has been a long delay between the offence taking place and the date of the trial, unless;
  - —   the offence is serious;
  - —   the delay has been caused in part by the defendant;

— the offence has only recently come to light; or
— the complexity of the offence has meant that there has been a long investigation;

(e) a prosecution is likely to have a very bad effect on the victim's physical or mental health, always bearing in mind the seriousness of the offence;

(f) the defendant is elderly or is, or was at the time of the offence, suffering from significant mental or physical ill health, unless the offence is serious or there is a real possibility that it may be repeated. The CPS, where necessary, applies HO guidelines about how to deal with mentally disordered offenders. Crown Prosecutors must balance the desirability of diverting a defendant who is suffering from significant mental or physical ill health with the need to safeguard the general public[1];

(g) the defendant has put right the loss or harm that was caused (but defendants must not avoid prosecution simply because they can pay compensation); or

(h) details may be made public that could harm sources of information, international relations or national security.

6.6. Deciding on the public interest is not simply a matter of adding up the number of factors on each side. Crown Prosecutors must decide how important each factor is in the circumstances of each case and go on to make an overall assessment.'

1.  See the discussion of this in 21.4

**15.4**  Although the Code states that 'by applying the same principles, everyone involved in the criminal justice system is helping the system to treat victims fairly, and to prosecute defendants fairly but effectively', it is clear that different police forces may well still apply different criteria in deciding which cases should reach the CPS in the first place. The Code stresses that review is a continuing process, so that Crown prosecutors should take into account changes in circumstances. Ashworth (1994) provides a useful comparison of jury acquittal rates, discontinuance rates, and judge-directed acquittals in an attempt to assess whether the CPS is too inclined to pursue weak cases, or drops too many. He makes clear that such comparisons are fraught with difficulties.

## Police cautions

**15.5**  Police—and other potential prosecutors or complainants—often deal with trivial offences by means of warnings or admonitions delivered on the spot. These may or may not be recorded by the officer concerned, but in either case do not find their way into the criminal statistics. What must be distinguished from them are official police cautions (which in turn are not to be confused with the 'cautions' given to suspects under the PACE 84, e g to inform them that what they say may be taken down and used in evidence). Three types of caution have to be distinguished:

a.  In the case of a traffic offence, a letter is sent to the offender. A record is kept of such 'written warnings', but even if the offender is later prosecuted for and convicted of another offence, no matter how similar, the court is not usually told of the offence for which he was warned. The decision to warn is almost always taken before and instead of a charge or the issue of a summons. More about such written warnings will be found in 23.7.

b.  A caution for 'loitering or soliciting in a street or public place for the purpose of prostitution' is the only kind of caution for an adult which is mentioned in a statute (s 2 of the Street Offences Act 1959). It is usually administered on the spot, without requesting the woman to go to a police station. Police have been instructed to caution women twice before prosecuting for this offence; so that policemen who see a woman acting in a way that seems to amount to the offence usually ask for her name and address so that they can check by radio whether she is recorded locally as having been cautioned for or convicted of an offence involving prostitution. If as a result she is cautioned and not arrested, this is reported on paper and recorded in local indexes, although her name may be removed from the records if she incurs no further police attention for prostitution during the next year or so. It is not too difficult, however, for a prostitute to avoid arrest for quite a long period by moving from district to district and giving false names. A cautioned woman can 'appeal' by applying to a magistrates' court for the expunging of the relevant entry in any police record. She must do so within 14 days; her application must be heard in camera unless she wishes otherwise, and the court must grant her application unless satisfied that she was in fact soliciting or loitering for the purpose of prostitution. The police, however, are not obliged to tell her of this procedure, and it is very seldom that a woman takes advantage of it. The caution may be referred to in court if she is subsequently prosecuted for soliciting and denies being a prostitute.

c.  An offender who is cautioned for any other type of offence is usually asked to go to a police station for the purpose, where he is told by a senior officer that he will not be prosecuted on this occasion, but is warned about his future conduct. The decision to caution is taken by an officer of inspector's or superintendent's rank, before the issue of a summons or the laying of information in a magistrates' court. HO Circular No 18/94 confirms that cautions should be confined to cases in which

    i.  the offender admits his guilt (though the pressure to admit may be great, to avoid a painful prosecution);
    ii.  there is enough evidence to justify a prosecution (though McConville (1991) suggests that the evidence is often weak and would not stand up in court); and
    iii.  the offender consents to being cautioned (but offenders so rarely refuse consent, in view of the alternative, that they may well be assumed to be giving it).

d.  'Caution-plus'. In some areas the police have made informal arrangements with the Probation Service whereby in addition to being cautioned the offender co-operates with local social work agencies or the Probation Service, or agrees to consult a doctor or clinic. While attractive at one level as a way of dealing with offenders suffering from mental disorder or social handicap, such schemes raise worrying questions about 'closed justice'. The decision-making process is normally invisible (to the offender) and unchallengeable, with juvenile liaison panels (composed of the police, probation, education and social services) advising on the cautioning of young adults and juvenile offenders.

## Home Office guidelines

**15.6** In 1985 the Home Office issued to police forces the first circular and 'guidelines' on the cautioning of juveniles and adults for offences other than traffic offences (HO Circ No 14/1985). These were based on a report of a working group of Home Office officials and chiefs of police. The main objects of the guidelines were to promote more effective and consistent cautioning practices throughout the country. The RCCP (1981) had drawn attention to wide variations between forces in the percentages of indictable offenders who were cautioned instead of being prosecuted: variations which did not seem to be wholly explicable by differences in types of offence or offender in different police areas. As a result of Evans and Wilkinson's research (1990), a new version of the circular was issued (HO Circ No 59/1990) urging greater use of diversion among adults as well as juveniles, and still encouraging greater consistency. As Table 15A shows, there was a sharp increase in the number of offenders cautioned between 1988 and 1993. More recently, this trend has changed: perhaps as a result of public and police concern at the practice of repeat cautions, the most recent version of the circular no longer stresses the benefits of cautioning to the same extent. The purposes of this circular are said to be:

- to discourage the use of cautions in inappropriate cases, for example for offences which are triable on indictment only;
- to seek greater consistency between police force areas;
- to promote the better recording of cautions.

**15.7** The 1994 circular (No 18/1994) revises the *National Standards* for cautioning (first issued in 1990), and although a purpose continues to be to achieve greater consistency, the circular stresses the need for flexibility:

'It is impossible to lay down hard and fast rules such as that first time offenders must be cautioned, or that certain minor offences should attract only a caution regardless of the offender's record. Nor does the presumption in favour of diverting juveniles from the courts mean that they should automatically be cautioned, as opposed to prosecuted, simply because they are juveniles'.

Evans (1994) fears that this 'tougher' approach to cautioning may well result in an increase of up to three times as many young offenders appearing in the youth court. Table 15A shows the latest figures for cautions, which reveals that adults are still much less likely to be cautioned than are juveniles.

**TABLE 15A: Persons found guilty of, or cautioned for, indictable offences[1] in 1993, (with equivalent 1982 percentages in brackets)**

| Sex and age | Number of cases (in thousands)[2] | | Cautioned as percentage of all found guilty or cautioned |
|---|---|---|---|
| | Found guilty or cautioned | Cautioned | |
| Males | | | |
| 10 | 1.8 | 1.7 | 94% (88%) |
| 11 | 3.5 | 3.3 | 94% (88%) |
| 12 | 6.5 | 6.0 | 92% (70%) |
| 13 | 10.4 | 8.9 | 86% (61%) |
| 14 | 14.7 | 11.5 | 78% (51%) |
| 15 | 18.1 | 12.9 | 71% (38%) |
| 16 | 19.8 | 12.0 | 61% (25%) |
| 17 | 25.3 | 12.2 | 48% (5%) |
| 18 | 27.7 | 10.0 | 36 % (3%) |
| 19 | 25.7 | 7.7 | 30% (2%) |
| 20 | 24.2 | 6.7 | 28% (2%) |
| 21 and under 25 | 76.3 | 18.3 | 24% (2%) |
| 25 and under 30 | 68.5 | 13.7 | 20% (1%) |
| 30 and under 40 | 58.6 | 13.8 | 24% (2%) |
| 40 and under 50 | 25.3 | 7.5 | 30% (3%) |
| 50 and under 60 | 10.1 | 4.0 | 40% (5%) |
| 60 and over | 5.2 | 3.4 | 65% (37%) |
| Females | | | |
| 10 | 0.3 | 0.3 | 100% (100%) |
| 11 | 0.9 | 0.9 | 100% (96%) |
| 12 | 2.2 | 2.2 | 100% (88%) |
| 13 | 4.3 | 4.2 | 98% (85%) |
| 14 | 5.7 | 5.3 | 93% (77%) |
| 15 | 5.6 | 4.9 | 88% (66%) |
| 16 | 5.1 | 4.2 | 82% (51%) |
| 17 | 5.2 | 3.8 | 73% (11%) |
| 18 | 4.7 | 2.7 | 57% (7%) |
| 19 | 4.3 | 2.2 | 51% (5%) |
| 20 | 4.0 | 1.9 | 48% (3%) |
| 21 and under 25 | 13.5 | 5.8 | 43% (4%) |
| 25 and under 30 | 13.5 | 5.3 | 39% (4%) |
| 30 and under 40 | 13.8 | 5.9 | 43% (6%) |
| 40 and under 50 | 6.1 | 3.3 | 54% (7%) |
| 50 and under 60 | 2.8 | 1.9 | 68% (15%) |
| 60 and over | 1.7 | 1.5 | 88% (62%) |

1. The sources for Columns 1 and 2 are CSEW 1993 Table 5.25. Unfortunately for strict accuracy, the figures in those columns include a small percentage of triable-either-way motoring offences, for which oral cautions are not administered, and the published information does not make it possible to deduct them from the figures in Column 1. If they were deducted the cautioning rates for the age groups most likely to commit such offences would be fractionally higher.
2. To the nearest 100.

## Other police and security forces

**15.8**  There is very little published information about the diversionary practices of special police forces or non-statutory security forces. Some of them simply hand over to the regular police all cases in which a prosecution seems possible. All of them hand over the prosecution of grave crimes, such as robberies involving violence. Those which undertake their own prosecutions exercise discretion or substitute warnings in certain types of case: but little is said publicly about the criteria by which such cases are identified. At one extreme, for example, the Royal Botanical Gardens Constabulary (Kew) deals with no indictable crimes and confines itself to oral warnings for all but a few summary offences.

## Diversion by other prosecutors

**15.9**  Other potential prosecutors often decide against prosecution even when it might well be successful. Potential private prosecutors often let offenders off with an informal warning: the commonest example is a shop where a juvenile or very elderly shoplifter has been detected. The CPS not only gives advice (both general and on individual cases) to police forces which may lead to a caution or non-prosecution: they also have the power to take over and then abandon prosecutions initiated by private persons.

**15.10**  The law enforcement practices of the major government departments were reviewed by the Royal Commission on Criminal Procedure (RCCP) in the late1970s. In a research study carried out for the RCCP, Lidstone, Hogg and Mawby (1980) reviewed the prosecuting policies of nine agencies in some detail. They pointed out the wide variations in prosecution policy, highlighting various factors which influenced the number of prosecutions an agency undertook: the population at risk of offending; the availability of alternative measures short of prosecuting; the resources available to investigate offences; the difficulty of proof; political pressure; the perception of the primary task of the agency; the perception of the offence; police reluctance to be involved.

**15.11**  Since then there has been significant academic work developing these comparisons. For example, Sanders (1985) compared the prosecution policies of the police and HM Factory Inspectorate, suggesting that while the former have a 'legally proper propensity to prosecute', the latter have an 'equally legally proper propensity not to prosecute'. Hutter (1988) developed this view of class bias in prosecution policy in her study of environmental health officers. Where the offender is seen as basically good, the enforcement agency adopts an accommodative approach, seeking compliance through negotiation. Cook (1989) analysed the different approaches taken to tax and social security frauds, suggesting that the differences can be explained in terms of the different histories of taxation and welfare: the ideological construction of taxpayers as 'givers' results in few prosecutions, whereas benefit claimants, perceived as 'takers' from the state, are more likely to be prosecuted.

## Serious Fraud Office

**15.12** Another body which does not currently come under the CPS umbrella is the Serious Fraud Office. Established by the CJA 1987, it investigates and prosecutes the most serious frauds in England, Wales and Northern Ireland. As Levi (1993) points out, measuring the prosecution policy of the SFO is not easy. Fraud trials are lengthy, expensive and often unsuccessful. Levi suggests that non-prosecutions may be due to political or other extra-legal factors, and fears that white collar crime prosecution decisions may be driven almost entirely by cost considerations.

## Local authorities

**15.13** It is difficult to obtain reliable figures about the prosecution policies of local authorities under the very miscellaneous statutes which they are expected to enforce. Lidstone et al (1980) found that trading standards departments in metropolitan counties cautioned almost as often as they prosecuted, while in non-metropolitan counties they cautioned far more often. Education departments, which have to deal with cases of non-attendance at school, have well-developed procedures for warning parents and enlisting the help of social workers before resorting to prosecution. In general, local authorities use many warning notices and other procedures but seldom resort to the criminal courts. One reason may be sheer shortage of the staff needed for prosecutions; another is almost certainly the complexity of the evidence needed for a successful prosecution.

## Administrative fines

**15.14** Some government departments and agencies not only 'warn' or 'caution' offenders but offer what are called 'mitigated penalties', which are in effect administrative fines. Most of the Inland Revenue's law enforcement work is concerned with tax evasion; but remarkably few cases result in prosecution. The Taxes Management Act 1970 (ss 93-107) officially recognised the Inland Revenue's long-standing practice of aiming at 'voluntary settlements' with offenders, and this practice has become increasingly widely used (e g under the Finance Acts 1986 and 1994). Such settlements have the status of a legal contract, and include payment of the actual tax liability, payment of any interest due on that sum, and usually also a financial penalty, which is likely to be a 'mitigated penalty' — i e less than the fine which a court would impose. Prosecutions are the exception, and are reserved for very serious cases (though see *Mead and Cook* [1992] STC 482 where the Divisional Court dismissed an application for judicial review of the IRC's policy of selective prosecution. The Court accepted that the IRC's primary objective is the collection of revenue and not the punishment of offenders). Customs and Excise proceed similarly in cases involving evasion of exchange control and excise duties; but are more likely to prosecute, especially in the enforcement of Value Added Tax or the laws against the smuggling of animals or drugs. Under s 152 of the Customs and Excise Management Act 1979 customs officers at ports levy 'on the spot' fines for minor attempts at smuggling.

## Fixed penalties

**15.15**   Minor traffic offences are normally dealt with by 'fixed penalties'. A detected offender is given a written notice that he has incurred the fixed penalty, and that it must be paid to a specified address within a certain time. The issue of the notice is a matter of routine, involving only occasional exercise of discretion (as for example when a traffic warden is persuaded to ignore illegal parking in an emergency). The system is dealt with more fully in chapter 23, which deals with traffic offenders. The London Regional Transport Act 1984 granted London Transport the power to impose 'on the spot' fines, and it may well be that fixed penalties will become increasingly used to combat minor offences.

## Courts' powers and practices

**15.16**   Courts have powers and practices which are sometimes called 'diversion', although this tends to confuse matters. Occasionally a judge—less often a magistrate—will query the justification for a prosecution (usually at the sentencing stage when more information about the case is available): but this has more effect on policy than on the case itself. More interesting are the formal powers of courts to defer sentence, bind over and discharge.

## Deferred sentence (s 1 PCCA 73, as amended)

**15.17**   A court 'may defer passing sentence on an offender for the purpose of enabling the court to have regard, in determining his sentence, to his conduct after conviction (including, where appropriate, the making by him of reparation for his offence) or to any change in his circumstances'. Deferment must be until a specified date not more than 6 months from the date of deferment; and cannot be extended[1]. The offender's consent is needed, as for probation, and the court must be satisfied, 'having regard to the nature of the offence and the character and circumstances of the offender that it would be in the interests of justice to exercise the power'. If he is convicted of and sentenced for another offence during the period of deferment the sentencing court can also sentence him for the original offence. Otherwise, when he reappears for the deferred sentence, the court's powers of sentence are exactly those which they originally were, except that if it is a magistrates' court it can no longer commit him to the Crown Court for sentence. A conviction which is followed by deferment of sentence cannot safely be treated as such (e g for the purpose of activating a suspended sentence: see *Salmon* (1973) 57 Cr App Rep 953) until it is known what measure the court eventually chose, since the court may yet choose to deal with the offence by way of discharge.

1.  Awkwardness arises if at the end of the period of deferment the court is awaiting information about the offender's behaviour during the period (as in the case of *Ingle* (1974) 59 Cr App Rep 306) who had still to be tried for the alleged commission of offences during the period). A short postponement of sentence is not improper in such cases.

**15.18**   In a guideline case (*George* (1984) 6 Cr App Rep (S) 211) the CA made several important points:

a.   'The purpose of deferment is .... to enable the Court to take into account the defendant's conduct after conviction or any change in circumstances and then only if it is in the interests of justice to exercise the power. It will ... seldom be in the interests of justice to stipulate that the conduct required is reparation by the defendant.'

b.   'The power is not to be used as an easy way out for a court which cannot make up its mind about the correct sentence'. If the principal object is to enable a PSR to be prepared, the proper way to achieve this is by adjournment, not deferment.

c.   'It is essential that the deferring court should make a careful note of the purposes for which the sentence is being deferred and what steps, if any, it expects the defendant to take during the period of deferment. Ideally the defendant himself should be given notice in writing of what he is expected to do or refrain from doing, so that there can be no doubt in his mind .what is expected of him'.

d.   In many cases a short probation order may be preferable. It enables the defendant's behaviour to be monitored by a probation officer, and ensures that formal notice of the requirements of the court are given to him.

e.   'A deferment of sentence will be more appropriate where the conduct required of the defendant is not specific enough to be made the subject of a condition imposed as part of a probation order without creating uncertainty in the mind of the probation officer and the defendant as to whether there has been a breach of the order, for example where the defendant is to make a real effort to find work, or where the sentencer wishes to see whether a change in the defendant's attitude and circumstances, which appears to be a possibility at the time of the deferment, does in fact come about'. Deferment may also be the proper course where the steps to be taken by the defendant could not of their nature be the subject of a probation requirement: 'for example where he is to make reparation, or at least demonstrate a real intention and capacity to do so'.

f.   In general, deferment 'should not be adopted without careful consideration of whether the sentencer's intention could not best be achieved by other means, and ... if deferment is decided upon care must be taken to avoid the risk of misunderstanding and a sense of injustice when the defendant returns before the court'.

g.   When a court has to deal with the defendant at the end of the period of deferment it must ascertain the purpose of it and any requirement imposed by the deferring court.

h.   Then it must determine whether the defendant has 'substantially conformed or attempted to conform with the proper expectations of the deferring court... If he has, then the defendant may legitimately expect that an immediate custodial sentence will not be imposed. If he has not, the court should be careful to state with precision in what respects he has failed'.

**15.19** When deferring sentence the court should not make any other order except, when appropriate, a restitution or compensation order (see 16.41ff). It is also inadvisable to sentence the offender on one count but defer sentence on another. If possible the offender should after deferment be brought before the same judge or magistrate, and be represented by the same lawyer. Otherwise, there may be nobody present—with the possible exception of the offender— who recalls what was expected of him during the interval. Corden and Nott (1980), however, found that, at least in West Yorkshire courts in 1977, nearly half the deferments resulted in eventual sentence by benches which did not have a single member in common with the deferring bench; and this was especially so in the case of Crown Court deferments. In the Crown Court at Bristol three-quarters of the cases came back before a different judge (Jones, 1983).

**15.20** Deferment is not very frequent: the CC resorts to it in about 2 per cent of cases, and MCs in less than 1 per cent of cases involving indictable adults or young adults (but more often in juvenile cases). It is rarely used for summary non-motoring offences, and even more rarely for motoring offences. Most often it is used for offences of dishonest appropriation of property, usually by offenders who have been convicted on a previous occasion, and are already on probation or under a suspended sentence; but it seems to be used occasionally for a first conviction of people who have defrauded their employers (Jones, 1983). In most such cases the court is deferring sentence in the hope that the offender's conduct during the period of deferment will persuade it not to impose a custodial sentence. The period of deferment is usually 6 months, but quite often 3 months.

**15.21** Since a custodial sentence is almost always a possibility in the mind of the deferring sentencer, the court before which the offender appears after deferment is usually provided with a PSR, which deals in particular with what has happened to the offender in the interval. If the report satisfies the court the eventual disposal by a MC is usually a conditional discharge, a probation order or a fine: in the CC it is usually probation or a fully suspended sentence of imprisonment. Normally it is only if the offender's behaviour in the interval has been unsatisfactory that the court resorts to an actual custodial sentence. In 1982 only about 9 per cent of MCs' deferments ended in this way, and about 24 per cent of the CC's deferments. Recent figures have not been published.

**15.22** Deferment has been used in one or two areas in order to encourage offenders to use facilities intended to help them to be law-abiding. The most striking of these schemes was the Newham Alternatives Project. By arrangement with the courts and probation offices in this part of London, some of the offenders who seemed likely to get prison sentences were referred instead to the NAP workers. If the offender turned up and seemed willing to participate an NAP worker would appear in court to ask for 'deferment to NAP'. If this was granted the offender was expected but not compelled to attend frequently at the NAP building, where he could get advice, take part in discussion groups and engage in other activities. At the end of this deferment NAP presented a report to the court, and if this was favourable the sentence was usually a conditional discharge. Dronfield, who described the project and its history (1980) emphasised the voluntary nature of participation, although participants must have been aware of the very real possibility of imprisonment if NAP's report was not favourable. It is clear that at the very least the Project, during 3¹/₂ years, saved about ²/₃ of 30 offenders from imprisonment for the offences for which sentence was deferred, even in some cases in which the offender was reconvicted during deferment. What this demonstrated was the persuasive effect which the project had on sentencers, in cases in which the Probation Service was either less optimistic or less persuasive. Efficacy in terms of subsequent convictions was not discussed by Dronfield.

## Discharge (s 1A PCCA 73)

**15.23** When a court 'is of opinion, having regard to the circumstances including the nature of the offence and the character of the offender, that it is inexpedient to inflict punishment and that a probation order is not appropriate [it] may make an order either (a) discharging him absolutely, or, (b) if the court thinks fit, discharging him subject to the condition that he commits no offence during such period, not exceeding three years from the date of the order, as may be specified'. If the discharge is conditional, it must explain to him in ordinary language that if he commits another offence during the specified period he will be liable to be sentenced for the original offence (s 1A(3)). If he is so sentenced, the order ceases to have effect. The court is not, however, obliged to sentence him for the original offence, and if it does not do so the conditional discharge continues to have effect.

**15.24** The defendant can appeal against the conviction, but not against a discharge, unless his case is that it was not valid (*Marquis* [1974] 1 WLR 1087). The conviction is deemed not to be a conviction for any purpose other than those of the proceedings in which the discharge order is made (or any later proceedings for offences committed during the period of a conditional discharge) (s 13 PCCA 73 and see 19.8). The rehabilitation period following absolute discharge is 6 months from the date of conviction: for a conditional discharge it is one year or the period specified for the observance of the condition (s 5 ROA 74). If, however, a conditionally discharged offender is eventually sentenced for the original offence, the conviction counts as such (eg if his criminal record is before the court in the later case); and the rehabilitation period is that appropriate to his sentence.

**15.25** A discharge can be combined only with a disqualification from driving (s 102 RTOA 88), a restitution or compensation order (ss 13,35 PCCA 73) or an order to contribute to the costs of prosecution (s 12(4) PCCA 73). If, however, the offender is at the same time dealt with for another offence or offences, he may be sentenced for these.

15.26    Absolute discharges seem to be used when the offence seems very trivial, when the circumstances seem to make it difficult to blame the offender, or where there is a great deal to be said by way of mitigation. Conditional discharges may be used in circumstances which are similar but in which the court feels that an absolute discharge would be too lenient, or that the offender needs some sort of indication that he will not in future be treated as a first offender. Their other typical use is as a tariff sentence in cases of minimal gravity, when imprisonment would be unjustified, probation inappropriate, and a fine out of the question because of the offender's situation. Conditional discharges are far commoner in the CC than absolute discharges, which are rather rare. The same is true of MCs, although absolute discharges are far from uncommon there. The proportionate use of the discharge for indictable offences has risen from 14 per cent in 1986-88 to 22 per cent in 1993.

## Binding over to keep the peace (s 1(7) Justices of the Peace Act 1968)

15.27    Any 'court of record having criminal jurisdiction' (which includes both MCs and the CC) has the power to bind over to keep the peace, and the power to bind over to be of good behaviour, provided that the person or his case 'is before the court' (that is, is a defendant, witness or complainant: see *Pawittar Singh* [1984] 1 All ER 941). It is not necessary that the person should have been convicted of an offence (he or she could even have been acquitted); but he or she must be told what the court has in mind, and given the opportunity to make representations (*Sheldon* [1964] 2 QB 573). A time-limit of a year is usually specified, but does not seem to be obligatory. He is required to enter into his own recognisances or to find someone else to act as a surety, or both; and this involves a specified sum of money, which is not paid at the time but is forfeited if he is later found not to have kept the peace or been of good behaviour, as the case may be. If he refuses to enter into recognisances or find sureties he can be committed to prison; but this power does not extend to imprisoning him for breach of a recognisance into which he has entered, although he could be imprisoned in default of payment. The facts which constitute a breach of the bind-over must be proved in court (*McGarry* (1945) 30 Cr App Rep 187).

## Binding over parent of offender aged under 16

15.28    Section 58 CJA 91 obliges a court to bind over the parent or guardian of a child under the age of 16, whenever the court is satisfied that to do so would be desirable in the interests of preventing the commission by the young offender of further offences. The court is empowered to order the parent or guardian to enter into a recognisance in a sum not exceeding £1,000 to take proper care of the offender and exercise proper control over him. The maximum period of the recognisance is until the offender reaches 18, or for a period of 3 years, whichever is shorter. The parent may refuse to enter into the recognisance, but if the court considers the refusal to be unreasonable the parent risks a fine not exceeding level 3 on the standard scale (see 16.3). While the Government sees this power as a useful way to encourage parents to stop their children offending, many critics see it rather as an attempt to lock the stable door after the horse has bolted: by the time children are offending sufficiently seriously to be brought before the court, they have normally proved themselves to be beyond the control of their parents. Nonetheless, the power was extended by para 50 of Sch 9 to the CJPOA 94: the courts may now add a condition to the parental bind-over requiring the parents to ensure that their children comply with any community penalty imposed on them. The condition may be used for example when a court thinks it appropriate that a parent should take steps to ensure that a child attends an attendance centre or keeps an appointment with a supervisor.

## Binding over to come up for judgement

**15.29**   The CC also has a common law power to bind over a convicted offender, with his consent[1], to come up for judgement when called upon. No time-limit need be specified (although a year is normal) and he is brought back to court again only if he misbehaves. Unlike a conditionally discharged offender he can be sentenced for the original offence even if he has not been convicted of a subsequent one. The power is thus, in effect, a common law power to defer sentence, but for some reason was not abolished when that option was introduced by statute. The use of the common law bind-over has declined, no doubt because of the introduction of conditional discharges and suspension and deferment of sentence. Certainly its only point nowadays seems to be that it allows the CC to do what those other powers do not: e g to place the offender under what is in effect an unspecified suspended sentence for an indefinite period.

1.   The offender must consent to be bound over to come up for judgement, but even if he does so under the threat of imprisonment his consent is not invalid (*Veater* (1981) 72 Cr App Rep 331).

**15.30**   The Law Commission has carried out a protracted study of binding-over provisions. Their final report, published in 1994 (Law Com No 222) and still awaiting Government decision, recommended that binding over should be abolished without replacement. They reached two main conclusions: first, that a number of recent Acts of Parliament (e g s 5 Public Order Act 86) have criminalised the sort of anti-social conduct which was previously only susceptible to a binding-over order. Secondly, that 'those aspects of the binding-over procedure which make the institution most attractive to its supporters are open to very substantial objection under the principles of natural justice'. Despite this, the procedure is still used: in *Percy v DPP* [1995] Crim LR 714 a peace campaigner who entered an air base was arrested under bye-laws and removed. She was not charged under the bye-laws, the validity of which were being challenged at the time. Magistrates committed her to custody for 14 days when she refused to agree to be bound over to keep the peace. Although the Divisional Court allowed her appeal since there was no evidence before the magistrates that violence was the natural consequence of any of her actions, the case does highlight what J C Smith calls 'the slightly confusing thing about the terminology of the law': 'the person responsible for a breach of the peace, and who may be arrested and bound over to keep the peace, is not necessarily, or usually, the actual breaker or apprehended breaker of the peace, but the person who has provoked, or may provoke, the violent response of others by his improper, though not necessarily unlawful, conduct' (at [1995] Crim LR 715).

**15.31** The only information about the efficacy of discharges and bind-overs comes from the Phillpotts-Lancucki follow-up described in chapter 7. As Table 7B showed, the 6-year reconviction rates of adult male 'first offenders' were very slightly below 'expectation' (97 per cent). For adult males with one, two, three or four previous convictions they were considerably above expectation (136 per cent); but not surprisingly the numbers of such recidivists discharged by courts was not large (44)[1]. The most that can be said is that when discharging Phillpotts and Lancucki's 'first offenders' in the early 1970s courts were not incurring worse reconviction rates than when fining other 'first offenders', and were incurring fewer than when they used the suspended sentence or probation.

1. For recidivists with 5 or more previous convictions, reconvictions were 98 per cent of expectation; but (i) the number at risk was very small (13) and (ii) in any case it was clear that no choice of disposal made much difference to the high general reconviction rate (88 per cent).

## Suspended sentences

**15.32** In the context of diversionary measures the suspended sentence deserves a mention, since it involves no penalising of the offender unless he is reconvicted. The law and practice governing this form of sentence have been described in 10.28 ff. What bears repeating is the fact that, however discouraging the reconviction rates after suspended sentences, and however substantial the numbers of suspended sentences which are activated, they do avoid imprisoning or otherwise penalising a sizeable fraction of the offenders for the offences for which they are imposed. This is almost as much as could be said for some other forms of diversion.

## General considerations

**15.33** It is time, however, to consider what English diversionary procedures have in common, what differences there are between them, and what is to be said for and against them. What they all have in common is that they are intended to avoid the penalising of an offender by a court, and are discretionary. The important distinction is between those which avoid a court appearance and those which involve prosecution; and the distinction is important because appearance in court is believed to stigmatise, and stigma is believed to be undesirable, however much of an oversimplification that may be (see 19.18 ff). Another distinction is between revocable and irrevocable forms of diversion: that is between measures which can be replaced by penalties for the original offence if the offender does not behave in the required way, and those which cannot. The difference between conditional and unconditional discharge is one example. Police cautions are irrevocable, in practice if not in law; and so, apparently, are warnings and cautions by other potential prosecutors, although an individual private prosecutor is presumably free to change his mind. Finally, unlike most forms of diversion in the USA, English varieties do not normally require the offender to engage in any therapeutic activity or 'programme' (though see 15.5.d).

**15.34** The underlying justification for diversion must be reductive. It certainly cannot have an expressive effect, except possibly upon the offender himself. In some cases the reasoning which favours it is retributive: for example when the offence is trivial, or the offender's culpability minimal. Usually, however, the decision is based on the hope that a mere warning—or the shock of detection—will be a sufficient individual deterrent. In the case of revenue offences the reasoning may simply be that the sums due—or something more—can be recovered without the cost of prosecution.

**15.35** What retributive reasoning does is to raise doubts about the distributive justice of the various practices. In the first place, why should an indictable adult in one geographical area have a much better chance of a caution than some one in another area? The courts have shown a clear reluctance to interfere with the discretion of either police or CPS. Thus, in *L; B* [1993] 1 All ER 756 (see 15.2) one applicant was a 16-year-old boy, who had been charged with assault occasioning actual bodily harm. Although the criteria for cautioning were made out in his case, the CPS had upheld the decision of the police to prosecute him. The other applicant was a 12-year-old girl charged with a minor shoplifting offence. She was not cautioned as she did not admit the offence. Watkins L J, in the Divisional Court, refused to interfere: 'I find it very difficult to envisage ... a circumstance, fraud or dishonesty apart, which would allow of a challenge to a decision to prosecute or to continue proceedings ...'. However, in *C* [1995] 1 Cr App Rep 136 the Divisional Court was prepared to strike down a decision not to prosecute because the CPS had failed to act in accordance with the 'settled policy' as set out in the Code for Crown Prosecutors. A greater willingness to intervene is also seen in *P* (1995) Times, 24 May, where the decision to caution a 12-year-old who had not made a clear and reliable admission was set aside. Yet even in these cases the courts have been at pains to stress that a successful challenge of the legality of a decision to caution will be very rare.

**15.36** There remain striking disparities between the practices of police and other prosecuting authorities. A man who is late in buying a TV licence or a car-licence, or in paying his income tax, has a much greater chance of being let off prosecution than an elderly shoplifter, even when there is clear evidence of dishonest intention. It is worth noting, too, that he may be detected in such dishonesties in quick succession by the different bodies and by the police without the news reaching any of the other prosecuting authorities; so that for all they know they are dealing with an 'out-of-character' lapse. Add to this the haphazard overlaps between conditional discharges, the two kinds of bind-over and deferment of sentence, and it becomes abundantly clear that there is a great need for rules or practices which are embodied in legislation. Nor should the constitutional implications be ignored: diversion plays an important part in the criminal justice process and yet has never been subject to Parliamentary scrutiny.

**15.37** Diversion has probably been of most value when (i) it was a substitute for a custodial sentence and (ii) it did not merely exempt the offender from prosecution or simply place him under supervision, but involved him in a programme of positive rehabilitation. This leaves the remaining question, whether diversion should be revocable if the offender does not play his part satisfactorily; and if so how satisfactory participation is to be assessed. The prosecuting authority will be faced with reports which say that he frequently fails to show up; that when he does he simply 'goes through the motions' of whatever activity is expected of him; and that he discourages other participants. Yet a decision to 'undivert' him will involve a delayed prosecution. Should he then be able to plead not guilty, or should his admission of guilt be held to preclude that? Should he be able to argue that he has in fact done what the diversion programme demanded of him, and has not breached any requirements? Probation officers know the difficulties of prosecuting for breach of probation orders. These problems make irrevocable diversion sound preferable; but if it is to be used to steer the offender into co-operating with positive efforts to help him it will be a formality without any force.

**15.38** Even if these problems can be solved, however, positive diversion should not distract attention from the development of diversion pure and simple: that is, discretionary non-prosecution without requirements and without the threat of later prosecution. This may not save many offenders from imprisonment: but it is arguable that the choice between custodial and non-custodial measures should be taken by a court and not by a prosecuting authority. What it does is to save many excusable or petty offenders from stigma, and what it could do is relieve enforcement agencies and courts of a considerable volume of trivial cases.

# Chapter 16

# Financial measures

**16.1** The financial payments which can be imposed on offenders are of six kinds:
   a. fines, payable to the state, imposable by higher and lower courts for any offence for which the sentence is not fixed by law;
   b. recognisances (in effect, suspended fines), which are imposable by higher and lower courts when offenders are bound over (see 16.40);
   c. compensation, payable to the victim for personal injury, loss or damage, imposable by higher and lower courts;
   d. contributions to the cost of the prosecution, imposable by higher and lower courts;
   e. fines imposed by police or other potential prosecutors without prosecution;
   f. 'mitigated penalties', accepted by the Customs and Excise, the Inland Revenue etc. in lieu of prosecution for certain types of offence.

Payment of type (a)–(e) are collected and enforced by magistrates' courts (even when imposed by the Crown Court); but 'mitigated penalties' are not. The amounts of payments of type (a)–(d) can be, and often are, reduced by courts to take account of mitigating circumstances including the limited means of offenders; but a fixed penalty cannot be reduced, although in practice it is occasionally decided not to enforce it.

### Fines

**16.2** Fines are by far the most common of penalties, being imposed in more than 91 per cent of motoring cases, 85 per cent of non-indictable non-motoring cases, and 41 per cent of indictable cases disposed of by MCs (1993). It is only in youth courts and the CC that fines account for less than half of all disposals. The percentage of disposals of indictable cases which take the form of fines has decreased since the mid-70s, largely because of increasing unemployment. What is certain is that, numerically, fines will continue to be the most important penalty for adult offenders; and they bring in more than £100,000,000 a year.

## The standard scale for summary offences

**16.3**   For most summary offences the maximum amount of the fine for any one offence was originally specified by the statute creating the offence. However, these amounts often proved inadequate as a result of inflation, and s 37 CJA 82 therefore allotted maximum fines[1] for summary offences to one of the levels on a 'standard scale', of which the maxima could be increased (or reduced) by an order of the Home Secretary under s 142 MCA 80:

| Level | Original maximum | 1984 maximum | 1991 maximum |
|-------|------------------|--------------|--------------|
| 1 | £25 | £50 | £200 |
| 2 | £50 | £100 | £500 |
| 3 | £200 | £400 | £1,000 |
| 4 | £500 | £1,000 | £2,500 |
| 5 | £1,000 | £2,000 | £5,000 |

But if the maximum fine is specified in subordinate legislation, that maximum is unaffected by the scale or by increases in it[2]. The Act also (in ss 35, 36) abolished 'enhanced penalties'[3], in the sense of maxima which were higher for a second or subsequent summary offence: in future the higher maximum was to apply to the first offences as well. Unlike the standard scale this applies to subordinate legislation.

1.  With some exceptions, listed in ss 38, 39 CJA 82.
2.  Again with a few exceptions.
3.  Again with exceptions: ss 33-36 Sexual Offences Act 56, and s 1(2) Street Offences Act 59, all of which relate to prostitution.

## Maximum fines for indictable offences

**16.4**   Unless a statute prescribes a special maximum for an indictable offence, there is no limit to the amount of the fine which the CC can impose for it, apart from the guidelines in case-law summarised below. MCs, however, are subject to a limit of an amount not exceeding the prescribed sum for any one offence (s 32 MCA 80, as amended). This sum, £2,000 in 1980, is now £5,000, with lower limits for 'young persons' and 'children'.

## Fines in magistrates' courts

**16.5**   It is only the smallest maxima, however, which are used as the normal fines for the offences to which they apply: the higher maxima are regarded as hardly ever appropriate. Disparities in fines have long been noted: see Softley (1978); Hood (1972). Efforts have been made to reduce such disparities, particularly by the Magistrates' Association. In 1966 they produced *Suggestions for Road Traffic Penalties*, and in 1989 a *Sentencing Guide for Criminal Offences (other than Road Traffic)*, together with a table of suggested compensation levels (see Table 16A). These guides have been amended following first the introduction of unit fines, and then their abolition (see 16.6). For all types of cases, the *Sentencing Guides* suggest a precise 'entry point' for an offence of average seriousness. Justices are then encouraged to consider a number of aggravating and mitigating circumstances which might make the case before them more or less serious. Having considered the seriousness of the offence, the bench will then consider any personal mitigation and, if a fine is still the appropriate penalty, they must then consider the offender's means. The guidelines are based on a first-time offender pleading not guilty. Thus for being drunk and disorderly the guideline fine is £90; for careless driving, obstructing a police officer, and the cultivation of cannabis, £180; for abstracting electricity, theft and criminal damage, £270; for failing to stop and report an accident, £360; and for driving without insurance £540. Although the guidelines state specifically throughout that they reflect the average seriousness of an offence of each type, such generalisations may often be of little help in practice.

## Unit fines

16.6. For many years it was accepted that since the amount of the fine should be limited by the gravity of the offence, the means of the offender should be taken into account only by way of mitigation. In *Fairbairn* (1980) 2 Cr App Rep (S) 315 a fine of £7,500, more than 10 times the value of the stolen goods, which the offender appeared to the trial judge to be capable of paying, was reduced to £1,000 because it was 'out of scale in relation to the gravity of the offence'. The implication was that a millionaire must be fined no more than the standard amount of, say, £100 for careless driving, or that he must go to prison because that is an inadequate penalty in his case (as the CA seemed to be saying in *Messana* ((1981) 3 Cr App Rep (S) 88). For many years there were increasing calls for the introduction in this country of a scheme similar to the Swedish day fine scheme, which has been in place since 1931. The essence of the scheme is that the amount of a fine is expressed in terms of the offender's estimated income for one day, the number of days being determined by the court's view of the gravity of the offence and the offender's culpability. The Home Office carried out a research study in four courts between 1988 and 1990 in order to test the feasibility of introducing a similar scheme in England (see HORPU Paper 59, Moxon, Sutton and Hedderman (1990)). The results were encouraging, and the CJA 1991 introduced a unit fine system, designed to ensure that the amounts of fines are not only less than average for the poor but more than average for the rich.

The scheme came into force in October 1992, but ran into difficulties soon after implementation. The Home Secretary, under fire from widespread newspaper criticism of apparently very high fines being imposed for minor offences, announced the abolition of the scheme after it had been operational for only seven months. It is a great pity that the scheme was dumped so swiftly and unceremoniously: if the upper levels were lowered, and the system had been amended suitably, the unit fine had much to commend it. Many of the highly publicised inappropriate fines had been imposed on offenders who had refused to fill in the means form, and therefore had been subject to the maximum fine. These were reduced on appeal, but by then the media harm to the scheme had been done. For the history of the ill-fated scheme see Wasik (1993), Appendix 1.

## The current tariff

**16.7**   The law, applicable in both MCs and CCs, is now as stated in s 18 CJA 91, as amended by s 65 CJA 93:

> '(1) Before fixing the amount of any fine, a court shall inquire into the financial circumstances of the offender.
> (2)   The amount of the fine fixed by a court shall be such as, in the opinion of the court, reflects the seriousness of the offence.'

The main rule is therefore that the fine should reflect the seriousness of the offence. Fines may still be imposed for offences of intentional violence where the injury is not very serious, for threats to murder, for causing death by reckless driving, for arson and other criminal damage even of the kind that endangers life, and for most kinds of sexual offence, to name only the more serious indictable offences. However, in most such cases, a fine will be inappropriate as the seriousness of the offence will require a custodial sentence (see 10.15) or a community penalty (see 17.1 ff).

## Mitigating fines

**16.8**   The court may reduce the amount of the fine by way of mitigation. A common reason for doing so is that the offender is also being ordered to pay compensation to the victim. Where a court considers that it is appropriate to impose both a fine and a compensation order, but that the offender's means are insufficient to pay both an appropriate fine and appropriate compensation, the court is to give preference to compensation[1], though it may impose a fine as well (s 67 CJA 82). In practice. many fines are reduced by courts for this reason, even in some cases in which the court has little or no information about the offender's means: MCs seem to have regard to the total amount to be paid by the offender, although without actually applying a tariff to this.

1.   Thus reversing the principle which had hitherto applied.

## Ascertaining offenders' means

**16.9**   The commonest reason for reducing fines, however, is offenders' means. Courts are expressly enjoined by s 18 CJA 91 (as amended by the CJA 93) to 'inquire into the financial circumstances of the offender' and to 'take into account the circumstances of the case including, among other things, the financial circumstances of the offender so far as they are known, or appear, to the court'.

However, this was further amended by para 42 of Sch 9 of the CJPOA 94 so that courts are now only required to inquire into the means of an offender 'who is an individual'. This seems to be a further move away from the unit fine principle of fining offenders (whether or not individuals) according to their means.

What offenders tell the court about their means is not subject to penalties for intentional deceit. When it is realised that applications for legal aid, which require information about income and financial commitments, carry penalties for deceit, the absence of similar penalties where fines are concerned is hard to defend. However, s 20 CJA 91 allows a court to make a 'financial circumstances order' after a person has been convicted. Intentionally or recklessly giving false information under such an order may result in three months' imprisonment or a fine not exceeding level 4 or both. HO Circular 13/1984 encouraged all courts to provide defendants with a 'preconviction means enquiry form'. It seemed likely at the time that these would be adopted as standard practice, and that defendants would be required to complete the form. However, the Government has been so alarmed by the brief experiment with unit fines that such forms are not only not a statutory requirement, but even the Magistrates' Association has been wary of producing a standard form. The 1993 Senten*cing Guidelines* state merely that 'the Association is aware that there are many local means forms in existence and suggests that courts build on these'.

## Relating fines to means

**16.10** Even if the offender's financial situation is known, however, there are few rules to help courts to adjust the fine to it. Until relatively recently it was considered that a fine should be capable of being paid within a year (*Knight* (1980) 2 Cr App Rep (S) 82), but the courts now recognise that longer periods (ie heavier fines) may be appropriate. This brings the guidance on fines into line with the CA's attitude to the amounts in compensation orders: see 16.43 (g). As Lord Lane CJ explained in *Olliver and Olliver* (1989) 11 Cr App Rep (S) 10:

'There is nothing wrong in principle in the period of payment being longer, indeed much longer that one year, providing it is not an undue burden and so too severe a punishment having regard to the nature of the offence and the nature of the offender. Certainly it seems to us that a two-year period will seldom be too long, and in an appropriate case three years will be unassailable, again of course depending on the nature of the offender and the nature of the offence ... this is particularly important in the present climate, where every effort is required in the face of the growing crime figures to find alternatives to custody.'

Capital assets may be taken into account as well as income: but so must likely charges on those assets. Being unemployed does not protect one against being fined: more than a third of Softley's (1978) sample of indictable offenders fined by MCs in 1974 were unemployed, and this percentage is likely to have increased. On the other hand, the amount of the fine should not be such as to reduce the offender's income below subsistence level.

## Payment by others

**16.11**  The amount should not be fixed on the assumption that someone else—even a spouse—will help to pay it: see *Baxter* [1974] Crim LR 611; *Charalambous* (1984) 6 Cr App Rep (S) 389. On the other hand, there is nothing to debar anyone else from paying an offender's fine. There have even been cases in which offenders who have deliberately defaulted as part of some act of protest, and therefore been imprisoned, have been released as a result of the anonymous payment of their fines by others. Companies whose employees are likely to incur fines because of the nature of their work—eg drivers of haulage vehicles or buses—often pay their fines. The Benefits Agency will not, however, increase payments to meet fines.

## Fining the affluent

**16.12**  Section 18(5) of the CJA 91 (as amended) provides that the level of the fine should be adjusted to reflect means 'whether taking into account the financial circumstances of the offender has the effect of increasing or reducing the amount of the fine'. This means that an offender's means should be taken into account—it does not mean that a fine may be imposed when an immediate prison sentence is the proper choice. What is clearly objectionable is an offender with ample means being able to 'buy himself out of being sent to prison' (*Markwick* (1953) 37 Cr App Rep 125).

**16.13**  The fine is so commonly used for such a variety of offences that there seem to be few 'contra-indications'. There are only two statutory prohibitions. Section 30 PCCA 73 rules out a fine for an offence for which the sentence is fixed by law (eg murder), or for which the court is precluded from sentencing the offender by its exercise of some other power. The example given in the statute is probation, which at that time was not a 'sentence' in its own right; however, the CJA 91 makes clear that a fine may now be combined with any community penalty (see 17.1 ff). The options which are still presumably considered to preclude a fine are absolute or conditional discharges (*McClelland* (1951) 35 Cr App Rep 22). As for a custodial sentence, courts are advised to think twice before combining it with a fine. In *Maud* ((1980) 2 Cr App Rep (S) 289) the CA said

> 'It bears very harshly upon a person who is serving a sentence of imprisonment to have to pay a fine as well, when there is no evidence that he has the means ... and he is ordered to undergo very nearly a year's imprisonment in default ... If it is clear, as it is to this Court, that this appellant was totally unable to pay ... then he gets no remission in respect of the additional sentence ... in default ... So that he is worse off compared with other prisoners serving somewhat similar sentences'.

However, there are times when the CA does uphold a substantial fine as well as a custodial sentence if it is clear that the offender has made a substantial profit from the offence (eg *Fox* (1987) 9 Cr App Rep (S) 110, where the Court upheld fines of £16,000 as a well as a sentence of five years' imprisonment on a drug smuggler who had had £23,000 hidden in his house at the time of his arrest.

## Fine enforcement

**16.14** As soon as a MC imposes a fine (or forfeits a recognisance or makes an order for compensation or payment of costs) it becomes due for payment; and some offenders pay their fines before leaving the court (in cash or by cheque: credit cards are not accepted). In some cases magistrates who suspect that the offender will evade payment use their power to order a search of his person[1], and authorise court officials to take any money found on him by way of payment. This must not be done, however, if the MC is satisfied that the money does not belong to him, or that its loss would be more injurious to his family than his detention (s 80 MCA 80). Offenders who are aware of this possibility usually empty their wallets beforehand[2].

1. By an officer of the same sex.
2. If the offender has been arrested instead of summoned to court, the charge sheet should tell the MC how much money he had on his person.

**16.15** That is the only method of enforcement which does not involve the court in lengthy procedures. MCs not only can, but are expected to, ask offenders if they want time to pay; to grant them at least a week if they ask for time; and to allow payment by instalments[1] if the amount is substantial (s 75 MCA 80). Out of 40 courts about which the Howe Working Party (1981) got information, 14 were said always to give time, and 13 to refuse it in less than 1 per cent of cases. It is usually foreign visitors and offenders serving or about to serve custodial sentences who are given no time.

1. But if the offender defaults on any instalment, proceedings can be taken as if he had defaulted on all instalments then unpaid (s 75 MCA 80).

**16.16** In certain circumstances (see s 82 MCA 80) an MC can issue a warrant of commitment to prison for default as soon as it has convicted the offender, so that he is under immediate threat of imprisonment unless he pays. This is permissible in the case of an imprisonable offence if he appears to the court to have sufficient means to pay 'forthwith'; or—whether the offence is imprisonable or not—if he appears unlikely to remain long enough at a 'place of abode' in the UK to make other means of enforcement possible. Thirdly, if he is also being sentenced to imprisonment for another offence, or is already serving such a sentence, a warrant of commitment can be issued. If in any of these situations payment is not made forthwith, the offender is taken to prison. 'Forthwith' in practice usually means 'on the same day': the offender will be allowed to telephone for money, but not to leave the court buildings. Whether a cheque is accepted in these circumstances depends on the clerk's assessment of the likelihood that it will be honoured.

**16.17** The period of imprisonment depends on the amount of the fine. It does not matter if the addition of this period to a prison sentence already imposed results in a total period of custody which exceeds the statutory maximum for

MCs (*Green* [1977] 1 All ER 353). The maximum periods permitted for default (by Sch 4 MCA 80 as amended) are

| For an amount not exceeding | Period |
| --- | --- |
| £200 | 7 days |
| £500 (but exceeding £200) | 14 days |
| £1,000 (but exceeding £500) | 28 days |
| £2,500 (but exceeding £1,000) | 45 days |
| £5,000 (but exceeding £2,500) | 3 months |
| £10,000 (but exceeding £5,000) | 6 months |
| £20,000 (but exceeding £10,000) | 12 months |
| £50,000 (but exceeding £20,000) | 18 months |
| £100,000 (but exceeding £50,000) | 2 Years |
| £250,000 (but exceeding £100,000) | 3 years |
| £1 million (but exceeding £250,000) | 5 years |
| For an amount exceeding £1 million | 10 years |

A court fixing the term to be served in default should exercise discretion. Latham J said in *Szrabjer* (1994) 15 Cr App Rep (S) 821 that

'in determining the right figure in default, we have to consider the circumstances of the case, the overall seriousness of the matter; but in particular we bear in mind that the purpose of the imposition of a period of imprisonment in default is to secure payment of the amount which the court has ordered to be confiscated. We consider that it is not necessarily appropriate to approach the case on a simple arithmetical basis, in other words providing a sort of ladder up the scale ....'

Any period specified is however automatically reduced proportionately if part of the fine is paid: 30 days would be reduced to 16[1] if half the fine had been paid.

1.  Not to 15 because s 79 MCA 80 deducts half the days 'less one day'.

## Means inquiries (ss 82-84, 85A, 86 MCA 80)

**16.18**  Normally, however, the MC must not issue a warrant of commitment to prison until it has inquired into the finee's means since his conviction. What it can do when fining him, with time to pay, is to fix a date for the holding of a means inquiry if he does not pay what is due. The inquiry must take place in his presence, and he can be brought to court either by summons or by a warrant for his arrest[1]. Before or at the means inquiry he can be ordered to submit a statement of his means (and be penalised for failing to do so, or for submitting a misleading statement). Some MCs use a form for this purpose in order to assist both themselves and the offender. As a result of a means inquiry a MC may grant more time to pay, allow payment by instalments, or reduce the amount of instalments; but cannot remit any of it (that is, reduce the amount) unless the conditions of s 85 MCA 80 are fulfilled (see 16.29), and in no circumstances can it increase the amount. If not satisfied that the offender is making enough of an effort to pay, it may tell him what period of imprisonment it has in mind for the default.

1.  Some courts issue reminder letters before taking this step: others consider this a waste of time. Means warrants, on the other hand, usually take more than 6 weeks to execute, and Softley (1982) suggests that a reminder or summons should be tried first.

## Commitment warrants (ss 76, 77, 82, 92 MCA 80)

**16.19** It may even grant a warrant for his commitment to prison, either for immediate execution or with a direction to postpone the actual commitment (in the hope that the granting of the warrant will have the desired effect). But a commitment warrant must not be issued for execution unless

   a.  the offender has been present at a hearing, whether this takes the form of a means inquiry or another form (but this is not obligatory if the court has already, in his presence, fixed the term of imprisonment to be served in the case of default, or if the defaulter is already serving a prison sentence); and

   b.  he seems to have the means to pay forthwith (in the case of an imprisonable offence) or (in the case of any sort of offence) the MC is satisfied that the default is due to his wilful refusal or culpable neglect; and

   c.  the MC has tried or at least considered all other permissible methods of enforcement and concluded that they are inappropriate or unsuccessful.

Telling the finee, however, what term of imprisonment to expect is often enough; and if not the arrival of the police to take him to prison is another stage at which he often pays. If he does, the police simply refrain from executing the warrant. Finally, he may 'buy himself out' after entering prison.

**16.20** Other methods are distress warrants, attachment of earnings, money payment supervision, overnight detention in police cells, and civil proceedings; but, for reasons which will become clear, not all of these are seriously considered in the case of the ordinary finee.

## Distress warrants (ss 76-78 MCA 80)

**16.21** A distress warrant allows the finee's goods to be seized and sold to meet the fine. As a means of enforcement, however, it is not liked either by magistrates, who see it as harsh, or by those who have to execute it, who know the difficulties. If a defaulter has valuable property, such as a car or television set, it is usually on hire purchase or hire; and its removal often causes more inconvenience to his family than to the offender himself. Police frequently return distress warrants to clerks with the comment 'no goods'. Distraint is a sanction which is more often used against small businesses which fail to pay fines. A means inquiry is not obligatory.

## Attachment of earnings (s 14 Attachment of Earnings Act 71)

**16.22** A common method of enforcement—usually after a means inquiry—is by an attachment of earnings order. It can be made by a MC for payment of maintenance, legal aid contributions and any sum adjudged to be paid by a conviction, including fines, compensation, forfeited recognisances or costs. It instructs the person's employer to deduct specified sums from his attachable[1] earnings and pay them to the clerk of the MC. The order does not lapse if the person subject to it leaves his employer for another employer; but he is required to tell the court of his change of employment within 7 days, and if his new employer knows about the order he too is required to communicate with the court (s 15 A of EA 71). In practice the court is usually told by the former employer, who wants to avoid further paperwork.

1.  Ie what is left after deductions of income tax, certain social security contributions, and the 'protected earnings' which the court must specify in the AEO as the limit below which what is actually paid to him should not be reduced, having regard to his resources and needs. The employer is allowed to deduct 50p from the attachable earnings to cover his administrative costs whenever he makes a payment under an order (s 3 and Sch 3, A of EA 71).

## Deduction from income support (s 24 CJA 91)

**16.23** Following the recommendations of a HO report (Moxon, Sutton, and Hedderman, HORPU Paper 60 (1990)), s 24 CJA 91 gave the courts a new power to make an application to the DSS for direct payment of the fine by deduction from the offender's income support payments. The details of the scheme are laid out in the Fines (Deductions from Income Support) Regulations 1992 and in HO Circular 74/1992. If the DSS accepts the court's application, the court will be informed that deductions at a standard rate have begun, and payments will be made to the court at quarterly intervals. The HO estimated that the number of defaulters imprisoned each year could thus be reduced by up to 13,000, though this does not appear to be reflected in the latest (1993) Prison Statistics.

## Overnight detention (s 136 MCA 80)

**16.24** An alternative to imprisonment is overnight detention in a police station. This is authorised by warrant of an MC, and can be used—with or without a means inquiry—in any case in which the MC has the power to imprison for default, so long as the payment in question was the result of a summary conviction. The offender is taken to a police station and released at 8am next day[1]. This very mild sanction is not often used, and in some courts is unheard of.

1.  Or any time after 4am if the officer in charge decides that there is good reason, such as the need to get to work on time.

## Money payment supervision orders (s 88 MCA 80)

**16.25**  Commoner is the money payment supervision order (MPSO). This places the fine under the supervision of a named person, usually a probation officer, whose responsibility it is to help him to budget and use his resources so as to meet the payments. It can also be used for compensation or costs. It can be made without or after a means inquiry. In the case of a person under 21 it must be tried before issuing a commitment or distress warrant, except in those cases in which the MC is allowed to commit a defaulter to prison forthwith (see 16.19). The number of people commencing a money payment supervision order has fallen each year since 1989; there was a fall of 13 per cent between 1992 and 1993 to 4,100, which was the lowest total since 1979. For most types of supervision males heavily outnumber females. However, 30 per cent of all offenders beginning a money payment supervision order in 1993 were female.

## Fine enforcement officers

**16.26**  Some of the busier courts employ full-time or part-time fine enforcement officers (FEOs), whose task it is to collect fines, act on warrants of distress or commitment, or supervise under MPSOs. Most FEOs are retired policemen with experience of enforcing warrants. Where MPSOs do not name an FEO they usually name a probation officer, although financial supervision is not a task that is welcomed by probation officers, who consider that nagging a finee to pay is detrimental to a more constructive relationship: they often delegate the work to ancillaries (see 18.7).

## Civil recovery (s 87 MCA 80)

**16.27**  Infrequently used is a procedure whereby, after a means inquiry, the clerk of an MC can apply to the High Court or a county court for enforcement as if the sum had been due in pursuance of a judgement or order of one of those courts. This is a way of arranging an order which allows the money to be taken from the bank account of an unwilling offender: but it is not seriously considered by clerks of the courts unless the amount is large.

## Community service orders

**16.28**  As an alternative to the issue of a commitment warrant for non-payment of a sum adjudged to be paid by conviction of a MC, s 49 CJA 72 would have allowed the MC to make a community service order (see 17.16 ff). This provision, however, has not so far been brought into operation; and when the Home Secretary considered doing so in 1984 he was dissuaded by the objections of the Probation Service, who did not relish the inclusion of unco-operative fine-defaulters in groups of community service workers.

## Remission of fines (s 85 MCA 80)

**16.29** Sometimes a finee is able to persuade the clerk of the court that enforcement of the fine—or the unpaid part of it—would be unduly harsh: for example because he has lost his job since it was imposed. If the clerk is satisfied that there has been a genuine change in the finee's circumstances, he can suggest to the MC that it use its power to remit the fine in whole or part. Before doing so it must have held a means inquiry or a precommitment hearing of the kind described in 16.18. The Howe Working Party (1981) emphasised that remission is not a substitute for an appeal against the original decision to fine. In order to ensure this they recommended that the power should be used only in two situations: when there has been a change of circumstances since the imposition of the fine, or when the fine has been imposed without knowledge of the offender's means (as often happens in the case of driving offences). The latter recommendation has not been implemented. In practice remission is rare, chiefly because magistrates do not like to appear to be interfering with each other's penalties.

1.  The power to remit in s 85 MCA 80 expressly excludes other kinds of sums adjudged to be paid on conviction, such as compensation. If the fine was imposed by the CC the latter's consent must be obtained (s 32 PCCA 73).

## Writing off fines

**16.30** More often, permission is obtained from the Home Office's Accounts Branch to 'write off' a fine as 'irrecoverable'. This is usual if the finee cannot be traced—as often happens in London, for example—of if he dies or is known to have gone abroad. (In 'untraceable' cases the fine is in effect suspended, and can be enforced if the finee turns up again, eg in court.) It is also the practice to write off the unpaid fines of young offender institution inmates, so that they are not burdened by them on release.

## Enforcement of Crown Court fines (ss 30-2 PCCA 73)

**16.31** The enforcement of fines, forfeited recognisances and compensation orders imposed by the CC is treated as if they had been imposed by a MC specified by the CC, or, if no MC has been specified, by the MC which committed the offender to the CC. There are, however, minor differences. The CC may allow time for payment, or payment by instalments, and in the case of a recognisance may 'discharge' it (ie forgo payment) or reduce the amount. What the CC does not appear to have power to do is to remit a fine: that can only be done later by the MC, with the consent of the CC. When fining or forfeiting a recognisance the CC must (not may) make an order fixing the term of imprisonment for default, which must not exceed the maximum appropriate to the amount (s 31(2)). But the offender must not as a result be committed to prison on the occasion of the fining or forfeiture, except in the circumstances defined in 16.19. On the other hand a fine or forfeiture imposed by the CC on appeal against a MC's decision is governed by the statutes applying to MCs' fines. A fine or forfeiture imposed by the CA or HL is subject to the requirement to specify a prison term for default, and also to the maxima in 16.3.

**16.32** The system is designed to ensure that defaulters are not committed to prison until (a) the MC has made sure that they have or have had the means to pay; (b) it has tried to secure payment by less drastic means, especially in the case of young adults. In practice, although prison receptions for default numbered 22,403 in 1993 these represented only 3 per cent of all persons fined by courts in the year. But the relationship between the number of fine defaulters received into prison and the total number of offenders fined is not straightforward, since the courts may take some years before they take the final step of committing a defaulter to prison, and the MCs are also responsible for the enforcement of fixed penalties (see 16.65) as well as those fines imposed by courts. Although 31 per cent of all receptions are defaulters, their periods of detention are so short (more than half serving less than two weeks) that they account for only about 1.7 per cent of the prison population. In 1993 the average time served in prison service establishments by fine defaulters in 1993 was 7 days for men and 6 days for women, compared with 14.1 and 10.1 days in 1983.

### Avoiding imprisonment

**16.33** The imprisonment of defaulters—whose offences are in some cases non-imprisonable—is regarded by everyone as a regrettable last resort. Some people—for example a minority of the Wootton Committee (1970)—are so opposed to it as to argue that it should not be available as a method of enforcement unless the defaulter has been the subject of a further prosecution, for persistent refusal or neglect to pay when having the means to do so. The majority of that committee, however, and the later Howe Working Party (1981) did not accept this. The experience of DHSS with a provision of this kind in the Ministry of Social Security Act 1966 had shown the difficulties of prosecuting for persistent refusal or neglect to pay family maintenance. To adopt it would be to introduce yet another troublesome step before the defaulter could be threatened with imprisonment. Clerks of courts find that recalcitrant payers are very apt to produce the money when told that a warrant of commitment has been granted. This was confirmed by Softley's (1978) study of fined indictable offenders (who are worse payers than summary or traffic offenders). Only 51 per cent of his sample paid up in full or part after the initial letter of reminder. A summons or warrant for attendance at a means inquiry produced a lower response—39 per cent—which is not surprising when it is considered that most of those who were involved had failed to respond to at least one reminder. An 'adjourned hearing' (which usually involves a warning of the likelihood of imprisonment) produced a much better response: 65 per cent. Those for whom commitment warrants were actually granted were thus recalcitrants who had come through reminders, means inquiries and the threat of a warrant without paying any part of what was due. Yet among this group the news of the granting of a commitment warrant produced at least some payment in 64 per cent of cases. It might be thought that the remaining 36 per cent who had not paid by this stage would be a 'hard core' of non-payers; but when warrants of commitment were issued, and they were faced with the prospect of immediate imprisonment, 55 per cent made some payment.

**16.34**   Interestingly, although about 1 in 3 of Softley's finees were unemployed when fined, the unemployed were only slightly more likely to default than the employed (60 v 49 per cent). What distinguished the non-payers more sharply from the payers was a record of previous convictions (70 v 34 per cent) and a fine of more than £25 (63 v 40 per cent). Since unemployed finees were more likely to have been fined smaller amounts, it was clear that it was not unemployment which was the main reason for non-payment. The sharp difference between finees with previous convictions and those without suggests that an important factor was an acquaintance with the workings of the system, and in particular the knowledge that payment could be deferred without any inconvenience until the warrant of commitment was granted or issued.

**16.35**   Softley's indictable finees were more likely to be non-payers than traffic offenders, of whom less than 1 in 200 go to prison for default. It seems to be burglars and robbers who are most likely to do so (nearly 9 per cent), with men of violence next (at about 5 per cent)[1]: the amounts of their fines may have something to do with this. Wilkins (1979) provides good descriptions of a number of fine-defaulters whom he interviewed in Winson Green Prison, and who seemed to fall into two main groups, the 'feckless' offender and the inadequate drunk.

1.   These figures are Wilkins' (1979) for 1977: Softley did not analyse defaulters by type of offence.

## The efficiency of enforcement

**16.36**   The efficiency with which fines are enforced varies greatly from one court to another, and even at different times in the same court[1]. The collection of fines has a lower priority than keeping up with court business; and when the latter is heavy other activities have to be neglected. Even accounting for received fines takes precedence over collecting unpaid fines. The identification of defaulters may still depend on a manual system usually involving a card for each finee—which requires periodic searches: but courts with computerised systems are not always speedier in enforcement (Softley, 1982). Most courts, too, depend on the police rather than their own FEOs for the execution of warrants, whether for attendance at hearings or commitment to prison; and among police this work has an understandably low priority[2]. A rough estimate of the amount of unpaid fines in 1995 would be £50,000,000.

1.   In Softley's (1982) sample of courts, the percentage of finees who paid within 3 months ranged from 53 to 90 per cent, and the percentage of amounts due which were paid ranged from 33 to 83 per cent. But a more accurate index of effectiveness was the 'accounting ratio': the ratio of fines recovered to amounts imposed plus arrears brought forward. This varied from 0.26 to 0.66.
2.   But courts with FEOs did not have better accounting ratios in Softley's (1982) sample. Nor did courts in which the staff had lower workloads concerned with fines.

## Corrective efficacy of fines

**16.37**  Enforcement apart, how effective are fines? Several studies have found that adults who have been fined or ordered to pay compensation for indictable offences are less likely to be reconvicted than those sentenced in other ways: Hammond (1964), Softley (1978), Phillpotts and Lancucki (1979). In the last of these, the actual six-year reconviction rates for adult men who received financial penalties for indictable offences were consistently below 'expectation', even for multiple recidivists: see Table 7B. This is consistent with the belief that financial penalties are not entirely ineffective as an individual deterrent. What has to be taken into account, however, is the possibility that when courts content themselves with financial penalties they are selecting offenders who are less likely to be reconvicted than those, for example, whom they put on probation, or in prison. Even an analysis which allows for age, previous convictions and type of offence cannot rule out the possibility that courts are influenced in their choice of financial or other measures by some factor which is also associated with a higher or lower reconviction rate. Softley's study (Table 4, p 5) shows that this is in fact so: a factor which is strongly associated with being fined is being in employment at the time of sentence, and this same factor is also associated with a lower reconviction rate . Since 566 of his sample had been fined in spite of being unemployed, he was able to make a comparison between them and the unemployed offenders who had received non-financial sentences. For the unemployed adults with no previous convictions, the two-year reconviction rates were significantly better (p <0.01) if they were fined than if they received non-financial disposals. For the recidivist unemployed, however, the results were equivocal, perhaps because of the operation of chance among small numbers. Among the unemployed offenders aged 21 or older, the finees had somewhat lower reconviction rates than the others (p <0.05); but for the younger adults the comparison was equivocal. In short, when the factors most strongly associated with being fined—type of offence, previous convictions and unemployment status—are allowed for, the odds are still in favour of the belief that financial penalties are followed by fewer reconvictions than other measures, although the difference is not substantial.

**16.38**  Whether this is true of summary offences we do not know, and cannot hope to, since the fine is the standard penalty for them, and it is hard to see what alternative could be substituted, having regard to sheer numbers. In their case the most we can hope to establish by research is the relationship between the severity of the fine and the probability of the offender's repeating the offence. It might also be possible to compare the efficacy of actual and suspended fines (see 16.40 on recognisances).

**16.39**  Even so, fines are preferable to some other measures. To the extent that they are effective, it must be because they operate as individual or general deterrents. As such, they have very few of the unwanted side-effects which are attributed to custodial deterrents. At worst, an excessive fine may result in hardship for a family, although the means inquiry should make this rare. The greater danger is that tariff fining, especially when coupled with the old doctrine that the well-to-do should not be fined more than the next man, has the result that the typical fine is a tax rather than a disincentive. The indications are that if the calculation of fines could be rationalised their efficacy would increase. On the other hand, merely increasing the statutory maxima seems unlikely to improve the calculation of amounts, when one compares the present maxima with the recommendations of the Magistrates' Association (see 16.5).

## Recognisances

**16.40**   In some other countries—for example France—a fine can be suspended, and enforced only in the event of a further conviction. In England something like this is achieved by binding over with recognisances: a measure which has been described in 15.27. The recognisance is in effect a bond to forfeit a specified sum of money if the offender fails to comply with the terms of the bind-over. If it is the offender himself who has entered into the recognisance he is in effect being fined, but required to find the money only in the event of a breach of the bind-over. There is no limit to the amount of a recognisance which the CC may stipulate, but unless the amount is trivial the court should inquire into the person's means in order to arrive at a proper sum (*Boulding* (1983) 5 Cr App Rep (S) 433). Payment of an 'estreated' (ie forfeited) recognisance can be enforced by any of the means used to enforce a fine. If the CC estreats a recognisance, and does not discharge it (ie forgo payment) it must fix the term of imprisonment which the MC which has to collect the sum may impose if all else fails.

## Compensation orders (ss 35-38 PCCA 73; as amended by s 67 CJA 82)

**16.41**   Compensation orders in effect direct an offender to pay money to the court for transmission to a victim who has suffered personal injury, loss or damage as a result of an offence. While provision for such an order has existed since the Prosecution of Offences Act 1907, few orders were made before the CJA 72. The offence must be one of which the offender has just been convicted, or which has been taken into consideration by the sentencing court (s 35 PCCA 73). The order may be made as a result of an application by the victim, or without one, although victims cannot safely assume that the court will always remember to consider compensation. A compensation order can be made either in addition to or instead of any other sentence or disposal (s 67 CJA 82), so that it may be the only penalty imposed for an offence. If the court thinks it appropriate to impose both a fine and a compensation order, but considers that the offender's means are insufficient to pay both an appropriate fine and an appropriate compensation, it must give preference to the latter, although this does not prevent it from imposing a reduced fine (s 67 CJA 82). As with a fine (see 16.10), the compensation order may be paid by instalments. If so, the compensation order will be paid off before the fine. The amount of compensation should be what the court considers appropriate having regard to any evidence and to any representations made by or on behalf of the accused or the prosecutor (s 67 CJA 82). This means that even in cases in which the amount claimed has not been proved, or agreed by both parties, the court is no longer prevented from ordering the payment of an amount which it considers appropriate, as it seemed to be by the ruling in *Vivian* [1979] 1 All ER 48. Since the CJA 88 courts have had to give reasons if a compensation order is not made. Despite this, in 1993, only 13 per cent of all those sentenced (excluding those sentenced for summary motoring offences) were ordered to pay compensation.

**16.42** There are limitations. An order cannot be based on loss suffered by the dependants of a person in consequence of his death; or on injury, loss or damage 'due to an accident arising out of the presence of a motor vehicle on a road', which must cover virtually all traffic offences[1] (s 35 PCCA 73). An order cannot be made by a MC for an offence for which it is committing the offender to the CC for sentence (s 56 CJA 67). Nor can one be made for an offence for which the offender has merely been cautioned by the police: a defect which is discussed in 16.51 ff.

1. An exception is damage to property while out of the owner's possession which is treated as having resulted from the offence; so that, for example, the owner of a car which was taken without his consent can obtain a compensation order for accidental damage to it: see s 35(2), (3) PCCA 73.

**16.43** What amounts to a practice direction on the use of compensation orders was given by the CA in *Miller* (1979) 68 Cr App Rep 56:
   a.   they are not an alternative to a sentence (superseded by s 67 CJA 82);
   b.   they should be made only when the legal position is quite clear;
   c.   regard must be had to the offender's means;
   d.   the order must be precise, relate to an offence, specify the amount, and the instalments if there is to be payment by instalments;
   e.   the order must not be oppressive. The court has to bear in mind that a discharged prisoner is often short of money, and he must not be tempted to commit further offences to provide the cash to satisfy an order;
   f.   there might however be good moral grounds for making an order, including payment by instalments, to remind the offender of the evil he has done. This might apply particularly when a non-custodial sentence is imposed and the order is for not too great a sum;
   g.   an order must be realistic. An order for payment by instalments over a long period is to be avoided.
In later cases the CA has offered what sound like further guidelines:
   h.   when counsel is instructed by a client to offer compensation in his plea for mitigation, counsel should 'press' him in order to make sure that he is genuinely able to pay (*Coughlin* (1984) 6 Cr App Rep (S) 102);
   i.   if the case is one in which immediate imprisonment is the right course it should be imposed notwithstanding that the offender is in a position to pay some compensation (*Copley* (1979) 1 Cr App Rep (S) 55);
   j.   if the offender puts before the court evidence of reasonable prospects of employment, a compensation order may be made even if he is sentenced to imprisonment (*Townsend* (1980) 2 Cr App Rep (S) 328);
   k.   a compensation order should not be made on the assumption that the money will be raised by disposing of an asset unless the court has an

accurate assessment of the value of the asset (*Chambers* [1982] Crim LR 189); and it should not be made when the asset is the matrimonial home, since this may be the subject of a claim by the spouse (*Harrison* (1980) 2 Cr App Rep (S) 313);

l.  but a compensation order may be made against an offender who does not appear to have income from which to pay if he is in possession of property which is in effect the proceeds of the crime in respect of which the order is made (*Workman* (1979) 1 Cr App Rep (S) 335);

m.  a compensation order may be made even when the offender would not be held liable for compensation in civil law (*Chappell* (1984) 80 Cr App Rep 31);

n.  the value to be set on the victim's loss must be formally proved (for example by a bill for repairs), unless the defendant agrees (*Vivian* [1979] 1 All ER 48); but this rule does not apply to small sums for personal injury, shock or suffering (*Bond* [1983] 1 All ER 456).

## Amount of compensation

**16.44**  MCs cannot order compensation of amounts exceeding £5,000 in respect of any one offence. If a MC orders compensation for offences taken into consideration it must not exceed the difference between any compensation which *has been* ordered for offences for which the offender has been convicted, and the maximum sum which *could have been* ordered (that is £5,000 multiplied by the number of offences of which he stands convicted) (s 40 MCA 80). The CC is not subject to such limits; but both CC and MC must have regard to the offender's means.

**16.45**  Personal injury cases give courts most difficulty. In 1978 the Magistrates' Association first published a table of guidance for MCs when calculating the sums to be awarded for common types of bodily injury. The amounts suggested were criticised for being too low, and have been increased regularly. The current compensation table in the Association's *Sentencing Guidelines* (see 16.5) is reproduced in Table 16A, with the generous permission of the Association.

**TABLE 16A**

|  | Type of injury | Suggested award |
|---|---|---|
| Graze | Depending on size | up to £50 |
| Bruise | Depending on size | up to £75 |
| Black eye |  | £100 |
| Cut: no permanent scarring | depending on size and whether stitched | £75-£500 |
| Sprain | depending on loss of mobility | £100-£1,000 |
| Loss of a non-front tooth |  | £1,000 |
| Facial scar | however small—resulting in permanent disfigurement | £750+ |
| Jaw | fractured (wired) | £2,750 |

| | Type of injury | Suggested award |
|---|---|---|
| Nasal | undisplaced fracture of nasal bone | £750 |
| Nasal | displaced fracture of bone requiring manipulation | £1,000 |
| Nasal | not causing fracture but displaced septum requiring sub-mucous resection | £1,750 |
| Wrist | simple fracture with complete recovery in few weeks | £1,750-£2,500 |
| Wrist | displaced fracture—limb in plaster for some 6 weeks; full recovery 6 -12 months | £2,500 + |
| Finger | fractured little finger; assuming full recovery after a few weeks | £750 |
| Leg or arm | simple fracture of tibia, fibula, ulna or radius with full recovery in three weeks | £2,500 |
| Laparotomy | stomach scar 6-8 inches long (resulting from exploratory operation) | £3,500 |

### Criminal Injuries Compensation Board (CICB)

**16.46** Courts are encouraged to order offenders to compensate the victim whether or not the injury comes within the scope of the CICB. The CICB, created in 1964, considers claims for compensation for bodily injuries resulting from crimes of violence which have been reported to the police, whether or not the perpetrators have been identified. Its discretionary awards are met from State funds. The provisions of the CJA 88 putting the CICB on a statutory footing were not brought into force, but even so the Home Secretary's attempt to change the system subsequently resulted in the HL holding the Home Secretary to be in contempt of court (see *Fire Brigades Union* [1995] 2 All ER 244)[1]. The minimum award is now £1,000 (excluding many potential claimants) and details of the CICB's criteria and procedure can be found in its annual reports. For accounts of the problems bedevilling the CICB (largely a lack of financial resources), see Newburn (1989), Miers (1989), Barclay (1991). CICB victims who submit claims to the CICB do not usually ask criminal courts for compensation orders: but if one is made before the CICB's award the latter is reduced accordingly. If one is made after the award the CICB is reimbursed to that extent.

1. The Criminal Injuries Compensation Act 1995 creates a new statutory framework.

### Enforcement of compensation orders

**16.47** Compensation orders are enforceable by the same procedures as fines, with minor differences. A MC's compensation order is 'suspended' until the end of the 21 days allowed for appeals against its decisions. This does not seem to prevent the justice's clerk from accepting the sum due within the 21 days; but he should not pay it to the victim until that period has elapsed. MCs have power to reduce the amount in the order, or discharge it (ie free the offender from obligation to make any payment) but only if injury, loss or damage has been held in civil proceedings to be less than it was taken to be for purposes of the order (a very rare occurrence) or, in cases of loss of property, if the property has been recovered by the person in whose favour the order was made (s 37 PCCA 73).

## Use of compensation orders

**16.48** In 1993 90,200 compensation orders were made by MCs and some 6,300 in CCs (compared with 1980 when the figure in MCs was 121,700 and some 6,000 by the CC)[1]. They were most frequent in cases of violence against the person (64 per cent in MC, 28 per cent in CC); criminal damage (56 per cent in MCs, 25 per cent in the CC), fraud and forgery cases (56 per cent in MCs, 20 per cent in the CC). At the time of Newburn's 1985 study, despite continued pressure on the courts to award compensation in all suitable cases, only 17 per cent of assault cases in MCs resulted in an award of compensation, compared with 75 per cent of criminal damage cases (Newburn, 1988). A survey by Softley (1978) found that in 1976 the majority of those who benefited from compensation orders in property cases were corporate entities such as government departments, commercial enterprises and local authorities. Orders were much less frequent in cases of personal violence (18 per cent in MCs, 11 per cent in the CC), perhaps because of the availability of CICB awards, but perhaps mostly because non-corporate victims were less often aware of their right to claim. A survey by Shapland (1982) in 2 midland cities found that half of the 278 victims of grievous or actual bodily harm, mugging, rape and indecent assault in her sample did not know of any source of compensation. The Victim's Charter (1991) and other attempts to publicise victims' rights may well be responsible for the increasing number of awards in cases of personal violence.

1.  Excluding summary motoring offences. The information about orders made in 1980 was supplied by the HO.

## Defects in the system

**16.49** What the present system of compensation orders does is to save the victim the trouble and cost of instituting proceedings in a civil court. They also have an important symbolic value as indicating the court's recognition of the victim's needs and rights (see Victim Support, 1993). The procedure however is by no means perfect. Victims are not always told that compensation can be awarded by a criminal court. If the defendant is known to be pleading guilty the victim may not even be notified of the date on which the case is to be dealt with. In some areas the police routinely inform the victim of his right to put his claim to the court; in others they do not. Failure to inform the victim is particularly likely if the offence is merely one which is to be 'taken into consideration'. Courts should, but do not always, remember victims' possible claims.

**16.50** Payment by instalments means that victims cannot count on being compensated quickly even under criminal proceedings. Approximately 75 per cent of Softley's sample in 1978 had paid in full within 18 months, and this had only risen to 80 per cent in Newburn's 1985 study. Of the 550 case in Newburn's sample, 45 ended in custody in default, and 41 of these orders were written off. Custody is therefore not an effective way of ensuring payment to victims. They are only eligible for compensation from the CICB (see 16.46) if they suffered personal injuries worth more than £1,000 and even then only about 50 per cent of claims are successful (Barclay (1991). Many commentators (the Hodgson Committee (1984), Samuels (1984), Newburn (1988) to name but a few) have called for a fund from which courts could pay the compensation, so that the fund and not the victim would have to wait for the instalments to come in from the offenders. This would involve the State in bearing the loss of interest on sums while the offender was paying instalments, and the somewhat greater loss in cases of default. It might encourage courts to fix the amount of compensation with more regard to what the victim deserved and less for the offender's means, knowing that the State would pay what the offender could not or would not. Newburn (1988) points out that, because of the clear relationship between the size of compensation orders and the likelihood of payment, if the size of awards rises the rate of default is also likely to increase. Given this country's present economic condition a system which more or less guaranteed victims full compensation would doubtless be regarded as too costly.

**16.51** A situation for which the system does not even attempt to cater is that in which the police are considering merely cautioning the offender. They may consult the victim to find out whether he objects to a mere caution; but they may fail to tell him that a caution deprives him of the right to claim compensation from a criminal court, so that his only recourse will be to civil proceedings. The problem cannot be entirely dismissed by arguing that a caution is unlikely if the victim has suffered serious loss, damage or personal injury, for this would not be true, especially in the case of juvenile offences. The Hodgson Committee (1984) recommended that it should be possible for evidence of a caution to be produced to a MC when the complainant has a clear case for compensation and for the MC to make a compensation (or restitution: see 16.52) order as if the offence had been taken into consideration. With this in view an offender who is cautioned should sign an admission of his offence. Alternative solutions would be to instruct police to explain to complainants that a caution would deprive them of their right to compensation from a criminal court, and to prosecute if as a result the complainant objected to a caution; or to instruct police to delay the decision whether to caution or prosecute until the offender has paid the compensation claimed, and to prosecute if he does not. Both solutions, however, would allow the complainant too much influence on the decision whether to prosecute, and the second solution would involve delays.

## Restitution orders (s 28 Theft Act 1968)

**16.52** A court can order anyone having possession or control of stolen goods to restore them to any person entitled to recover them. Alternatively, it can, on an application by a person entitled to recover goods from the convicted person, order goods directly or indirectly representing the stolen goods to be delivered or transferred to the applicant. Another alternative open to the court, if money was taken from the convicted person when apprehended, is to order a sum to be paid out of it, not greater than the value of the stolen goods, to the person who is entitled to them. The goods must have been stolen, and the person who is made the subject of the order must either have been convicted of the theft or had it taken into consideration in the determination of his sentence (see 2.10). The power can be exercised even when the sentence itself is deferred. It must not, however, be used unless in the court's opinion the relevant facts 'sufficiently appear' before sentence (*Church* (1970) 55 Cr App Rep 65), and unless there is no doubt of the rights of the parties (*Ferguson* (1970) 54 Cr App Rep 410). Nor must the result be that the victim gains more than he lost (*Parsons and Haley* (1976) CSP J3–2F01).

## Forfeiture of property used in the offence (s 43 PCCA 73)

**16.53**  The court has a general power[1] to order the confiscation of property used by or intended by the convicted person to be used for the purpose of committing of facilitating any offence. It can do so, however, only when convicting him of an offence punishable with two years' imprisonment or more, although the property may have been used or intended for use in 'any' offence. The property must have been in the possession or under the control of the offender *at the time of his apprehension* (with ridiculous results in *Hinde* (1977) 64 Cr App Rep 213). The effect is to deprive the offender of his rights in the property, and place it in the possession of the police. Anyone else with an interest in the property can apply within six months for the return of it. It is motor vehicles which are most frequently confiscated under this provision, and it is sometimes a moot question whether they were used 'for the purpose of facilitating or committing' an offence. The confiscation should be regarded as part of the penalty for the offence, and is sometimes quashed because the total effect on the offender seems excessive (eg in *Buddo* (1982) 4 Cr App Rep (S) 268). By the same token, it is regarded as inconsistent with an absolute discharge (*Hunt* [1978] Crim LR 697). The number of forfeiture orders has risen in nearly each year from 2,900 in 1983 to 15,500 in 1993 (with a total value of £9,678,118).

1.  Special powers of confiscation are contained in the Misuse of Drugs Act 1971, s 27; the Firearms Act 1968, s 52; the Prevention of Crime Act 1953, s 1; the Immigration Act 1971, s 25; the Incitement to Disaffection Act 1934, s 3; the Obscene Publications Act 1964, s 1.

**16.54**  The CJA 88 added a new s 43A to the PCCA allowing the court, where the offender has been convicted of an offence which has resulted in a person suffering 'personal injury, loss or damage' or where such an offence has been taken into consideration by the court, to order that any proceeds which accrue from the disposal of the forfeited property shall (up to a certain specified sum) be paid to that person. The court may only exercise this power where it would have made a compensation order (of that specified sum) but was unable to do so because of the offender's lack of means (s 43A(2)).

## Confiscation: Drug Trafficking Offences Act 1994

**16.55** Confiscation orders may be made under two different, mutually exclusive, provisions. First, the Drug Trafficking Offences Act (DTOA) 1986, as amended by the Drug Trafficking Act 1994: once the offender has been convicted, the trial judge receives written submissions from prosecution witnesses on the question of the offender's benefits from drug offences. The court then receives submissions from the defence, but may make use of certain assumptions to help it in its task of assessing the extent of the defendant's benefit (see *Dickens* (1990) 12 Cr App Rep (S) 191, where Lord Lane CJ described the law as 'intentionally draconian'). Sallon and Bedingfield (1993) conclude that the offender then 'faces a mini-trial without a jury for crimes for which the defendant has not been indicted and that may in the end add years to the sentence'. They argue that removing the offender's right to silence and his right to trial by jury does little towards fighting the war on drug abuse. In 1994 4,835 confiscation orders were made under the DTOA 1986, which represented only 26 per cent of eligible offenders (an increase from the 22 per cent of eligible offenders who received a confiscation order in 1993). Not only do these orders raise serious concerns about the due process rights of the offender, they are also clearly difficult to enforce. Thomas (at [1995] Crim LR 514) points out that Parliament took the easy option of adopting the existing procedure for the enforcement of fines and applying it to confiscation orders. But he questions the wisdom of giving magistrates the power to commit a person to prison in default of payment.

## Confiscation: CJA 88 (as amended by the Proceeds of Crime Act 1995)

**16.56** Such a confiscation order is the successor to the criminal bankruptcy order which was available from 1973 to 1988. A criminal bankruptcy order specified the amount of loss or damage appearing to result from each offence; the identified persons appearing to have suffered; the amount due to each; and the earliest date on which the offence, or the earliest offence, appears to have been committed. The effect was to make available the machinery of civil bankruptcy administration for the recovery of money for the benefit of victims. The DPP then acted as official petitioner, and made inquiries to see whether he should present a bankruptcy petition to the High Court, which almost invariably granted it, and appointed an official receiver to administer the bankruptcy. These orders were not a success: they were rarely imposed and difficult to enforce, especially on a prisoner serving a long sentence who had no interest in co-operating with the official receiver.

**16.57** Under Part VI of the CJA 1988 (ss 71-103), and the Proceeds of Crime Act 1995, a court has the power to make a confiscation order if
   i.   the offender is convicted of a 'specified offence' (an indictable offence other than a drug trafficking offence (see 16.55); a summary offence listed in Sch 4 of the CJA 88; certain offences under the Prevention of Terrorism (Temporary Provisions) Act 1989);
   ii.  it is satisfied that the offender has benefited from that offence;

iii. it is satisfied that he has benefited to at least the minimum amount (currently £10,000).

There is no upper limit to what may be seized. Section 72 sets out the procedure which must be followed by the court: the prosecution must give written notice to the court that an order of at least £10,000 could be made against the offender. The standard of proof required to determine any issue arising under these provisions is the civil standard (s 71 (7A)).

## Costs

**16.58** Defendants—even if acquitted—may suffer financial loss in meeting the costs of being tried. This can happen in the following ways:

a. they may have to meet the cost of legal advice and representation without being granted legal aid;
b. they may be granted legal aid but required to contribute part or even all of the costs;
c. they may be required to contribute to the costs of the prosecution, in addition to (a) or (b).

These paragraphs are confined to decisions which affect *defendants* in one of these ways, and do not deal with decisions as to whether prosecution costs should be met out of central funds.

## Legal aid (LAA 88)

**16.59** In criminal cases, legal aid usually means representation and advice by a solicitor, and also in certain kinds of case by counsel (a barrister), who are paid from public funds. An application can be written or oral, and is considered in the first place by the justices' clerk[1], who may grant it himself or refer the matter to a JP or the MC. Legal aid cannot, however, be granted unless the clerk or a JP has considered the applicant's means; and applicants are required to state these in detail on a form, unless they appear incapable of doing so by reason of their physical or mental condition. Legal aid *must* be granted when committing someone on a charge of murder; when the prosecution appeals or applies for leave to appeal from the CA to the HL; when someone charged before a MC and remanded in custody is brought before a MC on an occasion when he may be again remanded or committed in custody, not being already legally represented; or when someone who is to be sentenced or dealt with for an offence by a MC or the CC is to be kept in custody, including custody in a hospital for the purpose of inquiries or a report to assist the court. The factors which the court should apply in deciding whether to grant legal aid (previously known as the Widgery criteria) are set out in s 22(2) LAA 88:

'(a) the offence is such that if proved it is likely that the court would impose a sentence which would deprive the accused if his liberty or lead to loss of his livelihood or serious damage to his reputation;
(b) the determination of the case may involve consideration of a substantial question of law;

(c) the accused may be unable to understand the proceedings or to state his own case because of his inadequate knowledge of English, mental illness or other mental or physical disability;

(d) the nature of the defence is such as to involve the tracing and interviewing of witnesses or expert cross-examination of a witness for the prosecution;

(e) it is in the interests of someone other than the accused that the accused be represented.'

Case-law also makes it clear that legal aid should be offered when a MC is considering a recommendation for deportation (*Edgehill* [1963] 1 QB 593); when the defendant lives abroad with no experience of English courts (*Phillippe* [1965] Crim LR 109); when a hospital order is being considered (*Fysh* [1964] Crim LR 143); and when committing for sentence (*Serghiou* [1966] 3 All ER 637n). Notwithstanding all these guidelines, there seems to be scope for substantial variation in the readiness of different courts to grant legal aid, and in the level of contributions and down payments which they demand.

1. Unless made at the CC, CA or HL in which case it is made to the appropriate officers of those courts.

### Acquittals and costs

**16.60** There is more concern about defendants who have to bear or contribute to their costs in spite of being acquitted. If this happens in the CC, or if a MC summarily dismisses the information in an indictable case, or decides against committal for trial, the court may, but is not obliged to, order defence costs to be met from central funds. Section 16 of the Prosecution of Offences Act 1985 empowers the courts to make defendants' costs orders. Whether it does so or not, a court may order central funds to meet the expenses of witnesses. The CA may similarly defray the costs of an appellant. The same, roughly speaking, is true when an information charging an indictable offence is laid before a JP but not proceeded with.

**16.61** The principles governing the award of costs in cases of acquittal are set out in a *Practice Direction (Crime: Costs)* [1991] 1 WLR 498. There is also a *Guide to the Award of Costs in Criminal Proceedings* (1991), published by the Royal Courts of Justice. A successful defendant should normally have his or her costs paid, though the *Practice Statement* does single out examples of when this would be inappropriate:

i.  where the accused brought suspicion upon himself and misled the prosecution into believing that the evidence against him was stronger than it was;

ii. where the accused was acquitted on a meritless technicality when in fact there was ample evidence to support a conviction.

**16.62** There are no national statistics to tell us how often acquittals result in awards of costs in favour of defendants. A survey of 15 Petty Sessional Divisions by the Justices' Clerks' Society in 1977 or 1978 (cited in Levenson, 1981), which include four major cities, seemed to show that this is not common. Levenson describes examples of cases in which acquitted defendants have had to bear either the whole cost of defending themselves in MCs or a substantial contribution under the legal aid scheme. The Cobden Trust's study of four busy CCs in 1978 found that about 6 per cent of acquitted defendants had to make legal aid contributions out of their own pockets; and only 10 per cent had their costs paid out of central funds (but Levenson says that these were unusual cases). Unless it is argued that all of the remainder were in some way to blame for being prosecuted, it seems that meeting (or contributing to) the costs of one's defence is regarded as one of the risks of being a citizen of this country. Under s 21(4A)(a) POA 1985, where the accused has made a contribution to the costs of his legal aid such contributions do not count as costs recoverable under a defendant's costs order. This means that, save in exceptional cases, defendant's costs orders are only relevant to those who have funded their own defence.

## Prosecution costs

**16.63**   Section 19(1) of the POA 1985 provides that the court may award a prosecutor such amount out of central funds as it considers reasonably necessary to compensate him for any expenses properly incurred by him in the proceedings. Section 18 authorises the making of orders that a convicted accused or an unsuccessful appellant shall pay costs. For the convicted defendant an order to contribute to the costs of the prosecution is a real possibility. The court orders the payment of an amount that it considers 'just and reasonable'. If the defendant elects trial by jury (with its higher prosecution costs) he risks a larger award against him (*Hayden* (1975) 60 Cr App Rep 304). The amount should bear a reasonable relationship to the defendant's means and to any fine imposed on him. Indeed, where he is fined less than £5, he may not have a costs order made against him (s 18). Costs should not be awarded against someone when he will be unable to pay them until after release from a prison term, if ever (*Judd* (1970) 54 Cr App Rep 512). The payment of costs by defendants is enforceable in the same ways as the payment of fines.

## Fines without court appearance

**16.64**   For some kinds of offence fines can be levied without taking the offender to court. The 'fixed penalty' system for dealing with certain traffic offences, much expanded in 1986 and described in 23.8 ff, resulted in an increase in the number of fixed penalty notices issued from 4.5 million in 1985 to 5.8 million in 1987, at which level the annual figure has roughly remained. The Inland Revenue Department's 'mitigated penalties' and the Customs and Excise's 'on-the-spot' fines for petty smuggling are mentioned in 15.15ff, together with on-the-spot fines for fare-dodgers on London underground railways. The attraction of these expedients for those who have to administer them is that they save the cost of prosecutions. They have of course their own problems. It is not easy to settle on a level of payment which will function not merely as a tax on the conduct in question, but as a general deterrent: there is a risk of setting the level so high that enforcement of payment becomes a nuisance. Secondly, if persistent offenders have to be brought to court at last, what can courts be told about their persistence?

# Chapter 17

# Community penalties

**17.1** The next two chapters deal with the different kinds of supervisory and community measures to which adult offenders can be made subject; with hostels, day centres and community service; and with the Probation Service, which is responsible for providing or organising most of the necessary personnel and facilities. The first of these chapters is more concerned with a description of the various options, the next with the underpinning philosophies. The general principles applying to all community penalties are found in s 6 CJA 91:

'(1) A court shall not pass on an offender a community sentence, that is to say, a sentence which consists of or includes one or more community orders, unless it is of the opinion that the offence or the combination of the offence and one or more offences associated with it, was serious enough to warrant such a sentence.

(2) Subject to subsection (3) below, where a court passes a community sentence—
   (a) the particular order or orders comprising or forming a part of the sentence shall be such as in the opinion of the court is, or taken together are, the most suitable for the offender; and
   (b) the restrictions on liberty imposed by the order or orders shall be such as in the opinion of the court are commensurate with the seriousness of the offence, or the combination of the offence and one or more offences associated with it.

(3) In consequence of the provision made by s 11 below with respect to combination orders, a community sentence shall not consist of or include both a probation order and a community service order.

(4) In this Part 'community order' means any of the following orders, namely:
   (a) a probation order;
   (b) a community service order;
   (c) a combination order;
   (d) a curfew order;
   (e) a supervision order [see 20.12]; and
   (f) an attendance centre order [see 20.15].'

For a discussion of the key ideas of 'seriousness' and 'commensurability', see 10.17. It is enough to point out here that sentencers may not impose a community order unless the offence was serious enough to warrant it. No attempt is made within the Act either to define 'serious enough' or to rank the various community penalties.

## Probation

**17.2**   An offender over the age of 16[1] convicted of any offence other than one for which the penalty is fixed by law (i e, in practice, murder) may be made the subject of a probation order. In practice, probation is little used for motoring offences, revenue offences, railway offences, poaching or breaches of administrative prohibitions. Most probationers have been convicted of indictable dishonesty: 45 per cent of people starting a probation order in 1993 had been convicted of indictable offences of dishonesty, including theft, handling stolen goods, burglaries but not often robbery; 9 per cent had been convicted of offences of violence (mostly minor, but including, now and then, a manslaughter or a threat to kill). The number of probation orders imposed for summary offences has increased steadily from 10 per cent of sentences in 1985 to 30 per cent in 1995 (but this increase reflects both the changing definition of summary offences which now include more offences of assault and criminal damage, and the greater use of cautioning of minor offenders by the police).

1.   The juvenile equivalent is a supervision order, which may place the offender under the supervision of a probation officer or a local authority social worker, depending on whether the juvenile is over the age of 13 or not (see 20.12). The CJA 91 reduced the minimum age for a probation order to 16.

**17.3**   Probation is no longer a measure designed for one's first conviction. Two-thirds of all probationers have records of at least one previous conviction. Indeed, probation is slightly less likely for a first standard list conviction than for a subsequent one. It is recognised by sentencers as a sensible way of dealing with people whose repeated offences are not a serious threat to public safety, but are attributable to problems—economic, domestic or personal—with which they cannot cope.

**17.4**   The court may make a probation order if it is 'of the opinion that the supervision of the offender by a probation officer is desirable in the interests of—
  (a)  securing the rehabilitation of the offender;
  (b)  protecting the public from harm from him or preventing the commission by him of further offences' (s 2 PCCA 73, as amended).
It usually decides this after obtaining a PSR (see 2.15 ff, where it was noted that the original requirement that a probation order could not be imposed without a PSR has now been diluted but it remains good practice; see *National Standards*). By comparison, a court cannot make an order requiring an offender to submit to medical treatment or guardianship under the Mental Health Acts without psychiatric reports which advise this: a difference which is not easily justified.

In practice most sentencers would hesitate to order probation without a favourable PSR, but this is by no means unheard of.

## Consent

**17.5** Having decided on a probation order the sentencer must then explain to the offender in ordinary language
   (a) the effect of the order (including any additional requirements proposed to be included in the order);
   (b) the consequences which may follow under Sch 2 of CJA 91 if he fails to comply with any of the requirements of the order (see 17.26 below); and
   (c) that the court has under the Schedule power to review the order on the application either of the offender or of the supervising officer.
The order cannot be made unless the offender 'expresses his willingness to comply with its requirements' (s 2 PCCA 73). The offender must be given 'a fair opportunity to make his choice': if for example the offender thinks that the only alternative is a custodial sentence when this is not so, he is not being given this fair opportunity (*Marquis* (1974) 59 Cr App Repep 228). One reason for the requirement of consent was that probation was originally an alternative to a sentence, a voluntary undertaking accepted by the court on condition of good behaviour. As the HO Green Paper, *Strengthening Punishment in the Community* (1995), points out 'it is open to doubt whether the consent given by a defendant is, in the circumstances of a court appearance, either meaningful or unconstrained, given that the effective choice is often between consenting to a community penalty or risking imprisonment' (at page 18). The Paper argues that it is more important that the offender shows continued willingness to comply with the supervisor throughout the sentence. For that reason, the Government proposes to abolish the need for consent to any community penalty. (For the rather different arguments concerning consent and community service orders see 17.16.)

**17.6** A copy of the order must be given to the offender as well as to the probation officer assigned to the court, to the supervising officer, and to the person in charge of any institution (such as a hospital or hostel) in which the order requires him to reside (see 17.38ff).

## Incompatible disposals

**17.7** Because, until 1991, a probation order was made 'instead of sentencing' the offender, there were certain measures, such as a fine or a CSO, with which it could not be combined. However, it is now acceptable to combine a probation order with other community penalties either formally in a combination order (see 17.21) or separately with, for example, a curfew order (see 17.23). It continues to be improper to combine a probation order with a custodial sentence on the ground that a custodial sentence would prevent the probation order from beginning to operate forthwith, as it should (*Evans* (1958) 43 Cr App Rep 66). Nor should a probation order be made by a court which passes a suspended sentence on the same person for another offence (s 22 PCCA 73). (What it can do is to supplement a suspended sentence—if it exceeds 6 months in length—with a suspended sentence supervision order: see 17.30 ff.) Obviously a conditional or absolute discharge for the same offence would be a nonsense: and statute expressly deals with the substitution of a conditional discharge for a probation order (see 17.27).

## Compatible disposals

**17.8** It is expressly permissible to make a compensation order for the same (or another) offence, so long as payments of compensation for loss or damages for injury are not made a requirement of the order (see 16.41 ff). The same is true of an order to pay costs (see 16.60). A disqualification (e g from driving), a deportation order (see s 6(3) IA 71) or a disability which a court is allowed to impose for certain kinds of offence are also permitted. Being on probation already does not prevent an offender from being made the subject of a second probation order. In such cases the first order becomes ineffective for the purpose of supervision, but if reconvicted while it is still in force he can be dealt with for the offences which led to either or both of the orders (see 17.26).

**17.9** These lists of compatible and incompatible measures raise various questions. The original reason why a probation order could not, as it now can, be combined with a fine was purely formal: that a fine was a sentence, probation was a substitute for a sentence. However, there is some evidence to support a practical objection to fining probationers. Davies (1970) compared the one-year reconviction rates for SL offences of 278 probationers who had also been fined with those of 215 who had not been fined, making due allowance for other variables associated with reconvictions. The rates were markedly worse for those who had been fined. Admittedly the samples were confined to young adult males; it is possible that the difference would have been absent, or less marked, in the case of adults, or women. Again, Davies was not able to say exactly why the rates were worse. In 60 per cent of cases the arrangement seemed 'to work reasonably well'. Difficulties arose when the probation officer himself was involved in inducing the offender to pay; and Davies suggested that this probably interfered with the 'casework relationship' (see 18.14 ff). On the whole, the evidence suggests that coupling fines with probation risks an increase in the likelihood of reconviction. It was disappointing that Lloyd et al (1994) did not look at fines in their critical analysis of reconviction rates.

**17.10** Another question is why a short custodial sentence or hospital order should not be combined with probation. Again there is a formal reason: that a probation order begins to operate forthwith. But that is artificial: its operation could be postponed until release. There are sounder objections, however: the offender should be willing to be on probation; and however willing he might be (or say he is) at the time of sentence, he is likely to be less willing when released from custody. Secondly, since the circumstances in which ex-inmates are subject to compulsory after-care have been defined by statute, it is arguably inconsistent to use a probation order in such a way as to provide this.

**17.11**  A probation order directs that the accused is to be under the supervision of a probation officer appointed for or assigned to the petty sessions area in which he will be living[1]. One of the MCs in that area is designated as 'the supervising court'. The order remains in force for the period specified by the court, which must be not less than 6 months nor more than 3 years. The frequencies of the periods used by courts is shown in Table 17A. This table demonstrates that the most frequently specified period, which used to be 2 years, is now 1 year (but the CC uses periods of 2 or 3 years with relatively greater frequency than do MCs, perhaps because of the more serious nature of the cases with which it has to deal). In either kind of court, periods of 2 or 3 years are somewhat less frequently used for women than for men. Young adults are slightly more likely to get a 2- or 3-year order than are adults.

1.  If he goes to live in another petty sessional area the order must be amended in accordance with Sch 1A PCCA 73.

**TABLE 17A: Percentage of people sentenced to different periods specified in probation orders (excluding probation orders which are part of a combination order[1]) in 1985 and 1993**

|      | Under 1 year | 1 year | 2 years | 3 years |
| --- | --- | --- | --- | --- |
| 1985 | 6 | 35 | 56 | 4 |
| 1993 | 12 | 49 | 38 | 2 |

1.  The longer periods (i e 2 or 3 years) are somewhat more frequent if such orders are included.

**Requirements**

**17.12**  In addition to the direction that the accused is to be under supervision most orders include requirements. Section 3 of the PCCA 73 provides that an offender may be required to comply with such requirements as the court, having regard to the circumstances of the case, considers desirable in the interests of—
  (a)  securing the rehabilitation of the offender; or
  (b)  protecting the public from harm from him or preventing the commission by him of further offences.
Albeit not mandatory, courts frequently include the following, although the requirement to be of good behaviour and lead an industrious life is now regarded by many probation officers as inappropriate, especially since so many probationers are unable to find work:
  1.  The accused shall be of good behaviour and lead an industrious life.
  2.  The accused shall inform the probation officer immediately of any change of home address or employment.
  3.  The accused shall comply with the instructions of the probation officer

as to reporting to the officer and as to receiving visits from the probation officer at home.

## Special requirements

**17.13**   Specific requirements are mentioned in Sch 1A of the PCCA 73:
  (i)   requirements as to residence: before making a probation order containing any such requirements, the court must consider the offender's home surroundings. If the order requires him to live in an approved hostel or other institution, the period must be specified;
  (ii)   requirements as to activities etc.: a probation order may require an offender to participate or to refrain from participating in specific activities. He can be ordered to attend at a certain place for not more than 60 days;
  (iii)   requirements as to attendance at a probation centre: an offender can be required to attend at a probation centre which is defined in the Schedule as 'premises at which non-residential facilities are provided for use in connection with the rehabilitation of offenders; and which are for the time being approved by the Secretary of State as providing facilities suitable for persons subject to probation orders'. The offender may be required to attend for up to 60 days (unless he is a sex offender, in which case no upward limit is specified);
  (iv)   requirements as to treatment for mental condition etc: the offender may be ordered to submit to medical treatment. Such orders, known as psychiatric probation orders, are dealt with in 21.28ff;
  (v)   requirements as to treatment for drug or alcohol dependency: provided that the court is satisfied that the offender is dependent on drugs or alcohol; that his dependency caused or contributed to the offence in respect of which the order is proposed to be made; and that his dependency is such as requires and may be susceptible to treatment, it can order him to undergo residential or non-residential treatment for that dependency.
Probation orders occasionally include what are called 'negative requirements': for example, to refrain from associating with a person or type of person, frequenting football grounds, entering a public house, or visiting a certain city area. What is often overlooked in discussions is that a 'positive' requirement may well impose more restriction on the probationer's freedom than a 'negative' one. A requirement to attend at a certain place at certain times is more restrictive than a requirement not to be at another place. This illustrates the rhetorical effect of words such as 'negative'.

## Day centres

**17.14**   A common form of requirement involves attendance at a day centre for not more than 60 days of attendance, with similar stipulations as to interference with work or education. A survey in 1980 by Fairhead and Wilkinson-Grey (1981) of the 73 day centres at that time open to offenders in England and

Wales found that the primary aim of each could be classified as follows, although many of them had more than one of these aims:

Containment 27
Improving employability 12
Alternative to traditional probation methods 11
Socialisation 10
Socialisation and containment 7
Alternative to custody 5
Education 1

Mair (1988) criticised the diverse objectives and organisation of day centres, but this probably reflects less on the individual centres than on the uncertainties underlying community penalties (see 18.11)

## Termination

17.15   The probationer may be brought back to court for one of four reasons:
   a.   a change in, or addition to, the requirements attached to his order. This is usually proposed by his supervising officer; but his consent is needed;
   b.   a conviction, either then and there or elsewhere, of an offence committed during the currency of the order;
   c.   a breach of one or more of the requirements in the order (see 17.26);
   d.   with a view to the court's discharging the order (under s 11 PCCA 73), usually because the probationer seems no longer to require supervision. The application may be made either by the supervising officer or by the probationer himself. According to *National Standards*, early termination of a probation order should be considered:

   '(a) where the offender has made good progress in achieving the objectives set out for the order and where there is not considered to be a significant risk of reoffending and/or of serious harm to the public. Early termination on these grounds should not be considered until at least half the order has been completed without breach or reoffending; or
   (b) where the supervising officer consider that the offender should be resentenced because the order is no longer appropriate.'

## Community service orders

17.16   Section 14 PCCA 73 provides that an offender over the age of 16 may be required to perform unpaid work for a specified number of hours (between 40 and 240) at intervals over the next 12 months. It can be made by the CC or a MC (and by a youth court if the offender is aged 16) provided that
   i.   the offender consents to the making of the order, the effect of which must be explained to him by the court. (Consent is needed because it has been accepted that the European Convention on Human Rights' prohi-

bition in Article 4 of compulsory labour, except in custodial establishments and certain other circumstances, would outlaw compulsory CSOs.
However, the Government's Green Paper *Strengthening Punishment in
the Community* (1995) suggests a belief that 'earlier legislators might
have been overcautious in their interpretation' and they recommend the
abolition of the need for consent (see 17.5));

ii.   the offence is of a kind which is punishable with imprisonment;

iii.  the court has been notified by the Home Secretary that arrangements for
community service exist for people who reside in the petty sessional area
in which the offender resides or will reside. All English and Welsh courts
are now in this position;

iv.   the court is satisfied, after considering a report by a probation officer (or
a local authority social worker, in the case of a juvenile) and, if the court
thinks it necessary, hearing a probation officer, that the offender is a
suitable person to perform work under a CSO. Note that it is the court,
not the probation officer, who must be so satisfied. But if a requested
report on suitability for CS favours it, the court should not impose some
other penalty instead (*Millwood* (1982) 4 Cr App Rep (S) 281);

v.    the specified number of hours is not less than 40 nor more than 240.
Normally they must be completed within 12 months of the date of the
order, but the period can be extended by a MC acting for the petty sessions
named in the order, if this appears to be in the interests of justice having
regard to circumstances which have arisen since the order was made.
Unless revoked, the CSO remains in force until the offender has completed
the specified number of hours.

## Incompatible and compatible measures

**17.17** A CSO should not be combined with a prison sentence, even a suspended
one (*Starie* (1979) 1 Cr App Rep (S) 179). It may not be combined with a
probation order except as part of a combination order (see 17.21). There is
probably nothing wrong with imposing a probation order in respect of one
offence, and a CSO in respect of another being dealt with at the same time. This
was possible before the CJA 91 (*Harkess* (1990) 12 Cr App Rep (S) 366).
However, Wasik (1993) suggests that such a combination would now be
undesirable since it allows the court to circumvent the obvious intentions of the
Act. A CSO may though be combined with a fine or a curfew order.

**17.18** In 1993 the number of people who began a CSO rose to almost 48,000;
this figure, the highest ever, represented a 9 per cent increase on 1992 and a 40
per cent increase on 1983. The use of CSOs has been upheld by the CA for
offences which are often penalised by imprisonment: for example, burglary (*Afzal*
(1981) 3 Cr App Rep (S) 93) or grievous bodily harm (*McDiarmid* (1980) 2 Cr
App Rep (S) 130). Some sentencers tend to increase the hours if the offender is
unemployed because he is regarded as having more time to spare for rehabilitation
(Jardine and Moore, 1983). Recent trends show the greatest increase in CSOs
for offenders over the age of 21, who now make up 72 per cent of the total.

This reflects not only the growing availability of suitable schemes for adult offenders, but also reflects the dramatic reduction in the number of suspended sentences being imposed (see 10.28 ff).

**17.19**   The types of work provided are very varied, being dependent on local opportunities and attitudes. Examples are
   a.   helping the elderly or the handicapped by gardening, decorating and repairing their homes, or providing them with a shopping service;
   b.   activities with handicapped or deprived children, such as help with swimming or sports;
   c.   helping the inmates of institutions such as hospitals or homes for the elderly;
   d.   assisting in nature conservation;
   e.   maintaining camp grounds;
   f.   making toys or equipment for deprived or handicapped children;
   g.   maintaining churchyards;
   h.   helping in youth clubs.
Sometimes organisers are able to offer the offender a choice of work, sometimes not. In some schemes offenders' first tasks are under close supervision, after which they may be allotted to work by themselves, helping some individual. Most of the activities, however, involve them in working with volunteers or paid staff from whom they can learn the satisfaction to be got from service to other people.

**17.20**   While subject to a CSO the offender is required to report to the 'relevant officer' (that is, a probation officer involved in CS), to keep her informed of any change of address, and to do whatever work, at whatever times, the relevant officer tells him to do, for the specified number of hours. This does not give the probation officer a completely free hand: her instructions to the offender must, so far as practicable, avoid conflict with the latter's religious beliefs and interference with the times—if any—at which he normally is at work or attending an educational establishment. What it does allow is the choice of times which interfere with the offender's way of spending his leisure. Since it is usually his leisure activities which have got him into trouble, this may seem quite justifiable. For example, some courts have expected young men convicted of offences at football matches to be given Saturday afternoon tasks. Some probation officers, however, regard this as an improper use of CS, since it functions as the equivalent of a 'negative requirement' in a probation order (see 17.13).

## Combination orders

**17.21**   Section 11 CJA 91 introduced a new penalty, in effect a mix between a probation order and a community service order. It is an order 'requiring him both (a) to be under the supervision of a probation officer for a period specified in the order, being not less than 12 months nor more than 3 years; and (b) to perform unpaid work for a number of hours so specified, being in the aggregate not less than 40 nor more than 100. The court must be of the opinion that the 'making of the order is desirable in the interests of—(a) securing the rehabilitation of the offender; or (b) protecting the public from harm from him or preventing the commission by him of further offences'.

### Incompatible and compatible measures

**17.22** The combination order, already complicated, cannot be further combined with probation or community service, nor presumably with a sentence of imprisonment. However, there is no reason why it should not be combined with a curfew order, a fine, a compensation order or suitable disqualification. The HO White Paper (1990) appeared to aim the combination order at those offenders who are in danger of receiving an immediate sentence of imprisonment, specifically mentioning 'persistent property offenders ... who have three or more previous convictions'. However, since it is likely to be a more demanding sentence than either probation or a CSO alone, it is not surprising that it is given to more serious offenders. In 1993 combination orders had higher proportions of offenders with violence against the person offences, sexual offences, burglary or robbery (38 per cent) than either probation or CSO alone. In 1993 some 41 per cent of those aged 16 or 17 commencing a combination order had burglary as their main offence, though this proportion fell to 32 per cent for those aged 18–20 and 18 per cent for those aged 21 or more.

### Curfew orders

**17.23** Night restriction orders were first introduced by the CJA 82. Once it is brought fully into force, s 12 CJA 91 will allow a court to impose a curfew order on an offender over the age of 16 who is convicted of any offence. The order may specify different places of curfew or different periods of curfew on different days, but the curfew order may not last for longer than 6 months from the date on which the order is made. It must not involve curfew periods of less than 2 hours' or more than 12 hours' duration. The court must explain to the offender in ordinary language the effect of the order and the consequences of failure. The court must have information about the place or places to be specified in the order, including the attitudes of persons likely to be affected by the enforced presence there of the offender (s 12(6)).

**17.24** Courts are not yet permiited to impose curfew orders since their effectiveness depends on effective enforcement. The measure has proved extremely controversial, both ethically and practically. Mair and Nee (1990) reported on the first three experimental electronic monitoring schemes, which were used as a way of enforcing bail conditions rather than as part of a sentence. They were not very successful: there was a low take-up rate by the courts and a high rate both of equipment failure and of offender violation. Mair and Nee raised several key problems: the risk of increased domestic friction; the involvement of the probation service in a counselling and information-gathering capacity; and the need to reduce the conspicuousness and discomfort of the transmitter-bracelets. Ethical concerns centre around the justice of imprisoning people in their own homes and on the burden it places on their families. The key ethical issue surrounds targeting: so long as tagging is targeted at those who would otherwise be in prison, the concerns diminish (Nellis, 1991). According to the Home Office (1990), the aim of the order is to

> 'enable them to go to work, to attend training courses or probation centres, to carry out community service or to receive treatment for drug abuse. Curfews could be useful in reducing some forms of crime, thefts of and from cars, pub brawls and other types of disorder. A curfew order could be used to keep people away from particular places, such as shopping centres or pubs, or to keep them at home in the evenings or at weekends.' (HO, 1990)

There have been further experiments, but whether and when tagging will be introduced remains to be seen.

### Incompatible and compatible measures

**17.25**  It is clear from the White Paper (1990) that the Government envisaged that curfew orders would be able to stand on their own and be combined with other orders. They can, like the penalties discussed earlier in this chapter, be combined with a fine, a compensation order, an order for disqualification or for forfeiture. On the other hand they could not be combined with either a sentence of imprisonment or a conditional or absolute discharge.

### Breach of community orders

**17.26**  The CJA 91 brought together existing provisions for the enforcement of the various community penalties. *National Standards* make clear that breach proceedings under the Act should be taken whenever a failure to comply is 'serious'. If breach action is not taken when an offender fails to comply with, for example, a term of his probation order, a written formal warning must be given. At most two formal warnings may be given in a 12-month period before breach proceedings may be instituted.

In breach proceedings, the MC may (see CJA 91, Sch 2, para 3(1)):
a.   fine him not more than £1,000;
b.   impose a CSO of not more than 60 hours;
c    where the offender is in breach of a probation order, make an attendance centre order. The original order continues;
d.   revoke the order and deal with him for the original offence, or, if the order was made by the CC, commit him in custody or on bail to appear before the CC, which can then deal with him for the original offence.

### Substitution of conditional discharge

**17.27**  Courts sometimes substitute a conditional discharge for a probation order. This is allowed by a special provision (s 11 PCCA 73). The court must be the court which has power to discharge the probation order (which normally means the supervising court: see 17.10); it must have before it an application by the probation officer or the probationer; it must 'appear to the court ... that the order is no longer appropriate in the case of the probationer'. If the application is granted the probationer is treated in all respects as if the original order had been a conditional discharge for the period of the probation order; and the new order is 'subject to the condition that he commits no offence between the making of the order ... and the expiration of the probation period'. (If he does, he is liable to be sentenced for the original offence). A court may be persuaded that a probation order is no longer 'appropriate' either because the probationer's conduct has been so good that further supervision seems unnecessary (although early termination is more often used in such cases: see Table 17B) or because for some reason continued supervision seems impracticable.

**17.28** Not all breaches of requirements, however, result in court appearances. Quite apart from those of which the probation officer is ignorant, he may well decide in known cases not to take the step of bringing the probationer before the court. 'Breaching' a probationer is very like prosecuting him. The probation officer must initiate a summons or a warrant of arrest. In court he is, in effect, the prosecutor, although he will act as the main witness, usually giving his evidence on oath. The probationer may be legally represented, and is sometimes allowed legal aid for this purpose.

**17.29** From a formal point of view, orders can be distinguished by the ways in which they terminate, for which national statistics are published annually in the HO *Probation and After-Care Statistics, England and Wales*:

**TABLE 17B: Ways in which probation orders terminated in 1993 (with 1982 figures in brackets)**

| | Specified period of order | | |
|---|---|---|---|
| | *1 year or less* | *2 years* | *3 years* |
| | % | % | % |
| Ran full course | 80 (83) | 59 (61) | 56 (52) |
| Terminated early— | | | |
| for good progress | 8 (5) | 17 (14) | 18 (17) |
| for breach | 2 (1) | 5 (3) | 5 (3) |
| for further conviction | 6 (8) | 13 (16) | 12 (19) |
| for other reasons | 2 (1) | 5 (3) | 7 (5) |
| Replaced by conditional discharge order | 1 (1) | 2 (4) | 3 (5) |

As can be seen, 2-year orders are twice as likely to end in a breach or further conviction as shorter orders; and the likelihood of this occurring in the course of a 3-year order is 1 in 4. The older the probationer the less likely is an unsuccessful termination.

## Suspended sentence supervision orders (s 26 PCCA 73)

**17.30** When a court passes a suspended sentence of more than 6 months, it may make a suspended sentence supervision order (SSSO) placing the offender under the supervision of a 'supervising officer' for a specified period. A SSSO can also be made when a court deals with an offender who is already subject to a suspended sentence, if the court does not activate the suspended sentence (see 10.31); the order then replaces any SSSO made when the suspended sentence was passed. The specified period must not exceed the operational period of the suspended sentence (see 10.28), but can be shorter. The requirements of the order are given in the statute as keeping in touch with the supervising officer in accordance with such instructions as he may give from time to time, and notifying him of any change of address. No other requirement may be added, either by the court or by the supervising officer, whose 'instructions' must be confined to 'keeping in touch'. If either requirement is breached the offender may be brought before a MC by the same procedure as a probationer: but the MC's power is limited to fining him. The supervising officer must be a probation officer of the petty sessions area specified in the order, which must be the area in which the offender lives or will be living (another area can of course be specified later if he moves). An SSSO ceases to have effect if, before the end of the specified period the suspended sentence is activated (see 10.31 ff) or if, on the application of the supervising officer or the offender, the SSSO is discharged. Applications for discharge are dealt with by MCs, except in the rare cases in which the CC makes a SSSO but reserves the power of discharge to the CC.

**17.31** The present restriction of SSSOs to suspended sentences of more than six months means that they can be made by MCs only in those rare cases in which they can pass a sentence of more than 6 months. The CJA 91 has discouraged the use of suspended sentences generally (see 10.30), so it is hardly surprising that SSSOs are rarely imposed. There was a fall in the number of people commencing SSSOs to just over 300 in 1993 (28 per cent of whom were women). This was a continuing effect of the CJA 1991 which had already caused a reduction of 26 per cent between 1991 and 1992. Of the SSSOs which came to an end in 1993, 75 per cent had run their full course, 11 per cent were terminated because of good progress by the offender, 5 per cent ended because the suspended sentence had been activated (i e had landed the offender in prison under sentence) and 8 per cent ended early for miscellaneous reasons (such as the offender's death or emigration). As with probation orders, the older the offender the more likely was a successful termination.

**17.32** An SSSO differs from a probation order in 4 respects:
  i.   it can be made without the offender's consent;
  ii.  the specified period cannot exceed the operational period of the suspension; but since this is normally 2 years, and only a small percentage of probation orders specify more than 2 years, this difference is unimportant;
  iii. the court cannot add any special requirements;

iv. a breach of a requirement can lead at most to a fine, whereas a probationer can be sentenced for the original offence.

SSSOs were introduced on the recommendation of the Wootton Sub-Committee (1970), in order that offenders who were dealt with by means of suspended sentences should not as a result be deprived of the guidance or help which a probation officer might be able to give. The Home Office were not, however, very optimistic about the value of this measure, commenting that 'where the offender's motivation to seek help is low the intervention of a probation officer is unlikely to be effective' (*The Sentence of the Court*, 1978). No attempt however seems to have been made at a systematic comparison of the success rates—by whatever criteria—of offenders under suspended sentence with and without SSSOs.

## Money payment supervision orders (s 88 MCA 80)

**17.33** One of the least popular duties of probation officers is the supervision of finees who have been made subject to a money payment supervision order (MPSO) because of non-payment or dilatory payment of a fine or other sum (see 16.27). Most such offenders are young adults, because of the statutory prohibition on imprisoning them for fine default unless an MPSO has been tried. The supervising officer is not supposed to collect instalments of the sum due: merely to 'advise and befriend him with a view to inducing him to pay ... and thereby avoid committal to custody': the supervisor may also be asked to report to the court on the offender's conduct and means (rr 47 ff of the Magistrates' Courts Rules, 1981 (SI 1981/552)). The order automatically ceases to have any force as soon as payment is completed or the offender is dealt with for default. If the duty of enforcement is transferred to another MC because the offender has changed his address, the MPSO lapses and the other MC may or may not make a fresh one. The supervisee is under no specific requirements and for this and other reasons the Morison Committee (1962) considered that 'the nature of the order severely limits the probation officer's relationship with the offender and his scope for constructive case-work'. Its report also criticised courts which automatically used MPSOs when fining young adults, without waiting to see whether they defaulted. Nowadays in some areas MPSOs are entrusted to fine enforcement officers or probation ancillaries, since the statute allows anyone to be appointed as supervisor. The number of people commencing a MPSO has fallen every year since 1989: the total recorded in 1993 were 4,100 (30 per cent of whom were women), the lowest total since 1979.

## Supervising parolees

**17.34** The release of prisoners on licence is dealt with in chapter 14. The probation officer who is to supervise the parolee will have been named before his release, and if the parolee's prison is reasonably accessible will have visited him there. Standard licence conditions are set out at **14.36**. *National Standards* emphasise that the supervising officer should see the offender where practicable on the day of release, and in any event on the next working day after release. The officer confirms the conditions of the license, provides written information setting out what is expected of the offender, and issues the offender with a copy of instructions setting out the required standards of behaviour. Within five days the probation officer should visit the offender in his home, and within 10 days have another meeting at which the supervision plan can be finalised. When the probation officer wishes to vary the terms of the licence, he must apply to the governor of the prison from which the prisoner was released (for offenders sentenced to 12 months to 4 years) or to the Parole Board (for offenders sentenced to 4 years and over).

## Recall to prison

**17.35** The licence may be revoked and the ex-prisoner recalled to prison. This can happen as a result of one of several procedures (see 14.37). Usually it is as a result of a recommendation by the Parole Board (s 39 CJA 91). This recommendation, however, is the result of a report to the Board, via the Parole Unit of the Home Office, on the parolee's behaviour. A serious breach of one of the conditions of his licence, or a conviction for an offence, will be the subject of a report by his probation officer; and if the report is sufficiently disquieting the Parole Unit will consult the Parole Board. A recalled parolee has the right to make written representations against his recall; and if he does so his case must be referred to the Board. If the Board so recommends, he must be released again immediately. Most recalls are the result of this procedure. Occasionally, however, the need for recall seems too urgent for consultation with the Board; and in such cases the Parole Unit itself can recall the parolee. Slightly more common are recalls which are the result of a court order for the revocation of the licence. Section 38 CJA 91 authorises a MC to fine a short-term prisoner released on licence who failed to comply with the terms of his licence, and it may order that he be recalled to prison for up to six months, during which time the licence is suspended.

**17.36** Recalls are usually enforced by the police, who take the parolee into custody and remove him to a local prison. A recalled parolee can be paroled again, and is usually regarded as eligible for parole a year after his recall, if he is still in custody. Approximately 10 per cent of parolees are recalled, to which should be added those who have rendered themselves liable to recall but who are merely warned of this. Of those released under the discretionary release scheme (ie serving fixed sentences of 4 years or more), the Parole Board recalled 256 parolees in 1994: 29 per cent had failed to stay in touch with their probation officer, and 25 per cent had been charged with or convicted of a further offence. About 56 per cent of the recalls in 1994 involved people who had been on parole for less than 6 months: clearly part of the explanation must be that some of the men recalled early were those most likely to get into further trouble. Part may be the difficulties of the first few months at liberty: but see 15.39.

## Voluntary after-care

**17.37** One of the prescribed duties of probation officers is to advise, assist and befriend ex-prisoners who are not under licence but willing to accept this help. This ceases to be an obligation on the service 12 months after the offender has been released from prison; but a request for advice or assistance from any ex-inmate of any sort of penal establishment is most unlikely to be rejected, even if the service is not always able to fulfil the ex-prisoner's expectations to the full. Most such requests are for money, lodgings or jobs, all of which are in short supply. Probation officers have private knowledge of local employers or landlords of rooms who are well-disposed towards ex-prisoners; but not every ex-prisoner can be recommended or if recommended found a place. Small sums of money can be provided out of charitable funds; but this has to be done with caution. Some probation services, especially in metropolitan areas, have units which specialise in helping offenders released from custody, especially the homeless.

## Hostels

**17.38** Little so far has been said about probation hostels. A residence requirement usually obliges the probationer to stay in a hostel. If it does so, or if it requires him to stay in any other kind of institution—but not if it specifies a private lodging—the order must specify the period for which he is obliged to do so, which may be equal to or less than the period of the order. Usually the residence requirement specifies an 'approved probation hostel': that is, a hostel approved by the Home Secretary for this principal purpose. At the time of HM Inspectorate of Probation's inspection of probation and bail hostels in 1991–92 there were 113 approved hostels in England and Wales, providing 2,582 places, a figure which was expected to rise to 3,200 by March 1996. Of those resident in hostels in 1991–92, 69 per cent were on bail, 25 per cent on probation and 6 per cent were under supervision on release from custody.

**Table 17C: Number of approved hostels in 1991–92**

|  | Bail only | Probation and bail |
|---|---|---|
| Mixed | 14 | 28 |
| Men only | 16 | 48 |
| Women only | 1 | 2 |

A further four probation and bail hostels provided sheltered work programmes, three for men only and one for men and women. There is a considerable degree of flexibility; most probation hostels accept residents on bail and they are all authorised to accept parolees and young offenders released from youth custody centres; some bail hostels are able to accept the occasional resident on probation. People under 17 years of age are not admitted as residents; but for most hostels the Home Secretary has not set an upper limit. Some hostels, however, prefer to operate more restrictive age-limits; and in practice, taking the approved hostel system as a whole, the majority of residents are under 30. Barry's (1991) survey of 21 representative hostels in the late 1980s found that their regimes varied from the 'restrictive' to the 'liberal'. Even those whose rules were strict did not always enforce them. Yet in many cases courts were using probation hostels as optimistic alternatives to custody for men whose records of offending and breaching orders clearly risked custody. The court's decision in favour of a hostel, and its choice of hostel, were determined by the advice of the probation service. The result, however, was that men whose history seemed to call for a restrictive regime were often sent to a liberal one (and vice versa). The explanation may have been the limited availability of vacancies.

**17.39** Accommodation remains a major problem for those on probation. Andrews' (1979) study of the use of hostels by probationers and ex-prisoners in four English counties in 1976 showed that roughly half of the men who seemed to their probation officers to be in need of lodgings were homeless, but the other half had homes which seemed unsuitable. Nearly 9 out of 10 of those considered to need a hostel place did not get one. Usually this was because they themselves were unwilling to go to a hostel. The next most frequent reason was that the officer could not find a hostel that could or would take the offender. Similarly those who needed to be found somewhere to live, but were not recommended for a hostel, were difficult to place: only about 1 in 5 were found lodgings, again because they were unwilling or nobody could be got to take them. Most probation departments have arrangements with experienced letters of bedsitters who will accept probationers or parolees; but they do not always have a room to spare when wanted.

**17.40** Concern at the disparate conditions in hostels led to the *National Standard on the Management of Approved Probation and Bail Hostels*, which should be read in conjunction with the Approved Probation and Bail Hostel Rules 1995 (SI 1995/302). The *Standard* applies to approved hostels run by probation committees and to those (17 in 1992) which are managed by voluntary organisations by means of a voluntary management committee. If the warden is himself a probation officer he will usually be the inmate's 'supervising officer': otherwise the probation committee will appoint a 'liaison probation officer' for the hostel, who will also be the supervising officer for those inmates who are on probation. He may also be the after-care officer for parolees. A medical officer must also be appointed to inspect the hostel periodically and each resident as soon as is practicable after his admission.

**17.41** Home leave is freely granted, usually for weekends, and while the supervising court should be consulted in the case of a probationer it usually allows the warden discretion in this matter. If a resident does not come back from leave or otherwise absconds, the warden should tell the supervising officer (and the resident's next-of-kin if he is under 18). Usually the absconder is simply traced and sent—or escorted—back to the hostel; but persistent absconding leads to breach proceedings. Residents make weekly payments for their keep, out of earnings or social security benefits; but the probation committee must also contribute a prescribed sum to the hostel for each resident who is on probation, bail or licence. Other residents must meet the full cost of their keep.

**17.42**   In spite of all these formalities, a hostel is quite unlike a prison or youth custody centre. Usually only one member of the staff sleeps at the hostel, in case of trouble. Relations between residents and staff are relaxed; traditionally the rules are fewer and more flexibly enforced. However, *National Standards* specify certain rules which must be prominently displayed. They also provide that there should be a requirement for all residents to return to the hostel by 11.00pm. 'For residents on probation, any failure to return to the hostel by the required time without an acceptable excuse should be the subject of a formal warning. No more than two warnings can be given before breach action is instituted' (see 17.26).

## Other work of the Probation Service

**17.43**   Other prescribed duties include participation in local arrangements for crime prevention and the relationships between offenders and their victims — or the community at large. *National Standards* provide that in cases involving serious sexual and other violent offences a probation officer should arrange for the victim or victim's family to be contacted within two months of sentence and offered the opportunity of being kept informed of the sentence and 'in due course, of expressing any concerns which they would wish to be taken into account when the conditions which might attach to the offender's release are being considered'. Probation officers may also be given tasks which have little or nothing to do with offending. Most of these duties are concerned with matrimonial proceedings, although officers may also be asked to act as guardians ad litem in adoption cases. Some officers specialise in 'civil' work of this kind. It seems out of place in a service which is otherwise concerned with offending; but it has its origins in the days when the probation service was the only agency to which people of slender means could be referred in matrimonial proceedings. There have been frequent suggestions (for instance in the *First Report of the House of Commons Expenditure Committee for the Session 1971-72*) that it should cease to be a task for the Probation Service; and in 1984 the HO's *Statement of National Objectives and Priorities* went so far as to say that civil work should be contained at a level consistent with local circumstances and the higher priorities which other tasks deserved. Under the Children Act 1989 the courts may require the Probation Service to undertake the supervision of those under 18 by means of family assistance orders and supervision orders. The Act also introduced welfare reports to replace 'custody and access' and some other types of report. These reports are prepared to assist the family court to determine the needs of children involved in separation and divorce. The Probation Service may also provide a mediation service for divorcing or separating couples, aimed at achieving an agreed settlement concerning their children's welfare, without recourse to the full court process. The service has also been involved in the development of intermediate activities for juveniles, in collaboration with local social services departments, chiefly because of probation officers' experience in organising community service schemes.

# Chapter 18

# Philosophies and effectiveness of supervision

**18.1**  This chapter is concerned with the philosophies and effectiveness of those community penalties described in the last chapter. The last decade has seen many developments, provoked both by a cash crisis and crisis of confidence in their effectiveness or their legitimacy (see Cavadino and Dignan (1992)). May (1994) identifies two key trends in recent developments in probation and community sanctions: the movement from a 'welfare' to a 'punishment' model of community corrections, and the political call for community sentences to be tough on offenders. Before discussing these trends, an analysis of the role of the Probation Service, which has statutory responsibility for the operation of community sanctions, seems relevant.

## Administration of probation

**18.2**  The officer by whom a probationer or parolee will be supervised will probably be one of the 6,442 main-grade probation officers employed by the service, although he or she (more than half are now women) may be one of the 1,227 senior probation officers. The number of probation officers has increased by 30 per cent since 1983 (Barclay et al, 1995). Their office will be one of a group, located either at the headquarters of the area's Probation Service or in a divisional office. There the probationer will find an enquiry office, manned by ancillary or secretarial staff, and a waiting room, where he (or she) will meet other clients. His visits, whether scheduled or not, and any phone calls he makes to the office, will be recorded in his file, together with a brief account of anything important that is said. His file is confidential, available only to the staff of the probation department, or to Home Office inspectors, although like any other personal file it would have to be produced if a court required it as evidence.

**18.3**  The probation officer is likely to be the person who wrote the PSR about the probationer, and has therefore met him already and knows quite a lot about him. Roughly half of her case-load will consist of adults or young persons on probation or the juvenile equivalent ('supervision'), the rest being mainly offenders released on licence from prisons or young offenders' establishments. Most of her supervising time will be spent on the probationers and young supervisees: offenders on licence seem to call for somewhat less time. She will make appointments to see the probationer or parolee for about half an hour in her office, usually on a weekday, at times that do not interfere with any work or family responsibilities which the latter may have. The recommended frequency of these appointments is set out in the *National Standards*, and will vary from about once a week in the first few weeks of the order to once a month towards the end of a 2-year or 3-year order; but she will probably insist on more frequent meetings if the probationer or parolee seems to be getting into difficulties or trouble. It is failure to keep these appointments which is one of the commonest grounds for breach proceedings: without such meetings a probation order becomes an empty formality. Nevertheless, the officer will tolerate the occasional missing of an appointment: if she did not, she would have to breach most of her case-load.

### The officer's handling of her cases

**18.4**    Officers have a good deal of autonomy in the handling of their supervisees. Apart from guidance from a senior probation officer, she will have the benefit of guidance from the probation liaison committee, consisting of at least three justices from each of the petty sessions areas served by the Probation Service concerned (or of the whole probation committee of justices and co-opted members if it serves only one petty sessions area). Its function is to 'review the work of probation officers and to perform such other duties in connection with the work of probation officers as may be prescribed'. These other duties may be
  a.   to strengthen the links between the local justices and the Probation Service;
  b.   to assist the courts by ensuring that they are adequately informed about the facilities provided by the Probation Service in its area;
  c.   to offer general guidance to the probation officers serving in its area;
  d.   to contribute towards an awareness of the work of the Probation Service by the local community, and to advise the probation committee of the needs of that community;
  e.   to promote discussion of such issues as may be raised by the probation committee or the Probation Service.

**18.5**    The 55 local Probation Services are not, like the regions of the Prison Service, part of a unified organisation, although the Home Office exercises an increasing degree of control over their management and senior appointments. The secretary of the probation committee is normally an officer of the county or metropolitan council for the area, whose chief financial officer is the committee's treasurer; and a justices' clerk is secretary of the probation liaison committee[1].

1.   The constitution and staffing of London's committees (Inner London, North-East London, South-East London, South-West London and Middlesex) are special.

**18.6**    The Probation Services range in size from Inner London, with 667 officers, to Powys, with 14. The probation committee is composed mainly of justices from various benches in the area, but required to co-opt persons experienced in after-care, and encouraged to co-opt people with other kinds of relevant experience. Each service is managed by a chief probation officer (CPO). The larger departments also have a deputy CPO, and most departments have one, two or three assistant CPOs. Specialised management responsibilities, such as the running of a day centre, are usually assigned to senior probation officers. All grades above the main grade are filled by selective promotion. Posts are advertised nationwide, so that most SPOs, ACPOs and DCPOs have served in more than one area. The appointment of probation officers in senior grades is subject to the approval of the Home Secretary (s 4(2) PSA 1993). The number of officers (whole-time equivalent) rose from just over 5,900 at the end of 1983 to almost 7,700 at the end of 1993, an increase of 30 per cent. At the end of 1993 the number of women probation officers exceeded that of males for the first time (on a whole-time equivalent basis).

## Other staff

**18.7**  The staff of Probation Services also include about 3,000 full-time and 1,770 part-time clerical or secretarial personnel. Other ancillary staff are supervisors of community work, but a substantial number are members of 'court teams', sitting for example in courts in case the services of a probation officer are called for, or conducting on-the-spot interviews with offenders immediately after they have been made subject to a probation order, SSSO, MPSO or CSO. They are also used in day centres and other projects, and as money payment supervisors. The increase in helpers of all kinds throughout the 1970s and 1980s—much greater than the increase in numbers of fully-trained probation officers—relieved the latter of many tasks which do not call for their special qualifications, but may well have changed the nature of probation and other supervisory measures in ways which are not easy to define or control.

## Home Office influence

**18.8**  The Home Office retains a substantial degree of control. Only 20 per cent of local expenditure is met by local authorities; the rest comes from the taxpayer via the Home Office, who are willing to contribute to some but not other kinds of expenditure. General advice to departments is given by means of circulars, and there is a great deal of consultation between CPOs and the inspectors about problems or developments which are specific to certain departments. HM Inspectorate of Probation was put on a statutory footing by s 23 PSA 1993. Inspectors are chosen usually from members of the service who have had experience both of field-work and management, but some have relevant expertise of other kinds. Their function is to advise the Home Office about the general efficiency of Probation Services and to see that government policies are implemented.

The Home office's determination to eradicate local differences in probation practice is clear. First there was the HO's Statement of National Objectives and Priorities (1984), and, more recently, *National Standards*. Over the last few years there has been a stream of reports, policy statements and circulars emanating from the Home Office, culminating in the cash-limiting of Probation Service budgets (see Part V CJA 1991), the Probation Service Act 1993, and more planned changes in community penalties (see 17.16).

## NAPO, NASPO and ACOP

**18.9** Salaries and conditions of service at not determined locally, but negotiated between the representatives of the employers—i e the local authorities—and the Home Office on the one hand, and the National Association of Probation Officers (NAPO) on the other: a system which seems to result in more uniformity, and less flexibility, than local authorities apply to the salaries of their own social workers. It has also resulted in dissension within NAPO: a substantial number of SPOs who felt that their interests had been disregarded by NAPO's main-grade negotiators seceded in 1981 to form their own association (NASPO). Chief, deputy chief and assistant chief probation officers, though many are members of NAPO, have their own Association of Chief Officers of Probation (ACOP). All three associations are consulted on policy matters by the Home Office. Although taking part in negotiations is an important function of NAPO, which represents not only probation officers but also many of the service's ancillary staff, it is also concerned with professional practice and standards, with sentencing law and new ideas for non-custodial disposal of offenders, both adult and juvenile. It has local branches, one for each large service or combination of smaller services.

## Objectives and priorities

**18.10** Inevitably, among 55 independent Probation Services and three distinct associations of their members there are widely diverging views on the relative importance of the services' many tasks, as well as on the ways in which they should be carried out. For some officers the traditional 'supervising, advising, assisting and befriending' of probationers is the prime function. Others attach more value to civil work in the divorce courts, or to the preparation of PSRs. As a response to what was seen by many as the Government's increasing interference, ACOP, CCPC and NAPO jointly produced a document in 1987 *Probation: the Next Five Years*. This was followed by ACOP's own *More Demanding than Prison* (1988) which adopted the Government's more punitive stand. All three organisations have continued to publish strong critiques of the Government's proposals, 'resisting or ameliorating the implications of the punishment in the community era' (May (1994)).

## The ambiguity of community penalties

**18.11** The history of community service orders well illustrates what may be called the 'ambiguity' of penal measures. When the Wootton Sub-Committee recommended the innovation they recognised its 'appeal to adherents of different varieties of penal philosophy. To some, it would be simply a more constructive and cheaper alternative to short sentences of imprisonment; by others it would be seen as introducing into the penal system a new dimension with an emphasis on reparation to the community; others again would regard it as a means of giving effect to the old adage that the punishment should fit the crime; while still others would stress the value of bringing offenders into close touch with those members of the community who are in most need of help and support.

... What attracts us, however, is the opportunity which it could give for constructive activity in the form of personal service to the community, and the possibility of a changed outlook on the part of the offender. We would hope that offenders ... would see it in this light, and not as wholly negative and punitive.' (ACPS, 1970)

Most of these aims were echoed by the official pamphlet *The Sentence of the Court*, although like the Wootton Sub-Committee it took as the primary purpose of the CSO the provision of a constructive alternative for those offenders who would otherwise have received a short custodial sentence. When probation officers and task supervisors in South Glamorgan were asked to rank four possible justifications for CS, the probation officers tended to give highest place to the reduction of the prison population, and lowest place to 'help to the offender', although the task supervisors did the opposite (Shaw (1980), cited by Pease (1981)). The justifications that CS was a 'penalty' or 'reparation to the community' were given intermediate places by both groups.

**18.12** The vast quantity of literature published on community punishments reflects the great diversity of expectations which underlie most of the measures at courts' disposal. For sentencers—as well as for legislators and most members of the public—the primary aim of a probation order must be to reduce—to nil if possible—the frequency and seriousness of the offender's law-breaking. It is true that statute simply defines the probation officer's duties as supervising, advising, assisting and befriending (s 14 PSA 93), and does not add 'with a view to the prevention of further offences'. To most other agents of the criminal justice system, however, it seems obvious that this is what was intended by 'supervision'. They can point out that a probationer who reoffends during the currency of his order is liable (even if by no means certain) to be sentenced for his original offence. The implication is that probation is 'another chance', and that further offending is an indication that it has failed in its purpose.

**18.13** The modern probation officer is the product of at least 2 years of full-time training in one of the universities or other institutions which offer CQSW courses[1]. Her course will have included the principles and practice of social work (which involve the equivalent of at least one academic year spent in supervised practice, dealing with real cases under the guidance of an experienced officer); human growth and behaviour; social policy, the social services and social administration; and aspects of the social sciences relevant to social work. If she was 'earmarked' as a candidate for the Probation Service her course will also have included some criminal law and information about sentencing. For most of the course, however, she will have shared classes with trainees who intend to do social work of other kinds, and most of those classes are based on the assumption that the knowledge and skills required of her are not essentially different from those of other kinds of social worker, although the senior officers with whom she will have to work in the Probation Service will not always share her view. After finding a place in the Service, she may have taken one or more specialised courses, for example in the handling of marital problems; but these are not obligatory. She may have served for 2 or 3 years as a prison probation officer, or as the local organiser of community service. Probation may be her first job, but she is just as likely to have entered the Service in her late 20s or early 30s, after working in some other occupation, or perhaps as an 'ancillary' in the Probation Service itself (see 18.7). The process of selection for her qualifying course is intended to ensure that she is not merely able to cope with the necessary studies but is also a person who has a genuine interest in helping people who have social problems.

1.  Ie courses leading to the Certificate of Qualification in Social Work, with curricula which have been approved by the Central Council for Education and Training in Social Work.

**18.14**   The way in which a probation officer handles her probationers will depend to some extent on the approach of her teachers and practical supervisors during her training. Equally important is her own outlook on crime and other social problems. She may have chosen the service because of a humanitarian or religious interest in the reformation of offenders, although religious motivation is less common than it used to be. She may regard criminal behaviour as largely determined by adverse economic and social conditions, by the political structure of English society, or by an upbringing in a family which is disrupted, incompetent at child-rearing or committed to criminal ways of life. The HO has proposed a move away from academically qualified probation officers in the *Review of Probation Officer Recruitment and Qualifying Training: the Government's Response* (1995):

> 'The Government believes that there are advantages in relating recruitment and training directly to the required competencies, rather than relying on a new or modified academic qualification to provide evidence of readiness to practice as a probation officer. In this way there should be scope for broadening the intake to the service, including permitting applications from people wanting to pursue second careers, those unable to attend a 2-year course at university, and those with non-academic backgrounds but relevant experience and the potential to be good quality probation officers, and those already working in the service as Probation Service officers.'

One of the implications of this will be a different breed of officer, perhaps one less inclined to the social work ethos of those trained on CQSW related courses.

### Occasionalism

**18.15**   Many officers take a stance which may be called 'occasionalism', using the occasion of an offender's conviction as an opportunity for looking after his welfare. The obvious example is the hospital order which provides him with psychiatric treatment (see 21.61ff). Another example is the care order for juvenile offenders. A probation order is arguably of the same nature. It has to be admitted that the probationer's liability to be sentenced for his original offence if he reoffends while on probation distinguishes him from a hospital order patient, or a juvenile under a care order: probation has more in common with measures of 'conditional diversion' (see 15.37). Nevertheless, since many probation officers see themselves as social workers rather than agents of law-enforcement, their outlook is occasionalist, and their prime concern is the offender's welfare, even if he is not a probationer but a parolee. This outlook is reinforced not merely by their daily recognition of the difficulties under which many offenders have to live, but also by the responsibilities which the Probation Service has for people who have not been involved in criminal proceedings: for example those in need of matrimonial conciliation.

**18.16**  The extreme version of this view is that the Probation Service should cease to be involved in carrying out any non-custodial measure which is ordered by a criminal court. Harris (1977) supported this with the argument that probation officers are ineffective as crime-reducers, but good at social work. He did not discuss who would bear the responsibility for carrying out non-custodial sentences if his proposals were implemented.

**18.17**  An extreme policy of another kind was offered by Hilary Walker and Beaumont (1981), who saw the primary task of probation officers as attacking the features of English society which create so many practical difficulties and disadvantages for petty offenders. 'Socialist probation practice' consists chiefly of campaigns and 'oppositional work', although the authors also advise officers to safeguard themselves against criticism and disciplinary action by co-operating with colleagues, keeping the minimum of required records, and shouldering their share of the day-to-day work of the Service, but 'setting realistic limits so as not to wear themselves out' (1981). Many probation officers, however, who believe in socialist probation practice are also genuinely committed to helping their clients.

**18.18**  Bottoms and McWilliams (1979) suggested that the notion of 'help' should replace that of 'treatment'. They would not abolish the crime-reducing function of the Service, but since they regarded both 'treatment' and help as ineffective for this purpose the only possibility for fulfilling this function seemed to them to lie in crime-preventive work with local communities, and only when local communities are willing co-operators. More recently, Bottoms (1989) has offered proposals for a Probation Service organised around the principles of intermediate sanctions; probation as a social work agency; and a service coherently related to other agencies and to courts. This need to relate to other agencies has led others to urge the Probation Service to move centre stage. Thus Faulkner (1989) suggested that probation officers should not see themselves as the 'good guys' of the criminal justice system; instead they should help make the system as a whole 'good'. Harris (1992) now argues that the Probation Service should engage increasingly with the police, sentencers, victims and others to develop community-based criminal justice provisions which may make a contribution to reducing the use of prison. However, belief in the rehabilitative ideal (see 9.27) lives on and many probation officers remain deeply sceptical about the underlying philosophy of punishment in the community. Nellis (1995) tries to balance the welfare ethic with the new management culture, which he calls 'benevolent corporatism'. He suggests that the Probation Service should develop its role as a community justice agency built around 'the linked notions of anti-custodialism, restorative justice and community safety'. These ideological uncertainties, coupled with financial constraints, leave the Probation Service confused. Add to this the lack of empirical support from the US for approaches which are premised largely on surveillance and control, and which fail to address the underlying social and personal correlates of offending behaviour (McIvor, 1992) and many are left sceptical.

## The efficacy of community disposals

**18.19** The efficacy of community penalties can be assessed either by reconviction rates or by the extent to which they persuade sentencers to reduce their use of custodial sentences without too obvious an increase in reoffending. As we saw in 7.37, Lloyd et al (1994) compared the 2-year reconviction rates of nearly 18,000 men and women aged 17 or older who had received either custodial sentences or community disposals, making due allowances for differences in gender, age and criminal histories (see Table 7C). Reconviction rates after probation or community service were slightly better than after a custodial sentence; but rates after probation with special requirements (ie of the kind now permitted by Sch 1A PCCA 73, as amended) were slightly worse. The explanation of these conflicting outcomes may be that sentencers, on the advice of probation officers, were adding special requirements in cases in which the offenders' likelihood of reconviction was greater than predicted by their criminal histories. The alternative—perhaps too cynical—explanation is that there was something about the addition of special requirements that increased the likelihood of reconviction—for example, forming associations with other offenders in ways which ordinary probation does not involve.

## Intensifying probation

**18.20** Ordinary probation, as we have seen, is not a very demanding experience. If it reduces reconviction rates at all, then—in theory at least—intensifying the experience should produce better results. Experiments on these lines, in the early 70s, involved four probation areas, 475 subjects and 425 controls. The supervisors of the 475 subjects had their case-loads reduced so that they saw their probationers much more often (Folkard et al, 1976). The chief finding of the IMPACT study, as it was called, was that the 1-year and 2-year reconviction rates were worse after intensified probation than after ordinary supervision. It may have been unfortunate that many of the subjects were young adult males, who do not usually respond well to supervision; but the hard-headed conclusion may be that probation, whether intensified or not, is unlikely to have much effect on young adult males. But 'intensification' can take more than one form. In 1990 a new attempt was launched to study the effectiveness of intensified probation (Mair et al, 1994). This time, however, 'intensified' meant 'with specially required activities' and not simply 'with more frequent contact with supervisors'. Reconviction data have not yet been published, though Mair et al conclude that the IP projects were 'reasonably successful'. However, they acknowledge that success is a matter of degree. One major criticism which they raised was of lack of innovation in IP programmes. They offer a variety of reasons why a conducive atmosphere or framework for innovation did not exist: lack of ability to innovate, lack of time, confusion with other initiatives, lack of resources, reluctance to commit resources, fear of failure, the constraints of the statutory framework, and disagreement with the concept. Somewhat ironically, at the same time, they suggest that IP can make a contribution to culture change in probation. However, there is a danger if the punitive approach is pushed too far: as Bottoms (1995) points out, 'the normative commitments of offenders (including the perceived legitimacy of legal institutions and those officials who put the law into practice) may be lost'.

**18.21** It is not surprising that many probation officers have taken the line of the Morison Committee (see 7.4), arguing that reconvictions are a misleading criterion of effectiveness, and that their work should be judged as social work. This poses severe problems for evaluators, since the objectives of social workers not only vary from client to client—as they should—but also are often defined in ways which make success very difficult to assess with any pretence to objectivity. The IMPACT team made an attempt to use social criteria. Some of their findings suggested that by these standards intensive probation was more effective than ordinary probation:

   i.   by the time their probation order ended 'intensive probationers' were better off financially than the controls;
   ii.  most of them were using their leisure in better ways;
   iii. more of them had non-delinquent male friends;
   iv.  more of them had been discharged early for good progress (this may of course have been due to the greater optimism of their supervising officers).

On the other hand

   v.   more of them were known to have unsolved family problems (but perhaps because their officers knew more about them through more frequent contacts);
   vi.  more of them were said to have had casual as distinct from steady jobs.

**18.22** This comparison was more encouraging. It is arguable, however, that if 'social criteria' are to replace reconvictions it is not *sufficient*—though it is probably *relevant*—to apply the same social criteria to the progress of every client. The objectives which the probation officer has in mind for individual clients should also be taken into account. For example, if she considers—better still, if the client also considers—that the latter's main problem is heavy drinking, his future alcohol consumption must be a criterion in his case, although not necessarily in another case.

**18.23** Another measure of success might be the extent to which community penalties replace prison. If cost is important, then certainly they are cheaper than prison. The National Probation Survey (1992) found that a probation order cost only £1,060 per annum in 1990/1 and a CSO only £1,020 per annum. Put another way, a CSO cost £810 per completed case and probation £1,410 per completed case (1992/3 costs). Yet are they being used as an alternative to prison? The evidence is again mixed. The prison population continues to rise (see 10.1). CSOs have tended to be used for offenders who would otherwise have been fined or put on probation, although sometimes for those who had breached a requirement of a probation order, or reoffended while under a suspended sentence. It was estimated by Pease et al (1977) that only about half of the CSOs in the mid-1970s actually diverted the offenders from custodial sentences. Perhaps the percentage would have been higher if legislators had enacted that CSOs were not to be used unless the appropriate sentence would otherwise have been one of immediate custody (as s 22(2) PCCA 73 did in the case of suspended sentences). Since this restriction on the suspended sentence was included in the Act which also introduced CSOs, it must have been decided not to apply it to CSOs, and thus to allow courts freedom to use it as they thought best. McIvor's Scottish research (1990) was in line with earlier studies which concluded that community service was diverting about 40-50 per cent of offenders from an immediate custodial sentence. She concluded that, in Scotland, the proportion so diverted between 1980 and 1986 had dropped from 47 per cent to 42 per cent. There is clearly a very real risk that as more community penalties become available, they may be increasingly used not for those at risk of going to prison, but for those who might otherwise have been dealt with by means of an alternative penalty such as a fine.

## Voluntary organisations

**18.24** The Home Office's discussion paper *Partnership in dealing with Offenders in the Community* (1990) raised concerns among many probation officers that the HO was determined to move key tasks away from the Probation Service to voluntary organisations. A percentage of a probation service's budget must now be earmarked to support 'the independent sector'. Thus, many voluntary organisations were used in the IP schemes discussed in Mair et al (1994). However, while *National Standards* stress the need for effective liaison with independent sector agencies, there has been little discussion of accountability when anything goes wrong.

## The future

**18.25** In March 1995 the Government produced a White Paper, *Strengthening Punishment in the Community* suggesting a single integrated community sentence—which might be designated 'the community sentence'—replacing and incorporating all the current orders available in the adult courts. Within this, courts would have an increased discretion to determine the content of the community sentence in individual cases and to decide what restrictions and compulsions should apply to offenders: 'the essential proposed change is that the Probation Service should provide the community sentences which the courts consider to be required for individual offenders, rather than the courts having to select from the restricted range of sentences which the Probation Service is able to offer'. The key question here must be how the courts will know what is required. The White Paper merely suggests the matching of sentence elements to the three principal purposes of punishment in the community: restriction of liberty, reparation and prevention of reoffending.

# Chapter 19

# The control of stigma

**19.1** In the belief that offenders suffer from publicity to an extent that is unjust or that impedes their rehabilitation (according to the standpoint of the believer), various efforts have been made to limit this publicity by statute.

## Youth courts (s 49 CYPA 33, as amended by s 49 CJPOA 94)

**19.2** The most thorough of these efforts has been to protect children and young persons who are tried in youth courts. Although they are outside the scope of this book, the nature of the provisions is worth noting. The main one is that no newspaper report or radio or television broadcast of any proceedings in a youth court is allowed to reveal the name, address, school or any particulars calculated to lead to the identification of any child or young person concerned in the proceedings (whether as defendant or as witness), or to publish any picture of the child or young person. The same restriction applies to appeals. Youth courts can allow exceptions in individual cases if, on an application by or on behalf of the DPP, they are satisfied that making the exception would avoid injustice to the child or young person, or is necessary to enable him or her to be apprehended. The result is that while reporters can attend the proceedings, and the news media can report the nature of them (for instance that a 15-year-old boy was found guilty of burglary), they may publish nothing that helps to identify him. Members of the public are not admitted to the proceedings, although research workers, trainees of various kinds, and other people with a professional interest may receive permission to be present. Official law reports use initials instead of names (eg *C v DPP* [1995] 1 AC 1).

## Juveniles in other courts (s 49 CYPA 33, and s 57 CYPA 63)

**19.3** If a child or young person is concerned in proceedings in another sort of court—such as the CC or an ordinary MC—the position is reversed. The public are not usually excluded from the court, and it requires a direction of the court to give the defendant or witness the protection against publicity described in the previous paragraph. Such directions are usually given, but sometimes forgotten or deliberately omitted: for example in the case of a girl of 11 who was convicted in 1968 of killing two small boys. The result was that her subsequent career was followed by the news media until her release from prison in 1981, at the age of 24, and for several years after. The boys who killed James Bulger in 1994 are likely to suffer the same attentions.

**19.4**  This distinction between youth courts and other criminal courts is an understandable result of the way in which youth courts developed, but is not easy to defend today. If the aim of the provision is to protect children and young persons from stigma, it is hard to see why they should receive automatic protection when dealt with for everyday offences in youth courts but not when tried for the most stigmatising offences—such as homicide or rape—in the CC. If this is defended on the ground that such grave offences deserve stigma as well as punishment, this begs a question which will be discussed later in this chapter. It also draws too sharp a distinction between the moral culpability of juveniles with whom youth courts deal and those who are tried in higher courts. A less moralistic defence would be that those whose offences require trial on indictment are dangerous; but again this assumes too much, as well as making a similarly exaggerated distinction between the clientele of higher and youth courts. It would be simple to remove the anomaly by applying section 49 of the 1933 Act to all criminal courts, if not to courts of other kinds as well.

## Adults

**19.5**  Where adult witnesses or defendants are concerned, ordinary criminal courts have no power to prohibit the news media from identifying individuals. They may decide to conduct proceedings in camera (ie without the presence of reporters or the public), as sometimes happens when children are giving evidence about sexual matters, or in trials concerned with state security[1]. Sometimes a witness is allowed to identify himself privately to the court, for instance by giving his name and address on paper instead of aloud: this is the regular practice in the case of witnesses who claim to have been blackmailed. Occasionally courts request the news media not to identify a defendant or witness, but the request has no legal force, and is occasionally ignored.

1.  And without sitting in camera they may order publication of reports of proceedings, or parts of them, to be postponed in the interests of the administration of justice (s 4 Contempt of Court Act 1981); but it is unclear whether the power can be used in such a way as to protect parties permanently against identification.

## Rape cases

**19.6**  There are only two kinds of case in which the news media can be restrained. One is when the identification of an adult would, because of the nature of the case, identify a juvenile who has been involved in the proceedings. In such cases an order made under s 49 CYPA 33 would apply to the adult as well as the juvenile. The other is the victim in committal proceedings and trials concerned with a 'rape offence' (ie rape, attempted rape, aiding rape etc). If still alive she must not be identified, unless the trial judge is satisfied that this would be in the public interest or (as a result of a defence application) that public identification is needed to induce potential witnesses to come forward, and that otherwise the conduct of the defence is likely to be substantially prejudiced (s 4 Sexual Offences (Amendment) Act 1976). Logical chauvinists inserted a similar protection (in s 6) for the defendant in rape trials, but it was unpopular, and was repealed 12 years later (although the rapist's anonymity is still sometimes protected because the victim was his wife, as in *R v R* [1992] 1 AC 599).

**19.7** In any case legal restrictions on the news media do not prevent friends, acquaintances or other people who know the defendant from attending the trial. It is not too difficult to find out when this is due; the only problem is being sure of getting one of the limited number of seats if the occasion has attracted public interest. The assumption that excluding the public would remove an important protection against injustice is very strong, although the procedural safeguards developed by English law go far beyond what is understood by the man in the street. It is only from youth courts that the public is excluded as a matter of course; and the extension of this exclusion to adult courts has never been seriously considered by the legislature.

### Cautioned and discharged offenders (s 1C PCCA 73)

**19.8** The identities of offenders who are cautioned instead of being prosecuted are confidential, although cautions are recorded, and may be mentioned in antecedents reports (see 2.3ff). Until 1991 offenders who were dealt with by means of a probation order or a discharge were 'deemed' not to be' convicted. But the increasing use of probation for fairly serious or repeated offending made this inappropriate, and s 8 CJA 91 deprived probationers of this privilege. When an offender is convicted and discharged, however, the conviction is still 'deemed not to be' a conviction (except for the purpose of the proceedings resulting in the discharge and any subsequent proceedings taken against the offender for a breach of the conditions of a conditional discharge or proceedings for a subsequent offence committed during the currency of a conditional discharge). The conviction is also to be disregarded for the purpose of any enactment which imposes, authorises or requires any disqualification or disability in the case of persons convicted; but an exception is a conviction which permits disqualification from driving or the endorsement of a driver's licence (ss 46 RTOA 88). Convictions leading to discharges have been held not to be convictions for purposes such as matrimonial separation orders (*Cassidy* [1959] 3 All ER 187), the proceedings of a professional tribunal (*Pharmaceutical Society of Great Britain* [1981] 2 All ER 805), or a recommendation for deportation (*Akan* (1972) 56 Cr App Rep 716). The provision does not affect the offender's right of appeal against conviction (s 66 CJA 82) or the restoration of property as a consequence of conviction (s 13 PCCA 73). Nor does the section debar police from including a mention of the offence in antecedents reports for sentencers. If the offender was over 17 at the time of the conviction, and if the conditional discharge is subsequently superseded by a sentence for the offence, the original conviction is no longer 'deemed not to be' one. Otherwise, however, the discharged offender can safely deny having been convicted, for example when applying for a job. Magistrates who want to protect a convicted offender from the stigma of conviction, while at the same time penalising him, sometimes discharge him with an order to pay costs, instead of fining him.

## The Rehabilitation of Offenders Act 1974

**19.9** The Rehabilitation of Offenders Act 1974 (ROA 74) is an interesting attempt to extend this sort of protection, with equally interesting exceptions. Under it an offender's conviction becomes 'spent' after the lapse of a period which varies according to the nature of his sentence. He then becomes a 'rehabilitated person', and is to be treated for all purposes in law as a person who has not committed or been charged with or prosecuted for or convicted of or sentenced for the offence (s 4). This applies even to judicial proceedings[1], but with exceptions, of which the most important are criminal proceedings (ss 4 and 7). Such proceedings apart, if he—or anyone else—is asked for information about his previous convictions, offences, conduct or circumstances the question is to be treated as not relating to spent convictions[2], and he is not subject to any liability or otherwise prejudiced in law because of any failure to acknowledge or disclose such convictions. Any obligation to disclose matters to anyone else does not extend to a spent conviction[2], and it is not a proper ground for dismissing or excluding someone from any office, profession, occupation or employment, or for prejudicing him in any occupation or employment. The Act applies to convictions incurred before it came into operation.

1. Including proceedings before a tribunal, body or person having power by virtue of enactment, law, custom, practice or rules of an association, institution, profession, occupation or employment, or arbitration agreement, to determine any question affecting anyone's rights, privileges, obligations or liabilities, or to receive evidence affecting the determination (s 4(6)). For the application of the Act to the law of defamation, see s 8.
2. Or 'any circumstances ancillary to' them. These include the offence(s) which were the subject of the conviction, the conduct constituting the offence(s), any process or proceedings preliminary to the conviction, any sentence for it, any proceedings for reviewing it or the sentence (eg by appeal) and anything done in pursuance of or undergone in compliance with the sentence (s 4(5)).

**19.10** The 'rehabilitation periods' after which a conviction becomes spent begin on the date of the conviction. They are detailed in Appendix B, and vary greatly according to the sentence, as some examples show:
- after an absolute discharge: 6 months;
- after a conditional discharge or binding-over: one year or the currency of the order etc., whichever is longer;
- after a detention centre order: 3 years;
- after a fine, probation order or community service order: 5 years;
- after a hospital order: 5 years or 2 years after the order ceases to have effect, whichever is later;

- after a sentence of imprisonment for not more than 6 months: 7 years;
- after a sentence of imprisonment for more than 6 months but not more than 30 months: 10 years;
- after a sentence of imprisonment for more than 30 months: never.

If the offender is under 18 when sentenced custodially, fined, or made subject to community service, the period for an adult is halved. It is not halved after a discharge or a hospital order.

**19.11**  The variations are striking, especially when compared with the simplicity of, say, Germany's rehabilitation periods: 5 years for minor offences, 10 years for serious ones, irrespective of the nature of the sentence. The reasoning which led to the complex British provision was that of the Gardiner Committee (1972): 'clearly the more serious the offence the longer it will be before one can be reasonably sure that the offender has reformed' (it was assumed that the seriousness of the offence would be reflected by the sentence). This was, however, contrary to the known facts. Crimes of serious personal violence or sexual molestation are the least likely to be repeated, with the exception of violence by terrorists or professional robbers. It is trivial offences such as further drunkenness, indecent exposure, pilfering or soliciting, which are the most repetitive. What the Committee could have said was that the more serious the offence the more serious for other people will be the consequences of mistakenly treating the offender as unlikely to repeat it. But that would have been relevant only to the protection of other people against serious harm. It is hardly arguable that everyone sentenced to more than 30 months' imprisonment is so dangerous that his or her conviction should never become spent. Again the Committee could have argued, retributively, that graver offences *deserve* a longer wait before 'rehabilitation'; but that would have been alien to their philosophy. The alternative argument which they did offer was that to treat all offenders alike as regards the waiting-time would be 'too radical to command general support'. This sounds like their real reasoning, and the rest like pseudo-science.

**19.12**  However that may be, there are plenty of exceptions to the protection afforded by the Act. First, it never applies to custodial sentences of which the nominal length exceeds 30 months. Second, a fairly long list of professions, offices and employments is exempted[1] from the provisions relating to questions asked outside judicial proceedings; so that, for example, would-be entrants to the medical or legal professions, and to most appointments connected with law-enforcement, are supposed to disclose any previous convictions, whether spent or not[2]; and in considering whether to dismiss someone from one of the listed professions etc it is no more improper to take account of a spent conviction than of any other conviction.

1   By the Rehabilitation of Offenders Act 1974 (Exceptions) Order 1975 (SI 1975/1022), as amended by SIs 1986/1249 and 1986/2268, s 39 Osteopaths Act 1993 and s 40 Chiropractors Act 1994. Further exceptions were made in the Financial Services Act 1986, the Banking Act 1987 and the National Lottery Act 1993.
2.  Provided that they are so warned when the question is asked.

**19.13**  Moreover some consequences of a conviction are unaffected by the protection in paragraph 19.9[1] (s 4 as read with s 7(1) ROA 74):

i. enforcement of a fine or other sum due to be paid as a result of a spent conviction;

ii. proceedings for a breach of a requirement or a condition attached to the sentence;

iii. disqualifications, disabilities, prohibitions or other penalties whose duration extends beyond the rehabilitation period.

In criminal proceedings, if evidence of a conviction or ancillary circumstances[2] can properly be given, this can be done even if the conviction is spent. A *Practice Direction* by the LCJ, however, (*Crime: spent convictions* [1975] 1 WLR 1065) said

'... (3) During the trial of a criminal charge reference to previous convictions, and therefore spent convictions, can arise in a number of ways. The most common is when the character of the accused or a witness is sought to be attacked by reference to his criminal record, but there are, of course, cases where previous convictions are relevant and admissible as, for instance, to prove system[3].

(4) It is not possible to give general directions which will govern all these different situations, but it is recommended that both court and counsel should give effect to the general intention of Parliament by never referring to a spent conviction when such references can be reasonably avoided. If unnecessary references to spent convictions are eliminated much will have been achieved.'

1. There is also an exception for child care proceedings , and for adoption, guardianship, wardship, marriage, custody and other proceedings relating to minors (s 7(2)). Moreover, any judicial authority can overrule the prohibition in non-criminal proceedings if it is satisfied that otherwise justice cannot be done (s 7(3) and s 7(1)).
2. See 19.9, note 2.
3. But Archbold (1995 ed, Vol 1, para 8.212) says that this was 'misleading'.

**19.14** Finally, none of the protections afforded to a rehabilitated person by s 4 of the Act 'affect ... any right of Her Majesty, by virtue of her royal prerogative or otherwise, to grant a free pardon, to quash any conviction or sentence, or commute any sentence' (s 7(1)(a)). In other words, the prerogative can be used in the usual ways whether or not the sentence is spent. What is paradoxical is that the royal pardon does not give the convicted person as much protection as s 4. In *Foster* ([1984] Crim LR 423) the CA held that a free pardon does not 'in any sense eliminate the conviction itself'. Yet such a pardon is granted only when substantial doubt has been cast on the justice of a conviction.

## Sentencing and spent convictions

**19.15** As for the sentencing stage, the effect of s 7 is that a spent conviction may be included among those of which the court is told. The LCJ's *Practice Direction* of 1975 (see 19.13) said

'... (5) After a verdict of guilty the court must be provided with a statement of the defendant's record for the purpose of sentence. The record supplied should contain all previous convictions, but those which are spent should, so far as practicable, be marked as such.

(6) No one should refer in open court to a spent conviction without the authority of the judge, which authority should not be given unless the interests of justice so require. When passing sentence the judge should make no reference to a spent conviction unless it is necessary to do so for the purpose of explaining the sentence to be passed.'

Home Office Circular HOC 98/1975 adds that

'... Courts will no doubt wish to take spent convictions into account in determining sentence only when they are satisfied that it is in the interests of justice to do so. In cases where the court proposes to take spent convictions into account, and where they are to be cited orally as a result, the defendant or his counsel should be given the opportunity to refer to them in mitigation of sentence ... . The Secretary of State believes that magistrates' courts may wish to give their reasons when deciding to take account of spent convictions, and to admit oral testimony of them.'

## Use of criminal records

**19.16**   Finally, s 9 ROA 74 makes it an offence for anyone who, in the course of his official duties, has or has had custody of or access to official records or the information contained in them, to disclose to another person 'specified information': that is, information imputing that an identifiable rehabilitated living person has committed, been charged with, prosecuted for, convicted of or sentenced for an offence which is the subject of a spent conviction. There are of course exceptions: no offence is committed

i.   if the rehabilitated person is dead when the information is given; or

ii.   if the rehabilitated person requests the disclosure (or the discloser reasonably believes this to be so);

These exceptions are explicit in the section. Home Office Circular 98/1975 also suggests that disclosures in good faith in the following circumstances would be in the course of official duties and would not contravene the section:

iii.   in accordance with a statutory duty;

iv.   to persons or authorities who, by virtue of exceptions provided in the Act or by order of the Secretary of State, clearly have a lawful use for the information;

v.   to persons or authorities who, though not covered by (iv) will continue to have a proper use for the information. The use, however, should not be one which is confined to assessing suitability for employment. The example given is disclosure to local authorities or other bodies who are assessing someone's suitability for care of children or young persons;

vi.   for official purposes, between officers of the same organisation or similar organisations. Examples given are court staff, police officers, probation officers and social workers;

vii.   by a subordinate official in accordance with clear instructions indicating that disclosure in certain circumstances would be in accordance with his official duties.

The Home Office's list is not meant to be exhaustive, so that there may be other justifications. Finally,

> viii. the Home Secretary can by order make express exceptions, although he has not so far done so.

## Disclosure of unspent convictions

**19.17** If a conviction is not spent, its disclosure is not an offence under ROA 74, but may be a breach of express instructions (as in the case of police officers) or of a general code of confidentiality (as in the case of probation officers). News media in Britain, however, have no code of conduct which discourages them from mentioning the unspent convictions of any adult. This contrasts with the codes of journalism in countries such as Sweden, where it is exceptional for offenders to be identified, even in newspaper reports of their trials.

## Discussion

**19.18** It is usually a conscientious retributivism that makes people worry about the stigma attached to appearances in criminal courts (reductivists' worries will be discussed later). Stigma is a burden on top of a penalty. If the penalty seems to be what is deserved stigma is in excess of that. Yet sentencers can hardly be expected (although they sometimes try) to adjust penalties in order to take into account something which varies incalculably from one offender to another: hence the crude and artificial attempts to prevent stigma or at least limit its duration. The law cannot of course protect offenders against the unpublished gossip of enemies or friends. Even so, the ROA 74 is a half-hearted measure. It assumes that a conviction will be a handicap, but allows it to have this effect at the stage when it will matter most and for a period which may be as long as 5 or 10 years, by which time it will have done any damage that it can do. The illogicality of the variations in rehabilitation periods has already been pointed out.

## Acquitted defendants

**19.19** Nor did the Act attempt to deal with an obvious and everyday injustice: the defendant whose name and situation have been featured by the news media but who in the end is acquitted. Acquittals do not always prevent suspicion and persecution. New Zealand made a brave attempt to tackle this problem in 1975, enacting that defendants must not be publicly identified (with commonsense exceptions) unless and until found guilty . This was too unpopular with the news media, and lasted only a year or so ; but New Zealand judges still have the power to suppress defendants' names in any sort of case, and not infrequently do so (Stace, 1976 and personal communication). The British news media are unlikely to allow even an experiment on these lines. As we said in chapter 5, discrimination can be the result of good intentions.

## The reductivist's worry

**19.20**   The pure reductivist need not worry about desert or unfairness, and tends to reason that stigma serves the useful purpose of warning potential victims of what an offender has done and may do again (see chapter 22). He can argue too that since stigma is feared by many people it is a deterrent which should be used. In 1995 a police force began, as an experiment, to send letters to the homes of car owners who were photographed while kerb-crawling (*Times*, 29 September). There are obvious objections to such damaging ways of using stigma. Among them must be mentioned the claims of what is called 'labelling theory': that the stigma of conviction is one of the factors which precipitate further offending. The difficulty which known offenders have in finding legitimate jobs had been recognised for a long time, before Tannenbaum (1938) even sowed the seeds of labelling theory. What the theory emphasises are non-economic mechanisms which may drive the known offender into further offending. He may find—or at least believe—that law-abiding friends no longer want his company, and may thus drift into associations with the less law-abiding (especially if he has made new friends in prison or on community service). He may come to label himself 'a thief' or 'an alcoholic', and so acquire a self-image which makes him less likely to resist temptation to steal or drink. Labelling theorists tended to ignore cases in which such labels have a beneficial effect, stimulating offenders to show by their conduct that their labels are not deserved. Calling someone a dangerous driver or an alcoholic can improve their driving or their drinking.

**19.21**   Empirical confirmation of either sort of effect is hard to find, as Tittle (1980) discovered[1]. There are studies which compare reconvictions or rearrests after custodial and non-custodial disposals because the former are supposed to be more stigmatising (for example, that of Babst and Mannering[2], 1965); but other factors are likely to be operating, such as friendships formed in prison. The best evidence which Tittle could find was an FBI report of 1968, which

> '... showed rearrest rates for all people released from custody in 1963, with the data broken down by type of release. Rearrest rates were substantially *higher* ... among those who escaped being labelled (were acquitted or had their cases dismissed) than among those who were labelled (incarcerated, fined or placed on probation) ... '

This counts against labelling theory, although other factors may have been responsible for the higher rearrest rates of offenders who were not convicted (for example their acquittals no doubt gave some of them a mistaken confidence in their ability to offend without incurring penalties). In short, the empirical support for this part of labelling theory is more or less non-existent, at least so far as adults are concerned[3].

1.  This may be why not all labelling theorists make so definite a claim. As Tittle points out, some of their leaders, for example Becker and Schur, 'eschew precise propositional statements in favour of "sensitising observations" …'
2.  Babst and Mannering's follow-up lasted for only one year, during which all of their probationers and some of their released prisoners were under supervision!
3.  Nor is it strong where juveniles are concerned: see Hirschi, 1980. Here the evidence is complicated by the greater protection of their anonymity.

**19.22**  What cannot be dismissed is the damaging effect of a known conviction upon a person's prospects of getting or keeping a job. From this point of view, however, it is not newspaper publicity that is the decisive factor. Employers do not scan the newspapers for the names of present or potential employees. If they want to exclude offenders from their employment they ask for references and for declarations about convictions. The promoters of the ROA 74 were trying to deal with this problem, but could not afford to face the most important fact, which is that the time when concealment of a conviction is of most use to an offender is immediately after the conviction has taken place. To concede this, of course, would have wrecked the possibility of getting any legislation through Parliament. Hence the paradoxical compromises which have been described.

Part IV

# Special categories

# Chapter 20

# Young adult offenders

**20.1** The following chapters are concerned with categories of offender for which the sentencing law makes special provision: the mentally disordered, the dangerous, and the traffic offender. Numerically, however, the most important are young offenders, including the age-group known as 'young adults', who at 18 have passed out of the jurisdiction of the youth court, but are distinguished from adults by the law until they reach their 21st birthday. Young adults, whether men or women, account for roughly a quarter of the entire population of inmates under sentence in Prison Service establishments. In recent years the Government has reduced the minimum age for various sentences, and blurred the traditional distinction between adult and juvenile offenders. This chapter therefore approaches its subject by way of measures which are used to deal with 'children' (aged 10 to 13) and 'young persons' (aged 14 to 17).

## Cautioning

**20.2** The cautioning of young offenders was discussed in chapter 15, and Table 15A shows the proportion of offenders cautioned for indictable offences in 1993. The proportion of offenders cautioned remains very high for young offenders: in 1993 over 90 per cent of those aged 10-13 were cautioned rather than prosecuted, and even for 18-year-olds this percentage was 36 per cent. In 1982 only 3 per cent of 18-year-olds were cautioned. While the proportion of those cautioned will decline following HO Circular 18/1994 (see 15.6), it will clearly remain an important part of criminal justice policy.

## Therapeutic optimism

**20.3** The growth in the use of cautions among young offenders is explained partly by therapeutic optimism. It has been assumed for generations that the prospects of preventing recidivism are better if offenders are detected and dealt with appropriately at an early age. Even the decline in therapeutic optimism has been less sharp where juveniles and young adults are concerned. In reality, the reconviction rates of young adults do not provide much support for therapeutic optimism, as Table 20A demonstrates. Indeed, research has shown that whatever measure the court chooses for them, the rates are higher than those of older offenders. When young adults are selected for the most therapeutically-oriented measure of all—probation—the difference is particularly disappointing (see 18.19). Reconviction rates (over 60 per cent within 2 years) are high, and although this is to be expected from the ages, previous histories and social backgrounds of these young offenders, they are higher than they should be. Having experienced a YOI seems to increase the probability of early reconviction more than the experience of ordinary imprisonment (Lloyd et al, 1994).

**Table 20A: Percentages of Lloyd et al's offenders[1] reconvicted by age and sex**

| Age | Sex | | Total |
|---|---|---|---|
| | *Male* | *Female* | |
| 17-20 | 67 | 41 | 65 |
| 21-24 | 57 | 39 | 55 |
| 25-29 | 50 | 34 | 48 |
| 30+ | 42 | 29 | 40 |
| All ages | 57 | 36 | 55 |
| Total | 15,328 | 2,483 | 17,811 |

1. Based on a sample of all adult offenders given community disposals or discharged from prison during 1987. There was a 2-year follow-up period. See Lloyd et al (1994).

**Back to the tariff**

**20.4** Over the same period the sentencing system has been influenced— especially during the decline in therapeutic optimism—by tariff thinking (see 10.20). In particular, the custodial provisions of the CJA 91 are designed to allow sentencers to pronounce custodial sentences of the same length as they would award to adults, while consigning young adults to regimes which are intended to differ from those of prisons. Faced with two accomplices, one in his late teens, the other in his mid-20s, the sentencer can now say '6 months' detention in a young offenders institution (YOI)' to one, and '6 months' imprisonment' to the other. The respect for consistency, which sentencers share with offenders (see 4.39 ff), is to some extent satisfied, even if one sentence is served in a modern YOI, the other in an overcrowded local prison.

**No suspension**

**20.5** Even consistency, however, can still be outweighed by therapeutic optimism. Unlike short prison sentences, it has never been possible to suspend custodial sentences for young offenders. A sentencer who has to deal with two offenders, one of 20, the other of 21, for the same offence can pass sentences of the same lengths on each; but only the sentence on the adult can be suspended. The illogicality of this was criticised in a note of dissent which accompanied the Report on *Young Adult Offenders* by the ACPS (1974)[1]: but the majority of the Council were so convinced of the benefits from the special regimes of detention centres and youth custody centres that they thought suspension wrong. One of the White Papers which embodied many of the ideas in the ACPS Report accepted the logic of allowing suspension, but the arguments which eventually prevailed when the CJA 82 was drafted were that:

i. the suspension of sentences was not especially successful, measured by reconvictions;

ii. the stringent provisions designed to limit custodial sentences for young adults to cases in which no other disposal is appropriate should ensure that they are imposed only in cases in which suspension would be inappropriate.

Behind these arguments seemed to lie the belief that detention centres and youth custody centres offered prospects so much brighter than those of imprisonment that to make and then suspend the offer would be against everyone's interests. It may indeed be better that a potential recidivist should go to a 'specialist' young offenders' institution while he is still young enough to be eligible, instead of prison when he is an adult. However, the statistics for suspended prison sentences show that, however high the reconviction rates, the outcome in a substantial minority of cases is that incarceration is avoided altogether. Despite this, as we saw in 10.30, the move away from suspended sentences after the CJA 91 means that there is little chance of their introduction for young offenders.

1. By Lady James and Nigel Walker. Lord Lane CJ seemed to agree: *Dobbs* (1983) 5 Cr App Rep (S) 378.

**20.6** The chief consequence however of therapeutic optimism where the young are concerned has been the allocation of more resources and a greater variety of disposals to their age-groups. So far as young adults are concerned, this has meant

a. the provision of remand centres and YOIs to take the place of prisons, replacing borstal, detention centres and youth custody centres;

b. the provision of attendance centres, originally for juveniles only, but now also for young adults;

c. the creation of community service orders, which were designed with young offenders chiefly in mind. Community service has already been described (17.16 ff).

## Segregation

**20.7** Almost as important as therapeutic optimism has been the assumption that the young are likely to be influenced for the better or the worse by association with their elders. In its optimistic form this inspired what was called 'the house-master system' in borstals, which laid emphasis on grouping inmates under staff on whom they could model themselves and their values. The pessimistic corollary was the belief that association with older recidivists was likely to increase young offenders' commitment to, and skill in, law-breaking. This has had an even more marked influence on the custodial handling of young males, who are segregated from adult prisoners as much as conditions allow. (Many adult prisoners also approve of the segregation of age-groups, finding young adults too obstreperous or violent for their peace of mind; and nowadays the young, with their quicker appreciation of new technical possibilities for illicit enjoyment—for example with new drugs or weapons—can corrupt their elders.) By contrast, the Prison Department was persuaded by women governors during the 1960s that in many cases association between young adult women and older women prisoners could have a desirable effect on both; so that in their case the segregation of age-groups—which in any case created logistic problems because of the smaller numbers of establishments for women—is subject to many exceptions.

### Remand centres

20.8  Segregation can begin before sentence. Defendants of 17 or over who are refused bail—and the law of bail makes no distinction in favour of young offenders—spend their time on remand in remand centres or in separate parts of local prisons[1]. Remand centres suffer less from overcrowding; but since there are fewer of them their 'catchment areas' are larger, so that their inmates are often less accessible to their families and solicitors than they would be at a local prison. The populations of remand centres are subject to a faster turnover than those of prisons or YOIs, and the only long-term inmates are those who are kept after being sentenced in order to perform essential services. The rest hardly have time to get to know fellow inmates or staff before they are moved on. This, and anxieties about the outcome of their appearances in court, make life in remand centres tense and insecure (see for example HM Inspector of Prisons 1989 and 1993 Reports on Feltham. The 1989 Report in particular called Feltham an unacceptably poor regime. A more positive note is struck in his Report on Lancaster Farms (1995).)

Juveniles under the age of 17 are normally remanded to local authority accommodation. The local authority may place the juvenile in secure accommodation for up to 72 hours in any 28-day period, although secure accommodation must be a last resort. A court may impose a 'security requirement' which allows longer periods in secure accommodation if the child has a history of absconding or is likely to harm himself or another (s 25 Children Act 1989). If local authority secure accommodation is not available, and other accommodation would not be adequate to protect the public from serious harm, and the child is over the age of 12, he or she may be held in police custody. Section 23 CYPA 69 has allowed a court to issue a 'certificate of unruliness' on a defendant over the age of 15. If the defendant was 'of so unruly a character that he cannot safely be committed to the care of a local authority', he can be held in prison, but this procedure will be abolished when s 60 CJPOA 94 is brought into force, so ending the imprisonment of juveniles.

1.  Legally, remand centres *are* prisons, and are subject to the Prison Rules, 1964.

## The youth court

**20.9** The CJA 91 replaced the old juvenile courts with youth courts. All 10–17-year-old offenders who are prosecuted are tried in the youth court unless:
(a) they are charged with homicide (s 53(1) CYPA 1969); or
(b) they are charged with an offence which carries a maximum of 14 years or more (s 53(2) CYPA 33); or
(c) they are charged jointly with an adult.
In these cases, they must be committed for trial in the Crown Court. The youth court is presided over by three magistrates selected from the Youth Court Panel (the bench should include both sexes). The procedure is much more informal than that of the adult court, and young offenders enjoy much greater privacy than do adults: see 19.2ff.

## Sentencing in the youth court

**20.10** As Table 20B makes clear, the range of sentences available for young people is somewhat wider than those for adults. At the bottom of the scale, young offenders may be given absolute or conditional discharges and compensation orders, as may adults.

**Table 20B: Summary of sentences available for young offenders[1]**

| Age | Sentences available |
| --- | --- |
| 10-13 | Absolute discharge |
| | Conditional discharge |
| | Bind-over (of offender or parent) |
| | Fine (for which parent can be made responsible) |
| | Compensation order (for which parent can be made responsible) |
| | Money payment supervision order |
| | Attendance order |
| | Supervision order with conditions such as: |
| | —psychiatric treatment |
| | —educational requirements |
| | —night restriction orders |
| | —specified activities |
| | —residence requirements |
| | Detention under s 53 CYPA 33 for manslaughter and murder |
| 12- 14 inclusive | Secure training order |
| 14 years | all the above plus |
| | detention under s 53 CYPA 33 for serious crimes carrying 14 year maximum |
| 15 years | All the above plus |
| | Detention in a young offender institution (up to 12 months) |

| Age | Sentences available |
|-----|---------------------|
| 16 and 17 years | All the above plus<br>Probation order with:<br>—requirement of residence<br>—activity requirement<br>—probation centre requirement<br>—mental treatment requirement<br>—requirement of treatment for drug and alcohol dependency<br>—community service order<br>—combination order |

1.  Based on an appendix in Home Office's *Strengthening Punishment in the Community* (1995).

In addition some young offenders beyond parental control may meet criteria set out in the Children Act 1989 for the making of a care order in civil proceedings. Children subject to care orders may in certain circumstances be placed in secure local authority accommodation.

## Fining and binding over parents

**20.11**   The maximum fine payable by an offender under the age of 14 is £250, and for an offender aged 14 to 17 is £1,000. Under s 55(1) CYPA 33 the parents or guardians of a juvenile must be ordered to pay a fine, compensation order or costs imposed on a juvenile (though s 57(1) CJA 91 introduced a new s 55(1B) stating that if the young offender is over 16, the court has a power (not a duty) to order the parent to pay). If the juvenile is under 16, it is the duty of the court to order that the fine be paid by the parent unless the court is satisfied that

a.   the parent or guardian cannot be found; and

b.   that it would be 'unreasonable to make an order for payment, having regard to the circumstances of the case'.

In 1988 courts ordered parents to pay in only 13 per cent of cases when juveniles were fined, and 21 per cent of cases when they received compensation orders. The Government's White Paper *Crime, Justice and Protecting the Public* (1990) commented that these percentages were 'surprisingly low' since the statutory provision was expressed as a duty (subject to certain exceptions) rather than as a discretionary power. For this reason the CJA 91 put beyond doubt that, in deciding upon the level of the payment to be made, courts must take account of parents' means and not just the means of the children (s 57(3) CJA 91). Section 58(2) CJA 91 also allows courts to bind over parents to take proper care of and exercise proper control over children. The courts may add a condition to the parental bind-over requiring the parents to ensure that their children comply with any community sentences imposed on them (para 50 of Sch 9 CJPOA 94). This may be imposed for example when a court thinks it appropriate that a parent should take steps to ensure that a child attend an attendance centre or keep an appointment with a supervisor.

## Supervision orders

**20.12**   Since probation orders may now be imposed on offenders aged 16 and 17 (see 17.2), there is considerable overlap between probation orders and supervision orders, which may be imposed on offenders aged 10 to 17 inclusive. The offender may be required to be under the supervision of a social services department or a probation officer for a period of up to 3 years. The *National Standard on Supervision Orders* specifies that the aims of the order are:

- to encourage and assist the child or young person in his or her development towards a responsible and law-abiding life, thereby promoting the welfare of the offender and seeking
- to secure the rehabilitation of the offender
- to protect the public from harm from the offender
- to prevent the offender from committing further offences.

Additional requirements may be included in a supervision order: that the offender should:

(i)    reside with a named individual (s 12(1) CYPA 69);

(ii)   live at a specified place for a specified period; present himself to a specified person at a specified place and on a specified day; participate in specified activities on specified days (s 12(2) CYPA 69);

(iii)  do, on up to 90 days anything that under s 12(2) the supervisor has power to require; remain, for up to 30 days, at a specified place for specified periods between 6pm and 6am; refrain from participating in specified activities on specified days or for specified periods (s 12A(3) CYPA 69);

(iv)   live in local authority accommodation for up to 6 months (s 12AA CYPA 69);

(v)    submit to treatment of a mental condition (s 12B (1) CYPA 69);

(vi)   comply with arrangements for education made by the parent and approved by the local education authority (s 12C);

(vii)  comply with such provisions (prescribed in Rule 29(3) of the Magistrates' Courts (Children and Young Persons) Rules 1992) as the court considers appropriate for facilitating the performance by the supervisor of his or her functions under s 14;

(viii) notify the supervisor of changes of address and to keep in touch according to his or her instructions (s 18(2)(b)).

The rules governing breach proceedings are similar to those for probation orders and were discussed in chapter 17.

## Other non-custodial penalties

**20.13**   As for psychiatric disposals, the availability of special units or clinics for adolescents in some large cities sometimes decides a court in favour of a psychiatric probation order or hospital order (see 21.29 21.36). The Home Office are unlikely to accept a recommendation for deportation which would separate a young offender (even a young adult) from parents with whom he is living in this country. If it does seem desirable that he should leave this country, a young adult with no previous convictions is slightly more likely than an adult to be allowed a 'supervised departure' to avoid the stigma of a deportation order.

## Secure training orders

**20.14**   Created by the CJA 91, these remain very controversial and at the time of writing had not been introduced (and indeed were subject to an application for judicial review, initiated by the Howard League for Penal Reform who argue that the draft rules do not comply with the principles of child protection introduced by the Children Act 89). Under the Act, a secure training order may be made if a child or young person aged 12–14

    a.   is convicted of an imprisonable offence committed when he or she was at least 12 years old; and

    b.   has been convicted of at least three imprisonable offences (not necessarily on separate occasions); and

    c.   has been convicted of an imprisonable offence committed while he or she was subject to, or has previously failed to comply with the requirements of, a supervision order made in criminal proceedings.

The maximum length of the order is 2 years, and the minimum length 6 months. The first half of the order will be served in detention in a secure training centre, the second under compulsory supervision in the community. If the offender fails to comply with the requirement of his or her supervision in the community, the court may order the offender to be further detained in a secure training centre for up to three months or it may impose a fine up to level 3 (see 16.3) Secure training orders will not be introduced until the first suitable premises have been opened. The Home Office has allocated £30 million for start-up costs, and it is estimated that each place will costs £2,000 a week.

## Attendance centres (ss 16-19 CJA 82)

**20.15**   An attendance centre order may be imposed on an offender between the ages of 10 and 20 inclusive. Although attendance centres were introduced, by the CJA 48, primarily for juvenile offenders, two were opened later for young adult men. The maximum number of hours is 36 for those aged 16-21 (reduced from 17 to 16 by s 67 CJA 91), and 24 hours for those aged under 16. The minimum number of hours is 12, except where an offender is under 14 and the court is of the opinion that 12 hours would be excessive. Until the CJA 88 an attendance centre order could only be imposed on those who had no previous custodial experience, but despite the relaxation of this requirement the use of attendance centre orders has continued to drop. Essentially the centres, usually run by police officers in civilian clothes, assisted by civilian teachers, are places to which offenders are ordered to report for directed activities lasting between 1 and 3 hours until they have completed the number of hours specified by the court. Activities usually include physical education, classes in useful subjects such as first aid, motorcycle maintenance and traffic law. The premises are in use for other purposes during the week, and for this purpose on Saturdays. The days and times are chosen by the officer in charge of the centre: alternate Saturday afternoons are the usual choice. The offender must not be required to attend more than once on a given day, or for more than 3 hours. Travelling time does not count.

**20.16** The conduct of offenders and staff is subject to the Attendance Centre Rules 1958, as amended by the Attendance Centre Rules 1992. These Rules are much less detailed than the Prison Rules. In particular discipline is to be 'maintained by the personal influence of the officer in charge and staff'. An offender can be required to leave the centre, and be brought before the court again to be sentenced for his original offence (as he can be for non-attendance). Lesser penalties are 'separation' from other persons attending the centre (which in practice means working or exercising by oneself), or being given a 'less attractive form of occupation'. These lesser penalties can be applied on the spot; the Rules do not provide for adjudications of a formal kind. Return to court however is usually the outcome of repeated absences and discussions between staff and offender.

### Use and efficacy

**20.17** The proportionate use of attendance centres has never been high, and has remained remarkably constant over the last 10 years. In 1994, 1 per cent of sentenced females aged 14-17 were given an attendance centre order; for males, the figures were 2 per cent of 10–13-year-olds; 5 per cent of 14–17-year-olds; 1 per cent of 18–20-year-olds. These numbers remain too small, and the other information too sketchy, to allow of any reliable conclusion that attendance centre orders are more or less effective than other disposals.

### The artificiality of age-groups

**20.18** The statutory distinction, however, between offenders just under 21 and those who are a little older is obviously artificial, as are all distinctions based on birthdays. As ACPS (1974) pointed out, most of the special provisions which are made for the young adult in the sentencing system would be equally appropriate for the majority of men and women in their 20s, and would be extended to them if resources allowed. Even if YOIs are no more efficacious than prisons as places for correcting or temporarily incapacitating their inmates, the quality of life in most of them is closer to the standard which has been called 'humane containment'. In the past improvements in custodial conditions have quite often been introduced in establishments for the young but extended later, as improved resources and staff attitudes allowed, to the prisons: a process which will no doubt continue.

## Detention in young offender institutions

**20.19**  A variety of custodial regimes have been used in recent years: borstal (abolished in 1983); youth custody, detention centres (both abolished in 1988). These have all now been replaced by a single custodial sentence: detention in a young offender institution. This does not mean that all regimes for young offenders are now identical: there are wide variations in regime, from short stay open institutions to tougher, more secure regimes. Although the sentence is to 'detention in a young offenders' institution' it does not prevent the service from reclassifying the offender and allocating him to a specialised unit if his behaviour or security category calls for this (YOIs are 'open' or 'closed', but do not offer the highest degree of security). In any case, if the young offender is not due for release before or soon after his 21st birthday he will be reclassified and sent to a prison. Offenders under 18 are allocated to units for juveniles. Young women however are not segregated from their elders, for the reasons explained in 11.39.

Although some YOIs are purpose-built, some are in buildings which date from the borstal era. What matters more, however, to the new arrival is the inmate subculture. The more selective the system becomes in using custody for this age-group (and perhaps for any age-group) the more formidable the inmates are; and in a closed unit for medium or long sentences the result can be formidable indeed. The new arrival will be exposed to all the risks described in chapter 11, but especially to bullying and to drug trafficking. Ethnic tensions may be another problem. It is in these units that suicidal behaviour is commonest. For greater detail, see Leech (1995) or the reports on different institutions by Her Majesty's Inspector of Prisons.

**20.20**  Table 20C shows the reduction in the use of imprisonment for young adults since 1982, reflecting the changes of the CJAs 82, 88 and 91. The CJA 82 had introduced a new framework for the sentencing of young offenders, allowing a custodial sentence for offenders under 21 only if there was no other appropriate method of dealing with them, because either they were unable or unwilling to respond to alternatives, or if 'only a custodial sentence would be adequate to protect the public from serious harm from him'; or the offence was so serious that a non-custodial punishment could not be justified.

The CJA 1988 made it even less likely that young offenders would be sentenced to a custodial sentence. The details have been amended further by the CJA 91 and the CJPOA 94 such that the position is now that:

   (i)  the normal maximum sentence for an offender aged 15–17 (inclusive) is 24 months, with a minimum period of 2 months ;

  (ii)  the maximum for an offender aged over 18–20 (inclusive) is the maximum which would be available for an adult being sentenced for the same offence, with a minimum period of 21 days.

## Consecutive terms

**20.21**  Under s 1A(5) CJA 82, if a young offender is convicted of more than one offence for which he can properly be sentenced to detention in a YOI, or while serving such a sentence is convicted of one or more further offences for

**Table 20C: Receptions into prison service establishments of young offenders under sentence 1983–1993[1]**

| Age | 1983 | 1984 | 1985 | 1986 | 1987 | 1988 | 1989 | 1990 | 1991 | 1992 | 1993 |
|---|---|---|---|---|---|---|---|---|---|---|---|
| *Males* | | | | | | | | | | | |
| Under 17 | 6,544 | 6,360 | 5,681 | 4,206 | 3,825 | 3,120 | 2,131 | 3,709 | 3,621 | 3,344 | 3,564 |
| 18-20 | 21,072 | 21,647 | 23,200 | 19,815 | 19,458 | 17,924 | 15,053 | 10,290 | 10,998 | 9486 | 9,222 |
| Total under 21 | 27,616 | 28,007 | 28,881 | 24,021 | 23,283 | 21,044 | 17,184 | 13,99 | 14,619 | 12,830 | 12,786 |
| *Females* | | | | | | | | | | | |
| Under 17 | 71 | 101 | 103 | 71 | 59 | 60 | 45 | 95 | 97 | 79 | 102 |
| 18-20 | 695 | 750 | 778 | 709 | 642 | 527 | 445 | 286 | 312 | 265 | 317 |
| Total under 21 | 766 | 851 | 881 | 780 | 701 | 587 | 490 | 381 | 409 | 344 | 419 |

1. Taken from *Prison Statistics, England and Wales*, 1994, Table 3.11.

which imprisonment can properly be imposed, the court has the same power to pass consecutive sentences as it would have if they were prison sentences; and the CA has not so far made any distinction. However, s 1B(4) CJA 82 makes clear that a court shall not pass a sentence of detention in a YOI where its effect is to impose a total term in excess of the 24 month maximum, where that applies.

## Custody for life (s 8 CJA 82)

**20.22** If a young adult of 18, 19 or 20 is convicted of murder or any other offence for which imprisonment for life is the mandatory sentence, the court must sentence him to 'custody for life'. If he is convicted of an offence for which an adult could at the court's discretion be sentenced to life imprisonment, and the court considers custody for life appropriate, it is required to impose that sentence. The court is not obliged by statute to state its reasons for choosing this sentence, but it would be regarded as good practice to do so. Custody for life is usually spent in a prison, although the Home Secretary can and often does direct that the young adult spend the early period in a YOI.

If he is under 18, the sentence must be detention under s 53 CYPA 33 (as amended). The distinction between murderers under 18 and those of 18 or older dates from the provision exempting those under 18 from capital punishment. The only important difference is that whereas custody for life must be spent in a YOI or a prison, detention under s 53 can be spent 'in such place and under such conditions as the Secretary of State may direct', which usually, but not always, means a custodial institution.

## Long-term detention of children and young persons

**20.23** Section 53(2) of the CYPA 33 provides that where a young person is convicted on indictment of any offence punishable in the case of an adult with 14 years' or more imprisonment or is convicted of manslaughter, and the court is of the opinion that none of the other available methods by which the case may legally be dealt with is suitable, then the court may sentence the young person to a period of detention which may not exceed the maximum available for an adult. The section was amended by s 16 of the CJPOA 1994, which extended the scope of s 53(2) to apply to offenders aged between 10 -13, as well as those aged 14-17 (all ages being inclusive). The Act (Sch 10, para 40) also made the necessary amendment to the MCA 1980 to allow such children to be tried on indictment, so bringing them within the ambit of s 53(2). Whereas this power was only used on 105 offenders in 1992, the figure rose to 330 in 1993 and 405 in 1994: this increase may show that judges are becoming less keen to avoid long custodial terms for young offenders than they used to be.

## Payment defaulters and contemnors of courts

**20.24** Young adults who default in payment of fines or other payments ordered by criminal courts may, subject to the same safeguards[1] as adults, be committed to custody, and so may those who commit contempt of court (s 9 CJA 82). The periods for which they may be committed are the same as those for adult defaulters (see 16.32). The committal, however, is to 'detention', so that the period may be spent in a remand centre, young prisoners' wing of a local prison or a YOI.

1. Plus an additional safeguard if the payment to be made is the result of a summary conviction and the court does not commit him to detention forthwith in default. In such cases the court must try a money payment supervision order (see 16.27 and 17.23), unless satisfied that this would be undesirable or impracticable, before committing him to detention (s 88(4) MCA 80 as amended by CJA 82).

## Release from young offenders institutions

20.25   The criteria for the release of young offenders are not materially different from those used in the case of adults (see chapter 14). Young offenders who have been sentenced to less than 12 months' imprisonment will be released on automatic unconditional release at the halfway point in their sentence; those sentenced to more than 12 months but less than 4 years' imprisonment will be released on automatic conditional release at the halfway point in their sentence. Their licences will have no special features, and the local probation service will supervise them.

# Chapter 21

# Mentally disordered offenders

**21.1**  The mentally disordered offenders who are dealt with in criminal courts, and especially in MCs, are for the most part foot-soldiers in a smallish stage army, making repeated appearances as vagrants, shoplifters, drug abusers, alcoholics, burglars, beggars or brawlers. Many have already been in-patients or out-patients at NHS hospitals, either voluntarily or under civil procedures which nowadays do not involve the courts. In order to understand the ways in which courts can or cannot dispose of them it is necessary to see them in a wider context.

### Undetected offenders

**21.2**  Since most of the identified offenders with disorders seem to commit their offences without much in the way of precautions against detection, it is a reasonable inference that few such offenders remain undetected for long. There are examples, however, of exceptions. In the 1970s Graham Young poisoned people over periods of months before arousing suspicion, both before and after his time in Broadmoor, and Peter Cook, also ex-Broadmoor, and known to the Cambridge police as a burglar, raped on at least seven occasions before a chance encounter led to his arrest. Paranoid or sadistic offenders whose disorder does not impair their intelligence and resourcefulness may well succeed in avoiding identification; but they are fortunately in a minority.

### Unreported offences

**21.3**  Even detected offenders are sometimes not reported to the police by members of the public. In such cases the offence is usually trivial and the reason for non-reporting is compassion. If the offender is known to be under treatment— and especially if he is known to be an in-patient of a mental hospital—people often simply report the matter to those who are regarded as responsible for him.

## Unprosecuted offences

**21.4** Even when police are in a position to charge they may refrain because the offender is already under treatment or care, especially if the offence is trivial and he does not seem dangerous. The Butler Committee (1975) approved, adding that if the offender was in urgent need of treatment and was no danger to the public it should always be asked whether prosecution would serve any useful purpose. The CPS *Code for Crown Prosecutors* (1994) deals cautiously with this issue, under the heading 'Some common public interest factors against prosecution':

'6.5 A prosecution is less likely to be needed if ... (f) the defendant is elderly or was *at the time of the offence* suffering from significant mental or physical ill health, unless the offence is serious or *there is a real possibility that it may be repeated*. The Crown Prosecution Service, where necessary, applies Home Office guidelines about how to deal with mentally disordered offenders. Crown prosecutors must balance the desirability of diverting a defendant who is suffering from significant mental or physical ill health with the need to safeguard the public'.

The italics are ours. They emphasise the reluctance of the CPS to follow the spirit of the Butler Committee's recommendation. Mental disorder is to be a consideration weighing against prosecution only if it was present at the time of the offence, and not if it merely developed before the decision to prosecute. It is not to be a consideration if the offence, though not serious, may be repeated (but perhaps 'or' should have read 'and'?). Successful efforts, however, to encourage diversion have been made in several areas, notably as a result of an initiative by NACRO (Home Office, 1994).

### 'Places of safety' (ss 135 and 136 MHA 83)

**21.5** It is possible for a disordered person to be admitted to a mental hospital without the intervention of a court, relative or doctor. This happens 'if a constable finds in a place to which the public have access a person who appears to him to be suffering from mental disorder and to be in immediate need of care or control ...' If he 'thinks it necessary ... in the interests of that person or for the protection of other persons' he can remove the sufferer to a 'place of safety', which for this purpose usually means either a police station or a mental hospital, although it can mean certain other types of accommodation or indeed 'any other suitable place the occupier of which is willing temporarily to receive the patient'. If the sufferer is taken to and accepted by a mental hospital without a preliminary medical examination, he can be detained there for not more than 72 hours in order to let him be examined and observed, and so that any necessary arrangements can be made for his treatment or care. This procedure used to account for more than 1,500 admissions a year, but the number had declined to 859 in 1992–93. Some hospitals are very reluctant to admit patients in this way. The people involved are usually in a very disturbed and sometimes violent state, but not infrequently turn out to be merely drunk or drugged; and the incident often occurs in the middle of the night. If the police are aware—as they usually are—that the local hospital is likely to be unwelcoming, they will probably take the sufferer to a police station and try to arrange for a medical examination there[1]. Once that has been done, any admission to hospital must be 'informal', or 'in emergency' or 'for observation' or 'for treatment', and is thus lost in the statistics for one or other of those procedures. So the true figure for admissions arranged by police is greater—perhaps considerably greater—than the official figures suggest. This mode of admission deserves more attention than it has received, especially since it is the only mode which does not require the attendance of a doctor, at least until the prospective patient arrives at the hospital.

1. Alternatively, the police may decide to charge the sufferer with an offence, such as criminal damage or conduct likely to provoke a breach of the peace, with the result that he is in the end dealt with by a criminal court.

**21.6** The procedure just described applies only to people found in public places. If it is believed that a disordered person is living alone somewhere and is unable to care for himself, or, though not alone, is being or has been ill-treated or neglected, anywhere within a magistrate's jurisdiction, s 135 MHA 83 provides a legal (but more complicated) way of removing him to a 'place of safety'. This is, however, rarely used—from 10 to 20 times a year and hardly ever in circumstances which lead to the prosecution of the disordered person.

## The leniently sentenced

**21.7** If the offender is prosecuted, the information which the court gets about his mental state may lead it not to make a psychiatric order (which may not be possible, for reasons given below) but simply to choose a lenient disposal of an ordinary kind: a bind-over or a discharge. Occasionally sentence is deferred when it is said on the offender's behalf that he intends to seek treatment. Since the statistics do not give courts' reasons for such choices we do not know how often the offender's mental state accounts for them. The last estimate—about 3,000—was made by Salem in 1982, as a result of a survey of 14 MCs.

## The undiagnosed

**21.8** Unfortunately another possibility is that the offender's disorder is not recognised at all while he is being charged, prosecuted and sentenced. Some disorders are not obvious at any time (eg mild degrees of mental impairment), and some are episodic (eg manic outbursts). The offender may refuse to discuss his behaviour with anyone, sometimes for fear of being stigmatised as disordered, sometimes through a more general antagonism to law enforcement. It is even possible for people with histories of mental hospital admissions to escape diagnosis, especially if they use different names. The confidentiality of the central records of mental hospitals' admissions does not allow automatic searches to see whether an offender has a psychiatric history. Psychiatric examinations are routine only for very serious offences of violence or sexual molestation, and even in such cases the offender can refuse to talk to the psychiatrists. So that unless his or her history is known to police, court staff, local probation staff or prison staff, or unless the oddity of his or her offence or demeanour betrays the disorder, or relatives disclose it, it may well go unrecognised. If he or she gets a custodial sentence it may eventually become apparent to the staff; and if it is severe it is usually possible to arrange for a transfer to a mental hospital, or admission to one on release; but that does not always happen.

## Remands for psychiatric reports

**21.9** Suppose, however, that the possibility of mental disorder enters the mind of someone connected with the case before the courts dispose of it. It may occur to the police, to a friend or relative of the offender, to his legal adviser, to a probation officer, to a member of the prison staff (if he is in custody) or to the magistrates or their clerk. If anything is to be made of this possibility the court must be provided with a psychiatric report; for some purposes, two reports (see 21.37ff). In some areas 'panel assessment schemes' operate to alert courts, the probation service and other agencies when a mentally disordered person has been arrested, and to present MCs with co-ordinated recommendations for dealing with them (Hedderman, 1993).

**21.10** It is very rarely that relatives themselves directly make arrangements for a psychiatric report, although they may initiate the process by what they say to an official. Usually it is the defence solicitor or a probation officer who suggests to the court that a report is advisable. The defence solicitor may himself arrange for a report or—especially if payment for this raises difficulties—may ask the court to arrange for one. Sometimes the police or clerks of court are able to tell the magistrates that the defendant has already been the subject of psychiatric treatment, a hospital order or a psychiatric probation order (see 21.28ff).

**21.11** MCs are expressly empowered (s 30 MCA 80) to remand the defendant for medical examination, but subject to limitations:
   a. the court must be satisfied that he did the act or made the omission charged, but need not have convicted him;
   b. the offence must be one which is punishable with imprisonment on summary conviction;
   c. the adjournment must not be for more than 3 weeks at a time if he is to be in custody, otherwise 4 weeks: but this does not preclude more than one such adjournment.
The object of such remands is 'an inquiry into his physical or mental condition before the method of dealing with him is determined'. Sometimes, however, the result is that the court decides to refrain from proceeding to convict him: see 21.60.

**21.12** MCs also, however, have a more general power in s 10(3) MCA 80 to adjourn *after convicting the defendant* in order to enable inquiries to be made or to determine the most suitable method of dealing with the case; and this is often used when psychiatric reports are needed. It is not limited to imprisonable offences. The remand is subject to the same time-limits as a s 30 remand. If, however, it seems necessary to obtain psychiatric reports before proceeding to decide whether the defendant did the act or made the omission—as sometimes happens if the defence objects to that step—the magistrates must use their general power to adjourn under s 10(1) MCA 80. No time-limits are set by this subsection. Whichever procedure is used, the defendant may be remanded in custody, on bail, or to hospital (see 20.15).

## Whose reports?

**21.13** The contents of psychiatric reports are described and discussed in 2.33ff. The usual sources of such reports are

a. consultant psychiatrists, with NHS appointments. Unless they are required by their contracts of service to examine and report for courts they have to be paid for doing so, whether from legal aid funds (if the report is arranged by the defence) or from court funds (if the report is requested by a court). If the defence is not assisted from legal aid funds the report may have to be paid for privately; but it is often possible for the defence to arrange for the report to be asked for and paid for by the court;

b. prison medical officers, especially but not exclusively if the accused is remanded in custody. The medical staff of every large local prison and remand centre include doctors with psychiatric qualifications, who can be asked to render reports to courts as part of their contracts of service. Since prison medical officers see more non-disordered offenders in their everyday work than do hospital psychiatrists, and in addition have had the discouraging experience of trying to persuade NHS hospitals to accept unwelcome patients, their approach to diagnoses and recommendations sometimes differs from those of consultants.

Neither the defence nor the court, however, is restricted to these reports. The 'Harley Street consultant', though no longer a familiar figure in court, is still occasionally brought in by the defence. Moreover it is open to the defence to 'shop around' for another opinion if dissatisfied with a report; and even courts sometimes do so, if given a report which they regard as unhelpful (Salem, 1982).

**21.14** Whichever section of MCA 80 is used, the remand may be in custody—that is, in a prison or remand centre—on bail or in hospital. Bail can be granted on an undertaking that the remanded person will keep any appointment made for interview; but quite often the court insists on an undertaking to enter hospital as an in-patient. In such cases the patient's status is 'informal'—that is, voluntary— so that he cannot be restrained from leaving without invoking the little-used procedure in s 5 MHA 83. So long as he presents himself in court again at the due time he cannot be penalised for absconding or missing appointments.

## Remands to hospital (ss 35, 36 MHA 83)

**21.15** Because hospital admissions on bail so often resulted in absconding, ss 35 and 36 MHA 83 allow courts in certain circumstances to remand defendants compulsorily to hospital for the purposes of a report (s 35) or for treatment (s 36)[1]. The following conditions, however, must be satisfied:

a. the defendant must be on trial or arraigned but not yet sentenced for an offence punishable with imprisonment, or, in a MC, the court must have convicted him of an offence punishable with imprisonment on summary conviction, or else be satisfied that he did the act or made the omission charged (otherwise he must consent to this step by the MC);

b. the written or oral evidence of a medical practitioner must already have satisfied the court that there is reason to believe that the accused is mentally ill, psychopathic or (severely) impaired (labels which will be explained in 21.19ff). The suspicions of the police or a probation officer are not enough;

c. the court must be of opinion that it would be 'impracticable for a report on his mental condition to be made if he were remanded on bail'. Presumably evidence that he is unlikely to keep appointments, or that a period of continuous observation by trained staff is needed, would satisfy the court on this point;

d. the medical practitioner who is to be responsible for the making of the report on the accused (or some other person representing the hospital's managers) must assure the court that arrangements have been made for his admission within 7 days of the date of remand[2]. Hospitals are not obliged to admit patients under ss 35 or 36 MHA 83.

If instead of (b) the court has written or oral evidence from two practitioners that the accused is suffering from mental illness or severe mental impairment (mere mental impairment or psychopathic disorder will not do) which makes it appropriate to detain him in hospital for treatment, the court can remand him for treatment[3]. Whichever of these sections is used, each remand lasts for 28 days, and is renewable, but with an overall limit of 12 weeks. The recommendations of the Reed Committee (1992) would simplify and extend the provisions of ss 35 and 36.

1. But note that persons *convicted* of murder—or any other offence for which the sentence is fixed by law—cannot be so remanded; nor can persons in custody awaiting trial in the CC for offences with fixed sentences be remanded for *treatment* (ss 35(3), 36(2) MHA 83) .

2. If he or she cannot be received immediately by the hospital the court can direct that he or she be taken to a 'place of safety' (see 21.5), which in such cases will usually be a prison or remand centre.

3. If he or she is merely remanded for assessment and not for treatment, he or she can be given only treatment which he or she is willing to accept: the provisions for compulsory treatment outlined in 21.57 do not apply.

## Disposal to the National Health Service

**21.16** A psychiatric disposal after a finding of guilt (ie a hospital or guardianship order or a probation order with a requirement of in-patient or out-patient medical treatment) in effect hands over the offender to hospitals or clinics, usually one of those which are part of the National Health Service. The exceptions are

a. offenders sent to one of the three special hospitals: see below;

b. offenders for whom treatment has been arranged at a private hospital or clinic, as happens occasionally, the cost usually being met from public funds;

c. offenders made subject to guardianship orders, which entrust them to the care of local authorities. Although it was hoped in the1950s that local authorities would develop a guardianship service for the mentally disordered they have been slow to do so. Only 366 non-offenders were accepted into guardianship by local authorities under s 7 MHA 83 in 1992–93 and only 16 into guardianship by other people or agencies. Under s 37 MHA 83 a MC or the CC can make a guardianship order for an mentally disordered offender aged 6 or older; but in 1992–93 only five such orders were made. Efforts to encourage local authorities to develop this service have failed, partly because of costs and partly because of uncertainty about the powers conferred by such orders. CJA 91 gave courts the power to compel social services authorities to say whether they or any approved person in their areas are willing to act as guardians (s 39A MHA 83); but not to compel anyone to do so;

d. offenders serving custodial sentences who receive treatment in prisons or young offenders' institutions: see 21.55.

## The special hospitals

**21.17** There are three special hospitals for patients subject to compulsory detention under the MHA 83 'who, in the opinion of the Secretary of State[1], require treatment under conditions of special security on account of their dangerous, violent or criminal propensities' (s 4 of the National Health Service Act 1977). Broadmoor, Rampton and Ashworth[2] are administered by the Special Hospitals Service Authority. They provide a high degree of security and their escape rate is very low. Most of their patients have come to them via the criminal courts or the prisons; but quite a number (fully 1 in 6 in 1990) are patients transferred from ordinary mental hospitals because their behaviour has been too violent for those relaxed regimes. Criteria for admission to the special hospitals, however, are strict, and they receive many more applications than they can accept. Even so, in 1990 they held about 1,700 patients, most of them under 'restriction orders' for the protection of the public (see 21.51).

1. In this case, the Secretary of State for Health, not the Home Secretary.
2. Ashworth combines two formerly separate special hospitals, Moss Side and Park Lane.

## Secure units

**21.18** The NHS also provides 'medium secure units' for offenders (and non-offenders) whose behaviour is too disruptive or potentially harmful to allow them to be looked after in ordinary mental hospitals, but who do not need the high degree of security provided by the special hospitals. There are 26 such units in the various conurbations of England and Wales, with a capacity of more than 700 patients; and they are supplemented by about 250 places in the 'interim secure units' which some regional health authorities set up before central funds were provided for secure units.

## The sub-divisions of mental disorder (s 1 MHA 83)

**21.19**　The effect of psychiatric disposals by criminal courts cannot be fully appreciated without some knowledge of the general provisions of the MHA 83. In the first place the Act does not define mental disorder: all it does is to distinguish five sub-divisions of it, only three of which are defined. The distinctions are needed because the Act applies in different ways to different sub-divisions. The first of the three defined sub-divisions is 'severe mental impairment':

'a state of arrested or incomplete development of mind which includes severe impairment of intelligence and social functioning and is associated with abnormally aggressive or seriously irresponsible conduct on the part of the person concerned'.

**21.20**　Next, 'mental impairment' is defined as

'a state of arrested or incomplete development of mind (not amounting to severe mental impairment) which includes significant impairment of intelligence and social functioning and is associated with abnormally aggressive or seriously irresponsible conduct on the part of the person concerned.'

In this chapter these will be referred to as '(severe) impairment' for the sake of brevity. They must not be mistaken for precise clinical diagnoses, such as 'Downs' Syndrome': they are merely generic groups of diagnoses for legal purposes. The statutes governing psychiatric disposals do not require testimony to specify precise diagnoses: only to identify the generic group or groups into which the disorder seems to fall.

**21.21**　Thirdly, 'psychopathic disorder' is defined as

'a persistent disorder or disability of mind (whether or not including impairment of intelligence) which results in abnormally aggressive or seriously irresponsible conduct on the part of the person concerned.'

Although 'psychopathic disorder' is nowadays no more than a generic group of diagnoses, and no longer figures in the World Health Organisation's International Classification of Disorders (1990), many psychiatrists use it also as a diagnosis of a rather vague kind in their reports to courts, perhaps because it figures in the Act. Even so, they are usually prepared to be more specific about the type of aberrant behaviour to which the individual in question is prone (e g 'explosive aggression', 'paedophilia','inadequate personality'). The loose use of 'psychopathic' by some psychiatrists—especially in the USA—together with the very low success rate of techniques intended to improve 'psychopathic' conduct, has caused courts to react sceptically. Nevertheless there is ample evidence that there are many individuals whose frequent objectionable—and sometimes criminal—conduct is the result of very abnormal desires or is less subject to self-control or rational considerations than the objectionable behaviour in which most people occasionally indulge. Lack of success in treating or deterring conduct does not rule out the possibility that it is pathological. Nor does it justify rejecting the condition as an excusing or mitigating consideration. These points are of special importance when courts have to consider defences such as diminished responsibility.

**21.22**  Nevertheless this is the most controversial of the defined categories of mental disorder. What sort of conduct is *abnormally* aggressive, or *seriously* irresponsible? The answers must depend to some extent on the sort of company one keeps, although every sort of company draws a line somewhere. While generalisations about diagnostic practices will always be faced with unorthodox exceptions, it can be said that in criminal courts British psychiatrists tend to reserve the label 'psychopathic' for people who exhibit one or more of the following characteristics:

a.   motives (or the more short-lived mental states called 'impulses') which are very unusual: for example, the enjoyment of the infliction of pain ('sadism'), or sexual desire for animals ('bestiality');

b.   motives or impulses which, though not necessarily unusual, seem to be much stronger (ie more'compulsive') than they are in the great majority of people. Thus mercenary motives are very widespread, but only occasionally so strong that they induce people to murder their spouses for the sake of a legacy or insurance payments;

c.   self-control which seems to be unusually weak, yielding to motives or impulses in situations in which the majority of people would not. This is distinguishable from (b), in which all that is known is that the person yields to a motive or impulse of a fairly specific sort; but of course a person who at first appears to be an example of (b) may on further enquiry, observation or experience turn out to belong to (c);

d.   infringement of the law—or other normally accepted standards of conduct—without the regrets or anxieties about consequences which the great majority of people would feel in such a situation. It is this category which sentencers find especially hard to distinguish from 'criminality' or 'wickedness'; but it does seem to be the case that whereas the great majority of people experience remorse and anxiety about the consequences of misbehaviour there are a few people to whom remorse (and in even fewer cases, anxiety) is an unknown feeling. The most awkward sort of case is that in which the person concerned seems to feel remorse for some kinds of conduct (such as dishonesty) but not for others (such as personal violence).

**21.23**  'Mental illness', unlike the three groups just discussed, is not defined, mainly because of the difficulty of drafting a definition which would be sufficiently wide to satisfy psychiatrists and yet sufficiently precise to have any legal effect. (The possibility of defining it was discussed in a DHSS Consultative Paper in 1976, but eventually dismissed again in the 1978 DHSS *Review*)[1]. Under this heading psychiatrists group such diagnoses as schizophrenia, depressive states, mania, and a miscellany of other disorders.

1. Hoggett (1990) notes a case (*W v L* [1974] QB 711) in which Lawton LJ concluded that 'mentally ill' must be construed not as having any special medical or legal meaning, but as meaning what 'ordinary sensible people' would take them to mean. She calls this 'the man-must-be-mad test'.

**21.24** It is sometimes overlooked that s 1 MHA 83 also refers to a fifth category:'any other disorder or disability of mind'. Psychiatrists diagnose and treat mental states which some of them prefer not to call 'impaired', 'psychopathic' or 'mentally ill': for instance the mental disabilities of old age. What is important is that for some legal purposes 'any other disorder or disability of mind' is not by itself sufficient (see the next paragraph).

**21.25** These five generic groups are collectively referred to in s 1 as 'mental disorder'. For some legal purposes it is sufficient if a medical practitioner simply categorises the patient as 'mentally disordered': e g when trying to arrange 'emergency admission' (s 4) or an admission 'for assessment' (s 2). Similarly, removal by the police from a public place to a 'place of safety' requires only that the individual 'appears to be suffering from mental disorder and to be in immediate need of care or control' (s 136). In these three cases, however, the permissible period of detention is very limited, and for any form of compulsory admission which allows longer detention the medical certificates must at least specify (severe) impairment, psychopathic disorder or mental illness: 'any other disability or disorder' will not do.

**21.26** Many disordered people are found by psychiatrists to be suffering from more than one kind of disorder, just as a patient can have both pneumonia and rheumatism. Some—but by no means all—'psychopaths' are impaired. Some schizophrenics are also depressed, and a minority are impaired. Recognising that for some psychiatrists the most important feature may be the impairment, for others the personality disorder or the schizophrenia, the MHA 83 does not insist that medical certificates must in each case agree exactly on the diagnostic group: only that they must agree on at least one such group (ss 11(6), 37(7), 47(4), the last of which also applies to s 48). Thus if one certificate mentioned only 'impairment' and the other 'mental illness', that would not do; but if one mentioned 'impairment' and 'psychopathic disorder', the other 'impairment' and 'mental illness', that would do.

## Excluded conduct

**21.27** Both the defined and the undefined forms of mental disorder allow psychiatrists great latitude in their application; and they are sometimes under pressure—from relatives, social workers and others—to invoke one or other of the procedures for compulsory admission under Part II of the MHA 83 in order to restrain or remove someone whose behaviour is causing distress or outrage. The definitions in s 1 therefore end with the warning that they are not to be construed as implying that a person may be dealt with under the Act as suffering from mental disorder, or any form of it, by reason only of promiscuity or other immoral conduct, sexual deviancy or dependence on alcohol or drugs. This rules out the compulsory detention, in institutions for the mentally impaired, of girls who are embarrassing their families by their sexual behaviour: a fate which sometimes befell them in the past even when their intelligence was not much below average. Again, homosexual activity—even if the psychiatrist himself regards this as pathological—is not to be a ground of compulsion to enter a hospital. Nor are addictions, although the psychoses which can result from the prolonged abuse of alcohol or some drugs are not ruled out. Exactly what 'other immoral conduct' means has never been made clear in court or out of it. Since it is coupled with 'promiscuity' it was probably meant to refer to sexual misbehaviour; but it could be interpreted very literally as covering any sort of conduct which incurs moral disapproval. If so, a psychiatrist who is wondering whether to classify someone as psychopathic because of 'seriously irresponsible conduct' should consider carefully whether he is distinguishing clearly between irresponsibility and immorality. Such points, however, have not been the subject of legal decisions. Part of the explanation must be that compulsory procedures are seldom invoked in borderline cases.

## Informal admissions

**21.28**  The great majority—about 9 in every 10—of the 260,000 or so annual admissions to mental hospitals are 'informal': that is, under no legal compulsion (DHSS 1995), and the procedure for them is not laid down by law. Quite a few patients who enter under compulsion stay on as informal patients after the power to detain them has been allowed to expire. Psychiatrists prefer patients— except those whom they regard as dangerous to others or themselves—to undergo in-patient or out-patient treatment voluntarily, as this means that patients place more trust in staff, give less trouble, and probably make better progress. It is possible for a hospital doctor to detain an informal patient compulsorily if he thinks that the patient's disorder fulfils the necessary conditions; in particular, that it would be in the interests of his health or safety or the protection of others (s 5); but this expedient is used with great reluctance.

## Psychiatric probation orders (ss 3, 6(7) PCCA 73)

**21.29**  Informal patients include probationers who are under psychiatric probation orders. They must have consented to the making of the order, with its requirement that they 'submit to treatment by or under the direction of a duly qualified medical practitioner'; but if they leave hospital or break off out-patient treatment the MHA provides no power to bring them back. The only legal sanction that can be applied is proceedings for breach of the order's requirement under s 6 of the PCCA 1973; and this is rarely used in such cases.

The absence of legal compulsion is the main reason why psychiatrists prefer such orders to hospital orders, even for in-patients. They are also easier to arrange because only one 'duly qualified medical practitioner' is needed to give the necessary evidence, although he must be one of those listed under s 12(2) of the MHA 83 as 'having special experience in the diagnosis or treatment of mental disorder'.

**21.30** The necessary conditions for the making of a psychiatric probation order by the court are

a. the evidence of one 'duly qualified medical practitioner' to the effect that the offender's 'mental condition is such as requires and may be susceptible to treatment but is not such as to warrant ... a hospital order ...' (s 3(1) PCCA 73). This distinction between cases suitable for psychiatric probation orders and those suitable for hospital orders is often ignored because of psychiatrists' preference for psychiatric probation orders. In many cases it would be awkward if the court asked 'Would a hospital order be warranted?'; but since the psychiatrist is often not in court there might be no answer;

b. what is offered (not necessarily by the practitioner who gives the evidence) must be

   i. treatment as a resident patient in a hospital or mental nursing home (ie not necessarily under the NHS) but not one of the special hospitals (s 3(2)); or

   ii. treatment as a non-resident patient at an institution or place which the order must specify; or treatment by or under the direction of a duly qualified medical practitioner or chartered psychologist, who must be named in the order;

c. the court must be satisfied that one or other of the kinds of arrangement described in (b) have been made (s 3(3)): but note that s 3(5) allows later changes in the arrangements);

d. as in the case of any probation order, the offender must 'express his willingness to comply with its requirements' (s 2(6)). This willingness often evaporates soon after the offender leaves the court and realises that he can walk off with impunity; but Lewis (1980) found that if the offender had been got to understand the implications of the order and the nature of the treatment before consenting he was likely to make a genuine effort to persevere with it;

e. the requirement to undergo psychiatric treatment can be added later to a probation order, but only within 3 months of the making of the probation order (Sch 1 PCCA 73). It sometimes happens that the need for treatment becomes apparent only while the offender is on probation. The Butler Committee recommended the removal of the 3-month limit (1975), but the recommendation has not been implemented.

### Gravity of the offence

**21.31** Where psychiatric probation orders seem suitable the gravity of the offence is seldom regarded as relevant nowadays. While the CA has not provided 'guidelines' for the use of psychiatric probation orders, it has itself agreed to substitute them for more severe sentences in cases of considerable gravity: wife-stabbing, blackmail, arson (see *Hoof* (1980) 2 Cr App Rep(S) 299). Even when an important consideration was the protection of children against a paedophilic rapist it has taken 'a calculated risk' and substituted a 3-year order for a 5-year prison sentence (*Nicholls* (1981) CSP F1–2BO1). On the other hand, in cases in which the psychiatrist has not convinced it that the chances of success are high, the CA has refused to use such orders (see for example *West*—an alcoholic embezzler—(1975) CA: cit Thomas, 1979, p 293).

## Duration of the requirement

**21.32**   The duration of the psychiatric requirement can be that of the probation order itself or a shorter period: but in practice most are for 2 years, and 6-month orders are rare. Some probation officers see advantage in an order which gives them some supervision of the offender after his psychiatric treatment has ceased; but of course the duration of the requirement does not mean that treatment will last as long as that (nor on the other hand that it will stop at that point).

## Form of treatment

**21.33**   Most psychiatrists' reports to courts do not specify the form of treatment which they have in mind. The type of treatment must not be specified in the order (s 3(2) PCCA), which usually says 'as directed' or the equivalent. If the doctor or psychologist responsible for treatment comes to the conclusion that treatment should be continued longer than the order requires, or is no longer required, or that the probationer is not susceptible to treatment, or needs a different kind of treatment (of a kind to which he or she could be required to submit[1]), or if the doctor or psychologist is unwilling to continue treating or directing the treatment, he or she is required to report this in writing to the offender's probation officer, who is supposed to apply to the court for the variation or cancellation of the requirement (Sch 1(4) PCCA 73). According to probation officers this obligation is often overlooked by psychiatrists, who assume (as indeed do some probation officers) that all responsibility for the offender's progress has passed to them. In fact, all that the statute says is that while the probationer is under treatment *as a resident patient in pursuance of the probation order* the probation officer shall carry out the supervision to such extent only as may be necessary for the purpose of the discharge or amendment of the order. This restriction on the probation officer's function—which does not apply to out-patient treatment—was intended to prevent interference with the psychiatrist's responsibility; but it has been strongly criticised, especially by the Butler Committee (1975), which found that in practice it was largely ignored by officers who saw the need to establish their own relationship with the offender as early as possible.

1. A probationer who later refuses to take part in treatment can be dealt with as in breach of his order: but he can argue that his refusal 'to undergo surgical, electrical or other treatment ... was reasonable having regard to all the circumstances' (s 6(7) PCCA), and if the court agrees he is not in breach.

**21.34**   In order to make sure that the probationer's commitment to treatment is genuine some courts use the deferred sentence, and make a psychiatric probation order only when told that the offender has been co-operating in treatment. In a case of this kind, however (*Skelton* [1983] Crim LR 686), the CA disapproved of deferment 'on the basis of an undertaking'; so that courts which find this expedient useful must be careful what they say.

**21.35**   The most recent sample of psychiatric probation orders to be described— Lewis' 118 Nottingham cases (1980)—may or may not still be representative. Although nearly half the probationers were under 30, there were a few in their 60s. Their disorders were usually depression, personality disorder, addiction of one sort or another, and less commonly mental impairment or some form of psychosis. A few had anxiety neuroses, sexual problems or even brain disorders. The variety of their offences was considerable; but theft was the commonest, with personal violence second, and fully a quarter of the personal violence was domestic (psychiatric probation orders are sometimes used even for infanticidal mothers and manslaughters attributed to diminished responsibility, especially when the offender is a woman). Three-quarters of the Nottingham probationers had previous convictions, and usually more than one. Nearly half had previous histories of mental disorder. Lewis' follow-up did not assess the efficacy of psychiatric probation orders, nor do we know of any recent study which has attempted this[1]. What is clear from the statistics is that psychiatric probation orders are much less frequently used than they used to be: only 122 residential orders were made in 1992, compared with 278 in 1981, and only 686 non-residential orders, compared with 927 in 1981.

1.   Grunhut and McCabe's (1963) follow-up of a 1953 nationwide sample has never been repeated.

## Hospital and guardianship orders (s 37 MHA 83)

**21.36**   Unlike psychiatric probation orders, hospital and guardianship orders confer on the hospital or guardian certain powers of control. The offender's status becomes that of a person compulsorily received into guardianship or compulsorily admitted to hospital for treatment under the non-criminal sections of the MHA Part II, although with several important differences. In 1992 the number of hospital orders was 717. Guardianship orders have already been dealt with in 21.16.

**21.37**   A hospital order can be made by the CC or a MC (including a youth court)[1]. The conditions which must be fulfilled are set out in s 37 MHA 83:
    a.   the offence must be imprisonable. This limitation has been criticised by Walker and McCabe (1973) because non-criminal compulsory admissions are not restricted in this way; but it was partially endorsed by ACPS

(1977), which thought that hospital but not guardianship orders should be limited to imprisonable offences;

b. the offence must not, however, be one for which the sentence is fixed by law: i e not murder or treason. If on the other hand a homicide is found to have been merely manslaughter, infanticide, criminal involvement in suicide, or child destruction, a hospital or guardianship order can be made;

c. the necessary evidence must be given by two medical practitioners, at least one of whom must be approved under s 12(2) MHA 83 as having special experience in the diagnosis or treatment of mental disorder. (This is similar to the requirement for non-criminal admission for treatment under s 3 MHA 83). Written evidence (on forms provided) is usually enough; but the defendant may require one or both practitioners to give oral evidence; and can produce rebutting evidence (s 54(3)). Copies of the medical reports must be given to his or her counsel or solicitor; and if he or she is not so represented the substance of the reports must be disclosed to him or her (or to parents or guardians if the defendant is a juvenile and if they are in court (s 54));

d. the offender must first be convicted. The exceptions are offenders who are mentally ill or severely impaired, in which case a MC may (not must) make the order without proceeding to a conviction. Even so, the MC must at least be satisfied that the offender 'did the act or made the omission charged' (s 37(3)). The offence must be one which an MC can try (*Thompson* (1995) Times, 6 December). The discretionary power to make the order without conviction is an acknowledgment of the fact that some offenders with whom MCs have to deal are so disordered that the magistrates cannot be sure that they understand the proceedings sufficiently to be fairly tried, or, if they understand the proceedings sufficiently, had the necessary mens rea when they did the act or made the omission. It is thus a crude equivalent of the procedure by which the CC can find that the defendant is unfit for trial or should be acquitted on the ground of insanity. For this reason it is not a procedure which is open to the CC. Usually, however, MCs convict even the mentally ill or severely impaired before making hospital orders;

e. the court must be satisfied that arrangements have been made for the offender's admission to a specified hospital within 28 days of the making of the order. This condition is often an obstacle, since some hospital staffs are unwilling to accept offenders who are personally known to misbehave, or whose offences make them sound dangerous. If the court has difficulty in finding an acceptant hospital it can require a health authority to supply information about the hospitals in its region to which the offender could be admitted (s 39 MHA 83); but it cannot compel any hospital to accept an offender; only the Secretary of State can do that. If after a hospital has agreed to take the offender this becomes impossible, the Secretary of State can substitute another hospital. If for any reason the offender is not conveyed to the specified hospital within 28 days, the order lapses, although that does not prevent the making of a new order if all the necessary conditions are fulfilled. The Reed

Committee (1992) recommended that in exceptional circumstances the court itself should have power to direct an unwilling health authority to provide a hospital bed for the offender;

f.  the evidence must satisfy the court that the offender's disorder is of a nature or degree which makes it 'appropriate' for him to be detained in a hospital for medical treatment[2]; and in the case of psychopathic disorder or mental impairment (but not mental illness or severe impairment) that the treatment is likely to alleviate or prevent a deterioration of his condition[3]. Exactly what 'appropriate' means is not clear: it is easier to see what it does not mean. Since the court must *also* be 'of the opinion, having regard to all the circumstances including the nature of the offence and the character and antecedents of the offender, and to the other available methods of dealing with him' that a hospital (or guardianship) order is 'the most suitable method of disposing of the case', 'appropriateness' is not to be judged by the circumstances. This seems to restrict it to medical considerations. The word is also used in s 3, which deals with non-criminal compulsory admission for treatment; but there

i.  it is the doctors, not the court, who decide whether it is 'appropriate' for the patient 'to receive medical treatment in a hospital' (and whether, in the case of psychopathic disorder or impairment, the treatment is likely to alleviate or prevent a deterioration of the patient's condition);

ii.  it must also be considered 'necessary for the health or safety of the patient or for the protection of others that he should receive such treatment': a consideration which is not stipulated in the criminal procedure;

iii.  it must also be considered that the necessary treatment cannot be provided unless the patient is compulsorily detained: another consideration which is absent from s 37.

It would be going too far, however, to argue that a criminal court must not have such considerations in mind when accepting or rejecting medical testimony about the appropriateness of admission to hospital (or guardianship). All that can be inferred is that 'appropriate' allows the court to take into account anything which the doctors consider relevant so long as it is distinguishable from 'all the circumstances'. The CA has not provided guidelines for the interpretation of this part of s 37.

1.  But when sentencing for contempt of court only a 'superior court' (i e the Court of Appeal, the CC or the High Court) has the power to make a hospital (or guardianship) order, MCs, which cannot imprison contemnors for more than 1 month, have no such power (s 14 Contempt of Court Act 1981). On the other hand, there seems to be nothing to prevent a MC (or a CC) from using its powers to remand a contemnor for psychiatric examination.

2.  Or in the case of an offender aged 16 or older that the disorder is of a nature or degree which warrants reception into guardianship; in which case, of course, there is no stipulation about alleviation or prevention of deterioration.

3.  A stipulation introduced in 1983 in order to save hospitals from being asked to receive offenders (or civil patients) whose conditions were unlikely to benefit from medical treatment. In practice most hospitals were already protecting themselves against this by refusing beds in such cases.

**21.38**  So long as conditions (a)–(f) are fulfilled, the court is free to choose between an order under this section and some other measure, such as imprisonment or probation. (Strictly speaking it should not attach a psychiatric requirement to a probation order if the offender's disorder is such as to warrant a hospital order; but as has already been said this stipulation is usually ignored in the medical evidence.) In particular, the court is not required to take into account the extent to which the offender can be regarded as responsible for his offence, although courts have sometimes done so (see, for example, the obiter dictum of the CCA in *Morris* (1961) 45 Cr App Rep 185). Indeed, it has been held proper to make a hospital order even when the disorder has nothing to do with the offence: see *Hatt* [1962] Crim LR 647. If the court has good reasons for wanting the offender to be kept under secure control, but is offered only a place for him in an ordinary NHS hospital, it will be justified in refusing to make a hospital order and sentencing him to prison instead (*Parker, Griffiths and Rainbird* (1975) unreported: cit Thomas 1979 p298).

### Incompatible disposals

**21.39**   When making a hospital (or guardianship) order the court is prohibited by statute (s 37(8) MHA 83) from fining, sentencing to custody or making a probation order; but is expressly allowed to make any other order which it could otherwise make. For example, it can order the payment of compensation; but like a fine this might well be difficult or impossible for the offender-patient to pay. The CA has not given guidance on this, and is unlikely to be required to do so in view of the unambiguous wording of the subsection. The subsection does not, however, apply to the sentencing of offender-patients who are already subject to a hospital order: see 21.47).

### Legal consequences of hospital orders

**21.40**   The legal consequence of a hospital order is that the offender is in the same position as he would have been if he had been a non-offender compulsorily admitted for treatment under Part II of MHA (s 3), the important exception being that his nearest relative does not have the power to order his discharge under s 23 MHA 83. What his nearest relative does have is the right to apply to a mental health review tribunal (MHRT: see below) for his discharge, but only if he is detained for more than 6 months (s 69 MHA 83); and he himself cannot apply to the MHRT during the first 6 months of his detention, unlike a patient admitted under the civil procedure of Part II. For the effect of the Rehabilitation of Offenders Act 1974 where hospital or guardianship orders are concerned, see 19.10.

### Leaving hospital

**21.41**   Consequently, like any other compulsory patient, the offender-patient under a hospital order may become free in one of six ways. Firstly, he or she may be allowed leave of absence from hospital indefinitely or on specific occasions or for specific periods by the RMO, subject to any conditions the RMO considers necessary (s 17). This power is often used to ease a patient's transition from hospital care to outside life, since it preserves the power to compel his or her return to hospital, and thus provides something analogous to the after-care of a parolee.

### Discharge by RMO

**21.42** Compulsorily detained patients may be discharged whenever the RMO thinks this advisable, unless they are offenders subject to a restriction order (see 21.51ff). Discharge (under s 23) is unconditional, and brings the power of compulsory detention to an end, although it can be recreated by compulsory readmission. Once formally discharged they are not subject to compulsory supervision (although they may voluntarily accept it). Recently, however, concern about the numbers of ex-patients who do not co-operate with efforts to care for them—and in particular do not take the drugs prescribed for them—led to the passing of the Mental Health (Patients in the Community) Act 1995, which allows RMOs to apply for compulsory supervision when 'there would be a substantial risk of serious harm to the health or safety of the patient or the safety of other persons, or of the patient being seriously exploited, if he were not to receive the after-care services provided...' The after-care is to be provided by local 'after-care bodies (sic)', who can require the ex-patient to live in a specified place, and attend at a specified place for medical treatment (which can no doubt include medication), occupation, education and training. Supervisors must not be denied access to their supervisees. The power of supervision lasts for 6 months in the first place, but can be renewed for 6 months, and thereafter for periods of 1 year. The ex-patient has the right of appeal to a MHRT (see 21.45). Since the powers conferred by the MH(PC)A 95 were the subject of disagreement among psychiatrists, and between psychiatrists and the Department of Health, it remains to be seen whether it will be invoked in enough cases to make an impact on the problem.

### Expiry of compulsion

**21.43** A patient may be discharged or become an informal patient when the power to detain comes to an end through passage of time, as it does at the end of the patient's first 6 months[1] in hospital. It can, however, be renewed if within the last 2 months of the period the RMO certifies to the hospital managers that further detention is necessary in the interest of the patient's health or safety or for the protection of others. The first such renewal is for 6 months: subsequent renewals for 1 year (s 20). In most cases, however, the power is allowed to lapse at the end of the first 6 months, the DHSS (as it then was) having expressed the view that '... any significant improvement is likely to take place in the first 6 months' (1976 Review of the MHA).

1. In the case of hospital orders the period begins with the date of the order, even if admission does not take place at once: see 21.39(e).

## Discharge by operation of law (s 18 MHA 83 as amended by MH (PIC)A 95)

**21.44** A patient may become legally free by absenting himself without leave. The open-door regimes of NHS hospitals make this easy, since they are reluctant to impose physical restraints, even on compulsory patients. If a patient absconds, the hospital has the power (s 18) but is under no legal obligation to recapture him, and will usually do so only if there is anxiety about his safety or that of others. The 'retaking' can be done either by a constable or by an 'approved social worker' of the local authority (see s 138). If he remains free for 6 months or until the end of the period of compulsory detention, whichever is longer, the power to retake lapses, although a new compulsory non-criminal admission is not of course ruled out. The origin of this rule is the 19th-century anxiety about patients who were wrongly detained at the instance of rapacious relatives. It was believed that if they had the intelligence to escape from secure custody and maintain themselves at large for a substantial period (originally 14 days but extended to 28 by the MHA 59) their condition could not be such as to justify compulsory detention. Nowadays it calls for little competence to abscond from an ordinary NHS hospital, and in a welfare state even quite disordered persons can maintain themselves at large, with or without a little help from relatives or friends. Even if the rule is retained for non-criminal admissions, it is arguable that it should not be used as a loophole by offenders. However that may be, 'discharge by operation of law' is a not uncommon way in which hospitals are relieved of responsibility for compulsory patients; and if the patient is troublesome, as many offender-patients are, the staffs' relief is one reason why often little or no effort is made to recapture him or her.

## Discharge by mental health review tribunal (MHRT)

**21.45** A patient may apply for discharge to the local MHRT after he or she has been detained for 6 months from the date of the hospital order, and thereafter once during each period for which his or her detention is renewed. The nearest relative also has the right to apply to the MHRT if detention is renewed (s 69). The MHRT *must* direct the discharge of a hospital order patient if satisfied

   a. that he or she is not then suffering from mental illness, psychopathic disorder or (severe) mental impairment or from any of those forms of disorder of a nature or degree which makes it appropriate for him or her to be liable to be detained in a hospital for medical treatment; or
   b. even if the patient is still so suffering, that it is not necessary for his or her health and safety or for the protection of others that he or she should receive such treatment (s 72(1)(b)).

### The protection of others

**21.46** Note that (a) and (b) are alternatives; so that an MHRT might be satisfied that the offender-patient was still suffering from a disorder which make it 'appropriate' for him to be liable to be detained in a hospital for treatment, yet be obliged to order his discharge because it is satisfied that the medical treatment is not necessary for his or her health or safety or for the protection of others. This means that the phrase 'for the protection of others' is of great importance. Protection against what? As will be seen (21.51) the CC has the power to attach a special restriction to a hospital order if this appears necessary to protect the public against 'serious harm'; and MCs can commit an offender to the CC with a view to a restriction order. This seems to imply that in the case of an ordinary hospital order without restriction the protection of other persons which the MHRT must consider means protection against harm whether serious or less than serious. A MHRT could therefore take the view that it means protection against whatever conduct led to the hospital order, even if this was mere pilfering; or it could set a higher standard and consider only whether there was a risk of, say, 'substantial' harm.

## Discretionary discharge

**21.47** The ambiguity of the criteria which *oblige* MHRTs to order discharge is compounded by their *discretion* to do so 'in any case', even—apparently—if satisfied both that the patient is still so disordered that continued detention for treatment is 'appropriate' and that his discharge would threaten his health or safety or 'other persons'. In practice, however, it is difficult to imagine a tribunal acting so irresponsibly. The membership of MHRTs includes legally-qualified men and women of considerable experience, psychiatrists—also of considerable seniority and experience—and laymen, all appointed by the Lord Chancellor. At any sitting one of each group must be present, the lawyer presiding. A person must not take part in dealing with an application if he has a personal connection with the patient, has recently treated him in a professional medical capacity or is a member or officer of any of the responsible authorities. The procedure is also governed by Rules, and applicants have a right not only to appear in person but also to be represented by anyone they choose (organisations such as MIND offer the free services of experienced representatives). MHRTs may thus be persuaded on occasion to use their discretion to discharge when they are not entirely satisfied that the criteria which oblige them to do so are satisfied but consider that the risks are small. For a full-scale study of MHRTs see Peay (1989), and for a discussion of their legal powers see Hoggett (1990).

## Discharge by custodial sentence (s 22 MHA 83)

**21.48** Hospital order patients may be prosecuted for offences committed before or while they were patients; and this is by no means unheard of, especially if they commit violent offences. If as a result of custodial remands or sentences (or combinations of these) they spend at least 6 months in custody, their hospital orders lapse at that point. If they are made subject to new hospital orders the original orders lapse (s 40 MHA 83). Otherwise, the sentencing of a hospital order patient presents courts with problems, since he or she is seldom in a position to pay a fine or compensation, and a probation order or community service order is obviously inappropriate. Hence courts sometimes resort to an absolute or conditional discharge *faute de mieux*. Deferment of sentence in the expectation that the offender will be discharged from hospital within the next 6 months is a theoretical possibility; but the propriety of this is doubtful.

## Interim hospital orders (s 38 MHA 83)

**21.49**   A defect of the hospital order (and in theory of the guardianship order also) is its irrevocability. It commits to hospitals a few offenders who turn out to be malingerers and rather more who are so unco-operative that hospital regimes do them no good while they do positive harm to the regimes. Yet unlike a psychiatric probation order it does not allow the offender to be brought back to court. All the hospital can do is to discharge him or her, or hope that he or she will abscond. This could have been remedied simply by providing that an RMO could ask for an offender-patient to be brought back to court to be disposed of in some other way. Instead, however, on the recommendation of the Butler Committee (1975), the courts have been given the power to make 'interim hospital orders'. The important differences between interim and ordinary hospital orders are that:

   a.   instead of testifying that the criteria in 21.36 (f) are satisfied, medical witnesses need merely say that 'there is reason to suppose' that the offender's disorder is such that a hospital order is appropriate;
   b.   at least one of those medical witnesses must be employed at the receiving hospital;
   c.   the interim order is in force for a period specified by the court (instead of the normal 6 months, renewable); but the court must not specify more than 12 weeks, although it can renew it for periods of not more than 28 days, up to a maximum of 6 months (including the initial period), with or without the offender's appearing in court again;
   d.   if the patient absconds from hospital while the interim order is in force the court can terminate it and deal with him or her as if no such order had been made;
   e.   in any case, since the power is exercisable 'before making a hospital order or dealing with him in any other way' the court can follow an interim order with another disposal. Whether it can do so before the expiry of the specified period of the order in circumstances other than (d) has still to be determined by case-law;
   f.   MCs cannot use interim orders without convicting the accused (see 21.37(d)).
   g.   interim orders cannot be the subject of an A-G's reference (s 35 CJA 88).
Interim hospital orders, however, have not proved popular: only 66 were made in 1992. Probably remands to hospitals for reports (under s 35 MHA 83) have made it somewhat easier for staff to tell which offenders are likely to be manageable.

## A stage army

**21.50**   It is important to realise that for most offenders who are made subject to hospital orders this is not their first involvement with the criminal courts or the NHS. Walker and McCabe's (1973) study of a cohort of hospital orders made in 1963–64 (still, surprisingly, the only national sample) found that nearly $3/4$ of the men (but only half the women) had been in mental hospitals before, while nearly $2/3$ of both sexes had previous convictions for SL offences. Only 1 man in 9 and 1 woman in 5 had no record of either a conviction or a hospital admission; and many of these were either immigrants or quite young. In short, most belonged to what has been called 'the stage army', which circulates between hospitals, prisons and public appearances in the courts. Most of the stage army moves with remarkable speed. More than 2 in 3 left hospital with the approval of their RMOs within 12 months and some others absconded or were resentenced. Those with affective disorders (e g depressions) were especially likely to leave early: quite a few in the first 6 months[1]. On the other hand, the impaired, whose condition improves, if at all, only under long-term training, were likely to stay for more than a year.

1.   Soothill et al (1980) found even higher percentages of early discharges in a 1969-70 cohort of hospital orders made by Inner London and 'Wessex' courts.

## The dangerously disordered

**21.51**   If the CC regards a mentally disordered offender as dangerous, and wishes to ensure that he remains in custody until he represents less of a risk to others, it may be able to take one of 2 courses. If the conditions for a hospital order are fulfilled, and if the court considers that the step is 'necessary for the protection of the public against serious harm', it can add a 'restriction order' to the hospital order, with the effect that the offender-patient cannot be discharged, given leave of absence or transferred from one hospital to another without special authority (s 41 MHA 83). Sometimes the offence is of a kind which allows the CC the alternative of a life sentence. Otherwise a determinate prison sentence may be the only recourse. These choices and their complications are discussed in the next chapter.

## Transfers to hospital (ss 47-53 MHA 83)

**21.52**   By no means all 'restricted patients', however, have been dealt with as dangerous by the CC. Most admissions under such restrictions (632 in 1992) are the result of transfers from prisons, remand centres and young offenders' institutions, or occasionally, in the case of juveniles, from local authority care. A transfer direction is usually accompanied by a restriction on discharge, directed under s 49, which has the same effect as a restriction order made by a court under s 41; and in the case of prisoners transferred before sentence a restriction on discharge *must* be directed. If the sentence is determinate, the restriction on discharge ceases to have effect when the parole system would have released the prisoner, taking account of any 'added days' incurred before transfer (s 50). At this stage, even if he remains in hospital, a licence is issued which makes his local probation service responsible for supervising him. In a few cases the transfer takes place without a restriction on discharge, usually because the expected date of release is so near that this would seem oppressive. If so, the transferred prisoner's status is like that of an ordinary hospital order patient. Only prisoners whose transfer carries a restriction on discharge can be 'remitted' back to prison. This is uncommon; but sometimes a transferred prisoner makes a quick recovery while he has still to serve a substantial time before he can be considered for parole: and sometimes his behaviour in hospital is unacceptable to the staff. On the other hand, he may find himself still in hospital long after he would have been released from prison; and in such cases he is regarded as a 'restricted patient' for MHRT purposes (ss 70, 79 MHA 83).

**21.53** Before authorising a transfer the Home Secretary must be satisfied both that the person is suffering from one of the usual four categories of disorder (not merely 'any other disorder or disability of mind') and also that this makes hospital detention for medical treatment 'appropriate'. In the case of transfers before sentence only mental illness or severe impairment will suffice, and the need for transfer must be urgent. (The Reed Committee (1992) disapproved of these limitations, and wanted it to be possible to transfer prisoners to hospitals for assessment as well as treatment.) Transfers to guardianship are not provided for, although in some cases this might be more appropriate than parole. The most common transfer involves sentenced prisoners, although payment-defaulters and people committed to custody for failure to comply with recognisances to keep the peace or be of good behaviour are also eligible. The prison medical officer is expected to find a NHS hospital willing to receive the prisoner or — if a special hospital place seems advisable — to apply for this through the Department of Health. When a place has been found, the Home Secretary is asked to make a transfer direction, although it is open to him to refuse, since he must also be satisfied that the transfer is expedient, having regard to all the circumstances and the public interest. A more common obstacle, however, is the reluctance of any hospital[1] to accept the prisoner; so that at any given time there is a substantial number of prisoners who, in the view of prison doctors, ought to be in hospital, but for whom beds have not yet been found.

1. A transfer is possible without the hospital's consent, and the Home Secretary sometimes insists on it.

### Treatment or care in prison

**21.54** Overcrowding in the special hospitals and the inhospitality of other hospitals means that at any given time there is a substantial number of disordered prisoners who should but cannot be transferred, or who are awaiting transfer. An ordinary prison cell or dormitory is an unsuitable place for them. Their special difficulties and needs are unlikely to be understood by fellow inmates or by many prison officers, although some officers have as much experience, tolerance and skill as mental nurses. Advantage may be taken of an impaired or schizophrenic prisoner: he or she may be suicidal or violent to others; and for whatever reason he or she will need more surveillance than the ordinary prisoner. This is usually possible only in a hospital wing; and some large prisons have hospital wings where disordered prisoners are kept for considerable periods. There are also many cases however of milder disorder which do not qualify for these special wings, especially anxiety neuroses and depressions (a frequent reaction to the impact of imprisonment or the refusal of parole).

### Offender-patients' rights

**21.55**  The regimes of ordinary hospitals are planned with voluntary patients in mind: their slogan is 'the open door'[1]. Compulsory detainees are in a minority. Unfortunately some patients—and especially some offender-patients—are a nuisance: one reason why staff are sometimes reluctant to accept a well-known *revenant*. Rules have to be adopted, made known and enforced. They do not have the backing of statute, are not published, and vary from hospital to hospital, even from wing to wing. Penalties usually take the form of denial of amenities; but occasionally, as in prison, staff lose their tempers and commit assaults, for which they may be prosecuted. The ethical and practical problems of 'disciplining' disordered patients are discussed by Crichton (1996).

1.  Although there are procedures (in s 5 MHA 83) for detaining an 'informal' patient compulsorily if this seems necessary for his health or safety or for the protection of others

### Correspondence

**21.56**  The statutes do, however, allow a few kinds of interference with patients' freedoms. Normally their correspondence is not censored or withheld; but since some patients write threatening or abusive letters members of the public can ask the hospital to 'withhold from the Post Office' communications addressed to them by patients (s 134 MHA 83). (This does not prevent patients from telephoning, although staff may be able to prevent this unofficially). In the special hospitals experience has shown that the withholding of both outgoing and incoming mail is sometimes necessary, to shield either patients or their correspondents from distressing letters; and s 134 gives the necessary power to the special hospital managers. To ensure, however, that no patient is prevented from making complaints to outside authorities these powers of censorship do not apply to correspondence with ministers of the Crown, members of Parliament, MHRTs, the European Commission or Court of Human Rights and a number of other functionaries listed in s 134: and in any case patients have the right to appeal to the Mental Health Act Commission against censorship (see 21.59).

### Compulsory treatment (Pt IV MHA 83)

**21.57**  Patients—including convicted offenders—who are compulsorily detained under the Mental Health Act, otherwise than under the short-term emergency powers, can be treated for their mental disorder without their consent. There are exceptions for certain kinds of treatment, such as psycho-surgery and electro-convulsive therapy: special procedures are required if the patient does not consent to them. The subject is dealt with in detail by Hoggett (1990).

**21.58**   The protection of a patient's property—whether from mismanagement by him or misappropriation by relatives—is the responsibility of the Lord Chancellor and the judiciary, whose functions are set out in Part VII of the MHA 83. In practice it is only occasionally—and usually when a substantial amount of property is at stake—that they are asked to perform these functions. The approved social worker or probation officer, however, who is in personal contact with a patient's home, sometimes has to decide whether judicial intervention is needed to safeguard his interests.

## The Mental Health Act Commission

**21.59**   As a further safeguard for detained patients, however, there exists the Mental Health Act Commission, charged with various responsibilities by section 121 MHA 83. These responsibilities include keeping under review the powers and duties created by the Mental Health Act, investigating complaints made by patients, or by others about matters to do with the patient's detention, visiting detained patients, and various functions with regard to the 'consent to treatment' provisions outlined in 21.57.

## The conviction of the disordered

**21.60**   Remands apart, the powers of disposal which have been discussed are almost always exercised after the defendant has been found guilty. There are only four exceptions, none of which are common:

   a.   After a successful insanity defence in the CC the accused is not found guilty but is the subject of a 'special verdict'. The CC then has a choice between a hospital order (with a restriction on discharge), committal to a hospital specified by the Secretary of State for Health, a guardianship order, a 'supervision and treatment order' (similar to a non-residential psychiatric probation order), and an order for absolute discharge (s 5 CP(I)A 64 as amended by s 3 CP(IUP)A 91). There were only six successful defences of this kind in 1992 (Mackay, 1995). Only one led to a hospital order, and that without a restriction.

   b.   If the defendant is found to be 'under disability'—that is, so disordered as to make it impossible for him to participate in a proper trial—the CC has the same choices. In 1992 there were only 13 such findings (Mackay, 1995).

Procedures (a) and (b) are confined to the CC, the CA and courts martial. In the case of a MC, as was said in 21.36,

   c.   If it would have the power to convict the offender, and to dispose of him or her by means of a hospital order, but he or she is categorised as mentally ill or severely impaired (but not if he is merely impaired or psychopathic), it can make the order without convicting him (s 37(3) MHA 83).

d. Occasionally the CC or an MC decides that the defendant was in a state of 'automatism' when he or she did what has led to prosecution: that is, that he or she was not in control of his or her body (an everyday example is the convulsion of a sneeze). Sleepwalkers, epileptics and diabetics who drift into comas sometimes succeed with this defence; and when they do they must be acquitted. The prosecution, however, is sometimes able to argue successfully that the nature of the disorder makes the correct verdict one of insanity ('insane automatism'), in which case the defendant is disposed of in one of the ways listed in (a) above.

No statistics seem to be available for (c) and (d), but they too are rare. In short, diversion, psychiatric probation orders and hospital orders have more or less bypassed niceties about the offender's triability and degree of culpability.

## Occasionalism

**21.61** The question whether it is morally right to find virtually all disordered offenders guilty before disposing of them belongs to the jurisprudence of trial rather than the law of sentencing, and the evidential problems raised by the defences of insanity, diminished responsibility, infanticide and automatism are outside the scope of this book. Nowadays the approach of English courts to the problem is very pragmatic. If the offender's mental state seems to call for a psychiatric disposal rather than a sentence, it does not trouble courts or defending lawyers very much that the defendant is usually convicted before benefiting from psychiatry. What is called 'occasionalism' by Walker and McCabe (1973) treats the appearance of the defendant in court as a proper occasion for ensuring that he receives the care or medication which his state seems to need—or at least the nearest thing to this that the overloaded hospital system can provide. The same occasionalism is taken to justify the use of 'care orders' for juveniles who seem to need something other than a mere penalty for their offences. In the case of juveniles the triviality of the offence is not—in theory at least—a bar to using the court appearance as an opportunity for compulsory benevolence. In the case of disordered offenders the only bar is the limitation of hospital orders to imprisonable offences; but there is no such limitation when a psychiatric probation order is in question, and even the limitation on hospital orders can be circumvented by arranging a compulsory civil admission direct from court[1].

1. Hoggett (1990) dismisses occasionalism as 'too neat', but has missed the point. It is not a jurisprudential justification but a description of the way in which psychiatrists, probation officers and courts sometimes think.

**21.62** Even occasionalists, however, should be disquieted by at least one feature of the system. This is the frequency with which disordered offenders are found guilty only to be denied a psychiatric disposal because no hospital or clinic is willing to accept them as patients (or because facilities for guardianship are not provided by the local authority). The unwillingness of hospitals[1] is excusable when experience has taught them either that the nature of the disorder makes it unlikely that what they can provide will benefit the offender, or that the behaviour of the individual offender will interfere with the smooth running of the hospital or the peace of mind of other patients; both of which are often true, for example, of cases of personality disorder. But the alternatives open to the courts— conditional discharges, ordinary probation orders or custodial sentences—are seldom satisfactory solutions.

1.  It should be realised that it is often the nursing staff of hospitals, not psychiatrists, who insist that an offender should not be accepted as a patient, whether because the nature of his offence makes him or her sound dangerous, or because they believe from previous experience that he or she will be a nuisance.

**21.63** This being so, even an occasionalist should have doubts about the justice of a system which allows findings of guilt in the case of offenders whose disorder is such that
  a.   the system has no appropriate disposal to offer; but
  b.   the degree of the offender's disorder makes it arguable that he or she should be exempt from a penal disposal.
These doubts should be most acute when the only alternative to hospital which courts are prepared to consider is imprisonment. Clearly this troubles some judges, who will remand offenders several times while they press the NHS to find hospital beds for them, and will resort to custodial sentences only if this fails. There is a case, however, for a procedure—whether it takes the form of a special defence or occurs after conviction—that would debar the court from using a custodial sentence[1]. If hospitals have the power to refuse admission, it is arguable that either the Prison Department or some other competent authority[2] should have the power to deny the court the recourse of imprisonment. To legislate on these lines, however, without ensuring that there are facilities of some sort for housing and supervising the offenders in question would be irresponsible.

1.  Or a fine, by the same token; but courts seldom fine in such situations.
2.  Perhaps a prison medical officer, supported by another psychiatrically-qualified practitioner?

## How effective is court-ordered psychiatry?

**21.64** Part of the difficulty of answering this question lies in the choice of criteria for effectiveness. The occasionalist simply hopes that court-arranged psychiatry improves the quality of life for the offender-patient, as in many cases it must do. For the hard-headed utilitarian penologist the question is 'Does court-arranged psychiatric treatment reduce the nuisance or harm which offender-patients cause in the community to a greater extent than would mere detention or other restraints?' Nobody has attempted to match patients discharged from unrestricted hospital orders with a similar cohort of released short-term prisoners who should have been hospitalised but were not. In the 1960s Walker and McCabe (1973) achieved a 2-year follow-up of 456 male and female offender-patients who left hospitals in England and Wales within a year of being committed under hospital orders, but they were unable to compare them with imprisoned controls. Nevertheless the findings were interesting, and unlikely to become irrelevant even in the 1990s. For example, although the men's reconviction rate was much higher (42 per cent) than the women's (30 per cent) this was almost wholly explained by the women's better records and other circumstances. Women with diagnoses of mental illness and no previous convictions were seldom reconvicted, at least of SL offences (6 per cent), whereas men with diagnoses of subnormality or psychopathy and several previous convictions were often reconvicted (71 per cent).The less time offender-patients had spent in hospital the more likely they were to be reconvicted, which is consistent with the supposition that what was done to them in hospitals had some effect on their subsequent conduct. Those for whom hospitals claimed to have arranged some sort of voluntary after-care were also less likely to be reconvicted. Either the sort of offender for whom after-care seems a practical possibility (e g because he has a known home to go to) is more likely to keep out of trouble, or after-care itself prevents a substantial number of reconvictions, by arranging readmission when there are signs of relapse or by helping the ex-patient in other ways.

**21.65** Where ex-patients are concerned, however, there are complicating factors which mean that reconviction rates are less satisfactory measures of failure than in the case of non-disordered offenders. For one thing, an offender who is known to be an ex-patient may benefit by decisions to 'divert' rather than prosecute if he or she reoffends. For another, ex-patients are often readmitted to hospital without reoffending (or at least without being detected or prosecuted). This was what happened to 21 per cent of both men and women in the Walker-McCabe cohort, and it was particularly likely in the case of schizophrenics. Whether they would have been reconvicted but for readmission was of course an unanswerable question. What is possible, however, is that being identified as ex-patients, and probably being known to local hospital staffs, made them more likely to be admitted when they showed symptoms of disorder, and thus in some cases saved the community from more offences.

## Anti-psychiatry

**21.66** This chapter would be incomplete without a brief discussion of 'anti-psychiatry', a point of view commoner in the USA than in the UK, but represented here by some sociologists and even a few psychiatrists. It is critical not of forensic psychiatry in particular but of the role played by psychiatry in shaping attitudes to unusual behaviour and social control. Nevertheless, the acceptance of all or most of anti-psychiatry entails scepticism about both the utility and the justice of the procedures which this chapter describes.

**21.67** It is not a unitary point of view, but a collection of accusations: only the most extreme anti-psychiatrists would endorse them all. The gravest is that 'mental illness', 'mental subnormality', 'personality disorder' or their synonyms are figments, the by-product of the evolution of physical medicine. This discipline originally claimed expertise in the diagnosis and treatment of aberrations which it attributed to physiological disease or imbalance. Such causal attributions being usually surmises, they were discredited, but replaced either by new physiological explanations or by the concept of 'functional' disorders: i e disorders caused not by organic abnormalities but by faulty 'reactions', 'social learning' or theoretical equivalents. The anti-psychiatric argument is that to 'diagnose' functional aberrations as if they were each the symptom of a single underlying cause (in the way in which, say, pathologists diagnose tuberculosis) is a category mistake: it is as if an osteopath were applying his knowledge to the problems of a bad golf swing. No autopsy would find anything wrong with a slicing golfer; nor would it find any abnormality to explain a depression or a severe anxiety state. This argument makes a valuable point: that *some* psychiatric diagnoses should not be regarded as identifying a group of symptoms with a single explanation and are thus different from *most*[1] physical diagnoses. They are also 'context-bound', because they involve the assertion that the behaviour or mood is inappropriate or disproportionate to the situation. A broken leg or infected liver is context-free, whereas gloom may be appropriate, inappropriate or disproportionate, depending on circumstances. So may aggressive behaviour, anxiety, elation, suspicion.

1.    Not all: diagnoses of osteo-arthritis, for example, may be vague about causal factors.

**21.68**    The argument goes too far however when it claims
  i.    that all psychiatric diagnoses are context-bound. This is clearly not so in the case of Down's Syndrome (mongolism), Huntington's Chorea, Alzheimer's Syndrome, and many other disorders with a demonstrable physical cause;
  ii.    that to be context-bound is to be invalid. Some *physical* diagnoses are context-bound: examples are obesity, deafness, squints, constipation. Exactly how fat is obese is an awkward question: a Japanese wrestler seems obese to us but not to his fans; yet the use of the term by doctors and laymen is not challenged, only disputed *in certain instances*. Similarly the exact point at which gloom, grief, elation, suspiciousness, aggression cease to be regarded as appropriate and become matters of clinical concern is obviously open to discussion in individual cases: but there are cases whose pathological nature can be denied only by people who have taken up an extreme position.

**21.69**    What the anti-psychiatrist may nevertheless maintain is that in context-bound cases the psychiatrist's assessment should not be accorded a special status which places it above the layman's. Yet even this is going too far. A psychiatrist is practised and trained in making assessments. He will think of questions which might not occur to a layman, and which might reveal the full extent of the aberration. If the subject seems over-suspicious whom does he include in his suspicions? Have they a sexual content? Does he hear voices which other people do not? And so forth. Again, the psychiatrist is less likely to be swayed by affection, dislike or fear. He is also needed to say whether the aberration could possibly be attributed to physical illness, brain damage, drugs or lack of vitamins.

**21.70**    The second charge of the anti-psychiatrist is that psychiatry is one of the methods of social control. The charge implies either that all social control is a bad thing or—less extremely—that even when it is justified psychiatrists should not play a part in it. If this is carried to the length of saying that they should not intervene to save a defendant from conviction or a convicted offender from imprisonment, it seems unjust and inhumane. To be fair to the anti-psychiatrists what they usually have in mind is the use of psychiatry to control or discredit behaviour which is not really pathological but simply subversive from a political point of view or disturbing to people who are morally intolerant. The prime example of the former is the way in which some Soviet psychiatrists labelled political dissenters 'schizophrenic'. It is historically interesting that this practice was originally, in Stalin's time, a device for protecting dissidents from much worse fates; but this did not excuse the way in which it was later misapplied. In the eyes of anti-psychiatrists, all psychiatry is tainted by it.

**21.71**   In this country it is not so much the hospitalisation of offenders that is suspect as compulsory admissions under non-criminal procedure. The practice of labelling 'promiscuous' young women as 'mental defectives' under pre-1959 statutes has already been mentioned, together with the provision that is intended to prevent it (see 21.26). The dispute among American psychiatrists about the inclusion of homosexuality in their list of mental disorders—from which it was eventually removed—was essentially a disagreement about the desirability of trying to cure it. The problem of suicide will not be so easily solved. Some psychiatrists—such as Laing—argued that compulsory admission should not be used to interfere with the individual's choice, even if he or she is manifestly in an abnormal state; but this is not the view of most. Dangerousness to others also provides anti-psychiatrists with ammunition. Psychiatrists are accused of detaining people unnecessarily because they have been labelled violent. As will be seen, however, in the next chapter there are two variants of this view; that detention is never justified on this ground—a version which is obviously extreme; or that it sometimes is, but not as often as psychiatrists think. Most psychiatrists are prepared to concede the latter, and admit that they play safe. If so, they are certainly acting in accordance with the public's desire to be protected.

**21.72**   What is indisputable is that there are kinds of behaviour—violence being only the most obvious example—which almost inevitably provokes reactions of the kind called 'social control'. The question is whether psychiatrists should consent to take part, or should provide care or treatment only with the subject's consent. The fact that most British psychiatrists *prefer* to intervene only with this consent is not really an answer. The point is what would happen if *all* of them refused to intervene in any circumstances without that consent. One result would be the application of much less humane methods of control: imprisonment, strait-jackets, personal retaliation.

**21.73**   The third charge is that psychiatrists' claims to provide effective treatment are unjustified. Certainly the list of discredited cures is a long one: purges, douches, whirling chairs, floggings, insulin comas, are only a few examples. On the other hand, new drugs have made it possible to offer relief from the suffering which accompanies many of the psychoses and affective disorders, even if they do not attack the causes. Some disorders with known physical origins can be cured or kept at bay. To portray psychiatrists as charlatans purveying ineffective remedies is a gross distortion of the facts, by the device of selecting convenient examples and ignoring successes. The worst that can be said about the successes is that many of them should be credited to research chemists or psychologists—for example to chlorpromazine or behaviour therapy—rather than to psychiatrists, who merely make use of techniques invented by others. But that is true of many medical specialisms.

# Chapter 22

# Dangerous offenders

**22.1** Every jurisdiction has some statute or practice which allows it to deal in a special way with offenders who are considered dangerous. Statutes do not always define these offenders as dangerous. They may simply give courts special powers with or without definitions of the circumstances in which these are to be used. They may specify certain types of offence, and certain procedures (such as consideration of psychiatric reports on the offender, and the giving of notice to the defence that a special sentence is a possibility). In some jurisdictions a special sentence is mandatory when certain conditions are fulfilled ; but usually it is within the court's discretion[1].

1. Dangerousness may also be a consideration when police or courts decide whether to grant bail: see 10.6, and Padfield (1996).

## Reports to courts

**22.2** Sometimes the evidence of the offender's behaviour alerts the sentencer to his dangerousness; but often it does not, especially if he pleads guilty. Courts expect PSRs and psychiatrists' reports to indicate whether their subjects represent a serious risk to others; but this expectation is sometimes overlooked. HM Inspectors of Probation (1995) found that in a sample of 214 PSRs less than 40 per cent contained any comment on the likelihood of reoffending and the consequent risk to the public. One-third simply described the offence by repeating the offender's description of it 'even when this was at variance with the prosecution details and wholly implausible'. Psychiatrists too are not always fully informed about their patients' behaviour in the community, and in any case may be reluctant to give them a label which will delay their freedom. We shall discuss (in 22.29ff) the scruples which lead to this reluctance.

## Longer than commensurate (LTC) sentences (ss 2 and 31 CJA 91)

**22.3** The English penal code provides several kinds of custodial disposal for the protection of the public against serious harm (and, as we shall see later, some non-custodial precautions). For violent or sexual offences the court must (not may) pass a custodial sentence (i e of imprisonment or its equivalent for young adults or juveniles) which is longer than would be 'commensurate with the seriousness of the offence' (see 10.19), but not longer than any statutory maximum for the offence, if it thinks this 'necessary to protect the public from serious harm from the offender'. The mandatory wording of s 31, however, is deceptive, since it leaves the judge free to decide what additional period is called for (in *Mumtaz Ali* [1995] Crim LR 260 he decided on the extraordinarily short period of 3 years, which would have ensured parole after 18 months). The sentencer must say in open court why an LTC sentence is called for; and must give counsel notice that this step is being considered (*Baverstock* (1992) 14 Cr App Rep (S) 471).There must be evidence in the offender's record or elsewhere that if not so sentenced he or she is likely to do serious harm (*Swain* (1994) 15 Cr App Rep (S) 765, and *Bowler* (1993) 14 Cr App Rep (S) 78). The danger apprehended can be to a single person or small group: it need not be to the general public (*Hashi* (1995) 16 Cr App Rep (S) 121). Sexual offences are defined (in s 31 CJA 91) by listing the statutes which define them. A violent offence is defined as 'an offence which leads, or is intended or likely to lead, to a person's death or to physical injury to a person', and includes arson. What it does not include is psychological harm, so that robbers who have threatened their victims with knives but claimed that they did not intend to use them have had LTC sentences quashed (eg *Bibby* [1994] Crim LR 610); and so have men and women who threatened to kill (eg *Richart* [1995] Crim LR 574).

The length of the LTC sentence must not be 'out of all proportion to the nature of the offending' (*Mansell* (1994) 15 Cr App Rep (S) 771), and is often reduced slightly by mitigating considerations (eg in *Bingham* (1993) 15 Cr App Rep (S) 205). Both decisions seem inconsistent with the express aim of the statute. If a term of $x$ years is 'necessary to protect the public' it is hard to see how a somewhat shorter term is appropriate. This is a good example of the way in which legislators' utilitarian intentions can be diluted by the retributive reasoning of the CA.

### Sexual offenders' licences (s 44 CJA 91)

22.4   Sexual offenders (but not violent ones) are also singled out by s 44 CJA 91.When the whole or part of a determinate sentence is imposed for a sexual offence, the court can order that when the offender is released on licence it shall remain in force until the end of the sentence, not merely until the three-quarter stage is reached; and that if the ex-prisoner is recalled he or she shall be liable to be detained until the end of the sentence, and not merely until the three-quarter stage is reached. The court has this power whether or not its sentence is LTC; but it must have had regard to the considerations which are statutory for the Parole Board: the need to protect the public from serious harm, and the desirability of preventing further offences by offenders and of rehabilitating them (s 32 CJA 91).

## Indeterminate custody

**22.5** The CC can pass a sentence of imprisonment for life (or the statutory equivalents for offenders under 21: see s 8 CJA 82 and s 53 CYPA 33) if the offence is attempted murder, manslaughter, arson, criminal damage intended to endanger life, aggravated burglary, robbery, buggery, incest or sexual intercourse with a girl under the age of 13, kidnapping, possessing a Class A drug for supply and —in theory at least—unlawful abortion, infanticide and forgery of registers of births, deaths or marriages. The court must give due notice to the defendant that it is contemplating such a sentence, so that he or she can assemble a case against it. The CA has made it clear that normally 'life' should not be used 'unless there is clear evidence of mental instability, as opposed to mental disorder, which would indicate that the person was likely to be a danger to the public' (*Blackburn* (1979) 1 Cr App Rep (S) 205). The criterion is mental instability: medical evidence is usually expected, but the instability need not necessarily be a disorder which psychiatrists can name or treat (*Thornett* (1979) 1 Cr App Rep (S) 1). Parker LCJ explained that 'where no such condition exists … a judge should not pass the difficult matter of sentencing and the length of detention to others' (*Picker* (1970) 54 Cr App Rep 330): a surprising reason when the Parole Board had recently been created with the very purpose of advising the Home Secretary on the length of detention. Occasionally, however, the Court of Appeal has upheld a life sentence simply on the ground that the offender was dangerous and would be until an unforeseeable date (an example is *Allen* (1987) 9 Cr App Rep (S) 169, who was a persistently vengeful ex-lover). If the 'quality of the risk' is not such as to justify 'life' it may be justifiable to pass a LTC sentence (*Helm* [1995] Crim LR 441). The phrase 'quality of risk' seems to mean 'the probability plus the nature of the possible future harm'.

## Mandatory 'life' (s 1 M(ADP)A 65; s 8 CJA 82; s 53 CYPA 33)

**22.6** For murder, life (or its equivalent for murderers under 21[1]) is mandatory. The historical explanation is that it replaced the mandatory death penalty; but successive Home Secretaries have defended it on the ground that, unlike the discretionary life sentence, it symbolises the unique gravity of the crime and not the future risk from the offender. (If so, it should be extended to attempted murder.) Only one of the committees which have discussed it has supported the status quo, and that was the Home Affairs Committee of the House of Commons (1995), but with an important rider (see the next paragraph). Most have condemned it, notably one chaired by a former Lord Chief Justice (Lane, 1993). Their main argument has been a retributive one: that the culpability of murderers varies too greatly to deserve the same penalty; and that some—for example 'mercy killings'—do not deserve imprisonment at all. As for the symbolic role of the mandatory life sentence, this is a 19th century assumption unsupported by empirical evidence. It seems more likely (see 8.25) that the public relies on what it is told about individual cases, rather than on the nature of the sentence, to form an opinion about heinousness; and the fact that a life sentence is mandatory rather than discretionary is unlikely to convey any clear or authoritative message. The status quo apart, there are four solutions worth considering:

a. to make 'life' discretionary for all sorts of murder (as it is for attempted murder);

b. to make it discretionary — or even rule it out — for some defined categories of murder ('second degree murders');

c. to supplement provocation and diminished responsibility with another defence which would reduce murder to manslaughter: a defence of 'reduced culpability' (which could incidentally include cases of the sort that are nowadays straining the provocation defence);

d. to enact that mandatory 'life' should be appealable. It would still be mandatory on the sentencer to pass it, but would not debar the CA from varying it. (An analogy would be obligatory disqualification from driving: see 21.8ff.) A practical objection would be the large number of appeals with which the CA would have to deal; but it has its way of disposing of unmeritorious appeals.

1. In *Hussein and Singh* (1996) Times, 26 February, the ECHR applied the reasoning in *Thynne* to those detained under s 53(1) CYPA 33. They too should have the lawfulness of their detention determined by a court to comply with Art 5.4.

## Minimum periods to be served (s 1 M(ADP)A 65; ss 34, 43 CJA 91)

**22.7** Even less defensible is the difference between the statutory procedures governing the release of mandatory and discretionary lifers. When passing a mandatory life sentence the court may 'declare' the period which it recommends to the Home Secretary as the minimum time to be served before release. Originally this was intended to allow judges to recommend quite short minima for some murderers; but in *Flemming* [1973] 2 All ER 401 the CA disregarded that, and laid down that they should not make recommendations unless they had at least 12 years in mind. Such recommendations are not appealable, not being part of the sentence (*Bowden* (1983) 77 Cr App Rep 66). The Home Secretary must, however, consult the LCJ about any recommendation. He may accept, increase or reduce the period, but must give the lifer the opportunity to make representations to him, telling him what the judiciary have said about it, including their reasons; and the Home Secretary himself must give reasons if he is minded to depart from the judiciary's recommendation. Minimum periods — sometimes called 'tariff periods' — are meant to be such as to serve the need for retribution and deterrence, not the protection of the public, which becomes the main consideration only when the tariff period has been served. For a full discussion by the House of Lords see *Doody* [1993] 3 All ER 92. Contrast this with the minimum periods specified under s 34 CJA 91 for exactly the same purposes by a court which passes a discretionary life sentence for a violent or sexual offence. Though not required to do so it is expected to unless the seriousness of the offence justifies literal detention for life (*Practice Direction* of 1993 in [1993] 1 WLR 223). The defendant's counsel should be invited to address the court on the subject before it specifies the tariff period, and it is appealable (but not alterable by the Home Secretary). When calculating the tariff period the court is required by s 34 CJA 91 to take into account the period which a prisoner serving an appropriate determinate sentence for the offence would be likely to serve before being paroled. If the offence was not violent or sexual, or if by any chance the CC does not specify a tariff period, the sentence is not a 'discretionary' one; the tariff period is determined by the Home Secretary as if it were a mandatory sentence, and the Parole Board is merely invited to make a recommendation, not a decision (s 35(2) CJA 91). The Home Affairs Select Committee (see 22.6) thought that the Home Secretary should cease to play any part in determining the tariff period for any life sentence. For a discussion see Padfield (1993).

### Hospital orders with restrictions (ss 41-44 MHA 83)

**22.8**  When the offender's mental condition is of a nature or degree which persuades the CC to make a hospital order (see 21.35ff) it can prevent him or her from being discharged in the usual way by adding a 'restriction order' if it is of the opinion 'having regard to the nature of the offence, the antecedents of the offender and the risk of his committing further offences if set at large, that it is necessary for the protection of the public from serious harm'. Although an MC can make a hospital order it cannot make a restriction order, and can only commit the offender to the CC with a view to such an order, making no order itself (and cannot do even this if the offender is under 14). This does not prevent the CC from choosing some other disposal. But between committal and final disposal the offender can be remanded to a specified hospital.

**22.9**  A restriction order must not be made unless one of the medical witnesses has appeared in court to give oral evidence, so that he or she can be questioned about the need for the restriction or the degree of security which the proposed hospital can provide. On the other hand, even if both medical witnesses are opposed to a restriction order on the ground that the offender is not dangerous this does not prevent the court from making one (*Royse* (1981) 3 Cr App Rep (S) 58). By failing to appear in person, however, the medical witnesses can compel the court to think twice — a not unheard-of situation.

**22.10**  A restriction order may specify its duration or set no time-limit. Most orders are indeterminate: in *Gardiner* ((1967) 51 Cr App Rep 187) the LCJ said that a time-limit should be set 'only where the doctors are able to assert confidently that recovery will take place within a fixed period' (a point again emphasised by the CA in *Nwokia* [1995] Crim LR 668). The Butler Committee (1975) was convinced by the evidence it received that time-limits were always inadvisable; but pressure groups persuaded legislators otherwise.

**22.11**  The effects of a restriction order are that while it is in force
  (a)  none of the limitations on the compulsory detention of a non-criminal patient (see 21.40ff) apply to the offender-patient;
  (b)  the RMO cannot give him or her leave of absence, a transfer to another

hospital or a discharge without the Home Secretary's consent. If leave of absence is allowed the patient can be recalled by the Home Office as well as by the RMO;

(c) if discharge is allowed it can be subject to conditions (much as a parole licence can); and the discharged patient can be recalled either for a breach of a condition or for other reasons, such as a conviction.

**22.12**   What a restriction order does not do is to require the hospital to apply any special measures of security to the patient. If he absconds the police must be told and efforts made to recapture him or her. Only a special hospital, however, or a 'secure unit' (see 21.17ff) guarantees some degree of secure custody. Yet a substantial percentage of such orders commit the offender to ordinary NHS hospitals. This not as risky as it sounds. Many such patients present no immediate danger, and become likely to harm others only after being at large long enough to resume social—or anti-social—relationships, or return to heavy drinking or drug-abuse.

## Guidelines

**22.13**   What amount to guideline cases are *Gardiner* (1967) 51 Cr App Rep 187 and *Birch* (1989) 11 Cr App Rep (S) 202, which make several points:

1.  '... in the case of crimes of violence, and of the more serious sexual offences, particularly if the prisoner has a record of such offences, or if there is a history of mental disorder involving violent behaviour,....there must be compelling reasons to explain why a restriction order should not be made' (*Gardiner*);

2.  but ' there is nothing in the Act which requires a causal connection between the offender's mental state and ... the "index" offence' (*Birch*);

3.  and 'a minor offence by a man who proves to be mentally disordered and dangerous may properly leave him subject to a restriction' (*Birch*). This should be contrasted with the requirement for 'life', that the offence be one which the statutes treat as grave, and with the ruling that the length of an LTC sentence must not be 'out of all proportion to the nature of the offending' (*Mansell*, cited in 22.2);

4.  a restriction order should never be used as a punishment, or merely to mark the gravity of the offence (*Birch*);

5.  it is perfectly proper to take into account, when considering a restriction order, the powers of release which the MHRTs and the Home Secretary have (*Birch*: apparently a hint that it is possible to be too hesitant about adding a restriction order);

6.  the harm to be prevented must be serious, but 'need not be limited to personal injury. Nor need it relate to the public in general, for it would ... suffice if a category of persons, or even a single person, were adjudged to be at risk' (*Birch*);

7.  a restriction order can be made even when the psychiatrists are unanimous that it is not necessary (*Birch*).

## In practice

**22.14**   CSEW do not show the frequency with which the CC uses LTC sentences, but do provide information about the use of life sentences and restricted hospital orders. Table 22A assembles this:

**TABLE 22A: Indeterminate detentions in 1993 (with 1992 numbers in brackets)**

| Offence | Life sentences[1] | Restricted hospital orders[2] |
|---|---|---|
| Murder | 174 (158) | ineligible |
| Attempted murder | — (4 ) | 1 (2) |
| Threats etc to murder | 7 (- ) | 1 (5) |
| Diminished responsibility manslaughter | 2 (4) | 12 (3) |
| Other manslaughter | 8 (10) | 8 (16) |
| Woundings etc endangering life | 3 ( 8) | 8 (15) |
| Buggery | 3 (4) | 1 (-) |
| Rape | 13 (10) | 4 (5)* |
| Robbery | 6 (1) | 9 (9) |
| Kidnapping, abduction | 2 (2) | 3 (1) |
| Drug offence | 1 (-) | —(-) |
| Arson | 5 (8) | 8 (5) |
| Lesser woundings | These | 16 (17) |
| Cruelty to children | offences | —(1) |
| Concealment of birth | were | 1 (-) |
| Indecent assault | not | 3 (3) |
| Theft | eligible | —(3) |
| Burglary of dwelling | for | —(1) |
| Fraud by director | life | —(1) |
| Criminal damage | sentences | 3 (-) |
| Firearms offence | | —(1) |
| Blackmail | | 1 (-) |
| Rioting | | 1 (-) |
| Common assault | | 1 (-) |
| Summary traffic offence | | 1 (-) |
| TOTALS | 224 (209) | 82 (88) |

1.  Not including indeterminate detentions under s 53 CYPA 33.
2.  Including perhaps a few with time-limits (see 21.7).

## Other restricted patients

**22.15**   It must be remembered that, as 21.52 explained, most patients admitted under restrictions have come not from the CC but from prisons, remand centres and young offenders' institutions. By no means all of these patients are of a kind which psychiatrists or the CC would regard as dangerous: the intention is simply to prevent them from being discharged by the RMO as if they had been admitted in one of the ordinary ways (see 21.40ff). Transfers under restriction far outnumber restriction orders made by the CC: 632 in 1992.

## Release

**22.16**  The release of prisoners serving LTC sentences is considered by the Parole Board under the procedures which apply to all sentences of 4 years or more, although the knowledge that a sentence was passed with a view to protecting the public against serious harm makes panels approach their decisions with special care. It is lifers and restricted patients whose release is subject to specific statutory rules and directives. Release from a discretionary life sentence is also a matter for decision by the Parole Board, but only after the prisoner has served the period specified by the sentencing judge as appropriate to the seriousness of the offence (and any other offences associated with it), and after the case has been referred to the Board by the Home Secretary (which the prisoner can require the Home Secretary to do once the specified period has been served) (s 34 CJA 91)1. This provision, however, applies only to discretionary life sentences for violent or sexual offences (as defined by s 31 CJA 91), and courts are not obliged to specify any minimum period.If a court does not, or if the life term was for an offence not defined as violent or sexual, release is a matter for decision by the Home Secretary, as it was for all life sentences before the CJA 91. He refers the lifers' cases to the Board, and if the Board opposes release he cannot authorise it; but if the Board recommends it he is not bound to agree, and often does not (for example, in at least 7 out of 88 cases in 1993). Naturally the Board considers (and interviews) lifers of all kinds with particular care. The panels which deal with them are chaired by judges and usually include a psychiatrist and an experienced probation officer. The number released each year (114 in 1993) is very much smaller than the number of new lifers (see Table 22A), so that the lifer population in the prison system (3,000 in 1992) is growing at a rate which is causing concern. It is much larger than the lifer population of any other country in Western Europe, and although that is partly due to other countries' preference for very long determinate sentences part of the explanation is the mandatory life sentence for murder.

1.   But if the discretionary lifer has been transferred to hospital for psychiatric reasons (see 21.51) his case cannot be referred to the Parole Board unless and until his treatment has ended or is no longer appropriate (*Hickey (No 1)* [1995] 1 All ER 479).

## Reasons for adverse decisions

**22.17**  As in the case of determinate sentences the Parole Board and the Home Secretary can be required to give reasons for an adverse decision. A typical reason is the prisoner's recent behaviour. Lifers who seem likely to be fit for release are almost always transferred to open prisons and allowed work and sometimes recreation in the community. Some of them fail this test. Another reason—usually only temporary—is the difficulty of finding accommodation where they will be under satisfactory supervision. Recently the Home Secretary has admitted (in a directive published in the Parole Board's Report for 1993) that he may take into account the likely reaction of public opinion to the release of a particular lifer.

## Time served[1]

**22.18** Although in theory a lifer could be released within a matter of months, in practice very few are set free within 7 years. Since 1993 it has been the Home Secretary's policy not to agree to release before 20 years have been served in cases of terrorist murders, murders of police or prison officers, sexual or sadistic murders of children and murders by firearms in the course of robbery. About 1 in 20 lifers have served 20 years or more, and some 30 years or more. A few have been told not to expect release at all.

1.   Source: the Prison Statistics for 1992.

## Licences

**22.19** The standard conditions of a licence from a determinate sentence are set out in 14.36, and are similar, though differently worded, in a lifer's licence. Special conditions, however, can be added to both kinds of licence at the instance of the Parole Board or a supervisor: an example is one forbidding work or association with children under a certain age. A lifer's licence remains in force until death, although after some years of trouble-free conduct (usually about 5) its specific conditions will probably have been removed. He or she is liable however to recall at any stage for conduct which gives rise to alarm, although the ground is usually a breach of a specific condition or a new conviction. A recalled lifer can appeal to the Parole Board, which can cancel the recall, or advise the Home Secretary to do so in the case of a mandatory life sentence.

## Restriction order discharges (ss 73-79 MHA 83)[1]

**22.20** A restricted patient cannot be discharged simply by a decision of his RMO: only on the authority of the Home Secretary or the local MHRT (see 21.44ff). He has the right to apply to, and appear before, the MHRT at regular intervals; and his case can be referred to the MHRT by the Home Secretary. The prime consideration is of course his own health and safety and the protection of other persons; but the MHRT is obliged to direct his discharge if satisfied that he or she is not now suffering from mental illness, psychopathic disorder or mental impairment to a degree that makes detention in hospital for treatment 'appropriate'. Occasionally this obliges an MHRT to direct discharge even when it is not satisfied that this is safe (e g because the mental illness is of a kind that is likely to recur). The Home Secretary's discretion is not subject to this awkward constraint; but the patient can always resort to the MHRT. Another limitation of MHRTs' powers is that they cannot direct transfers from one hospital to another. Yet it is usually preferable for a restricted patient in a special hospital or secure unit to be transferred to a more open hospital as a first step to freedom. The MHRT may agree, but feel obliged to direct a discharge because it has not been found possible to persuade an open hospital to accept a transfer.

1.  The discharge of a patient who is under restriction as a result of being transferred to hospital during a sentence of 4 years or more is the responsibility of the Parole Board. If he or she is still in hospital at the date when he or she would have had to be released by law the restriction order lapses, and discharge from hospital becomes a matter for the RMO.

### Time spent in hospitals

**22.21**   Table 22B shows what periods had been spent in hospital by restricted patients who were still there at the end of 1992. The source (Home Office Statistical Bulletin 04/94) does not, unfortunately, show the periods spent by those who were discharged during the year. Nevertheless the table shows how long it is possible to be detained:

**TABLE 22B: Periods spent in hospital by restricted patients still detained at end of 1992**

| Time since original admission or last recall | Men | Women |
| --- | --- | --- |
| under 2 years | 426 | 46 |
| 2 to 5 years | 726 | 96 |
| 6 to 10 years | 340 | 60 |
| 11 to 20 years | 369 | 52 |
| 21 to 30 years | 164 | 9 |
| over 30 years | 39 | 6 |
| TOTALS | 2064 | 269 |

Roughly half of the men and women were in the special hospitals. It should not be assumed that all of them were unwillingly detained. When Mackay and Ward (1994) studied 85 men and women who had been restricted patients for 15 years or more after being found insane or unfit to plead (admittedly a rather extreme group: see 21.60), they found that 35 were recorded as having said that they wanted to stay where they were; and some even labelled themselves as dangerous.

### Conditions of discharge

**22.22**   A discharge may be—usually is—subject to conditions as to where the ex-patient must live and the appointments he or she must keep with a local psychiatrist or supervisor. A breach or a new conviction makes him or her liable to be recalled. A discharge may, however, be 'absolute' — ie unconditional — in which case the ex-patient cannot be recalled (although he or she can be readmitted compulsorily or voluntarily if his or her condition justifies this). An unconditional discharge is sensible if arrangements have been made for the patient to leave Britain, but is seldom without risk.

### Reconvictions and recalls[1]

**22.23** A follow-up (using the Offenders' Index) of lifers and restricted patients released in the years 1972-89 found that 3 per cent of the lifers and 5 per cent of the ex-patients had within five years been convicted of a 'grave offence' (ie homicide, serious wounding, rape, buggery, robbery, arson or aggravated burglary). Most (90 per cent) of the released lifers had been sentenced for homicides; but they were somewhat less likely than the others to be reconvicted of a grave offence, even when previous convictions were taken into account. The rates would almost certainly have been higher but for the 16 per cent of lifers and 14 per cent of ex-patients who had been recalled.

1.   Home Office Statistical Bulletin 18/94.

### Supervision

**22.24** Timely recalls are the responsibility of supervisors (usually experienced probation officers, even when an ex-patient is under the care of a local psychiatrist). Reasons for recall may be minor convictions, heavy drinking, drug abuse, leaving an approved address, persistent failure to keep appointments with supervisors (or psychiatrists) or other erratic behaviour. Some of these reasons sound trivial, but are often the precursors of recidivism. Warning signs vary of course with the crime: what would be worrying behaviour by a paedophile would not necessarily justify concern about a wife-killer. Not all supervisors, however, are adequately briefed. A survey of all 56 English probation services by Shaw (1991) found that 37 had no specific policies as regards the definition or handling of dangerous 'clients'. Many dossiers had no detailed account of the circumstances of the original offence, and were of little help to a new supervisor. There have been improvements; but this supports the conclusion of Coker and Martin's (1985) study of released lifers : 'the notion of, or belief in, "strict" supervision is nonsense'. On the other hand, supervisors are meant to be supportive as well as watchful. Probation services find lodgings or hostels for those who cannot rejoin their families, and if possible jobs. They give advice as well as warnings, advice which sometimes averts another offence or recall.

### Confidentiality

**22.25** The more people know about the supervisee's past the more alert they will be to report warning signs to his or her probation officer. Yet there is an understandable reluctance to burden the ex-inmate with the awareness that he or she is stigmatised in the eyes of those with whom he has daily contact. So far as ex-patients are concerned the Health Service Guidelines are strict:

'...all information relating to the patient is confidential. Such information should be disclosed within the NHS only to those who are involved in the care and treatment of the patient and then only on a strict need-to-know basis. Disclosure outside the NHS (for example to social workers, the police or the probation service) should occur only if the patient has expressed or implied consent, or where disclosure can be justified as *being in the public interest*.... Obtaining consent is essential in most cases.' (HSG (94) 27: our italics).

Clearly a member of the NHS needs courage to decide that it would be in the public interest to disclose vital information about an ex-patient. Where ex-prisoners are concerned information is less sacrosanct. Supervising probation officers are given fairly full histories, and feel free to decide how much should be passed on to hostel wardens or other people with whom the ex-prisoner will be living. (It is sometimes advisable to tell employers the relevant facts: Graham Young, the compulsive poisoner, was entrusted with tea-making for his fellow employees when he was found his first job, with fatal results.) The police are told the date of the prisoner's release, his or her previous convictions and his or her new address. If his or her crime gravely affected a victim (or relatives of a victim) and he or she is going to live or work near them, the local probation service is supposed to make sure that this will not be too disturbing for them. If it clearly will be this may alter the plans for release.

Understandably, most ex-inmates look forward to the day when they can move to an address and job of their own choosing, free of supervision and of stigma. Some try to do so without permission. Eventually, however, usually after 5 years of good behaviour, the Home Office may remove all the specific conditions, and allow this to happen.

### Supervision registers for ex-patients

**22.26** In 1994 health authorities were required to create 'supervision registers' for people aged 16 or older who are suffering from severe mental illness or personality disorder 'and are, or are liable to be, at significant risk of committing serious violence or suicide or of severe self-neglect in some foreseeable circumstances which it is felt might well arise in this particular case (e g ceasing to take medication, loss of a supportive relationship or loss of accommodation)' (HSG (94) 5 from the NHS Management Executive). It is not clear why this definition does not include mental impairment, and why the risk of non-violent sexual offences is not mentioned as a consideration. The decision to place someone on the local supervision register is the responsibility of the relevant consultant psychiatrist. The ex-patient must be told that he or she has been put on it, and can ask to be removed from it; but since the request is simply considered by the consultant psychiatrist 'in conjunction with professional colleagues' it is unlikely to succeed in most cases. The ex-patient's entry in the register is as confidential as any other health records, but may be communicated to non-NHS agencies—such as courts or probation services—if the patient consents or *if disclosure can be justified in the public interest.* Entries should be transferred from one local register to another if the ex-patient is known to have moved. The main aim of this innovation was to ensure that the special problems and risks presented by an increasing number of ex-patients were not overlooked by busy health and social workers. It is too early to tell how much effect it will have; and indeed the effect will be hard to measure.The same is true of the Mental Health (Patients in the Community) Act 1995, which allows offenders who have been subject to hospital orders without restriction orders to be discharged under compulsory supervision and after-care on the application of their RMOs, on grounds which include 'the safety of other persons'(see 21.41).

## Non-custodial precautions

**22.27** Although it is natural to think of precautionary sentences as custodial, since this offers the highest degree of incapacitation short of death or mutilation, there are a few non-custodial measures which are intended to make it less likely that an offender will commit similar offences. The best known is disqualification from driving, dealt with in 23.12ff. Others will be found in the Food and Drugs Act 1955, the Firearms Act 1968, the Licensing Act 1964, the Medicines Act 1968, the Dangerous Wild Animals Act 1976, the Company Directors Disqualification Act 1986, the Children Act 1958, the Licensed Premises (Exclusion of Certain Persons) Act 1980, the Domestic Proceedings and Magistrates' Courts Act 1978, and the Public Bodies Corrupt Practices Act 1889. Most of these statutes rely on courts to make the necessary order, but some entrust the necessary discretion to other authorities: to chief constables, for example, in the case of firearms, to the General Medical Council in the case of dangerous doctors, to the DES in the case of child-abusing teachers. An ACPS report (1970) recommended that courts should be empowered to impose 'prohibited employment orders' when convicting people of sexual, violent or cruel offences against children, thus making it an offence for them to seek jobs involving association with children; but successive governments have rejected the idea. In any case, disqualifications merely threaten: they do not disable. Disqualified drivers can still drive, and many do.

## Medical precautions

**22.28** Medical or surgical measures can sometimes be used by way of precaution. British law does not allow castration or the amputation of hands. What it does allow is the giving of drugs to sexual offenders to reduce their desires. This can be done only with the offender's informed consent, but the offender is often in the position of knowing that refusal will probably delay his release. Other drugs can be offered to counteract irritability of the kind which leads to violence, to avert the 'highs' of manic disorder or the lows of depression, and thus reduce the likelihood of violence. They need, however, to be administered at regular intervals, and if the offender is recalcitrant or forgetful this may not happen, one of the reasons for supervision registers and the MH(PICA)95 (see 22.26).

## Ethical aspects

**22.29** Incapacitation is the one aim which an individual sentence can be relied upon to achieve. But since custody is the only efficient way of incapacitating it raises ethical issues which have still to be discussed (for a fuller discussion see Walker, 1996).

One theoretical cliché can be disposed of fairly quickly. Dangerousness is sometimes said to be always 'conditional'—dependent on the occurrence of some provocation or some temptation. It is true that many violent assaults and sexual offences are responses to situations in which people with weak self-control find themselves. It is also true that some people have a tendency to drift into situations in which they are likely to be tempted or provoked—a phenomenon of interest to psychologists as well as social workers. But there are people of a third kind, the opportunity-seekers and opportunity-makers, who, if their inclinations are sexual, sadistic or aggressive, must be regarded as unconditionally dangerous.

**22.30** More important, however, is the ethical debate about the propriety of imposing precautions on unwilling people. This is one by-product of retribut-ivism's negative rule, which forbids (i) punishing those who have committed no crime, and (ii) punishing those who have more severely than they deserve. It has been argued, for example, that detaining offenders for longer than they deserve in order to protect others is punishment for offences they have not committed and may never commit (Swedish National Council for Crime Prevention, 1978). The fallacy in this argument is the assumption that the purpose of a sentence is and must always be retributive punishment, and nothing else: an assumption which would be rejected by any legislature, except perhaps an Islamic one.

**22.31** A somewhat less extreme view is Dworkin's (1977). He believes that restraining someone against his or her will is an infringement of a right to liberty and respect. He does not see this right as one that can be forfeited, and he merely tolerates the infringement of it in the case of people who cannot control their conduct, not as an infringement which can be justified but only as a 'compromise with principle', and only when the danger is 'vivid' (he does not indicate how to distinguish 'vivid' from 'non-vivid' danger, but Bottoms and Brownsword (1983) suggest that it must be mainly a synthesis of seriousness and probability). The Floud Committee (1981) also talked the language of rights but less one-sidedly. They saw the right not to be restrained as founded on the right to be presumed harmless: a right enjoyed only by those who have not done or tried to do serious harm. This presumption and this right are forfeited by those who do or attempt serious harm, thus giving others—ie society's courts—

the right to deal with them as potentially harmful. This is a right but not a duty. Courts must exercise discretion and decide who needs to be restrained.

**22.32** Yet the exercise of this discretion does not escape moral sniping. A great deal is made of the fact that most people who do grave harm to others do not do so again when at liberty. There are exceptions: a majority of males with more than three convictions for violent offences will eventually be reconvicted of violence. And there are a few identifiable opportunity-makers, especially among sexual offenders. By and large, however, considerably less than half of offenders who do grave harm are ever guilty of doing it again. This being so, a policy which prolongs their detention solely for the protection of others will make more mistakes than one which does not. The fallacy in this argument is its arithmetic, which lumps together two quite different errors under the term 'mistake'. A release which has disastrous consequences cannot be put in the same scales against a decision to prolong detention which, could one have known it, is unnecessary. What is less obvious is that any anti-protectionist argument which is based on probabilities relies on this arithmetical fallacy.[1] Underlying the arithmetical fallacy, too, is the covert assumption that a mistaken decision which is to someone's disadvantage is always a moral wrong, even when every effort is made to avoid it.

1. This is not an objection to the estimation and use of probabilities (although the difficulties are considerable, as we shall see in the next paragraph). It is merely a refutation of anti-protectionist reasoning which is based on probabilities.

**22.33** For efforts are made. Parole Board panels, MHRTs and Home Office staff use all the information which is available and seems relevant in order to select 'good risks' for release (with the results summarised in 22.23). The information is usually of the kind called 'clinical' — a mixture of facts about the offender's history and the impression he or she has made on psychiatrists, psychologists and other staff. Less reliance is placed on 'actuarial' information, consisting of statistics about the reconviction rates of offenders of comparable age, gender, record and so forth. In other sorts of prediction actuarial information has usually proved more accurate than clinical judgement; but attempts to predict the repetition of grave offences come up against great difficulties:
   a. experiments in which a random selection of grave offenders is set free early to see who will repeat his or her offence are out of the question;
   b. in real life, some released offenders have to be recalled, as we have seen, in case they are about to commit new offences of a serious kind, but without any certainty that they would have. They cannot be categorised as 'successes' or 'failures", and simply have to be discarded from calculations;
   c. since the question is whether subjects will ever commit another grave offence, the follow-up must be a very long one: at least 5 years, and preferably more (especially in the case of sexual offenders because of their low detection rate);
   d. for statistical reasons prediction formulae have the best chance of being usably accurate when about 50 per cent of subjects do what is being predicted. The smaller the percentage the greater the number of erroneous

predictions. Since the percentage of grave offenders who do grave harm again is small, actuarial predictions are bound to yield quite a lot of 'false positives' and 'false negatives'.

**22.34** Consequently hopes of providing decision-makers in this field with powerful information of an actuarial kind seem doomed. An individual's own history is still the most useful information. 'Nothing predicts behavior like behavior' (Kvaraceus, 1966). Not that it is a very accurate predictor. Taking into account other kinds of information—age, gender, use of alcohol or drugs, time inside and so forth—may be helpful; but where grave offences are concerned decision-makers must not expect prediction formulae which yield *reliably* quantified probabilities. Very occasionally some item of information may be reassuring in a really decisive way: for example that the offender has been disabled by injury or illness. But such cases are rare.

## Kinds of harm

**22.35** Less often discussed is the question 'What kinds of harm are such as to justify drastic precautions, and in particular prolonged detention ?' The answer in the CJA 91 (s 31) is 'death or serious personal injury, whether physical or psychological, occasioned by …[the offender]'. Yet there is at least one modern statute which allows an indeterminate sentence for a type of offence which does not fit easily into this definition. The Misuse of Drugs Act 1971 permits a life sentence for possessing a Class A drug with intent to supply it to others. It is of course arguable that the effect of abusing a Class A drug is likely to be 'serious personal injury'; but it is equally arguable that the supplier is not exactly 'occasioning' the injury. (It is in fact quite likely that this provision was intended as a deterrent rather than a prophylactic). It would be consistent with the 1971 Act, however, to permit a similar sentence—or at least a longer than commensurate one—for the dangerous disposal of toxic or radioactive waste; and a case could be made for LTC sentences for financiers who ruin pensioners or investors. It was proposed some time ago that precautionary sentencing should be allowable to prevent harms of kinds which (a) are lasting, (b) are irremediable and (c) seriously damage the quality of life (Walker, 1980). Another seldom discussed point is that as a rule nowadays—it was not always thus[1]—English statutes disallow precautionary custodial sentences unless the offence leading to the sentence is itself violent or sexual, although of course what the sentence is intended to do is prevent *future* harm. An interesting exception is a hospital order with restrictions, which is merely limited to any imprisonable offence by a person disordered enough to warrant compulsory hospitalisation. The CC must have regard to the nature of the offence (inter alia) but it does not have to be violent, sexual or even serious (*Khan* (1987) Cr App Rep (S) 455: *Birch* (1989) 11 Cr App Rep (S) 202). What is required is simply that the CC believe the restriction order to be necessary for the future protection of the public against serious harm. As Table 22A shows the CC is prepared to use such orders when dealing with offences which are not in themselves very alarming: an example is 'concealment of birth'. The degree of discretion seems wide but rational.

1.  The 'extended sentence', which was replaced in 1991 by the LTC sentence, could be used for any offence punishable with imprisonment for 2 years or more (but was limited to offenders whose criminal histories met strict and complicated criteria: see ss 28, 29 PCCA 73).

## Conditions of detention

**22.36** One final point remains to be made. When an offender's detention reaches a stage at which it is being prolonged solely for the benefit of others, it is arguable that the conditions of detention should be made as tolerable as practicable by way of recompense. In fact the Prison Service honours this principle to a certain extent in its handling of long-sentence prisoners, although in many cases considerations of security interfere with amenity. The same is true of secure mental hospitals.Unfortunately some prisoners and patients are dangerous to staff and to fellow inmates. The ways in which prisons can deal with them are governed by strict rules and procedures for ensuring that the rules are applied fairly. In hospitals, on the other hand, it tends to be assumed that staff will exercise humane control without being bound by statutory rules. It is only recently that it has been argued (e g by Richardson, 1993) that this is not sufficient. It is not only inmates' conduct, however, which limits amenities. Public opinion, or more precisely public opinion when stimulated by the news media, is critical of them where offenders are the beneficiaries. In both prisons and hospitals there are staff who are willing to sell information about them to the media, enabling the latter to use emotive descriptions such as 'holiday camps'. Nevertheless it is arguable that the special status of prisoners and patients whose detention is being prolonged solely for the protection of others should be accorded some recognition.

# Chapter 23

# Traffic offenders

**23.1** A category of dangerous offender not mentioned in the previous chapter is the bad driver. Since he or she is responsible for more deaths and injuries than any other single category of offender, it is remarkable how little attention is paid to this subject in books about crime or sentencing[1], in Parliament or in criminological research units[2]. The readiness of legislators to provide courts with new or tougher ways of dealing with indictable offenders—whether or not courts are prepared to make use of them—contrasts strongly with the opposition to attempts to improve the state of the Road Traffic Acts. Recent examples have been the requirement to wear a seat-belt and the random use of breath-tests. Private motorists are vigorously and ably represented by the Automobile Association and the Royal Automobile Club, each with a high percentage of offenders in its membership.

1.  The authoritative textbook on the law is the latest edition of *Wilkinson's Road Traffic Offences*. Hood's pioneering study of the sentencing of motoring offenders (1972) has now been rendered out of date by the guidance in the Magistrates' Association's *Suggestions for Road Traffic Offence Penalties* (1993).
2.  Most of the relevant research in this country has been carried out by the Transport and Road Research Laboratory (formerly the Road Research Laboratory), although references to other studies, such as Willett (1973) and Kriefman (1975) will be found in this chapter. There seems to have been little recent British research of a relevant kind. A minor but not insignificant problem is the driver who is mentally disordered or under the influence of psychotropic medication: see Humphreys and Roy (1995).

## Mere negligence?

**23.2** Sentencers, too, are apt to distinguish traffic offenders from other kinds. The reason is not simply that the sentencers know that they themselves—or at least their colleagues—have committed or could well commit traffic offences. There is also a tendency to assume that whereas most indictable offences are committed with intention, traffic offences are the result of mere negligence or, at worst, recklessness.

**23.3** In the case of at least one type of offence this assumption seems to be supported by empirical evidence. Quenault (1967) compared 50 car-drivers convicted of careless driving with a randomly selected sample of drivers, all from the area surrounding the Road Research Laboratory. The careless drivers drove, on average, twice the mileage of the control group, used their cars more for business as well as pleasure, and had had three times as many reported accidents. When accompanied by an observer they overtook more often, carried out more 'unusual manoeuvres' and experienced more 'near accidents'. Quenault thought he could sub-divide his drivers into

a. the safe;
b. the injudicious;
c. the dissociated active, who drove unpredictably and impatiently;
d. the dissociated passive, who were patient and stolid, but whose set pattern of driving sometimes ignored the needs of the situation.

The fact that these differences were observable when the drivers knew they were under observation strongly suggests that types (b), (c) and (d) were unaware of the defects of their driving, and it seems likely that their unconscious errors were even worse when they were not under observation.When the exercise was repeated two years later with the same drivers but different observers, every driver was placed in the same sub-division as before: striking support for the typology. A third study, of different drivers under less demanding traffic conditions, reached very similar conclusions (Quenault, 1968).

**23.4** The assumption of non-intentionality is less plausible however where reckless driving is concerned, and is an obvious over-simplification in cases of drunken driving. Many documentary offences—such as driving with an out-of-date licence—are the result of mere negligence; but most parking offences are committed with every element of mens rea.

## Leniency under pressure

**23.5** A third reason for leniency is the sheer impracticability of dealing as severely with traffic offenders as courts do with other criminals whom they regard as dangerous. Custodial sentences, even if reserved for drivers who have repeatedly demonstrated the hazard to others which they represent, would result in a degree of overcrowding in local prisons which this country has not experienced within living memory. In the case of drivers precautionary sentencing usually takes the form not of imprisonment but of disqualification. Even this is used very leniently. The ease with which a plea of hardship could persuade courts not to use it made it necessary to legislate so that in some circumstances it is not discretionary but mandatory: a feature which distinguishes it from most other disqualifications which courts can order. Even so, as we shall see, courts are allowed, and are very ready, to find 'special reasons' for disregarding the mandate (see 22.13ff); and unlike a mandatory life sentence a mandatory disqualification is appealable. The period of disqualification, too, is usually brief, and when it is not the offender has a good chance in the long run of persuading the court to remove the disqualification.

## Diversion under pressure

**23.6**   The sheer volume of traffic offences with which police and courts deal is responsible for other differences. Like the mentally disordered, traffic offenders who appear in court are only the tip of an iceberg, but in this case a huge one. In 1993 an unknown number received informal warnings on the spot, 200,000 were sent written warnings, 200,000 were told to rectify defects in their vehicles, and 4 million received fixed penalty notices. Only 2.4 million were dealt with by courts (in 99 per cent of cases by MCs). Even the minority of traffic offences which are prosecuted is so huge that the procedure of pleading guilty by post was introduced to cope with it, although it can now be used to deal with other kinds of summary offence.

## Written warnings

**23.7**   Written warnings are the equivalent of cautions for non-traffic offences (see 15.5), and are most often about 'documentary' offences, concerning licences, insurance or record-keeping, or else about the condition of vehicles; but about 12 per cent are about speeding. In most police areas they account for between 2 and 5 per cent of formal actions, but in one or two they account for more than 20 per cent, and are clearly being used in cases which in most areas would result in a fixed penalty. Similar to written warnings are Vehicle Defect Rectification Scheme (VDRS) notices.

## Fixed penalties (ss 51-59 RTOA 88 as amended by s 34 RTA 91)

**23.8**   Under the fixed penalty procedure the offender is served on the spot, or later by post, with a notice requiring payment of a standard sum, which varies with the nature and location of the offence. If the offence is one for which endorsement is obligatory the standard sum is greater, and the notice also awards penalty points (usually 3); but if the addition of these to points awarded earlier would lead to automatic disqualification (see 23.11) the offender must be brought to court. He or she can also ask for a court hearing if the notice seems unwarranted, but since that would risk a fine larger than the fixed penalty it is not a frequent response. Unpaid penalties can be converted by MCs to fines, usually 50 per cent greater than the penalties. Offences liable to fixed penalties are listed in Sch 3 RTOA 88: the common ones are

- illegal parking
- infringing speed-limits
- failing to comply with traffic signs
- failing to stop at the request of the police
- failing to comply with requirements as regards seat-belts or motor-cyclists' helmets
- having a motor vehicle in an unsafe condition
- not exhibiting the required vehicle licence
- driving a motor vehicle elsewhere than on a road.

The use of automatic cameras to detect and prove speeding and disregard of traffic lights has added to the numbers of fixed penalty notices. About 3 in 4 fixed penalties for endorsable offences are eventually paid. For some reason the rate is lower—about 2 in 3—for non-endorsable offences.

## Immobilising parked vehicles (ss 104-10 RTRA 84)

**23.9** Another penalty which can be imposed on the spot is the immobilisation of an illegally parked vehicle. The police may[1] attach an 'immobilisation device' (in practice a wheel-clamp), either to the vehicle where it stands or after moving it to another place. They may use contractors for this purpose. In order to recover the use of the vehicle the driver then has to make contact with the police by telephone and pay a 'release charge'.

1. With exceptions: for example if the vehicle carries a disabled driver's badge.

## Endorsement (ss 44, 46, 57, 58 and Sch 2 RTOA 88)

**23.10** When a conviction incurs endorsement the court must normally order particulars of it (and of any disqualification ordered) to be noted on any driving licence held by the offender. An offender who is discharged absolutely or conditionally is not exempt from endorsement. The endorsement remains on the licence either

- a. for 4 years after the conviction (not the offence) if disqualification was ordered; or
- b. if no disqualification was ordered, 4 years after the offence (not the conviction) or until disqualification, whichever is the earlier; or
- c. if the offence was causing death by reckless driving, or reckless driving, 4 years after the conviction (not the offence) irrespective of any disqualification;
- d. if the offence was for driving under the influence of drink or drugs, driving with excess blood-alcohol, or attempts at these, 11 years after a conviction, irrespective of any later conviction or disqualification for that conviction.

A driver who wants a 'clean' licence, however, showing no lapsed endorsements, must apply and pay for it, when the necessary time has elapsed. All endorsements involve penalty points (see 22.11), and they are always obligatory, but as in the case of obligatory disqualification the court is allowed to find 'special reasons' for not endorsing (see 23.14 ff).

## Penalty points

**23.11** Every offence[1] which is liable to disqualification or endorsement entails a number of penalty points, laid down[2] in Sch 2 RTOA 88. They are escaped only if

a. disqualification is ordered for the offence or for another offence which is dealt with on the same occasion; or

b. if the court decides against endorsement for special reasons: see 23.14ff.

In the event of endorsement for two or more offences committed on the same occasion only the points for the offence which incurs the most are endorsed. If the offences were committed on different occasions the points for each are endorsed. In the case of a few offences the court can choose from a range of points (3-6, 3-9, or 3-11) having regard to the seriousness of the offence (not, suggests *Wilkinson*, the offender's record). If and when the offender incurs a conviction carrying a number of penalty points which together with previously endorsed points totals 12 or more, he must be disqualified for

a. at least 6 months if no previous disqualification is to be taken into account (as it must be if imposed within 3 years preceding the commission of the offence incurring the latest points); or

b. at least 1 year if one such disqualification has to be taken into account; or

c. at least 2 years if more than one such disqualification has to be taken into account.

But the court may be satisfied that there are 'mitigating grounds' for not disqualifying or doing so for a period shorter than the statutory minimum.

1. Except the use of a motor vehicle for the commission of an offence: see 23.20.
2. But the number of points may be altered by the Secretary of State by statutory instrument approved in draft by both Houses of Parliament.

## Disqualification (ss 34, 34A, 34B, Sch 2 RTOA 88)

**23.12** Disqualification debars the offender forthwith[1] from holding or obtaining a licence to drive any sort of motor vehicle during the period of disqualification. It may be the automatic result of 'totting-up' penalty points, or obligatory or discretionary, depending on the offence. An absolute or conditional discharge does not prevent disqualification from driving (s 46 RTOA 88). A MC which is remitting a defendant to the CC or another MC may add an interim disqualification if the offence carries obligatory or discretionary disqualification. When it is automatic or obligatory the period specified by the court must be at least 12 months[2] and may be for any longer period, including life. When it is discretionary the court may specify any period, and usually specifies less than a year. Unlike custodial sentences disqualifications imposed by magistrates' courts are subject to no maxima: the only difference between their powers and those of the Crown Court in this respect is that only the Crown Court can disqualify for a non-traffic offence in which a motor vehicle was used for the purpose (s 44 PCCA 73): all that a magistrates' court can do in such cases is to commit the offender to the Crown Court with a view to this. Periods of disqualification may be concurrent but not consecutive (*Sandwell* (1984) 80 Cr App Rep 78).

1. So that an offender who has driven himself to court may find himself unable to drive away.
2. 3 years when the offence is driving (or attempting to) when unfit through drink or drugs or

with more than the prescribed level of alcohol in the blood and the offender has already been convicted of one of those offences within the last 10 years. Offences incurring obligatory or discretionary disqualification are listed in Sch 2, RTOA 88.

## Refraining from obligatory disqualification

**23.13** The obligation to disqualify is not absolute. A court may refrain for one of three reasons (s 93 RTA 72):
   a. if the offence is merely that of aiding, abetting, counselling or procuring the offence, and not of committing or attempting it;
   b. if the court makes a hospital or guardianship order without convicting a mentally disordered offender (see 21.36);
   c. if the court decides that there are 'special reasons' or 'mitigating grounds' for refraining. 'Mitigating grounds' may also allow the court to disqualify for a shorter period than the required minimum (see 23.16) .

## Special reasons

**23.14** 'Special reasons' for not ordering an obligatory disqualification or endorsement must be distinguished from 'mitigating grounds' for refraining from a disqualification which has been incurred by accumulation of penalty points ('totting up') or for disqualifying for less than the statutory minimum period: those are discussed in 23.15. *Wickens* ((1958) 42 Cr App Rep 236) confirmed earlier rulings that a special reason must fulfil all of four criteria:
   a. it must be 'a mitigating or extenuating[1] circumstance';
   b. it 'must not amount in law to a defence to the charge';
   c. it 'must be directly connected with the commission of the offence';
   d. it must be a matter 'which the court ought properly to take into consideration when imposing punishment'.
These should probably be regarded as 'guidelines' (see 1.24). An interesting feature of criterion (d) is the reference to 'punishment'. Originally, the aim of disqualification and endorsement was the protection of other road users from danger: the punishment consisted of a fine or imprisonment. This is no longer so, even in theory. The Court of Appeal's dicta in this and other cases (for example *Donnelly* (1975) 60 Cr App Rep 250) clearly imply that disqualification is now regarded as punitive in intention.

1. There does not seem to be any real difference between the meanings of these two adjectives.

**23.15** However that may be, these four criteria seem to allow a wide variety of special reasons. From the long list in *Wilkinson* some examples can be taken:
   a. driving for a very short distance and in circumstances when the driver was most unlikely to encounter other road users;
   b. being misled (for example as to the constituents of a drink);
   c. having to drive in an emergency when there was no practicable alternative.
More instructive, however, are clear statements of what are *not* acceptable as special reasons: for example

i.   being of good character, with a good driving record (*Whittall v Kirby* [1947] KB 194);
ii.  the hardship that will be experienced by the offender, his family or employer (*Whittall v Kirby* [1947] KB 194);
iii. the fact that the offender is a doctor or in some other occupation in which service to the public requires him to drive (*Holroyd v Berry* [1973] RTR 145);
iv.  the fact that, as a condition of bail, the offender has already been prohibited from driving (*Kwame* [1975] RTR 106);
v.   the fact that the offence itself was not serious (*Nicholson v Brown* [1974] RTR 177).

Unless the prosecution admit the facts constituting special reasons the defence must establish them by evidence on a balance of probabilities, and not merely as a reasonable possibility (*Pugsley v Hunter* [1973] 2 All ER 10).

## Mitigating grounds (s 35 RTOA 88)

**23.16** 'Mitigating grounds', which are relevant only when a court is considering whether to refrain from a 'totting-up' disqualification, or whether to disqualify for less than the statutory minimum period, must be interpreted in the light of s 35 RTOA 88, which
a.  says that the court must have regard to 'all the circumstances' not excluded by a later subsection; but
b.  in that later subsection, excludes
   i.   any circumstances alleged to make the offence or any of the offences not a serious one ('any of the offences' seems to refer to any of the offences which incurred the relevant penalty points). Note the similarity of this exclusion to the exclusion of non-seriousness as a special reason in *Nicholson v Brown*: see 23.12 (v).
   ii.  hardship, other than exceptional hardship: this includes hardship to people other than the driver, such as family, employer, customers. The distinction between 'hardship' and 'exceptional hardship' is interpreted by *Wilkinson* as the difference between the hardship likely to be experienced by anyone who is prohibited from driving and hardship experienced as a result of special circumstances, especially by persons other than the driver;
   iii. any circumstances which, within the 3 years immediately preceding the conviction, have been taken into account as mitigating grounds in connection with a disqualification.

This statutory exclusion of mitigating considerations is peculiar to traffic offences. In the case of all other kinds of offence it has been left to the CA to say what is or is not a proper mitigating consideration, and as we have seen in chapter 4 its guidance has been much more equivocal. Once again, the reason for this statutory peculiarity is the ease with which some courts can be persuaded to make exceptions to the obligatory.

## Removal of disqualification (s 95 RTA 72)

**23.17** Someone who has been disqualified by order of a court[1] can apply to that court for removal of the disqualification
    a.   after 2 years if the order was for less than 4 years (the effect is that it is not permissible to apply for the removal of a shorter disqualification: only to appeal against it);
    b.   after a half of the period of disqualification if that was for at least 4 but less than 10 years;
    c.   otherwise, after 5 years.
If the application is refused, 3 months must elapse before a renewed application. There is an analogy in parole, with the important difference that in this case the decision is taken by a court, 'having regard to the [person's] character ... and ... conduct subsequent to the order, the nature of the offence and any other circumstances of the case'. When an application is granted the licence must be endorsed accordingly: the exception is a disqualification for a non-traffic offence in which a motor vehicle was used for the purpose: the removal must then be reported to the Secretary of State[2]. Statistics of applications and their successes are no longer published; but in 1981 3 in every 4 succeeded.

1.   But not someone who has been disqualified until he passes a driving test: his licence is restored by the licensing authority when he produces evidence of this.
2.   Because such disqualifications are not endorsable, presumably for the reason that the offence does not involve any infringement of traffic precautions.

## Periods of disqualification

**23.18** Statutory minima apart, courts are given little guidance as to the lengths of the periods for which they should disqualify. The Magistrates' Association's *Suggestions for Road Traffic Offence Penalties* suggest 7 days for exceeding a speed limit by more than 29mph, 14 days for exceeding it by more than 34mph, and 18 months for refusing a specimen for a blood or urine test; but for most offences does not make any suggestion. No general 'guidelines' have been promulgated by the CA, and the most that can be said about its decisions is that it does not often uphold a determinate period of more than 10 years. On the other hand, it has held that there is nothing wrong with disqualification for life, even when this is intended to leave the driver with little hope of ever driving again (*Tunde-Olarinde* (1967) 51 Cr App Rep 249, and more recently in *A-G's Reference (No 2) of 1993* (1995) 16 Cr App Rep (S) 670). In practice, as Table 23A shows, life disqualifications are by no means unheard of, even in MCs. More than 70 per cent of MCs' disqualifications, however, are for periods of a year or less, and periods exceeding 3 years are uncommon. Indeed it seems likely that most of the 3-year disqualifications are imposed only because the statute makes this obligatory for repeated offences involving drunken driving. Contrary to what is sometimes argued on appeal, 'there is no rule that persons who are sent to prison and who are at the same time disqualified have a right to have the period of disqualification coincide ... with the period of the sentence'

(*Hansel* (1982) 4 Cr App Rep (S) 368). But the CA has been very ready to reduce the period because 'if a young man cannot drive a motor vehicle it is a grave handicap ... when he seeks employment' on leaving prison (*Weston* (1982) 4 Cr App Rep (S) 51). A striking example of lenient reasoning was *Thomas* [1983] 3 All ER 756, 'a young motorist seemingly incapable of leaving vehicles alone'. Because of his previous convictions a 2-year disqualification seemed inevitable, and was imposed by the CC. The CA, however, were persuaded to reduce this period to 1 year because he could not be expected to obey the disqualification for as long as 2 years. This illustrates the acceptability of reasoning in traffic cases which would not be entertained where other offences are concerned.

### TABLE 23A: Periods of disqualification from driving, 1993

|  | Magistrates' courts per cent | Crown Court per cent |
|---|---|---|
| Under 6 months | 11 | 2 |
| 6 months | 11 | 8 |
| Over 6 months, up to 1 year | 37 | 39 |
| Over 1 year, under 2 | 15 | 6 |
| 2 years and under 3 | 9 | 21 |
| 3 years | 15 | 15 |
| Over 3 years, under 5 | 1 | 3 |
| 5 years, under 10 | 2 | 4 |
| 10 or more years | (187 cases) | (23 cases) |
| Life | (27 cases) | (5 cases) |
| Totals[1] | 144,075 | 5,965 |

Source: Home Office's Supplementary Tables of Offences relating to Motor Vehicles)

1. Not including 31,824 'totting-up' disqualifications in MCs and 43 in the CC, for periods not specified in the published statistics.

## Disqualification until the test is passed

**23.19**   A disqualification for manslaughter, causing death by dangerous driving, dangerous driving or other offences which may be prescribed must be ordered to last until the driver has passed an extended driving test. Otherwise such an order is discretionary, to be used' in respect of people who are growing old or infirm or who show in the circumstances of the offence some kind of incompetence which requires looking into'. This dictum was repeated by the Court of Appeal in *Donnelly* ((1975) 60 Cr App Rep 250) with a degree of approval which seems to make it a 'guideline'; and the Court added that the power is not to be used for merely punitive purposes. On the other hand, in the case of a young and inexperienced driver the CA has upheld the addition of this requirement to a relatively short period of disqualification (1 year) on the ground that his driving skill should be checked before he returned to driving as an occupation (*Guilfoyle* (1973) 57 Cr App Rep 549).

## Confiscation

**23.20** Motor vehicles are sometimes confiscated by a court order under s 43 PCCA 73, which permits this when a person (not necessarily the owner) is convicted of an offence punishable with at least 2 years' imprisonment, was in possession or control of the vehicle when apprehended, and it had been used to commit or facilitate (or had been so intended by him or her) *any offence* (not necessarily the offence of which he or she is convicted). The confiscation is regarded as part of the penalty, so that it can be quashed because of the totality principle (see 4.3, and *Buddo* (1982) 4 Cr App Rep(S) 268). It is inconsistent with an absolute discharge (*Hunt* [1978] Crim LR 697). Usually the confiscation is the result of a conviction for a non-motoring offence: few motoring offences—only those involving homicidal or dangerous driving—carry 2 years' imprisonment or more. It is conceivable, however, that a valuable vehicle could be among assets confiscated under the Drug Trafficking Offences Act 1956, or s 71 of CJA 88.

## Other penalties

**23.21** Confiscation, disqualification and endorsement apart, the CC and MCs have the same sentencing powers in traffic cases as those they exercise in other cases; but as Table 23B shows they make less frequent use of some of them.

**TABLE 23B: Measures other than confiscation, disqualification and endorsement imposed on adults for traffic offences in 1993**

| | Magistrates' courts | | Crown Court | | |
| --- | --- | --- | --- | --- | --- |
| | Indictable offences by dangerous etc driving | Summary offences driving[1] | Causing death | Dang- erous | Summary offences |
| | per cent | per cent | per cent | per cent | per cent |
| Discharges | 7 | 3 | — | 1 | 3 |
| Fines | 81 | 92 | 7 | 13 | 24 |
| Probation | 2 | 1 | 1 | 10 | 20 |
| Community service | 5 | 1 | 14 | 18 | 14 |
| Combination orders | 1 | < 0.5 | 1 | 3 | 3 |
| Suspended imprisonment | < 0.5 | < 0.5 | 5 | 4 | < 0.5 |
| Unsuspended imprisonment | 3 | 1 | 71 | 51 | 28 |
| Otherwise | < 0.5 | < 0.5 | — | < 0.5 | 8 |
| Totals | 7,829 | 583,326 | 196 | 1,117 | 894 |

Source: CSEW, Supplementary Volumes.

1. Other indictable offences are not shown here: they account for only 6 per cent of all indictable traffic offences dealt with in the CC.

Note how seldom traffic offenders are discharged. More interesting still is the relative frequency of community service orders in the CC, even for offences which led to deaths, when compared with their infrequency in MCs. Custodial sentences are used in about 3 in 4 cases involving death or bodily harm, but suspended sentences are more frequent than one might expect, given that nowadays they are supposed to be reserved for exceptional circumstances (see 10.30). It is when driving which has resulted in deaths is dealt with non-custodially that the CC is most criticised, though not always fairly (see 4.20ff for the relevance or irrelevance of harm done).

**23.22** As for MCs, some of the advice in the Magistrates' Association's *Suggestions* (1993) is interesting. Community penalties, not imprisonment, are the 'entry point' (see 1.22) for dangerous driving. The only offences for which the 'entry point' is a custodial sentence are driving while disqualified[1] and aggravated vehicle taking[2]. In an effort to promote consistency in dealing with 'excess alcohol' cases a graph is provided, so that the period of disqualification (ranging from the statutory minimum of 12 months up to 36 months) and the level of the fine can be exactly determined by micrograms or milligrams of alcohol per 100 millilitres. Above a certain point on the graph imprisonment is to be considered. It is made clear that 'circumstances' should always be taken into account.

1. Until 1962 imprisonment was obligatory for this offence: a provision which the Magistrates' Association tried to revive in 1966.
2. The Aggravated Vehicle-Taking Act 1992 was aimed at teenagers' 'joy-riding'. The offence consists of injuring a person or damaging property as a result of driving a vehicle without the owner's consent. In practice in the first year (1993) only 34 per cent of the young adults convicted were dealt with custodially by MCs; but 63 per cent were in the CC. The guideline case—for the moment at least—is *Bird* (1992) 14 Cr App Rep (S) 343.

### Drinking drivers (ss 34A, 34B, 34C RTOA 88)

**23.23** Concern about the dangers of drink-driving has persuaded many MCs to impose prison sentences on drivers with high levels of blood-alcohol; and the Court of Appeal approved in *Short* ((1996) Times, 23 January). Probation used to be, and in many areas still is, a measure to induce alcoholic drivers to undergo remedial courses. Now, however, drinking drivers may be catered for by an innovation in the RTA 91. When a driver is sentenced for an offence involving driving under the influence of alcohol or a drug, and is disqualified for a period of at least 12 months as a result, the court may order that the period is to be shortened by 3 months in the case of a 12-months disqualification (or not more than a quarter in the case of longer ones) if the driver successfully completes an approved course by a specified date. 'Success' must be certified in writing to the clerk of the court. An order of this kind can be made only if the court is satisfied that a place is available in a course of this kind. By the end of 1995 there were 20 such courses, whose efficacy was being studied by the Transport Research Laboratory. In some areas courses for bad drivers are offered by police forces, but are outside the scope of s 34

A, B and C RTOA 88, so that probation is used to persuade offenders to attend them.

**23.24** In a guideline case in 1984 (*Boswell* (1984) 6 Cr App Rep (S) 257) the CA made it clear that in its view courts were not using prison sentences for reckless driving to the proper extent, and made points which apply nowadays to dangerous driving.. Aggravating factors which make imprisonment proper are

1. consumption of alcohol or drugs;
2. racing at a grossly excessive speed: 'showing off';
3. disregarding warnings from passengers;
4. a prolonged, persistent and deliberate course of very bad driving;
5. other offences committed at the same time (an example being driving without a licence);
6. previous convictions for motoring offences, particularly those involving bad driving or excessive consumption of alcohol;
7. where several people are killed as a result;
8. behaviour at the time of the offence, such as failure to stop;
9. causing death in the course of driving in an attempt to avoid detection or apprehension.

On the other hand, the offence can be mitigated

a. if the reckless driving was a 'one-off' action, a momentary error of judgement, briefly dozing off at the wheel or failing to notice a pedestrian at a crossing;
b. by a good driving record;
c. by good character generally;
d. by a plea of guilty;
e. sometimes by the effect on the defendant, if he was genuinely remorseful or shocked;
f. if the victim was either a close relative or a close friend and the consequent emotional shock is likely to have been great (an example of the 'natural punishment' mentioned in 4.30).

But only if no aggravating feature is present would a non-custodial penalty be appropriate. The current practice of imposing not more than 12 or 18 months' imprisonment was too lenient. In the very worst cases 7 to 10 years would not be too long. Yet as we saw in 23.22 the Magistrates' Association suggest 'community penalties' as the entry point for dangerous driving.

## Efficacy of measures

**23.25** As was emphasised in 7.2, efficacy must be distinguished from efficiency. We know a little for example about the efficiency with which fixed penalties are collected (about 75 per cent are when the offence is endorsable, but only about 65 per cent for non-endorsable offences); but we have no idea what percentage of the offenders who pay are deterred. Endorsements are now recorded centrally in a very high percentage of cases, but we have no estimates of the deterrent efficacy of penalty points. We know that legislation which creates new offences can sometimes affect people's moral attitudes: the Walker-Marsh survey (1984) did suggest that legislation to make the wearing of seat-belts compulsory would harden moral attitudes towards non-compliance: but the nature of the penalty did not seem to have any influence. Riley's (1991) study of the effectiveness of high rates of breath-testing (discussed in 8.7) was not concerned with the effectiveness of sentences for drunk driving.

## Driving while disqualified

**23.26** How efficient or effective is disqualification from driving? It is often cited as an example of an unenforceable prohibition. Some critics—such as Willett (1973: see 22.29ff )—even doubted whether it had much utility. The findings so far, however, do not justify complete scepticism. It is true that
  a. most disqualifications are for periods so short that they are mere penalties, not serious precautions against danger;
  b. if Willett's samples are representative[1], disqualification does not substantially reduce the likelihood of another offence by drivers who are convicted of serious traffic offences, with the possible exception of drunken drivers[2];
  c. at least half of Willett's disqualified drivers disobeyed the prohibition, probably more than once.
In short, as a way of incapacitating drivers who are dangerous to other road users disqualification is not very effective.

1. They were not very large, and they were collected in the 1960s.
2. Perhaps because of the smallish numbers, Willett did not separately tabulate the reconvictions of drunken drivers (almost all of whom must have been disqualified).

**23.27** On the other hand. Kriefman's (1975) study of the detection of disqualified drivers—in which the Lancashire police took special steps to achieve this, while the Metropolitan Police did not—arrived at several findings which are a mild antidote to complete scepticism:
  d. unauthorised taking of vehicles and uninsured driving were especially frequent offences in the histories of people convicted of disqualified driving, while drunken driving was most frequent in the records of those who were not;
  e. similarly, previous convictions for indictable offences, and unskilled, irregular manual employment were more frequent among people convicted of disqualified driving;
  f. once an offender had been detected in disqualified driving he was much less likely to be detected in it again than was someone who had been detected in drunken driving (and disqualified for it). Yet drunken drivers were less likely to be detected in disqualified driving than people convicted of other sorts of offence (such as dangerous or careless driving). These differences were observed whether or not the driver had received a custodial sentence: but those who did receive custodial sentences were even less likely to be detected later in disqualified driving.

**23.28** Kriefman's findings are fairly strong, if indirect, indications that while disqualified driving is fairly common, it is much more likely to be committed by the less law-abiding sort of driver (the sort who does not worry about the trouble he causes by 'borrowing' a car, or about the need for third-party insurance in case he injures someone). Rather surprisingly, drunken drivers seemed to belong, on the whole, to the sort of citizen who is sufficiently respectful or fearful of the law to abide by a disqualification. Of course the two groups cannot be sharply distinguished: some drunken drivers do drive while disqualified, and some unskilled manual workers with records of theft, car borrowing and uninsured driving obey their disqualification. On the whole, however, the findings suggest that disqualification deters a substantial number of people from driving.

**23.29** It is not easy to arrange interviews with disqualified drivers. Mirrlees-Black's (1993) study achieved only 90 interviews with 192 subjects; and those who could not be interviewed were likely to be less law-abiding. Even so, she found that nearly half of her interviewees admitted to driving while disqualified, but usually claimed to have driven less often or more carefully than they would have done before being disqualified. To avoid detection they avoided parking their cars outside their own homes, drove other people's cars, chose routes on which they did not expect to encounter police, or wore disguises. Some even obtained papers with false identities.

**23.30** It is clear that many disqualified drivers have a low estimate of the likelihood of being detected if they drive; and anything that will visibly increase the risk deserves serious consideration. The risk is now greater than it was when Willett and Kriefman carried out their researches, since police are now able, whenever someone is detected in a traffic offence, or involved in a traffic accident, to confirm by means of the national computer records whether he is subject to a disqualification. Yet unless the disqualified driver comes to notice in one of these ways his chances of being detected are far smaller than is desirable. On the other hand, it seems unsound to argue, as so many sentencers do[1], that longer-than-average periods of disqualification should be avoided because they tempt the offender to drive while disqualified. It is much more likely that if the offender is a person of the sort who will disobey the disqualification he will do so fairly soon, whatever the period.

1. Including the CA: see 23.18.

### Correcting drivers

**23.31** Corrective efficacy is usually measured by—*faute de mieux* (see 7.3 ff)—reconvictions. In the case of traffic offences, however, the validity of this measure is even more questionable than in the case of indictable offences because of the enormous 'dark figure': more precisely, the high percentage of offences in which offenders are not detected. Until recently, too, the arrangements for central recording did not facilitate the linking of recorded offences to individual drivers. Sentencers had to rely on endorsements of licences, much as mediaeval judges had to rely on branding, to tell them when they were dealing with recidivists. Only the most serious traffic offences found their way to the Criminal Record Office: others had to be traced through local police records. Now that the Driver Vehicle Licensing Authority at Swansea is in full operation more thorough follow-ups will be possible; and it is to be hoped that some will be carried out and analysed.

**23.32** In the late 1960s Willett (1973) carried out an unusually thorough 4-year follow-up of 173 men and eight women who had been convicted of dangerous, careless or drunken driving, failing to stop after an accident or driving while disqualified or uninsured[1]. Only 27 per cent of them were reconvicted of traffic offences at least once during the follow-up period, including 9 per cent who were convicted of one of the serious offences chosen by Willett[2]. This is markedly lower than the 4-year reconviction rate which one would expect for SL offences; but in all probability the explanation is simply that detection rates for traffic offences are even lower than for thefts. The only numerous group with a significantly different reconviction rate was the drunken drivers, of whom only 11 per cent were reconvicted of traffic offences, although nearly all of these were serious[3]. The reconviction rates of offenders who were disqualified were not significantly lower than those of the rest.

1. The sample was taken from the areas of Durham, Burton-on-Trent and Reading, and the offenders were interviewed twice during the follow-up, and completed a personality inventory (the Cattell). As controls 641 men and women with no traffic convictions other than parking. (or other 'stationary' offences) were taken at random from the licensing records of Durham, Oxford and Derby.
2. If non-traffic reconvictions are ignored, there was not a significant difference between the reconviction rates of 'first offenders' and others. This too, however, may have been due to very low detection rates.
3. If they are omitted, the reconviction rate for the rest of the sample was 32 per cent.

**23.33** Willett asked members of his samples 'What influence would you say that your sentence has had on you?' Out of 112 answers about a third were encouraging: the driver claimed to be more careful or more conscious of the law. About half, however, denied that the sentence had influenced them, and the rest described undesirable effects (for example, 'I'll take a bit more care in future. I won't phone the police, I'll just clear off'). Very few—about 1 in 9— expressed any guilt or contrition about their offence, even when this was dangerous or drunken driving. Willett's study strongly suggests that a valid distinction can be drawn between convicted drivers who are more or less law-abiding and those who are not, at least in the sense that they have little regard for ownership, insurance, disqualifications and other regulatory requirements. This impression is supported by Kriefman's study of driving while disqualified (see 23.22).

**23.34** A similar question was put by Griffiths et al (1980), but their interviews were with 1,055 drivers aged 16 or older, selected by 'probability sampling' from all adults in Great Britain (and thus more likely to be representative). The 1,114 who reported having been the subject of police action for a traffic offence were asked 'As a result of all this do you feel you took more or less care ... with your driving (or of your vehicle, or of your documents, according to the offence) … or did it make no difference to you?' The responses from those who had committed driving offences are shown in Table 23C:

**TABLE 23C: Drivers' estimates of effects of police action for traffic offences**

| | Nature of police action | | |
| Responses | Verbal warning per cent | Warning letter per cent | Prosecution per cent |
| --- | --- | --- | --- |
| 'more care' | 62 | 81 | 61 |
| 'less care' | - | - | 1 |
| 'no difference' | 36 | 19 | 36 |
| 'don't know' | - | - | 1 |
| refused to answer | 2 | - | 1 |
| Totals (=100 per cent) | 295 | 21 | 320 |

At their face value, these responses suggest that verbal or written warnings are as effective as prosecution[1]; and Griffiths et al were able to cite another independent study to the same effect. But their respondents were clearly less frank than Willett's, of whom about 1 in 6 reported *undesired* effects of prosecution[2].

1. Not that written warnings are *more* effective than other types of action: 81 per cent of 21 is not significantly different from 61 per cent of 320. A safer interpretation is that about 60 per cent of drivers will say 'more care' and 36 per cent 'no difference' whichever type of action they have experienced, and that the 81 per cent is a chance result of sampling.
2. The explanation may be differences in the way in which interviews were conducted.

## Incapacitation

**23.35** Since custodial sentences for traffic offences are not very common, and when imposed tend to be short, they cannot be taken seriously as measures of incapacitation. Disqualification, though originally introduced with this aim, has long since ceased to be used in a way that is consistent with it; and in any case, as we have seen, is too often disobeyed. An extension of courts' powers to confiscate vehicles (see 23.20) has not been seriously considered, for obvious reasons (the driver is often not the owner, and would in many cases be able to use another vehicle). Devices have been invented which make it difficult for drunks to start their cars; for example by electronic combination locks which require them to punch a series of numbers: but unless this becomes a widespread fixture it cannot keep many drunks from driving.

## Hazard-plates

**23.36** Yet if incapacitation is hard to achieve, more could be done to warn road-users of the proximity of drivers who represent a hazard. This is the objective of the L-plates which learners are required to display. It would be consistent, and reasonable, to require drivers whose licences are endorsed for driving without due care—and similar offences—to display H-plates for a minimum period thereafter, so that other drivers and pedestrians could keep a watchful eye on them. Since drivers are unwilling to admit to incompetence, the stigma of an H-plate would add to the deterrent efficacy of endorsements. Deliberate stigmatising is apt to arouse ethical emotions; but a society which tolerates—for good reason—the stigmatising of innocent learner drivers cannot consistently object to a similar precaution where the guilty are concerned. The proposal is less objectionable than stigmatising kerb-crawling drivers in the way described in 19.20.

## General deterrence

**23.37**  There remains—at least so far as sentencers are concerned—general deterrence. The fashionable scepticism about the efficacy of such a policy has already been discussed in chapter 8, and shown to be exaggerated. In countries such as Sweden it is claimed that a policy of automatic custodial sentencing for drunken driving has greatly reduced the incidence of this offence. Yet the Magistrates' Association's *Suggestions* do not suggest that it should be considered until the level of alcohol in breath, blood or urine is more than twice the illegal minimum.

**23.38**  It must be conceded that a policy of general deterrence has to contend against heavy odds. So far as dangerous traffic offences are concerned the likelihood of prosecution is extremely low. Even when such offences are observed by members of the public who are in a position to report them together with the registration number of the vehicle, they seldom do so. It is accidents or police observation which select the unlucky offenders for official action. Dix and Layzell (1983) regard fear of death, injury or damage as more powerful deterrents than fear of official action; and there have been studies of common risks which are either overrated or underrated by drivers (for example, Watts and Quimby, 1980). Having an accident however 'does not seem to improve the generally low level of knowledge about driving dangers'.

**23.39**  The most optimistic thing that can be said about subjective probabilities of detection is that most drivers seem to overestimate their chances of being detected by the police in driving offences. Hogg (1977) found that most of his sample of drivers believed that their chances of being detected in speeding was almost fifty-fifty, whereas it is more likely to be about 1 in 7,000. Subjective probabilities can be sharply increased by the sight of police cars or notices about speed traps, although the effect wears off with the passage of time. It is possible that other ways of increasing and maintaining subjective probabilities could be devised. They will not have much effect on the high-mileage driver who has learned to estimate his chances realistically; but they would have some influence on the less experienced. Fooling some of the people most of the time is cynical, but preferable to killing or injuring them.

**23.40** As for the probabilities of penalties, if one is detected in a driving offence the likelihood of a fine is very high; but there are many for whom this is more like a tax than a penalty, and a tax which is sometimes paid by an employer (a transaction which is not yet criminal). The certainty of disqualification for the more serious offences is ostensibly very high; but again, as we have seen, the reality is less frightening, especially if one can afford a lawyer of one's choice. Even when disqualification strikes, there are too many drivers who are prepared to take the risk of disobeying it. Dix and Layzell (1983) found that not even involvement in accidents seems to improve 'the generally low level of knowledge about driving dangers'. It is 'the onset of parenthood ... when personal responsibility widens to include the driver's family' that seems to result in 'a major change'. The main difficulty to be overcome is the male driver's belief in his own competence, which is one of the things that age does not wither.

# Chapter 24

# The executive and the judiciary

**24.1** England's criminal justice system exemplifies the usual tensions: between objectives and resources, between police and social workers, between 'managers' and 'front-line' workers, and of course between the ideologies of just deserts and crime reduction. One sort of tension, however, seems to be particularly taut in England, and to have developed since the first edition of this book was published.

## The special relationship

**24.2** Until the 1980s the working relationship between the executive and the judiciary was co-operative. By tradition judges—and to a lesser extent magistrates—were allowed scope for discretion in their choice of sentences. Civil servants found the tradition useful when Home Secretaries wanted to force innovations upon the courts. If and when innovations were decided upon the executive provided the facilities—for example detention centres for teenagers—and persuaded Parliament to empower, but not compel, courts to use them. It was exceptional for courts to be obliged to use a measure. Disqualification from driving was a rare example, and it was magistrates rather than judges whose leniency towards motorists made this step necessary. On the whole the judges played the game. New powers were not ignored, although sometimes used with reluctance, and not quite in the way intended (the extended sentence was an example). Even when the introduction of parole meant that prisoners sentenced by a judge could be released after one third of the time specified instead of two thirds, most judges did not, as had been feared, lengthen their sentences to compensate for this (Walker, 1984). When restraints were imposed on their discretion it was usually by the Court of Appeal, an example being the doctrine that discretionary life sentences should not be used unless the offender was at least psychologically unstable (see 22.5).

## The worsening relationship

**24.3** It was pressure groups which in the 1970s became influential enough to change this relationship. So far as the criminal courts were concerned the first important victory was the Bail Act of 1976, which placed strict limitations on courts' discretion to refuse bail (see 10.5ff): and again it was magistrates' courts which were chiefly affected. A few years later the use of custodial sentences for young offenders was restricted, for example by s 1 CJA 82; and in 1991 the restrictions were extended to adults. Sentencers were even forbidden—with a subtle exception—to take into account previous convictions or failures to respond to previous sentences (s 29 CJA 91). This curious by-product of 'just desert' theory was so resented by the judiciary that it had to be repealed in the CJA 93.

## The 1995 proposals

**24.4** More limitations on judges' discretion, however, were foreshadowed in the Home Secretary's address to the Conservative Party's 1995 Conference. He promised a White Paper which has still to appear; but from what he said then and later it seems that he had in mind legislation during the 1996–1997 parliamentary session which would include three measures for public protection:

a. *'stiff' minimum custodial sentences for domestic burglars with at least two previous convictions for such burglaries, and similar—but probably stiffer—minima for dealers in Class A drugs.* The main objective would be the protection of the public. Minima of this kind are common in some other jurisdictions, such as the USA, but would be a break with the English tradition. Courts would be allowed to make exceptions, and probably left to decide the circumstances in which this would be justified. Many domestic burglars, for example, are still in their teens and unlikely to benefit from 'stiff' periods of detention. Even so the minima would be resented by the judiciary, who are well represented in the House of Lords. It is not clear why these two kinds of offence were selected for this special treatment. The reason may simply be public concern.

b. *the replacement of the parole system with a much less generous system of remission for good conduct,* so that time spent in custody would correspond more closely to the periods specified in courts' sentences. Any compulsory supervision would extend beyond the nominal end of the sentence. Sentencers would be expected—perhaps directed—to adjust the lengths of sentences to take account of the fact that prisoners would no longer become eligible for parole at the halfway stage. One result would be that sentences would *sound* shorter, but might well *be* longer (for example because of a statutory minimum or a half-hearted adjustment). On the other hand 'time inside' would correspond more closely to time specified. At present automatic conditional release at the halfway stage means that a prisoner sentenced to two years spends only six months more inside than one serving one year. A system with remission of, say, one sixth[1] of sentence would widen the difference to 10 months.

The gain in public protection would be modest, but the increased differentiation between the effects of sentences would please just-deserters who want proportionality (see 9.13-9.14). It would certainly weaken prisoners' main incentive for good behaviour, and increase the numbers of unmanageable prisoners who had forfeited all their remission.

c.  *mandatory life sentences for certain kinds of violent or sexual offences by men or women convicted of such offences on at least one previous occasion.*Again the main objective would be the protection of the public. Release would be a matter for the Parole Board, not the Home Secretary, and no doubt the CC would be encouraged to specify minimum periods to be served, as it is in the case of 'discretionary' life sentences (see 22.7). This proposal would override the CA's guideline which discourages non-mandatory life sentences for offenders who are not mentally disordered or 'unstable' (see 22.5). It is likely to be opposed, and not only by judges. Mandatory sentences, like minimum sentences, are a breach with tradition, the only exceptions being some non-custodial disqualifications. The closest analogy which comes to mind from the past was the mandatory death sentence for a second conviction for a non-capital murder (see s 6 of the Homicide Act 1957)—a precedent which is unlikely to be cited in support. The proposal might be made more acceptable by providing for exceptions or appeals; but the unpopularity of mandatory life for murder (see 22.6), especially in the House of Lords, will not make the Home Secretary's task any easier.

1.  The fraction proposed in the Scottish Office's consultation paper *Making the Punishment Fit the Crime* (1996).

**24.5**  All three innovations seem certain to increase the prison population, and the abolition of automatic conditional release would make it more difficult to control. There would on the other hand be some gains by way of public protection, the one practical purpose which incarceration can be counted on to achieve. It is to be hoped that the fate of the proposals will be settled by pragmatic reasoning, not by appeals to tradition. Particularly misleading are claims that there is some sort of constitutional boundary beyond which the executive must not venture in its efforts to influence sentencers. It might be said to be a recognised principle that ministers should not interfere with the sentencing of individuals; but even so the executive is allowed to invoke the prerogative of mercy or other compassionate devices in deserving cases (see 1.26). There is certainly no constitutional principle which forbids or even discourages Parliament from limiting the discretion of sentencers if it can be persuaded -whether by a Home Secretary or by a humble private member—that this has advantages. The advantages may be real or imaginary; but Parliament has the last word.

# Examples of statutory maximum determinate prison sentences of 2 years or more[1]

| Statute | Nature of offence |
| --- | --- |
| **14-year maxima** | |
| Offences against the Person Act 1861, s 30 | Placing explosives near a building. |
| Explosive Substances Act 1883, s 4 | Making or possessing explosives in suspicious circumstances. |
| Firearms Act 1968, ss 17(2), 18(1) & Sch 6 | Possessing firearm while committing or with intent to commit indictable offence. |
| Theft Act 1968, ss 9, 21, 22 | Burglary, blackmail, dishonest handling of stolen goods. |
| Suicide Act 1961, s 2 | Aiding or abetting suicide. |
| Sexual Offences Act 1956, s 17 & Sch 2 | Abducting a woman by force. |
| Coinage Offences Act 1936, s 3 | Impairing gold or silver coin. |
| Misuse of Drugs Act 1971, ss 4(2), 4(3), 5(3), 6(2), 8, 9 | Producing, supplying, offering, exporting etc a Class B controlled drug: an occupier of premises permitting certain activities there connected with such drugs. Offences relating to opium. Cultivating cannabis plant. |
| Customs & Excise Act 1952, ss 45(1), 56(2) | Unlawful importation of a drug controlled under the Misuse of Drugs Act 1971. |
| | Unlawful exportation of a drug controlled under the Misuse of Drugs Act 1971. |

1.  For offences for which life imprisonment is the statutory maximum penalty see 22.5

381

| *Statute* | *Nature of offence* |
|---|---|

### 10-year maxima

| | |
|---|---|
| Public Order Act, 1986, ss 1, 38 | Riot. Contamination of goods. |
| Road Traffic Act 1988, ss 1, 3A | Causing death by dangerous driving. Causing death by careless driving while under the influence of drink or drugs. |
| Sexual Offences Act 1956, ss 14, 15 | Indecent assault. |
| Theft Act 1968, ss 9, 15 | Burglary (non-dwelling). Obtaining property by deception. |
| Criminal Damage Act 1971, ss 1(1), 2, 3, 4(2) | Destroying or damaging property. Threatening to destroy or damage property. Possessing anything with intent to commit criminal damage. |
| Offences against the Person Act 1861, ss 4, 16, 23 | Soliciting, encouraging, persuading or proposing to another to commit murder. Threatening to murder. Administering poison with intent to endanger life or inflict grievous bodily harm. |
| Prison Act 1952, s 39 and Criminal Justice Act 1961, s 22(1) | Assisting prisoners to escape. |
| Forgery and Counterfeiting Act 1981, ss 1 -5; 14-15 | Forgery. Making, copying, using false instruments etc Counterfeiting currency. |
| Trade Marks Act 1994, s 92 | False application or use of trade marks. |
| Hallmarking Act 1973, s 6 | Making or uttering counterfeit dies or marks. |

### 7-year maxima

| | |
|---|---|
| Sexual Offences Act 1956, ss. 10, 11, 30, 31, 37 & Sch 2 (as amended) | Incest by a woman, or by a man with a female over 13. Man living on earnings of prostitution. Woman exercising control over a prostitute. Attempted sexual intercourse with a girl under 13 years. |
| Theft Act 1968, ss 1, 19, 20(1), 20(2) | Theft. False accounting. False statements by directors. Suppression of documents. Procuring execution of a valuable security. |
| Perjury Act 1911 | Perjury. |

| Statute | Nature of offence |
|---|---|
| Misuse of Drugs Act 1971, ss 4(3), 5(3) & Sch 4 | Possessing a Class A controlled drug. |
| Criminal Law Act 1977, s 51 | Bomb hoax. |
| Offences against the Person Act 1861, s 57 | Bigamy. |
| Child Abduction Act 1984, ss 1, 2 | Child abduction |
| Sexual Offences Act 1967, s 5 | Man or woman living wholly or in part on the earnings of male prostitution. |
| Insolvency Act 1986, ss 206, 209, 353 | Fraud in anticipation of winding up. Officer destroying company books. Bankrupt failing to dislose property. |
| Forgery Act 1861, s 34 | Personation acknowledging bail. |
| Prevention of Corruption Act 1916, s 1. | Corruption where HM Government or a public body in concerned. |
| Unlawful Drilling Act 1819, s 1 | Assembling etc for unlawful drilling. |
| Immigration Act 1971, s 25(1) | Assisting illegal entry. |

### 5-year maxima

| | |
|---|---|
| Public Order Act, 1986, s 2 | Violent disorder. |
| Offences against the Person Act 1861, ss 20, 24, 59 | Supplying poison or instruments with intent to procure a miscarriage. Inflicting grievous bodily harm. Administering poison with intent to injure or annoy. |
| Offences against the Person Act 1861, s 47 | Assault occasioning actual bodily harm. |
| Theft Act 1968, ss 11, 13, 16 | Removal of articles from places open to the public. Abstracting electricity. Obtaining pecuniary advantage by deception. |
| Misuse of Drugs Act 1971, ss 4(2), 4(3), 5(2), 5(3), 8, and Sch 4 | Producing, supplying, offering to supply, possessing with intent to supply a Class C drug. Possessing a Class B drug. As occupier of premises and permitting certain activities therein connected with Class C drugs. |
| Customs & Excise Act 1952, ss 45(1), 304 & 56(2) | Unlawfully importing or exporting a Class C drug. |
| Children & Young Persons Act 1933, s 1(5) | Cruelty to or neglect of children under 16 years by persons with a financial interest. |

| *Statute* | *Nature of offence* |
|---|---|
| Firearms Act 1968, ss 1(1), 4, 19 & Sch 6 | Possessing a firearm or ammunition without a firearms certificate (if aggravated). Shortening a firearm. Carrying loaded firearm in a public place. |
| Sexual Offences Act 1956, ss 12, 13 & Sch 2 (as amended) | Buggery by a man of 21 years or over with another under 21 years with consent. Indecency by man of 21 or over with a man under 21. |

## 3-year maxima

| | |
|---|---|
| Public Order Act 1986, s 3 | Affray. |
| Theft Act 1968, s 25 | Going equipped for stealing. |
| Firearms Act 1968, s 1(1) & Sch 6 | Possessing a firearm or ammunition without a firearms certificate. |

## 2-year maxima

| | |
|---|---|
| Public Order Act 1986, s 18 | Stirring up racial hatred. |
| Theft Act 1968, s 12A | Aggravated vehicle taking. |
| Prevention of Crime Act 1953, s 1 | Having an offensive weapon in a public place. |
| Official Secrets Act 1989, s 1 | Disclosure of security information entrusted in confidence. |
| Road Traffic Act 1988, s 2 | Dangerous driving. |

# Rehabilitation periods

**Sections 5 and 6 of the Rehabilitation of Offenders Act 1974 as amended by the Criminal Justice Act 1982, the Criminal Justice Act 1991 and the Criminal Justice and Public Order Act 1994**

### 5   Rehabilitation periods for particular sentences

(1) The sentences excluded from rehabilitation under this Act are–

(a) a sentence of imprisonment for life;

(b) a sentence of imprisonment youth custody or corrective training for a term exceeding thirty months;

(c) a sentence of preventive detention; and

(d) a sentence of detention during Her Majesty's pleasure or for life, or for a term exceeding thirty months, passed under section 53 of the Children and Young Persons Act 1933 [1933 c 12] or under section 57 of the Children and Young Persons (Scotland) Act 1937 [1937 c 37] (young offenders convicted of grave crimes); and (e) a sentence of custody for life;

and any other sentence is a sentence subject to rehabilitation under this Act.

(2) For the purposes of this Act

(a) the rehabilitation period applicable to a sentence specified in the first column of Table A below is the period specified in the second column of that Table in relation to that sentence, or, where the sentence was imposed on a person who was under eighteen years of age at the date of his conviction, half that period; and

(b) the rehabilitation period applicable to a sentence specified in the first column of Table B below is the period specified in the second column of that Table in relation to that sentence;

reckoned in either case from the date of the conviction in respect of which the sentence was imposed.

**TABLE A: Rehabilitation periods subject to reduction by half for persons under 18**

| *Sentence* | *Rehabilitation period* |
|---|---|
| A sentence of imprisonment, detention in a young offender institution or youth custody or corrective training for a term exceeding six months but not exceeding thirty months. | Ten years |
| A sentence of cashiering, discharge with ignominy or dismissal with disgrace from Her Majesty's service. | Ten years |
| A sentence of imprisonment or detention in a young offender institution for a term not exceeding six months. | Seven years |
| A sentence of dismissal from Her Majesty's service. | Seven years |
| Any sentence of detention in respect of a conviction in service disciplinary proceedings. | Five years |
| A fine or any other sentence subject to rehabilitation under this Act, not being a sentence to which Table B below or any of subsections (3), (4A) to (8) below applies. | Five years |

**TABLE B: Rehabilitation periods for certain sentences confined to young offenders**

| *Sentence* | *Rehabilitation period* |
|---|---|
| A sentence of Borstal training. | Seven years |
| A sentence of detention for a term exceeding six months but not exceeding thirty months passed under section 53 of the said Act of 1933 or under section 57 of the said Act of 1937. | Five years |
| A sentence of detention for a term not exceeding six months passed under either of those provisions. | Three years |
| An order for detention in a detention centre made under section 4 of the Criminal Justice Act 1982, section 4 of the Criminal Justice Act 1961 or under section 7 of the Criminal Justice (Scotland) Act 1963. | Three years |

(3) The rehabilitation period applicable
(a) to an order discharging a person absolutely for an offence; and
(b) to the discharge by a children's hearing under section 43(2) of the Social Work (Scotland) Act 1968 [1968 c 49] of the referral of a child's case;
shall be six months from the date of conviction.

(4) Where in respect of a conviction a person was conditionally discharged, bound over to keep the peace or be of good behaviour, the rehabilitation period applicable to the sentence shall be one year from the date of conviction or a period beginning with that date and ending when the order for conditional discharge or (as the case may be) the recognisance or bond of caution to keep the peace or be of good behaviour ceases or ceased to have effect, whichever is the longer.

(4A) Where in respect of a conviction a person was placed on probation, the rehabilitation period applicable to the sentence shall be —

(a) in the case of a person aged eighteen years or over at the date of his conviction, five years from the date of conviction;

(b) in the case of a person aged under the age of eighteen years at the date of his conviction, two and a half years from the date of conviction or a period beginning with the date of conviction and ending when the probation order ceases or ceased to have effect, whichever is the longer.

(5) where in respect of a conviction any of the following sentences was imposed, that is to say—

(a) an order under section 57 of the Children and Young Persons Act 1933 [1933 c 12] or section 61 of the Children and Young Persons (Scotland) Act 1937 [1937 c 37] committing the person convicted to the care of a fit person;

(b) a supervision order under any provision of either of those Acts or of the Children and Young Persons Act 1963 [1963 c 37];

(c) an order under section 58 or 58A of the said Act of 1937 committing the person convicted to custody in a remand home or to detention in a place chosen by a local authority, or (as the case may be) committing him for a period of residential training;

(d) an approved school order under section 61 of the said Act of 1937;

(e) a care order or a supervision order under any provision of the Children and Young Persons Act 1969 [1969 c 54]; or

(f) a supervision requirement under any provision of the Social Work (Scotland) Act 1968;

the rehabilitation period applicable to the sentence shall be one year from the date of conviction or a period beginning with that date and ending when the order or requirement ceases or ceased to have effect, whichever is the longer.

(6) Where in respect of a conviction any of the following orders was made, that is to say—

(a) an order under section 54 of the said Act of 1933 committing the person convicted to custody in a remand home;

(b) an approved school order under section 57 of the said Act of 1933; or

(c) an attendance centre order under section 19 of the Criminal Justice Act 1948 [1948 c 58];

the rehabilitation period applicable to the sentence shall be a period beginning with the date of conviction and ending one year after the date on which the order ceases or ceased to have effect.

(7) Where in respect of a conviction a hospital order under Part III of the Mental Health Act 1983 [1983 c 20] or under Part V of the Mental Health (Scotland) Act 1960 [1960 c 61] (with or without an order restricting discharge) was made, the rehabilitation period applicable to the sentence shall be the period of five years from the date of conviction or a period beginning with that date and ending two years after the date on which the hospital order ceases or ceased to have effect, whichever is the longer.

(8) Where in respect of a conviction an order was made imposing on the person convicted any disqualification, disability, prohibition or other penalty, the rehabilitation period applicable to the sentence shall be a period beginning with the date of conviction and ending on the date on which the disqualification, disability, prohibition or penalty (as the case may be) ceases or ceased to have effect.

(9) For the purposes of this section—

(a) 'sentence of imprisonment' includes a sentence of detention in a young offenders institution in Scotland and a sentence of penal servitude, and 'term of imprisonment' shall be construed accordingly;

(b) consecutive terms of imprisonment or of detention under section 53 of the said Act of 1933 or section 57 of the said Act of 1937, and terms which are wholly or partly concurrent (being terms of imprisonment or detention imposed in respect of offences of which a person was convicted in the same proceedings) shall be treated as a single term;

(c) no account shall be taken of any subsequent variation, made by a court in dealing with a person in respect of a suspended sentence of imprisonment, of the term originally imposed; and

(d) a sentence imposed by a court outside Great Britain shall be treated as a sentence of that one of the descriptions mentioned in this section which most nearly corresponds to the sentence imposed.

(10) References in this section to the period during which a probation order, or a care order or supervision order under the Children and Young Persons Act 1969 [1969 c 54] or a supervision requirement under the Social Work (Scotland) Act 1968 [1968 c 49] is or was in force include references to any period during which any order or requirement to which this subsection applies, being an order or requirement made or imposed directly or indirectly in substitution for the first-mentioned order or requirement, is or was in force.

This subsection applies

(a) to any such order or requirement as is mentioned above in this subsection;

(b) to any order having effect under section 25(2) of the said Act of 1969 as if it were a training school order in Northern Ireland; and

(c) to any supervision order made under section 72(2) of the said Act of 1968 and having effect as a supervision order under the Children and Young Persons Act (Northern Ireland) 1950 [1950 c 5 (NI)].

(11) The Secretary of State may by order—

(a) substitute different periods or terms for any of the periods or terms mentioned in subsections (1) to (8) above; and

(b) substitute a different age for the age mentioned in subsection (2)(a) above.

## 6   The rehabilitation period applicable to a conviction

(1) Where only one sentence is imposed in respect of a conviction (not being a sentence excluded from rehabilitation under this Act) the rehabilitation period applicable to the conviction is, subject to the following provisions of this section, the period applicable to the sentence in accordance with section 5 above.

(2) Where more than one sentence is imposed in respect of a conviction (whether or not in the same proceedings) and none of the sentences imposed is excluded from rehabilitation under this Act, then, subject to the following provisions of this section, if the periods applicable to those sentences in accordance with section 5 above differ, the rehabilitation period applicable to the conviction shall be the longer or the longest (as the case may be) of those periods.

(3) Without prejudice to subsection (2) above, where in respect of a conviction

a person was conditionally discharged or placed on probation and after the end of the rehabilitation period applicable to the conviction in accordance with subsection (1) or (2) above he is dealt with, in consequence of a breach of conditional discharge or probation, for the offence for which the order for conditional discharge or probation order was made, then, if the rehabilitation period applicable to the conviction in accordance with subsection (2) above (taking into account any sentence imposed when he is so dealt with) ends later than the rehabilitation period previously applicable to the conviction, he shall be treated for the purposes of this Act as not having become a rehabilitated person in respect of that conviction, and the conviction shall for those purposes be treated as not having become spent, in relation to any period falling before the end of the new rehabilitation period.

(4) Subject to subsection (5) below, where during the rehabilitation period applicable to a conviction–

(a) the person convicted is convicted of a further offence; and

(b) no sentence excluded from rehabilitation under this Act is imposed on him in respect of the later conviction;

if the rehabilitation period applicable in accordance with this section to either of the convictions would end earlier than the period so applicable in relation to the other, the rehabilitation period which would (apart from this subsection) end the earlier shall be extended so as to end at the same time as the other rehabilitation period.

(5) Where the rehabilitation period applicable to a conviction is the rehabilitation period applicable in accordance with section 5(8) above to an order imposing on a person any disqualification, disability, prohibition or other penalty. the rehabilitation period applicable to another conviction shall not by.virtue of subsection (4) above be extended by reference to that period; but if any other sentence is imposed in respect of the first-mentioned conviction for which a rehabilitation period is prescribed by any other provision of section 5 above, the rehabilitation period applicable to another conviction shall, where appropriate, be extended under subsection (4) above by reference to the rehabilitation period applicable in accordance with that section to that sentence or, where more than one such sentence is imposed, by reference to the longer or longest of the periods so applicable to those sentences, as if the period in question were the rehabilitation period applicable to the first-mentioned conviction.

(6) Subject to subsection (7) below, for the purposes of subsection (4)(a) above there shall be disregarded—

(a) any conviction in England and Wales of an offence which is not triable on indictment;

(b) any conviction in Scotland of an offence which is not excluded from the jurisdiction of inferior courts of summary jurisdiction by virtue of section 4 of the Summary Jurisdiction (Scotland) Act 1954 [1954 c 48] (certain crimes not to be tried in inferior courts of summary jurisdiction); and

(c) any conviction by or before a court outside Great Britain of an offence in respect of conduct which, if it had taken place in any part of Great Britain, would not have constituted an offence under the law in force in that part of Great Britain.

(7) Notwithstanding subsection (6) above, a conviction in service disciplinary proceedings shall not be disregarded for the purposes of subsection (4)(a) above.

# The Offender Group Reconviction Scale (OGRS)

The OGRS, based by Copas on a large sample from the Offenders' Index (see 7.14), is Crown Copyright, but is reproduced here with the permission of the Home Office. It is designed to help probation officers when they are preparing PSRs (see 2.19); but it is not intended that a PSR should quote an exact figure from the scale as an estimate of the probability that the offender will be reconvicted. The author of a PSR is expected to take into account what he or she knows of the offender's circumstances, character and background.

To use the scale, start with the figure 31 (28 if the offender is female). Then
(a) subtract his or her age. Subtract the number of previous sentences to a YOI;
(b) divide the total of previous court appearances leading to a finding of guilt by the number of years since first conviction. Add 5. Calculate the square root of the result, and multiply it by 75. Round the result to the nearest whole number and add it to the result of (a);
(c) if the principal offence for which the offender is to be sentenced on this occasion is a
   • violent offence (including robbery or arson) subtract 5;
   • sexual offence subtract 12;
   • burglary add 7;
   • theft or handling offence add 6;
   • fraud or forgery offence subtract 2;
   • theft of or from a motor vehicle or unauthorised taking of a motor vehicle add 6;
   • criminal or malicious damage offence add 3;
   • drug offence subtract 6;
   • offence of some other type add 3.

Compare the total with the following scale:

| Total score | Percentage reconvicted within 2 years | Total score within 2 years | Percentage reconvicted |
|---|---|---|---|
| 0 or less | 4 | 50 | 46 |
| 2 | 5 | 52 | 49 |
| 4 | 5 | 54 | 52 |
| 6 | 6 | 56 | 55 |
| 8 | 7 | 58 | 58 |
| 10 | 8 | 60 | 61 |
| 12 | 8 | 62 | 64 |
| 14 | 9 | 64 | 66 |
| 16 | 10 | 66 | 69 |
| 18 | 12 | 68 | 72 |
| 20 | 13 | 70 | 74 |
| 22 | 14 | 72 | 76 |
| 24 | 16 | 74 | 78 |
| 26 | 17 | 76 | 80 |
| 28 | 19 | 78 | 82 |
| 30 | 21 | 80 | 84 |
| 32 | 23 | 82 | 85 |
| 34 | 25 | 84 | 87 |
| 36 | 28 | 86 | 88 |
| 38 | 30 | 88 | 89 |
| 40 | 33 | 90 | 90 |
| 42 | 35 | 92 | 91 |
| 44 | 38 | 94 | 92 |
| 46 | 41 | 96 | 93 |
| 48 | 44 | 98 or more | 94 |

The scale can be used not only to tell writers of PSRs how likely an offender is to be reconvicted but also to tell evaluators of regimes how many reconvictions to expect from a sample of offenders (see 7.33).

NAPO's National Executive Council, however, 'opposes the use of any predictive scale to monitor the effectiveness of supervision or in the sentencing process on the grounds that it makes monitoring and sentencing mechanistic and discriminatory ...' (NAPO News, February, 1996). Yet surely discrimination is just what the OGRS would prevent?

# Index

Numerals refer to chapters and paragraphs, not pages